WHAT IT MEANS
TO BE HUMAN

Also by Joanna Bourke

FEAR: A CULTURAL HISTORY

RAPE

WHAT IT MEANS TO BE HUMAN

Reflections from 1791 to the Present

JOANNA BOURKE

COUNTERPOINT
BERKELEY

First published in Great Britain by Virago Press

Library of Congress Cataloging-in-Publication Data

Bourke, Joanna. What it means to be human : historical reflections from
the 1800s to the present / Joanna Bourke. p. cm. Includes
bibliographical references. ISBN 978-1-58243-608-1
1. Human beings. 2. Humanism—History. 3. Human evolution.
4. Psychology, Comparative. 5. Human-animal relationships.
6. Equality. I. Title.
BD450.B6396 2011 128.09—dc22

Printed in the United States of America

COUNTERPOINT
1919 Fifth Street
Berkeley, CA 94710
www.counterpointpress.com

Distributed by Publishers Group West

10 9 8 7 6 5 4 3 2 1

For Costas

Contents

Preface

Intellectual inspiration and friendship are entangled. I am grateful to friends and colleagues for telling me stories about what it means to be human. Alas, because these discussions often took place late at night in restaurants, tavernas and bars, the precise details of their tales were often forgotten by morning. But I was always left with a sense that their insights had been both mischievous and outraged. I imagine that distorted versions of their stories are retold here.

Let me list just a few of these delightful storytellers: Efi Avdela, Alexandra Bakalaki, Rika Benveniste, Rosi Braidotti, Nicholas Brown, Ana Carden-Coyne, Phædra Douzina-Balalaki, Nikos Douzinas, Richard Evans, David Feldman, Vanessa Harding, Kostas Hatzykyriakos, Louise Hide, Yanna Kandilorou, Aglaia Komninos, Maria Komninos, Christos Lyrintzis, Carmen Mangion, Akis Papataxiarchis, Annik Paterneau, Dorothy Porter, Samis Taboh, Anna Tsigonias, Nikos Tsigonia and Slavoj Žižek. Anthropologist Alexandra Bakalaki, historians Ana Carden-Coyne, Chandak Sengoopta and Neil Penlington, lawyer and political philosopher Costas Douzinas and cardiothoracic surgeon Tom Treasure generously provided acute critiques of chapters, many of which required months of labour to restore to a fit state.

I have also been dependent upon the labours of other people. Particular thanks go to Zoe Dinga, without whom my life would be unbearably more complicated. With calm professionalism, Alan Forth, David Murray and Mansour Shabbak dealt with emergencies related to computer malfunctions and visual meltdowns. A writer needs an editor and Lennie Goodings is simply the best. I am immensely grateful for her support for the project and perceptive feedback. Zoe Gullen shouldered the burden of editing and coordinating editorial production, while Linda Silverman tackled the frustrating task of seeking out the images. The cover design is the inspired creation of Nina Tara. My agent Andrew Wylie and his team, especially James Pullen and Sarah Chalfant, have been of immeasurable help throughout the process. The Wellcome Trust's financial support and the advice of the team in the History of Medicine and Medical Humanities section of the Trust helped this research to be carried out.

Institutionally, I have also been blessed. The Department of History at Birkbeck, University of London, deserves its reputation as a world-renowned centre for historical research and teaching. The sociability and intellectual generosity of my colleagues has fostered my work over many years; and my students have consistently forced me to think anew about received wisdom. Finally, though, thanks go to my supportive, extended families in New Zealand, Australia, Switzerland and Greece. In particular, my parents have helped my understanding in innumerable ways.

But nothing happens without Costas. His intellectual acumen is breathtaking; his solidarity with the *sans papiers* and the *aganaktismenoi* (the 'indignant'), inspiring; and the ease with which he nurtures me, fulfilling. This is why this book is dedicated to him.

CHAPTER ONE

Introduction

'Are Women Animals?'

In April 1872, a woman known only as 'An Earnest Englishwoman' published a letter entitled 'Are Women Animals?' In it, she attacked the fact that certain people were treated as lesser humans. Indeed, she fumed, they might even be treated as inferior to animals. Her full argument will be developed in Chapter Four, but this extract gives a taste of the force of her rhetoric.

ARE WOMEN ANIMALS?

TO THE EDITOR OF THE TIMES

Sir, – Whether women are the equals of men has been endlessly debated; whether they have souls has been a moot point; but can it be too much to ask [for] a definitive acknowledgement that at least they are animals? . . . Many hon. members may object to the proposed Bill enacting that, in statutes respecting the suffrage, 'wherever words occur which import the masculine gender they shall be held to include women;' but could any object to the insertion of a clause in another Act that 'whenever the word "animal" occurs it shall be held to include women?' Suffer me, through your columns, to appeal to our 650 [parliamentary] representatives, and ask – Is there not one among you then who will introduce such a motion? There would then be at least an equal interdict on wanton barbarity to cat, dog, or woman . . .

Yours respectfully,
AN EARNEST ENGLISHWOMAN

The Earnest Englishwoman was angry because animals had more rights in law than did women. In fact, the status of women was much worse than that of the rest of the animal kingdom. Regulations prohibiting cruelty against dogs, horses and cattle were significantly more punitive than laws against cruelty towards women. The Earnest Englishwoman recognized that the all-male parliamentarians were not prepared to give women the vote. Her heartfelt cry, therefore, was for women to be allowed to 'become-animal' in order to reap the benefits that they were being denied on the grounds that they were not part of '*man*kind'.[1]

So who was this Earnest Englishwoman who railed against her sex's exclusion from full humanity? I have been unable to find out. All we know is that the author chose to cloak her anonymity in a character trait (earnest), a nationality (English), and a gender (woman).

The Earnest Englishwoman (or the newspaper's editor) titled her letter of protest 'Are Women Animals?' She was concerned with one group of sentient beings – women – who were not granted the status of being fully human. In my 'historical reflections', the Earnest English-woman's 'women' stands in for *all* sexes and genders. This goes against tradition. In the history of Western philosophy, as well as in common parlance, 'man' and 'mankind' have often been used to mean 'human', albeit only to the extent that women, intergenders and transgenders conform to various traits that have been coded 'male'. By using the female gender as indicative of the status of humanity, I am disrupt-ing this assumption. Instead of men being the norm for 'human', women become 'humanity'.

The implications of any investigation into what it means to be human are potentially immense. After all, two of the most distinguished tra-ditions of modern times – theology and humanism – were founded on espousing hierarchies of humanity. According to the great Chain of Being, everything in the universe was ranked from the highest to the lowest – from the Divine to the human, then to the rest of the animal kingdom and finally incorporating inanimate objects. As Alexander Pope exclaimed in his *Essay on Man*,

> Vast chain of being! which from God began;
> Natures ethereal, human, angel, man,
> Beast, bird, fish, insect, who no eye can see,
> No glass can reach; from infinite to thee;
> From thee to nothing.[2]

This Chain was, however, subject to countless disruptions. Throughout this book, theologians and others will be seen to be muddying the seemingly clear borders: some animals were placed above certain humans. The Supreme Creator might have fashioned 'the human' to reign over 'the animal', but powerful men, 'in endless error hurl'd', had elevated certain animals over their own human-sisters, non-white Europeans and children, to take just three common exclusions. Later in his *Essay on Man*, Pope observed that 'man' found himself poised 'on this isthmus of a middle state', doubting whether he should 'deem himself a God or Beast'.[3] People excluded from the status of being fully 'men' might be forgiven for bitterly concluding that they had been decisively demoted to 'Beast'.

What about humanism? Surely an ideology that was defiantly independent of the God of Natural Theology, choosing instead to celebrate human progress and rationality, was founded on the idea of a shared humanity. Unfortunately not. The humanist insistence on an autonomous, wilful human subject capable of acting independently in the world was based on a very particular type of human. Human civilization had been forged in the image of the male, white, well-off, educated human. Humanism installed only *some* humans at the centre of the universe. It disparaged 'the woman', 'the subaltern' and 'the non-European' even more than 'the animal'. As a result, it is hardly surprising that many of these groups rejected the idea of a universal and straightforward essence of 'the human', substituting something much more contingent, outward-facing and complex. To rephrase Simone de Beauvoir's inspired conclusion about women, one is not born, but *made*, a human.

Although theological and humanist modes of thought have predominated in the period discussed in this book, it is important not to see the trend as linear. It is too simple to posit a movement *from* the theological *towards* the rationalist and scientific. God keeps being resurrected; the glory of human progress always fails to live up to its narcissistic promise. It is equally wrong to posit a shift *from* the humanist *to* the post-humanist. Conceptions of the post-human retain elements of liberal humanism at their ideological core. None of these approaches are internally coherent or self-contained.

The Earnest Englishwoman with whom I started this introduction was writing in 1872. She was preoccupied with the status of women. If she had turned her gaze to the previous century, her critique could equally have been applied to slaves, who were loudly insisting that 'We ain' like a dog or a horse'.[4] If she could have seen one hundred years into the future, she might have contributed to debates about the human status of '*sans papiers*' – immigrants to the West – or chimeras created by transplanting animal fluids and organs into human bodies, or genetic research using stem cells. This book looks backward by a century from the Earnest Englishwoman's time and forward by more than a century in order to elaborate on her reflections.

This book is also narrowly focused upon Anglo-Americans; that is, two peoples historically responsible for many of debates about what it means to be human. However, understanding these cultures' debates is impossible without exploring the way they imagined cultural and ethnic outsiders. The roles played by subjugated colonies in the creation of 'the West' and the Western 'human' cannot be overestimated. In a book of this length I cannot do justice to the full range of imperial encounters that shaped Anglo-American notions of humanity. Therefore, I will be illustrating the role of subjugated outsiders by exploring the role that Saint-Domingue (the French colonial name) or Haiti/Ayiti (the name given upon its independence on 1 January 1804) played in Anglo-American cultures.

Why Haiti? My choice is deliberate. Haiti provides the earliest example of a nation whose very existence and identity was framed around notions of a universal humanity. The revolution in the French colony of Saint-Domingue started with slave revolts in August 1791 (the date chosen for the start of my historical reflections) and ended just over twelve years later with Haiti's Declaration of Independence. In 1804 Haitians became the first black peoples to wage a successful anti-colonial revolution, the first to liberate slaves, the first to create a black republic. The grand Declaration of the Rights of Man and of the Citizen, cobbled together by deputies of the National Assembly of France in 1789 and declaring both the 'natural, inalienable and sacred rights of man' and the right of 'resistance to oppression', saw its first trial by fire, sword and rifle on this small island in the Caribbean Sea. It is for these reasons that this book not only explores Anglo-American cultures between 1791 and the present, but also assimilates the history of Haiti as this civilization's 'other'.

Why Explore 'The Human'?

It turns out that the concept 'human' is very volatile. In every period of history and every culture, commonsensical constructions of 'the

human' and 'the animal' exist, but the distinction is constantly undermined and re-constructed. My point is not simply that there is a porous
boundary between the human and the animal (although there certainly
is), but that the distinction is both contested and policed with demonic
precision. In complex and sometimes contradictory ways, the ideas,
values and practices used to justify the sovereignty of a particular
understanding of 'the human' over the rest of sentient life are what
create society and social life. Perhaps the very concept of 'culture' is an
attempt to differentiate ourselves from our 'creatureliness', our fleshly
vulnerability. What philosopher Giorgio Agamben has called the
'anthropological machine', or the compulsive inclination to demarcate
the territory of the human from that of the non-human, is one of the
great driving forces of history.[5] Delimiting those territories not only
involves violence, but inspires it.

Most of this book, then, involves untangling varying interpretations
that emerged within human cultures in Britain, America and Haiti
between the late eighteenth and early twenty-first centuries. I explore
the different ways in which people have sought to declare '*here!* and not
there! is the place where the human starts and the animal ceases'. It
turns out to be a futile (albeit absorbing and captivating) exercise. The
creative and exhilarating desire for community and communion,
authenticity and certainty, is what creates humanity as understood at
any particular moment of time and topology.

To understand the instability of definitions of who is truly human,
we need history. Stories and myths enable people in the past (and
today) to make sense of a thoroughly bewildering world populated by
an unimaginable number and range of sentient beings. In the words of
Jacques Derrida, paying attention to the full community of sentient
beings 'poses grave definitional and practical threats to the discourse of
humanism' which attributes 'authority and autonomy . . . to the
man . . . rather than to the woman, and to the woman rather than to
the animal'.[6] By looking back into the past we can trace competing
ways in which 'the human' and 'the animal' have been imagined.

I will illustrate this point by looking at the ways that, historically, the
human has been most commonly marked as male. At the start of the
nineteenth century, for instance, the author of a pamphlet protesting
against cruelty to animals insisted that 'when humanity quits the man,
and chastity the woman; they are both soon deprived of their best pos-
sessions'.[7] The male is defined by his humanity; the woman by her
sexuality. If we jump forward to near the end of that century, another

leading science writer 'denied that women were even one half of the human race . . . The race were really men': women were simply creatures who '"produced" the human race'.[8] Fast-forward to the late-1960s and zoologist Desmond Morris can be heard claiming that the 'naked ape self-named *Homo sapiens*' is 'proud that he has the biggest brain of all the primates, but attempts to conceal the fact that he also has the biggest penis'. His assumption that 'human' equals 'male-human' is reinforced when he finally turns to female sexuality. He calls women's orgasms 'pseudo-male'; they are 'borrowed' from men.[9] The baseline for all these science writers is resolutely male. As Catharine MacKinnon put it in her collection of essays entitled *Are Women Human?*, women constantly find themselves confronted by a 'denial of their humanity'. Becoming human, she continues,

> is a social, legal, and political process. It requires prohibiting or otherwise delegitimating all acts by which human beings as such are violated, guaranteeing people what they need for a fully human existence, and then officially upholding those standards and delivering on those entitlements. But . . . seeing what subordinated groups are distinctively deprived of, subjected to, and delegitimated by, requires first that they be real to power: that they first be seen as human . . . The status and treatment of men still tacitly but authoritatively define the human universal.[10]

MacKinnon's title delightfully (although unintentionally) echoes the Earnest Englishwoman's question, 'Are Women Animals?'. However, although I wholeheartedly agree with MacKinnon's protest that women have been (and are) treated as inferior humans, her critique remains situated within the liberal tenets of equality, rights and species. I wish to disrupt the 'Human' of her book's title. I will also be disrupting the term 'Animal'. Indeed, I believe that this is exactly what the Earnest Englishwoman was doing in 1872.

In the 220 years explored in this book, definitions of what it means to be 'human' or 'animal' have generated a raucous amount of excitable babble. It turns out to be extremely difficult to state what differentiates the human. In the eighteenth and nineteenth centuries the designation of different species was based primarily on outward appearance. Thus the father of biological taxonomy, the eighteenth-century biologist Carl Linnæus, divided animals into six classes – Mammalia (meaning 'of the breast'), Aves, Amphibia, Pisces, Insecta, and Vermes.[11] He grouped humans with other animals possessing milk-producing mammæ, thus making the category female (males have only dry, vestigial breasts). Then, when Linnæus set out to *distinguish* humans from the rest of mammals, he invented the term *Homo sapiens* or 'man of wisdom'. In other words, for Linnæus and subsequent taxonomists, what *tied* humans to the rest of the animal kingdom was feminine, while what *distinguished* humans from other mammals was masculine.[12] Woman is an animal; man is the exemplary human.

Other conventional distinctions between human and nonhuman animals are applied inconsistently, or are simply wrong. Is intellectual ability the crucial criterion? Or self-consciousness? Or the possession of a soul? Or tool-making? Or private property? Or genetic inheritance? Aristotle prioritized language. This is one of the most common distinctions made, as I explore in the next chapter. For Aristotle, every living being has a *telos*: an appropriate end or goal. To be human was to belong to a *polis*, for it was only in that context that 'man' could truly speak. As he put it, 'mere voice is but an indication of pleasure or pain, and is therefore found in other animals' while

> the power of speech is intended to set forth the expedient and inexpedient, and therefore likewise the just and the unjust. And it is a characteristic of man that he alone has any sense of good and evil, or just and unjust, and the like, and the association of living beings who have this sense makes a family and a state.[13]

Others placed emphasis on the ability to 'apprehend . . . God'. To be religious, observed John Evelyn, 'is more truly the formal distinction between men and beasts, than all the philosophers have furnished to its definition; and, therefore, more adequate to his character than either polity, society, [or] risibility'.[14] It turns out that the link between the apprehension of God and the possession of language is closer than those of us born in the twentieth century might have thought.

René Descartes made yet another proposition. He insisted that, unlike 'men', animals were mere 'automata' or moving machines, driven by instinct alone. It is

> Nature which acts in them according to the disposition of their organs, as one sees that a clock, which is made up of only wheels and springs can count the hours and measure time more exactly than we can with all our art.[15]

His famous statement 'Cogito ergo sum', or 'I think, therefore I am', was an insistence that only humans possess minds. This is the Cartesian dualism, separating body from mind. Immanuel Kant, writing at the end of the eighteenth century, also emphasized rationality, stating categorically that the human-being was 'an animal endowed with the capacity of reason (*animal rationabile*)'. The human was

> markedly distinguished from all other living beings by his *technical* predisposition for manipulating things (mechanically joined with consciousness), by his *pragmatic* predisposition (to use other human beings skilfully for his purposes), and by the *moral* predisposition in his being (to treat himself and others according to the principle of freedom under the laws).

In case the magnitude of the distinction was not clear, he reminded readers that 'any one of these three levels can by itself alone already distinguish the human being characteristically as opposed to the other inhabitants of the earth'.[16] In contrast, Sigmund Freud complicated Descartes and Kant's mind/body dualism with his twentieth-century invention of the unconscious. Less well-known is his suggestion that human civilization only emerged once man stood upright. This led to the 'diminution of the olfactory stimuli' and the subsequent development of disgust and sexual repression, which, in turn, led to the founding of the family and so to human civilization.[17]

Whatever definition we choose, it excludes some creatures we want to include in the 'human', and excludes others. As Bertram Lloyd, author of *Humanitarianism and Freedom*, commented in the early 1930s,

> Deny reason to animals, and you must equally deny it to infants; affirm the existence of an immortal soul in your baby or yourself, and you must at least have the grace to allow something of the kind to your dog.[18]

My point is that the list of criteria for defining humanity and animality could go on and on, leading Derrida to conclude that

> None of the traits by which the most authorized philosophy or culture has thought it possible to recognize this 'proper of man' – none of them is, in all rigor, the exclusive reserve of what we humans call human. Either because some animals also possess such traits, or because man does not possess it as surely as is claimed.[19]

Figure 1. A Möbius strip, from a 1963 poster of the woodcut by M. C. Escher: 'Which side of the strip are the ants walking on?'

The Möbius Strip

It is helpful to think of these ideas with the Möbius* strip in mind. This strip is depicted in Figure 1.

The Möbius strip is named after the nineteenth-century mathematician August Ferdinand Möbius. As a topological space it is easy to make, but the result is aesthetically and philosophically astounding. Simply take a long, rectangular strip of paper, twist one end by 180 degrees and glue it to the other end. The result? A one-sided surface, with no inside or outside; no beginning or end; no single point of entry or exit; no hierarchical ladder to clamber up or slide down. The Möbius strip is a profoundly useful device, particularly if we want to think outside unhelpful dichotomies such as biology-as-inside/culture-as-outside,

---

* Pronounced 'MEU-bee-uhs'.

animal/human, and fe/male. The Möbius strip embodies the roller-coaster ride of life, or *zoe*. Most usefully for us, it deconstructs the human versus animal dilemma. The boundaries of the human and the animal turn out to be as entwined and indistinguishable as the inner and outer sides of a Möbius strip.

It would be wrong to conclude from the spiralling Möbius strip, with its indistinguishable borders, that all life is fundamentally the same. Quite the contrary. In the conclusion, I will elaborate on a central principle that infuses this book: that of 'negative zoélogy'* or radical otherness. The concept can be simply stated: face to face with the fundamental fluidity in definitions of human/animal (the twistings and turnings of that Möbius strip), we must move beyond comparisons based on similarities and dissimilarities and inject instability and indeterminacy into our discussions. The advantage of thinking in terms of the Möbius strip is that it encourages a celebration of difference and uniqueness.

This is also not to imply that we can understand the swirling motions of the Möbius strip outside of the material, ideological and historical contexts that brought it into being. There is nothing metaphysical or transcendent about the strip. Its existence depends, after all, on paper, scissors, glue, and the mental and physical labour of mathematicians like August Möbius and readers like you and me. It is a product of human labour, and that labour is political. In other words, *agents* are involved in determining what the Möbius strip of life actually means.

For me, then, the emotional tone and purported rationales given for tying a knot in that Möbius strip in order to declare '*here!* and not *there!* is the place where the human starts and the animal ceases' is what is fascinating. It is a process infused with human narcissism. Take, for example, the ways physiognomists (that is, those thinkers who strove to develop the science of the human versus animal through an analysis of the contours of their faces) paid homage to the greatness of human faces in comparison to those of other sentient creatures. 'God of perfection!', Johann Kaspar Lavater exclaimed in 1804. 'How supremely, how benevolently hast thou displayed thyself in man!' In case his readers had not quite grasped the full glory of their own humanity, he continued:

> Beyond the human body! that fair investiture of all that is more beauteous! − Unity in variety! Variety in unity! How are they there

* Pronounced 'zow-EE-low-gee'.

displayed in their very essence! – What elegance, what propriety, what symmetry, through all the forms, all the members! How imperceptible, how infinite, are the gradations that constitute this beauteous whole! . . . The likeness of God![20]

On the other hand, Charles Darwin's musings on humanity's animal inheritance were more reflective. As he put it in The Descent of Man,

The difference in mind between man and the higher animals, great as it is, is certainly one of degree and not of kind. We have seen that the senses and intuitions, the various emotions and faculties, such as love, memory, attention, curiosity, imitation, reason, &c., of which man boasts, may be found in an incipient, or even sometimes in a well-developed condition, in the lower animals.[21]

Darwinian arguments may have contributed to the deconstruction of the radical differences imagined between humans and animals, but humanism survived this attack. It did this, in part, by rejecting absolutist narratives of the human (the claim that people are utterly distinct from animals) and embracing relativistic ones (the idea of a continuum between the two states, with the fully human at one end and the fully animal at the other).

In more recent years, dramatic scientific and cultural initiatives have continued to require us to question earlier certainties about human identity. Work with primates has shown that they can communicate in sign language, they possess complex communities, and their cognitive abilities are greater than many humans'. Progress in xenotransplantation technologies and stem-cell research have muddled even the most basic human/animal border. Many scientists question the traditional demarcations of species itself. As physiologist Jared Diamond asks in The Third Chimpanzee, how did the 2.9 per cent genetic difference between two kinds of vireos (passerine birds) or the 2.2 per cent difference between two gibbons make for a different species, while only 1.6 per cent separates humans from the chimpanzees yet we occupy a different genus?[22] If Homo sapiens is genetically so close to the other great apes, why shouldn't these apes be accepted as 'persons' too?[23]

What should we be celebrating: equality or difference? In relation to women, it is a question that has been discussed by every generation of feminists. Expressed crudely, should we be celebrating women's difference from men or should we be emphasizing our common

humanity? Conversely, should animals be judged according to the
degree to which they resemble 'us', or is that also the wrong criterion?
I will be arguing that the concept of negative zoélogy can help us out of
the dilemma possessed by these knotty (in the sense implied by the
Möbius strip) questions.

In recent years an anti- or even post-humanist rhetoric has emerged.
In large part, this is due to the palpable failure of humanism, which is
seen to be corrupt ('humans' have been tortured and killed in the
name of 'humanitarianism') or obsolete (scientific and cultural shifts
have blurred any clear notion of a human–animal border).

Unfortunately, though, post-humanism has proved much more successful in identifying what is wrong with humanism than with setting
out its own coherent position. This is why I believe that history and philosophy need to come into dialogue. The most productive discussions
on what it means to be human have emanated from the great philosophers of late modernity. For me, the insights of Jacques Derrida have
proved particularly rewarding. More than any other modern philosopher, Derrida devoted his life to 'deconstructing', or intellectually
unpicking, the dogmas of traditional philosophy. His philosophical
writings have consistently sought to show how supposed dichotomies
are actually dependent upon each other, and are extraordinarily fluid.
For me, Derrida is the philosopher of the Möbius strip.

For our purposes, it is Derrida's deconstruction of the human/animal
dichotomy that is most relevant. Derrida has criticized two ways of
responding to 'the animal' – that is, either seeing them simplistically as
'the other' against whom humans are constituted, or turning them into
nothing more than anthropomorphized substitutes for humans. His philosophy is a powerful acknowledgement of the moral significance of
alterity or 'otherness': the recognition of the way in which radical difference creates what is the self or the same.[24] I follow Derrida in
deconstructing the 'human' – that is, in unpicking the various strands
that (in specific places and at various times in the past and present)
philosophers, scientists, politicians, feminists and 'Jane and John Smith'
claim to constitute 'the human'. This also involves critiquing the designation 'animal'. As Derrida reminds us, 'the animal' is nothing more (or
less) than 'a word that men have given themselves the right to give . . .
They have given themselves the word in order to corral a large number
of living beings within a single concept: "the Animal," they say.'[25] Erasing
the awe-inspiring variety of sentient life impoverishes all our lives.

Obviously, there are an 'infinite number of animal societies'.[26] In a single volume like this one, it is impossible to attempt to include more than a tiny number of animal cultures, and it is too clumsy to always put 'the animal' and 'the human' in inverted commas. Perhaps it is simplest to state that the animals of choice in my analysis will be cats, dogs and the great apes, although we will also come face to face with lizards, pigs, mice, sheep, cows, horses and vultures. Unfortunately, only a few of these individuals have names. Equally, the text would be encumbered if I introduced neologisms such as 'humanimal' or made too much use of lumbering terms such as 'human-animal' and 'non-human animal' (although I do use these terms occasionally as a useful reminder). These terms are anthropocentric, prioritizing the 'human', against whom there is a 'non-'. Instead, I shall take it as given that the words animal and human are not only highly problematic, shorthand concepts, but also remain indispensable in the task of rethinking the human and the post-human in the twenty-first century.

'The Cat Metamorphosed into a Woman'

So, how should we respond to the Earnest Englishwoman's question about whether women are animals? Her satire is an astute political critique of a society that denigrates women as lower than animals. Misogynist humour of her time and ours routinely classifies women as animals (pussies, chicks, birds, vixens, cows and bitches, for instance). At the other political extreme, and for profoundly different reasons, feminist critiques also often characterize women as animals, as did Mary Wollstonecraft in *A Vindication of the Rights of Woman* (1792), where she railed against the lives of ladies 'confined in cages like the feathered race' with 'nothing to do but to plume themselves, and stalk with mock majesty from perch to perch'.[27] Many purportedly scientific, legal, and sociological accounts continue to assume that 'man' is simply a synonym for human. Defenders of this usage claim that those of us who feel excluded from 'mankind' are simply falling prey to political correctness.

Fabulists, however, can provide more subtle meditations on what it means to be alive, whether in the bodily form of a human or of an animal. Occasionally, they also reflect on the nature of love between different genus and species – bonds of affection between *Felis catus* (the domestic cat) and *Homo sapiens*, for instance – bringing into question whether the conflict that arises in all attempts to reach out to other creatures is due to irreconcilable genders (female or male) or genera (*Felis* or *Homo*).

One of the wittiest of these fables dramatically inverts the Earnest

Englishwoman's question 'Are Women Animals?' by positing that animals might be women. 'The Cat Metamorphosed into a Woman' was written by the French fabulist Jean de La Fontaine (see Figure 2). La Fontaine's droll, yet profound, insights into the question of what it means to be human have meant that they have been read avidly by every generation since he penned them in the seventeenth century.

In La Fontaine's fable, the poet speaks of a man 'much enamoured of his cat':

> Her gentle beauty was a joy to see;
> Her meow, sweet, soft, as meow could be.

Through 'prayer, and charm, and spell', the lover transformed the cat into a woman, whom he immediately married. He admitted that, before her transformation, his love was merely 'passing fond' but, as a 'beast-turned-to-wife', a 'burning lust he bore' and he 'coddled, caressed her, and she him'. All was well until, while 'plying their pleasure on the mat of natted straw', some mice turned up for a nibble. What happened next grieved the husband:

> Up jumps the wife, unthinking . . .
> Lunges . . . Misses her prey . . . But when the mice
> Return, as soon they do, she stands in wait,
> And they, undaunted by her cat-free state,
> Are leapt upon and, in a trice,
> Done in: for they, thereby, excite
> The more milady's appetite.

The message is clear: 'nature' has 'such power, such strength' that it cannot be changed, although a person might 'flail . . . with lash and pitchfork':

> Slam shut the door: without ado, it
> Opens the window and climbs on through.[28]

'The Cat Metamorphosed into a Woman' introduces a number of questions that will appear in this book. Are women animals, as this fable would have it? Or are animals women, property to be petted and redesigned at the whim of their owners? Substituting the word 'slave' for 'women' draws our attention to two widespread forms of viciousness in Anglo-American history.

Figure 2. Jean de La Fontaine's 'The Cat Metamorphosed into a Woman', from Marmaduke Park, *Aesop, in Rhyme; or, Old Friends in a New Dress*.
Park, *Aesop, in Rhyme; or, Old Friends in a New Dress*

La Fontaine's young lover wrought the metamorphosis of his beloved cat through spiritual mysticism but, in more modern times, scientists and physicians wield real transformative power. What is the 'true nature' of chimeras conjured up by white-frocked surgeons who transplant organs or stem cells from animals to humans? When the ardent lover confesses that his devotion to his gentle Cat was but 'passing fond' when compared to his passion for the Woman, he subscribes to a widely held assumption that animals have lesser moral and aesthetic standing than some humans. Animal rights advocates disparagingly label such people 'speciesists'.

Finally, what does it mean to be a certain kind of human, or a certain kind of animal? Being a woman, an ape, a subaltern or a dog *matters*. La Fontaine seeks to question the pliability of 'human nature' and 'animal nature'. It is 'natural' for the Woman to respond to her husband's gentle caresses, and she enjoys 'coddling' him in return; equally, the Cat's 'natural' appetite for mice cannot be sated. On closer inspection, however, the unyielding 'nature' in the poem turns out to be extremely subtle. Who decides whether the female protagonist is human or animal? The mice recognize her as a woman because of her 'cat-free state'; the young husband grieves because her eagerness to play with, and eat, mice proves that she remains a cat 'by nature'. The Woman herself is silent.

Finally, I will not be pretending to say anything about what it means to be an animal. We simply do not know.

In a famous passage in 'The Animal that Therefore I Am (More to Follow)', Derrida strips himself bare for his readers, asking us to imagine him standing naked in his bathroom. Suddenly, Derrida admits, he became aware of the gaze of his cat. Who is this cat who dares to look at the great philosopher without any clothes on?

Derrida states categorically that this cat is not a cat from one of La Fontaine's fables. Neither did she emerge from one of 'Kafka's vast zoopoetics' (I discuss one of these in the next chapter). Derrida's cat is a 'real cat'. This living cat did not appear in the bathroom 'as representative, or ambassador, carrying the immense symbolic responsibility with which our culture has always charged the feline race, from La Fontaine to Tieck (author of "Puss in Boots")'. In other words, this cat is not a symbol; she responds to a specific name, not as 'the exemplar of a species called cat, even less so of an animal genus or realm' but as a 'real cat'. Equally, Derrida recognizes that he would be wrong to call the cat '*my* pussycat', as though the cat is an object to be owned (perhaps like the cat/woman in La Fontaine's fable). Derrida does, however, admit that he identifies the cat in his bathroom 'as a male or female cat', but even before assigning it a gender, he sees the cat

> as *this* irreplaceable being that one day enters my space, enters this place where it can encounter me, see me, even see me naked. Nothing can ever take away from me the certainty that what we have here is an existence that refuses to be conceptualized.[29]

The figure of 'the animal' disrupts human identity precisely because of the refusal of the full range of 'real animals' to conform to philosophical or, indeed, historical schemas. Contrary to La Fontaine's fable, a living Cat cannot be seen as simply a stand-in for Woman; the animal is not the 'other' against whom the human is constituted. Equally, it is not the case that when the female-being looks like a human, she is really an animal: the Woman is not an anthropomorphic animal. Both are 'real'. This acknowledgement of the unknowability of 'the animal' gestures towards a much broader point: the unknowability of all animals, including human ones. It is this celebration of the 'unsubstitutable singularity' of people and animals that permeates this book.

Primates and Language

CHAPTER TWO

Red Peter

Red Peter was an ape from the Gold Coast. He was not a real ape (indeed, he had a tail, unlike other members of his species), but had emerged from the imagination of Franz Kafka. Red Peter was one of those personalities who came to life within 'Kafka's vast zoopoetics'.

Kafka introduced the world to Red Peter in the short story 'A Report to an Academy'.[1] He published it during the First World War, when Enlightenment hopes for the perfectibility of humanity under the civilizing directives of reason, law and habits of decorum were being violently undermined. The key question in Kafka's story echoed the one asked by La Fontaine in 'The Cat Metamorphosed into a Woman': what does it mean to be a woman or cat, a man or an ape? What does it mean to be a member of the family of great apes, *Hominidae*: genus *Homo* (humans), *Pan* (chimpanzees and bonobos), *Gorilla*, and *Pongo* (orang-utans)?

Red Peter's life story – as he rehearsed it in front of the members of an unnamed but distinguished Academy – was a meditation on the question of whether an ape could truly overcome his apish nature. Could Red Peter become a man?

For Red Peter, the enquiry was deeply personal. He had been shot and captured while drinking from a river on the Gold Coast. His captors had been employed by Carl Hagenbeck, who was infamous for supplying European zoos with wild animals. Five years before making his report to the distinguished academicians, he had found himself on Hagenbeck's steamer, imprisoned in a small cage and bound for Germany (see Figure 1).[2]

Figure 1. Feeding caged animals on board one of Carl Hagenbeck's steamers on its way to Europe, c.1890. In his autobiography, *Beasts and Men*, Hagenbeck recalled how, after capturing 'baboons by waiting for them near rivers and other drinking places' (exactly how Kafka said that Red Peter had been shot and captured), his team would load them on to steamers bound for Europe. Many died en route. In Hagenbeck's aloof prose, 'Whether this [death] is due to the terror and strain which they underwent at capture, or to being confined in cramped cages, I cannot say. But the fact remains that not more than half of them arrive safely at their destinations, despite our utmost care.'[3]

Courtesy of Tierpark Carl Hagenbeck GmbH, Hamburg-Stellingen

En route to his place of exile, Kafka's Red Peter had plenty of time to speculate on what it meant to be an ape rather than a man. Why, he asked, were the humans on the steamer free to wander the decks while he was forced to 'squat, with bent and constantly trembling knees . . . while the bars of the cage cut into my flesh behind'. Gradually, a 'lofty goal began to dawn on me': if he could imitate humans, then surely he would attain similar freedoms. 'Very well, then', he resolved, by becoming proficient in 'aping' men, he 'would cease to be an ape'.

It turned out to be easier than he had expected. What did humans do? They shook hands. Red Peter learnt the gesture. They spat. After only a few days he could spit. Soon, he could smoke. The hardest task was learning to drink alcohol (see Figure 2). One day, though, he seized a gin bottle and, to the amusement of the sailors, Kafka's Red Peter recalled how he put it to my lips, and without hesitation, without grimacing, like a professional drinker, with eyes rolling and throat gurgling, really and truly drank it dry; then threw the bottle from me, not in despair this time but with artistic skill.

Then, 'because all my senses were reeling', he cried out a loud 'Hallo!'

With this word he 'broke into human speech, sprang with this cry into the community of men, and felt their echoing cry: "Listen, he's speaking!"' The ape said 'Hallo' and was catapulted into the 'community of men'. Humans, it turned out, are speaking apes. They are (as Red Peter certainly was) fond of 'using images', thus demonstrating the ability to think conceptually or in abstract terms. For Kafka's Red Peter, as well as many other thinkers throughout the centuries, what distinguishes *Homo sapiens* from other animals is language.

The centrality of language in distinguishing humans from other animals was Red Peter's most significant insight. But he had other things to report about what it means to be human. All creatures, Red Peter

Figure 2. 'Diogenes', an orang-utan from Borneo, who was captured and kept as a pet by Carl Hagenbeck, the man Kafka made responsible for capturing Red Peter. From Hagenbeck's *Beasts and Men*.

Hagenbeck, *Beasts and Men*

insisted, are the product of long evolutionary processes. He confessed that it was not possible for him to talk about his past life as an ape because, although only five years 'separate me from my apehood', his evolutionary progress in that period had been astoundingly fast. 'To speak plainly,' he exhorted the gentlemen of the Academy, 'your own apehood' (if they were honest enough to admit to it) 'cannot be further removed from you than mine is from me'. Indeed, every creature, 'from the little chimpanzee to the great Achilles', feels 'a tickling at his heel'.

However, Red Peter found himself in a harsh, Darwinian world, dominated by the struggle for existence and the inexorable forces of natural selection. As Charles Darwin wrote in *The Origin of Species*,

> Can we doubt (remembering that many more individuals are born than can possibly survive) that individuals having any advantage, however slight, over others, would have the best chance of surviving and of procreating their kind? On the other hand, we may feel sure that any variation in the least degree injurious would be rigidly destroyed. This preservation of favourable variations and the rejection in injurious variations, I call Natural Selection.[4]

In the struggle for survival, effective mimicry was essential. Darwin drew attention to the extraordinary variety of techniques and ruses that living creatures employed in order to survive and reproduce. Take insects, for instance:

> [They] often resemble for the sake of protection various objects, such as green or decaying leaves, dead twigs, bits of lichen, flowers, spines, excrement of birds, and living insects . . . The resemblance is often wonderfully close, and is not confined to colour, but extends to form, and even to the manner in which the insects hold themselves.[5]

Red Peter admitted to adopting some of these evolutionary strategies: imitation, adaptive behaviour, deception, rationalisation, and self-delusion were tools he used to survive. Flawless performance was indispensable. Other marginalized groups employed similar techniques in order to integrate themselves into more privileged strata of society. In human communities, for example, women strove to 'get ahead' in professional life or the army by becoming 'more manly than the men' and Jews attempted to fit into Christian communities by masking their culture (Kafka's story is often seen as an analogy of Jewish assimilation).[6] In Red

Peter's case, he imitated the sailors on board the steamer. He 'chose' least-bad options (deciding that a job in a variety show was preferable to incarceration in a zoo, for example); he shared a bottle of wine with the man responsible for his capture; he impressed the academicians with his elocution and metaphoric flourishes. All the time, he admitted that he was being deceptive and that his debasement was strategic. He boasted that, through mimicry and quickness of intelligence, he had 'attained the cultural level of an average European'. In fact, he had become superior to those he mimicked. He often employed as many as five teachers at once, especially after his first teacher 'became himself almost apish' as a consequence of teaching him and had to be 'removed to a mental hospital'.

As the struggle for mastery between Red Peter and his teachers suggests, Kafka's story adopts a pessimistic Darwinism. Language is acquired in order to imitate, deceive and dominate. Red Peter promises candour – including the handshake, which, he admits, 'betokens frankness'. However, he only offers imitations. The implication seems to be that the possession of language does not propel forward the evolutionary advancement of humans; rather, human civilization is driven by basic physiological needs and ignominious urges; language is little more than an instrument of domination.

The freedom that Red Peter sought while encaged on the company steamer also turned out to be mere whimsy. In the variety theatre where he was employed, he watched acrobats as they 'swung, they rocked, they leapt, they floated into each other's arms, one carried the other in his teeth by the hair', but this 'freedom' was nothing more than 'arbitrary movement'. What a 'mockery of mother nature', he exclaimed, adding that 'No building could withstand the laughter of the assembled apes at a sight like that'.

Although the liberties offered by the theatre were illusionary, Red Peter recognized that life in pantomime was preferable to captivity in a zoo. This even applied to the 'new zoos' designed by the man who captured him, Carl Hagenbeck. The animal parks that Hagenbeck designed from 1907 onwards became the model for zoos throughout Europe. Hagenbeck's zoos eliminated iron bars: instead, the animals and their audiences were separated by carefully hidden moats. Furthermore, these zoos displayed not only apes, tigers and flamingos, but people as well – Laplanders, Nubians, Eskimos, Patagonians, Fuegians, Sinhalese, Indians and other 'unspoiled children of Nature' and 'wild men' (as Hagenbeck called them).[7] These people were displayed as families and communities alongside the appropriate 'wild

Figure 3. A rare photograph of Hagenbeck's Egyptian exhibition of 1912. Such ethnographic exhibitions were extremely popular. Despite the fence around the display, historian Eric Ames convincingly argues that bourgeois spectators and 'performers' were not rigidly confined to their own designated space.[8]

Courtesy of Tierpark Carl Hagenbeck GmbH, Hamburg-Stellingen

animals' and 'authentic' tools, ornaments, cooking utensils, musical instruments, and costumes (see Figure 3). In both variety theatres and zoological gardens, Red Peter recognized that what humans called 'freedom' merely required them to internalize the bars of the cage.

This moral vacuity at the heart of human society was most palpable when Red Peter looked at the treatment of animals. People did not bother to distinguish between different animal species, he observed with scorn. As Jacques Derrida put it, humans give themselves the right to name animals: they 'have given themselves the word in order to corral a large number of living beings within a single concept: "the Animal," they say'.[9] Even acts of naming that *seemed* to differentiate animal personalities turned out to be nothing of the kind. Red Peter had been given a personal name, for instance, but his name merely cobbled together the identity of a recently deceased performing ape and the visual evidence of a dark red scar on his cheek (where he had been shot during his capture). He complains that his name was

A positively apish invention, as if to suggest that the only thing distinguishing me from that performing ape Peter, a creature with some
small reputation who met his end the other day, was this red mark on
my cheek.

These complaints aside, Red Peter did have some choices, albeit
extremely limited ones. Escape was not one of them. Fleeing was
impossible for the captives, though Hagenbeck admitted that he was
impressed by how frequently they attempted it. 'What further evidence,' he mused, 'could be required of the high intelligence which
these animals possess?'[10] Red Peter, however, observed that if he
escaped he would simply have been recaptured and banished to an
even worse prison. Or he might have been killed by the other animals,
such as the boa constrictor in the cage opposite him. Red Peter also
refused to contemplate suicide, although this seems to have been a
fairly common choice in other fictive accounts by incarcerated monkeys
and apes.[11] The only real options were variety theatre or the zoo. In the
end, Red Peter 'chose' the former, believing that 'the zoo is only
another barred cage; if you land there you are lost'.

Red Peter was unimpressed by claims that humans distinguished
themselves from other animals by possessing, and adhering to, a higher
code of morality. The needs and urges of Hagenbeck's hunters and the
coarse sailors on the steamer, he observed, were 'beastly'. They shot
animals; they found it hilarious to burn captured animals with their
pipes. They thought it was a hoot to witness apes drinking wine, beer
and spirits. As many nineteenth-century owners and observers of orang-
utans, baboons and chimpanzees seemed to believe, these animals
'relished' alcoholic beverages even though it 'hastened their death'.[12]

The cruelty of kidnapping and imprisoning wild animals, ostensibly
on the grounds of cultivating scientific insights and advancing understanding of the evolution of *Homo sapiens*, was incomprehensible to
Red Peter. Surely it was sadistic to imprison sentient creatures in cages
that were 'too low to stand up in and too narrow to sit down'. 'Such a
method of confining wild beasts', Red Peter caustically agreed, was
'considered advantageous' from 'the human point of view'. It forced
animals to submit to human desires.

The submission of animals is at the heart of human civilization.
Although written decades after Red Peter's account, the full brutality
of human dealings with animals in captivity is illustrated by Winifred
Felce's experience of working with chimpanzees in the Munich

Tierpark in the 1930s. Like Kafka, Felce believed in the 'bitter struggle for existence, full of hardships and dangers'.[13] In contrast, however, she celebrated this struggle as a way to ensure human superiority. She believed that apes did not suffer by their loss of freedom:

> Love of freedom is primarily a human characteristic and we fail to understand animals if, instead of studying their emotions, we credit them with ours. But even man, the highest of all animals, is normally willing to forgo much of his liberty in exchange for security and comfort. Animals are not given to abstract thinking; they quickly forget the past and it is unlikely that they would long for it even if they could remember it.[14]

Felce believed, like Red Peter, that 'freedom' was overrated: the bars of the cage might be invisible, but they were necessary for human contentment. Maintaining a strict hierarchy of humans and animals was also imperative. Felce insisted on asserting her authority over the chimpanzees in her charge, insisting that 'almost every chimpanzee needs one good beating':

> [Their] large ears are useful accessories for beatings: the left ear is held by the left hand and the blows administered with the right hand, or vice versa. This gives a firm hold on the culprit in a way that prevents his biting. They are very tough and the pain inflicted is little compared with what they receive, cheerfully, in the course of their rough games with one another.

To illustrate her techniques, Felce drew reader's attention to a chimpanzee called (like Kafka's ape) Peter. Felce's Peter was a 'merry four-year-old chimp'. When he arrived in the zoo, he was 'full of laughing impudence' which was, Felce disapprovingly noted, 'not far from being dangerous uppishness'. She admitted that Peter 'earned his first box on the ears from me soon after being released from his travelling case. Peter understood, and we were friends for ever after.' Another keeper, however, treated Peter more indulgently and, as a result, he bit her. 'Enraged with pain and humiliation', this keeper 'forgot all caution, turned on him and gave him the shaking up he had so long deserved. Peter was openly amazed and wailed entreatingly for mercy. From then on they were great friends.' Such treatment made the captive chimpanzees 'docile all their lives'.[15] 'Friendship' between humans and their nearest animal relatives was dependent on violence and the assertion of hierarchies.

Was that why people were so heartless? Red Peter was bewildered: 'Scratch yourself raw between the toes and you won't find the reason [for human cruelty]. Shove yourself back against the bar until it nearly cuts you in two and you won't find the reason.' Was pain integral to the civilizing process? Might the sacrifice of animal life be necessary in becoming human?

Humans could not even claim a higher sexual morality to other animals. Red Peter had been shot twice during his capture – once in his cheek and another, more serious wound, 'below the hip'. Red Peter rallied against a journalist who claimed that the fact that he would pull down his trousers to show visitors where he had been wounded was evidence that his 'ape nature was not yet wholly suppressed'. Red Peter insisted that he was allowed to

> remove my trousers before anyone I please; nothing will be found there save a well-groomed coat of fur and the scar . . . Everything is open and above board; there is nothing to conceal; where the truth is at stake, every high-minded person will cast refinements of behaviour aside.

In contrast, if the journalist 'were to take off his trousers when visitors come, things would certainly appear in a different light, and I will let it stand to his credit that he does not'.

In the process of 'aping' fully human representatives of humanity (that is, male ones), Red Peter also treated women like animals, or creatures who could be used as means to an end: *things*. When he would return in the evenings,

> a little half-trained chimpanzee is awaiting me and I enjoy her company after the fashion of apes. By day I have no wish to see her; for she has that wild, confused look of the trained animal in her eye; no one but me can recognize it, and it is more than I can bear.

These human pleasures (assuming, of course, a hierarchy of humanness in which man ranks far ahead of woman) were granted to Red Peter because of one thing: his ability to speak, to possess language. It was a theme explored by many writers and artists before and after Kafka's time (see Figure 4). For instance, Kakfa would have known of the civilized ape Milo, created by the German romantic author E. T. A. Hoffmann. Milo's

Figure 4. Sir Edwin Landseer's *The Monkey who had Seen the World*, 1827. The painting, showing a monkey dressed in livery among 'wild' monkeys, is a meditation on ideas about civilization and nature. Most of the monkeys seem to be rhesus macaques, but there is also a baboon and a brown capuchin.

The Travelled Monkey, 1827 (oil on canvas), Landseer, Sir Edwin (1802–73) © Guildhall Art Gallery, City of London/The Bridgeman Art Library

story also involved being 'liberated' from his animal existence and taught to speak, write and play music. Kafka may have also known of Thomas Love Peacock's *Melincourt* and Wilhelm Hauff's 'The Ape as Man'.[16]

What makes Kafka's story so brilliant, however, is its subtle deconstruction of an individual ape and a broader human society that turns out to be limited and imitative. In the end, the great loser is Red Peter himself, who (through adopting human language) is condemned to a life of dissimulation. He even becomes an animal oppressor himself. Is this what it means to become human? By acquiring language, Red Peter sought to ingratiate himself to the human members of an illustrious academy. Red Peter's imitative and inebriated 'Hallo!' catapulted him from ape society into the 'community of men'. Might the insistence on the importance of language as a marker of status, even full personhood, be an act of violence?

CHAPTER THREE

Talking Animals

An Ape with a pliable thumb and big brain,
When the gift of the gab he had managed to gain,
As a Lord of Creation established his reign,
Which nobody can deny.

'THE ORIGIN OF SPECIES. A NEW SONG'[1]

'The Origin of Species. A New Song', published in *Blackwood's Magazine* in 1861, succinctly identifies what many people believe constitutes 'the human'. The vast gulf between humans and the rest of the animal world is all due to the 'gift of the gab', or language. The anonymous author of 'Monkeyana' (1896) may have quipped that it was the monkey's 'unfortunate inability to discard his tail' (and Kafka's ape mysteriously gained a tail!) that meant that he had 'fallen hopelessly behind ourselves in the race for evolutionary honours',[2] but most commentators sided with Aristotle in declaring humans to be 'speaking animals'. As Aristotle put it, it was obvious that 'man' was

more of a political animal than bees or any other gregarious animals . . . Nature, as we often say, makes nothing in vain, and man is the only animal whom she had endowed with the gift of speech.

He was very wrong about bees, who turn out to possess a highly complex language of dance,[3] but his pronouncement has been immensely influential. Aristotle admitted that animals possessed 'mere voice', the most basic 'indication of pleasure or pain', but 'the power of speech is intended to set forth the expedient and inexpedient, and therefore likewise the just and unjust'.[4] For Aristotle, certain animals produce sound (*psophos*). Others have voice (*phone*). But only human animals have language (*dialéktos*).[5]

Speech was 'God's gift to man . . . the gift was to him alone, as distinct from all other living creatures', as a late-nineteenth-century commentator summarized the situation.[6] Language enabled humans to *respond*, not simply *react*, to the world. A secular version of this can be seen in the writings of John Stuart Mill. For Mill, what distinguished 'man' from 'animal and machine' was the ability to choose, reason, discriminate, decide, exercise self-control and display 'vigorous reason'. This was in

" NOW, HOW DID I COME TO WIN THAT WAR ? "

Figure 1. From *Our Empire. The Official Organ of the British Empire Service League* (1930). The purpose of the cartoon was satirical, an attack on a number of war memoirs published in the 1920s that depicted soldiers as 'bestial'. The cartoonist and the British Empire Service League were making the point that the men were not apes, but had fought a war in defence of human civilization. They strove to convince people that language – that superior trait possessed by humans but not apes, enabling people to articulate concepts such as honour and courage – removed human violence from the 'beast'.
Our Empire (May 1930)

contrast to the 'ape-like' faculty of 'imitation'.[7] Mill claimed that language testified to the possession of exquisite reason and willpower.

The question, though, becomes: what does it mean to truly 'speak', and is speaking the same as 'language'? Is speech merely 'a peculiar movement of certain organs of the body – a series of muscular contractions of the thorax, the throat, the tongue, the lips, etc.', as one commentator in 1907 would have it?[8] Or is language something more splendid? Is it the 'symbolic use of communicative signs; the use of signs in communicative settings to engage in acts of reference . . . The use of signs as symbols, as things that stand conventionally for other things', for instance?[9] Are humans the only animals capable of language? What about humans who cannot speak? As we will see throughout this book, the uncertainty of human identity encouraged people to seek out some trait that would provide a sense of certainty: '*there!* is the human'. Nowhere is this desperation more obvious than when we encounter our closest kin. This is perhaps what Agamben meant when he observed that human identity is 'constructed as a series of mirrors in which man, looking at himself, sees his own image always already deformed in the features of an ape'[10] (see Figure 1). The main 'deformity' many humans have identified in the ape is muteness. But what if the ape spoke?

Only Humans Truly 'Speak'

In one of the most dogmatic assertions about language – René Descartes' *Discourse on Method* (1637) – readers are chided for holding to the fantasy that 'beasts speak, although we do not understand their language'. How could that be, Descartes asked. Since the organs of many animals resembled those of humans, if they could speak, then surely they would be able to 'make themselves understood by us'. Speech, he scolded, must not be confused 'with the natural movements which express passions and which can be imitated by machines as well as by animals'. It was not that 'beasts have less reason than man'; in fact, they 'have *no* reason at all'.[11]

Seventeenth-century diarist Samuel Pepys was not so certain. Like many Europeans when they first encountered apes and monkeys, Pepys's first thoughts when seeing a baboon that had been brought to Europe from Guinea was about language. The baboon was 'so much like a man in most things', he wrote, adding that 'I do believe it already understands English, and I am of the mind that it might be taught to speak or make signs'.[12] Or, as naturalist philosopher Julien Offray De La Mettrie mused in *Man a Machine* (1748), an ape who was 'properly trained', in the same way as a deaf person was trained, could 'be taught to pronounce, and consequently to know, a language'. If this happened, the ape 'would no longer be a wild man, nor a defective man, but he would be a perfect man, a little gentleman, with as much matter or muscle as we have, for thinking and profiting by his education'.[13] For both Pepys and La Mettrie, the muteness of simians reminded them that not all adult *humans* possessed language either. As we shall see later in this chapter, apes and (human) deaf-mutes were constantly being conflated in debates about language and reason. Spoken language turns out to be a particularly tight knot tied in the Möbius strip, serving to categorize a particular definition of *zoe*.

Pepys was writing in the seventeenth century and La Mettrie in the mid-eighteenth, but commentators throughout modern history shared their concerns. Thomas Stewart Traill was a keen explorer, who went on to found the Liverpool Royal Institution and become a professor of medical jurisprudence at the University of Edinburgh. In the 1820s he published an account of the anatomy of what he called an 'Orang Outang', but was actually a chimpanzee. He was struck by the chimpanzee's 'striking appearance to man' and noted that, 'On reviewing the structure of the organs of respiration, of the tongue and larynx, there does not appear any reason why the Orang Outang should not speak.'

He concluded that 'if animal organization were alone necessary to speech', the chimpanzee 'ought to possess this faculty in an eminent degree'. The explanation for the chimpanzee's 'deficiency' must, therefore, be due to 'mental peculiarities' rather than physiology. Traill went on to link speech with the possession of reason, admitting that it was 'extremely difficult to point out the exact boundary between human intellect, and the faculties of the lower animal'. However, there was 'one grand distinction peculiar to the human species': humans were capable of abstraction or the 'expression of ideas by arbitrary sounds'. In other words, 'the want of speech in the Orang and other animals, with a corporeal organization so similar to that of man, is wholly to be attributed to the absence of the faculty of abstraction'.[14]

Why might God have designed the 'brute creation' to be languageless, with its associated inability to think in abstract terms? The answer can be found in the short ditty with which I began this chapter: with the 'gift of the gab', humans 'established his [sic] reign' over all other animals. In 1776, however, Humphry Primatt elaborated on this answer. He claimed it was due to 'the Wisdom and Goodness of GOD that the Brutes should be animals *Irrational*, and *Dumb*'. Primatt distinguished between the '*Brutes of Ferocity*' – that is, wild animals – and the '*Brutes of Humanity*', or domesticated animals. Imagine, he instructed readers, the effect if wild animals not only possessed 'Strength, Swiftness, and Sharpness of Tooth or Talon' but also were capable of speech. In such a world, 'Men, who are animals naturally defenceless, and comparatively slow of motion, would live in perpetual fear'.

Equally terrible, Primatt thought, would be if animals that people used in their everyday life (domesticated animals, such as dray horses, bulls, goats and dogs) proved to be capable of reflecting on their 'subordinate and servile Condition'. This would make them 'very unhappy in themselves; and perhaps less tractable'. These animals would be tempted to 'enter into combinations and conspiracies against mankind'. They would quickly recognize that they were superior in 'stature and strength' to humans. The 'sense of their hard slavery, and of the injurious treatment they meet from us, would probably awaken their resentment'. People would face a 'general insurrection' if not the 'total overthrowing of the human Yoke'. Humankind would be forced to 'submissively bow down before their magnanimity and power'.[15] It was a biblically inspired fantasy of brute creation rising up in combination to overthrow their human oppressors that was also influenced by more secular concerns about speech as potentially revolutionary. What would happen if *any* subaltern group – animals, women, the poor and disenfranchised, the colonized – spoke? Revolt.

Theological understandings of the function of language, and the anxieties they inspired, were dominant throughout Primatt's century and the next. In 1855 Edward Meyrick Goulburn, headmaster of Rugby School and a prominent churchman, also insisted that speech was 'the great organ of Reason', which not only distinguished humans from 'the inferior animals' but also 'allies him [sic] with God and holy angels'.[16] Goulburn admitted that the 'brute creation' was capable of expressing its feelings – they cry out when beaten, for instance – but these expressions were nothing when compared to the 'Discourse of Reason, in one sentence of which ideas are ordered, marshalled and communicated'. There was a 'great gulf fixed' between the 'sound expressive of feeling and the sound expressive of intelligence', and this gulf was 'far greater than that which separates man from man, the kindly but rough peasant from the acutest philosopher'.[17] And what was the purpose of language that was allegedly shared by peasant and philosopher? It was piety. After all, the 'highest form of Speech' was 'Prayer and Praise'. The 'noblest exercise of Speech, its most exalted function; its great final cause — is that it should be poured forth before the Lord in confession, supplication, thanksgiving and praise'.[18]

The idea that animals possessed no language whatsoever was increasingly met with disquiet. After all, the author of 'Language of the Lower Animals' (1888) noted, it was possible to understand the 'jabberings' of *other* lesser creatures — savages and women, for instance. The Godordained stewardship of humans over animals was similar to that of missionaries over 'savages', he implied. If missionaries could devote twenty years to deciphering the '"clicks" of the clicking races' (he was referring to the Khoisan languages of southern and eastern Africa), why shouldn't it be possible to eventually decode the 'jabber of an ape'?[19]

This idea that 'savages' did not truly possess language — and were, therefore, set outside the fully human and relegated to the land of the 'beasts' — was extremely common. In the words of theologian Frederic William Farrar, in *An Essay on the Origin of Language* (1860), 'savage languages' were characterized by a '*hopeless poverty of the power of abstraction*'. Their 'tongues' proved that they possessed minds 'incapable of all subtle analysis'. Even more devastating, he contended that

> Existing savage races could not have *sunk* into this condition, and there seems every ground for believing that they are morally, mentally, and physically incapable of rising out of it, since they melt away before the advance of civilization like the time of snow before the sunlight.[20]

This was also the view of James Ross of the Manchester Royal Infirmary in his essay *On Aphasia* (1887). Ross differentiated between two kinds of thinking. On the one hand, there were lower forms of thinking, which included the communication of feelings and perceptions: this form was shared by humans and the 'lower animals'. On the other hand, more exalted forms of thinking existed. In his words,

> Thinking, on the higher level, has for its subject matter the relations in which phenomena are presented to us when they are detached from all individual perceptions, and it can only be carried on by means of mathematical symbols and *abstract* nouns.

This kind of thinking was not only beyond the capabilities of animals but was also absent within the 'lower races' of humanity. Words such as 'co-efficient' and 'virtue' were 'not even capable of being expressed' in the languages of 'inferior' humans.[21]

The weird noises made by 'savages' and apes were one thing: what about the possibilities of translating the 'jabberings' of women and birds? This was what Herbert Maxwell (Scottish politician and country gentleman) asked in *Blackwood's Edinburgh Magazine* in 1892. Some people, he noted, 'arrogantly' claim that speech is 'the monopoly of man [sic]'. However, he defied readers to refuse to admit that birds conversed with each other. The sounds made by birds were 'part of a conversation at least as intelligible and intelligent as the confusion of tongues arising at a fashionable lady's reception', he insisted. Maxwell admitted that

> An Englishman standing close on the skirts of some entertainment in London, will hear snatches of conversation and disjointed words which he can understand; but let him pause and listen on the stairs outside, and the human chatter has no more significance to him than the cackle of a poultry-yard.[22]

For Maxwell, then, women's speech resembled that of animals: their prattle was as 'intelligible and intelligent' as that of chickens and other 'birds'. The Earnest Englishwoman got the answer to her question of 1871: yes, women are twittering animals.

Maxwell was speaking as a keen naturalist. He would have been profoundly conscious of the work on language that had been carried out by Charles Darwin, the greatest scientist of the nineteenth century. In *The Descent of Man*, Darwin claimed that the 'half-art and half-instinct of language' propelled human evolution. The 'large size of the brain in man . . . may be attributed in chief part . . . to the early use of some simple form of language'.[23]

Darwin admitted that apes could 'make other apes understand by cries some of their perceptions and simpler wants'. However, the 'notion of expressing definite ideas by definite sounds had never crossed their minds'. The 'continual use of a highly developed language', Darwin argued, led humans to acquire 'certain powers, such as self-consciousness, abstraction, &c.' These characteristics were 'peculiar to man [sic]'.

Nevertheless, Darwin warned against exaggerating the distinction between humans and other animals with respect to language. After all, he asked,

At what age does the new-born infant possess the power of abstraction, or become self-conscious and reflect on its own existence? We cannot answer; nor can we answer in regard to the ascending organic scale. The half-art and half-instinct of language still bears the stamp of its gradual evolution.[24]

It was a perceptive observation: if to be human means to possess language and self-consciousness, then what does this mean for infants, the comatosed or the severely intellectually impaired?

The satirical possibilities of Darwinian thinking on language were immense (see Figure 2). 'My Cousin the Gorilla', written by someone signing himself 'Sigma', was published in the same year as *The Descent of Man* and this satire was concerned as much with the 'rights of man' and animals as it was with language. In Sigma's story, a chimpanzee who picked the pocket of her zookeeper found herself with a copy of Darwin's book. After reading it, she handed the 'poisonous tome' to her 'second cousin the ape in the next cage', and so it passed through the zoo, as fast as 'the savoury romances of the present day go through a seminar in Clapham'. Peace and contentment vanished, as the animals clamoured for 'reform and a bill of rights'. They resolved to set up a college at the centre of the zoo to prove to the world the 'incontestable truth of the immortal Darwinian theory'. 'Hixley' (a satirical rendering of Thomas Huxley, the great popularizer of Darwin) was commissioned to draw up the curriculum, aimed at enabling chimpanzees, monkeys, apes and gorillas to attain 'the full-blown dignity of mankind'. Classes included one on speech, which set out to teach the 'Arts of Biting, Howing [sic], Grinning, and Screaming, as compared with imperfect human speech'. Sigma then called on Oxford philologist and Sanskrit scholar Friedrich Max Müller to begin the process of translating the 'thousand new dialects of the pre-Adamite world'. The prospect would 'fill the halls of Young Oxford with pæan of joy'.[25]

It was a brilliant satire, and one that would have even made Darwin's followers smile. In more serious works in the biological and social sciences, Darwinians were quick to embrace the notion that language was central to the struggle for existence. In the words of the influential American rhetorician Fred Newton Scott (1908),

We shall see hundreds and thousands of these little systems of speech springing up, competing one with another and passing away. In the struggle for existence we may conceive either that the fittest group

Figure 2. 'Evolutionary Electioneering (A Darwinian Drama – Part III), from *Fun*, 25 November 1885. The cartoon was part of a satire on what would happen if animals demanded their rights, including the right to vote and stand for parliament. The sign at the back reads, 'Orang Outang for White-Chapel'. In 1885, Whitechapel was a notoriously impoverished area, overcrowded with Irish and Jewish immigrants, and the site of the Jack the Ripper murders. Working-class men and women in Whitechapel did not have the vote. The second stanza of the accompanying poem focused on the absurdity of giving rights to animals who have no language. It reads:

> For while the said Candidate smirked and orated,
> And his views with a rough kind of eloquence stated,
> Yea, while burning questions he manfully tackled,
> His hearers quawed [sic], quacked, brayed and bellowed,
>   and cackled.

For readers of *Fun*, the link between impoverished human inhabitants of Whitechapel and 'orang outangs' would have been obvious: it was absurd to give either group 'rights'.

Fun (25 November 1885)

survives, together with its mode of speech, or, what is more probable, that (other things being equal) the group with the best language-system, since it is able to give more explicit instructions for the organization of defense and attack, gets the start of the rest, and perpetuates both itself and its system of communication.[26]

Or, as the pioneering primatologist Robert Mearns Yerkes insisted seventeen years later, 'man alone has developed to a highly useful degree spoken and written language'. Humans and other primates have 'a well-developed voice and various ways of using it, but in no instance is there systematic and elaborate use of meaningful sounds as in the case of human speech'. He went on to observe (as did Traill a century earlier) that 'language so favors the appearance of ideas' and has been crucial in enabling 'man to advance, while his strong, versatile, but relatively speechless kindred have gradually lost in the struggle for existence'.[27]

Darwinian approaches to language were gradualist, cautious about declaring dogmatically at what stage in 'the ascending organic scale' we say that '*there!* is language, and not mere sound or voice'. Opponents were more impatient. In 1877, anti-Darwinian Sir Frederic Bateman launched a major defence of speech as an attribute unique to humans. In his words, the 'faculty of Articulate Language' created 'an immeasurable gulf' between apes and people, and this was a difference '*not only of degree, but of kind*'.[28] The chatter of parrots was nothing more than evidence of their 'remarkable power of imitation', and monkeys ('whose structural organism so closely resembles that of man') have for ever remained mute, capable only of 'pantomimic expression'.[29] Importantly, language was a '*Universal Attribute of Man*', that is, it was shared by all 'races', even the 'lowest barbarians'. He exhorted readers to

> Bring a Fuegian to England, and give him time, and he will talk, for he possesses the healthy germs of speech, and has the capacity for evolving a language; [but] put a monkey under training for any number of years, and he will never evince the slightest capacity for the acquisition of language.[30]

He ventured that the faculty of speech might be similar to that of the soul. It was

> an immaterial *nescio quid*, the comprehension of which is beyond the limits of our finite minds . . . I pin my faith to the story of the Grand Old Book, which tells us that man was created in the divine image, and I accept the tradition that Man sprang *as Man* direct from the hands of his God.[31]

In his preface to Bateman's book, the Dean of Norwich added his voice to the debate, corroborating the view that this special facility of humans was linked to their possession of an immortal soul. Only humans possessed the ability to rise above mere materiality and acknowledge the presence of a God. Even the most 'debased' races of humans, with their 'superstitious regard to some fetish' possessed the germ of religiosity, which might, 'by pouring the light of Divine truth upon it', be made to 'recognize the true God as its Judge'. In contrast, there was not the 'faintest glimpse of so sublime a faculty' in any animal.[32] Language was the link between 'man' and 'his' Heavenly Father.

Bateman and the Dean of Norwich were strident critics of Darwin from a theological perspective. Arguably the most influential critique of Darwin, though, approached the question from a very different perspective. Friedrich Max Müller was the Oxford philologist satirized by Sigma in 'My Cousin the Gorilla'. Sigma predicted that Müller would be beside himself with joy if the animals in the zoo, all of whom had been radicalized by reading Darwin, offered him the chance to translate their 'dialects of the pre-Adamite world'. Denied that heavenly moment, Müller sounded grumpy. 'It required some courage', he admitted, to 'stand up against the authority of Darwin'. Nonetheless, 'all serious thinkers agree . . . that there is a specific distinction between the human animal and all other animals, and that difference consists in language'.[33] He sneered at Darwin for imagining that evolutionary processes could 'derive language, that is, real *logos*, from interjections and mimicry'. 'Defending so unfortunate a position', he continued, 'as the transition of the cries of animals into the language of man', misled 'even so great a general' as Darwin. Müller insisted that

> I may say without presumption that, to speak of no other barrier between man and beast, the barrier of language remains as unshaken as ever, and renders every attempt at deriving man genealogically from any known or unknown ape, for the present at least, impossible, or, at all events, unscientific.[34]

In other words, the fact that humans, and humans only, possessed language was proof that evolution must be wrong: the evolutionary jump from ape to humanity must be impossible because no ape could truly speak.

Müller's refutation of the reasoning powers of animals was built into the famous rule propagated by psychologist Conwy Lloyd Morgan. According to 'Morgan's Canon' of 1892,

> In no case is an animal activity to be interpreted as the outcome of the exercise of a higher psychical faculty, if it can be fairly interpreted as the outcome of the exercise of one which stands lower in the psychological scale.[35]

In other words, Morgan set the bar for the possession of complex psychological and reasoning powers higher for animals than for humans (such as human children, for instance). Morgan's Canon forbade the use of complex explanations if simple ones would suffice. Morgan concluded that

> By means of language and language alone has human thought become possible. This it is which has placed so enormous a gap between the mind of man and the mind of the dog. Through language each human being becomes the inheritor of the accumulated thought and experience of the whole human race. Through language has the higher abstract thought become possible.[36]

Richard Lynch Garner, American naturalist and amateur scientist, agreed with Müller and Morgan that language and reason were inextricably related. But, contrary to them, he sought to prove that monkeys possessed language, and therefore *did* possess reason and self-consciousness.[37] If he could show that monkeys communicated through their forms of language, then *ergo* they must be capable of thought, emotions and consciousness. He declared that he was 'willing to incur the ridicule of the wise and the sneer of bigots' by proving that '"articulate speech" prevails among the lower primates, and that their speech contains the rudiments from which the tongues of mankind could easily develop'. He predicted that, if he could prove his view, his research would 'rattle the dry bones of philology' (that is, presumably, Müller's).[38]

How was he going to do this? Garner conflated speech and language, defining both as 'any oral sound, voluntarily made, for the purpose of conveying a preconceived idea from the mind of the speaker to the mind of another'.[39] His research into animal language began in 1884, with a visit to the zoological gardens in Cincinnati.

After listening to the monkeys' chatter, he resolved that this must be a form of communication. He returned to the gardens a few years later, determined to capture the language of gorillas and chimpanzees on the cylinders of the Edison phonograph[40] (see Figure 3). He did not conclude that monkeys and humans were *equal* in language acquisition – indeed, he accepted that humans possessed 'the highest type of vocalisation, and just as we descend in the cranial scale the vocal type degrades into sounds less flexible, less musical, and less capable'.[41] Animals did not need 'intricate or abstract thought', but

Figure 3. R. L. Garner conducting phonographic experiments with monkeys in Central Park, New York City, December 1891. At the bottom is a sketch of what Garner proposed to do in the French Congo. He is sitting in his cage, observing apes 'in the wild' and recording their speech. In this way, he claimed to be able to observe them 'in perfect freedom'. He boasted that he had 'seen more of those animals in a state of nature' than any other 'white man' had seen in all of history. The illustration is by F. S. Church for *Harper's Weekly*.

Harper's Weekly (1891)

they did need to communicate using a limited vocabulary.[42] Garner explained that, unlike human speech,

> the Simian idea is expressed in a single word of one sound, or syllable. For example, the one sound . . . which sounds like *wh-oo-w* as nearly as I can put it in letters, not only means *food*, but anything which is connected with food, all the inflections of the noun *food*, all inflection of the verb *to eat*, the adjective *hungry*, the noun *hunger*, the results obtained from the act, &c., such as to express satisfaction, that it is good, and so on.[43]

His experiments in zoos were followed by a trip to Africa, in order to 'capture' the language of these primates 'in the wild'. According to his account, in July 1892 he set sail to the port of Gaboon, in the French Congo. From there, he proceeded up the Ogowé River until he arrived at the south side of Lake Fernan Vaz. By April 1893 he had taken up residence in a cage he had constructed in the 'heart of the primeval forest'. He was accompanied by a young chimpanzee called Moses and 'from time to time' a 'native boy as a servant'.[44] He remained in the 'jungle' for four months, claiming to have discovered that chimpanzees possessed a vocabulary of between twenty-five and thirty words, including words for food, drink, sickness, cold and alarm. More startling, he claimed that he could make himself understood by them in about ten words.[45]

Garner was an enthusiastic evolutionist, but was seduced by a racist form of Social Darwinism. Because he believed that the Cebus was 'the most intelligent of monkeys', he dubbed them the 'Caucasian of monkeys'.[46] He used Petrus Camper's 'facial line' (a highly chauvinistic way of measuring faces) to distinguish between 'higher' and 'lower' animals,[47] even though this was a terminology that Darwin had resisted.[48] For Garner, Europeans were the highest animals; apes and monkeys were lower ones. He insisted that 'negro infants' retained that 'instinct of prehension' (the capability to grasp objects with their hands and feet) for much longer than white babies, thus setting them in a lower category to their 'white' sisters and brothers.[49] In fact, he argued that he was working in the 'wilds' of Africa not only in order to record the speech of the great apes but to 'bring home the sounds of all the creatures of those deep forests that utter speech', including that of the 'natives of the same regions'. In this way, he would preserve for civilized man a faithful panorama of the royal families, of the warriors armed with their simple instruments of death, the beaux and belles of royal society in evening dress, the peasantry, slaves and social parasites, the wild beasts, the tropical birds, and even the slimy serpents that infest the Eden of tropical Africa.

With the help of phonographic records and photographs,

We may thus ascertain how much bondage and civilization have respectively wrought for this race, by comparing their condition with that of their kinsmen in America [African Americans], who have grown up under the influences of civilization.[50]

As Garner said elsewhere, it was not enough to 'get to the bottom of monkey talk': that would only reveal 'a single link in the [evolutionary] chain'. He also wanted to

Take down the speech of the lowest specimens of the human race – the pygmies, the Bush-men . . . the Hottentot cluck and click. If there be a family resemblance, structural relationship, between the Rhesus monkey, the chimpanzee, and the lower grades of humanity, there may be a correction of speech, philological kinship, and then – and then – the origin of man's talk may be found.

After all, 'human racial highness and lowness showed itself in body as well as mind, including language'.[51]

Garner's ideas proved popular, but failed to win over most other scientists, and not because of their inherent racism. In 1892 Lloyd Morgan outdid Garner's racism with his misogyny, arguing that Garner's 'contributions to science' consisted of nothing more than anecdotes 'with reflections thereon suited for the delectation of elderly spinsters'.[52] In 1894, Garner was even accused of fraud by well-known journalist and politician Henry Labouchère.[53] Two years later the anonymous author of 'Mr Garner and his Apes' sneered at whether Garner even travelled to Africa or knew anything at all about African animals.[54] Perhaps, journalists speculated, Garner had simply spent his time in a Catholic mission, swilling claret. Despite this, Garner's technique of recording animal voices on phonographs and then playing it back to the animals to see if it could be understood ('playback feedback') was successfully revived in 1970s investigations into animal languages.[55]

Speechless Humans

Garner, as well as most other nineteenth-century commentators, ranked humans and other animals according to a hierarchy of language. They expected 'primitive peoples' to possess less elaborate systems of communication. These peoples were, literally, less human than others. We have already seen how some human languages were denigrated, along with their speakers. The 'clicking races' are one example. The 'twitterings' of women are another. I could also point to the dismissal of Creole languages, such as Haitian Creole. As David Ker informed readers in his story 'In a Haytian Village' (1876), the Haitian language was a 'horrible native patois which would be the fit language of the baboon'.[56] Creole languages were hybrid ones, incapable of complex or abstract thought, and scarcely worthy of civilized (truly human) discourse.

The way language was used to create hierarchies among humans comes into even starker focus when commentators turned to Europeans who had been born, or who became through accident or illness, mute (see Figure 4). Were they fully human?

Figure 4. 'Self-portrait by a patient with aphasic mutism', from Yvan Lebrun, *Mutism.* Lebrun was a neurolinguist and he used this portrait to introduce his chapter on 'organic mutism'. Aphasic mutism is also called 'word mutism': the person cannot make verbal utterances, but may have partial or total speech comprehension.

Lebrun, *Mutism*

Speechless adult humans typically belonged to one of two categories: aphasics and deaf-mutes. People with aphasia were able to understand language but were unable to speak. As the *Lancet* put it in 1868, a person with aphasia possessed 'a brain that could think, and a tongue that could wag quite well, but without any power to make the thinking and the tongue-wagging coincide'.[57] The condition was only named in the 1860s; as the president of the Dublin University Biological Association explained in 1907, prior to the early nineteenth century the brain was 'looked upon as a dish of macaroni, all parts alike in texture and function'.[58] In 1825, however, Bouillaud concluded that the frontal lobes were crucial for 'the formation of words and of memory': damage to the frontal lobes seriously compromised a person's ability to think.[59] Then, in 1861, surgeon Pierre Paul Broca stood before the Société Anatomique in Paris to present his findings from a post-mortem on a patient called Leborgne. When alive, Leborgne had lost the ability to speak after suffering a major lesion in the third convolution of the left hemisphere of his frontal lobe (see Figure 5). The only syllable he was able to pronounce was 'Tan'. After conducting an autopsy on Tan, as Leborgne has become known, Broca

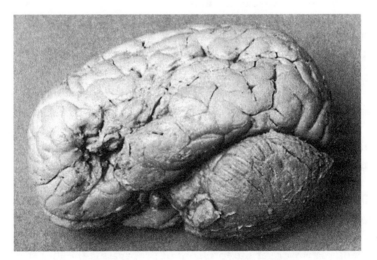

Figure 5. The brain of Leborgne ('Tan'), showing the lesion in the left frontal lobe. Paul Broca used this specimen to identify the part of the brain that enabled human speech. Image reproduced from Katrin Amunt and Karl Zilles' chapter in Yosef Grodzinsky and Karen Amunts (eds), *Broca's Region*.

Grodzinsky and Amunts (eds), *Broca's Region*

claimed that speech was localized in this region of the brain, an area that was subsequently labelled 'Broca's region'.[60] Crucially, in terms of what it means to be human, many scientists at this time believed (in the words of anatomist Carl Vogt) that 'in *apes* the third left frontal convolution actually is *entirely absent*'.[61] Lacking language was biologically determined. And, in turn, it defined the human.

No one doubted that people like Tan were members of *Homo sapiens* but, albeit through no fault of their own, they were distinctly lesser ones. Because aphasics could obviously understand language, and many had lost the ability to speak through brain lesions acquired in adulthood (and thus had established themselves within human culture), they tended to be accorded much greater consideration than the other group of speechless humans: that is, people who had been born deaf, or who had lost their hearing in early childhood.

Were people incapable of speaking, such as deaf-mutes, fully human? This question was relatively easy to answer if they could be identified as lesser humans on grounds other than speech. Thus some commentators stated that it was a 'known fact' that 'the Hebrew race' not only 'produces a larger number of blind and idiotic individuals than the European races among which it [sic] lives', but also 'produces' around four times more deaf-mutes.[62] In this way, deaf-muteness was evidence of lesser humanity according to 'racial' and eugenic criteria.

The problem still remained, though: not all mute Europeans were Jewish, Irish or other 'immigrants'. It was widely assumed that the simple fact of speechlessness meant that these people lacked a part of their humanity. The possession of language was fundamental to human identity for two main reasons: first, language was the facility that gave humans access to God and, second, language was tied to reason. As a result, mute humans were set outside full humanity, closer to the rest of animal life.

The first reason for setting mute people outside full humanity – the religious one – was loudly espoused. Humans were set above the animal precisely because of their intimate ties to the divine. Without language, how could any creature have access to God?

Theologians were at the forefront of propagating the idea that only humans possessed an innate awareness of religion. In 1850, *The History of Religion: A Rational Account of the True Religion*, authored by the eminent seventeenth-century diarist John Evelyn, was published. It proclaimed that religion was 'the highest reason'; it makes the human 'like his great Creator, rectifying the depravity of his nature, which, if uncultivated by religion, becomes fierce and sensual'.[63] This was why 'pigmies (those diminutive people, or sort of apes or satyrs) . . . are, therefore, not of the human race, because they have no religion'.[64]

It was a view repeated time and again in the nineteenth century. Leading commentators on deaf-mutism were adamant that 'without revelation or traditional knowledge there was no power in the human mind which could ever guide it to the idea of God as a Creator, or of a future state of rewards and punishments'.[65] In the words of an unnamed person reviewing John Kitto's *The Lost Senses* (1847), which drew on his experiences as a deaf-mute from the age of twelve,

> Experience furnishes no instance in which a deaf-mute, having nothing but the language of signs at his command, has ever attained to any distinct notion of a future world, of his own moral accountability, of man's ultimate destiny, or even of a Supreme Being.[66]

They were 'shut out from all the knowledge derived from history and tradition', including, most tragically, from knowledge of 'a future world, or a deity'.[67] In *The Happy Mute* (1835) evangelical writer Charlotte Elizabeth Tonna was equally blunt. 'Religious teaching seems to be out of the question, where words are wanting to convey it', she claimed. A deaf-mute child might be taught

> to kneel, to hold up his hands, to move his lips, and often he will do so with the most affecting aspect of devotion; but we can tell nothing of God the Creator and Preserver, the Redeemer and Sanctifier of our fallen race.[68]

As the Reverend Thomas H. Gallaudet, in 'A Sermon on the Duty and Advantages of Affording Instruction to the Deaf and Dumb' (1852), observed, deaf-mutes were ignorant even of 'natural religion', let alone 'revealed religion'. He recalled conversing with a deaf-mute, for whom 'a few glimmerings of truth had begun to dissipate the mental darkness in which it had been shrouded'. What had he felt when seeing a friend die, Gallaudet asked. The deaf-mute had responded (presumably by signs or writing), that he had seen only

> the termination of being; the destruction of all that constituted man. I had no notion of any existence beyond the grave. I knew not that there was a God who created and governs the world. I felt no

accountability to Him. My whole soul was engrossed with the gratification of my sensual appetites; with the decorations of dress; the
amusement of pleasure; or the anticipations of accumulating wealth,
and living in gayety [sic] and splendour.

As Gallaudet exclaimed,

A little while ago, this immortal mind had its vision bounded by the
narrow circle of temporal objects: *now*, its ken embraces the vast
extent of His immortal existence, with all the momentous realities of
that unseen world whither it is hastening. – *Then*, oh! what a degradation! it was kindred to the beasts of the field: *now*, what an
exaltation! we hope that it is allied to the spirits of the just made perfect; that it is elevated to communion with its God![69]

Throughout the century, commentators reiterated their belief that
the idea of God could not be 'innate', because it never appeared
spontaneously, without education.[70] No person 'conceived of a
First Cause' by simply 'viewing the works of nature': they were only
capable of looking at the wonders of nature 'like the brutes'.[71] As the
Reverend Colin Stone, of the Ohio Institution for the Deaf and
Dumb, put it,

The deaf-mute never reasons concerning the origin or the destiny of
the beings and things around him. Indeed, so heavy is the hand of his
calamity upon him, so nearly does it depress him to the level of mere
animal life, so dead are all the germs of thought and feeling in his soul,
that the great facts and truths relating to God and a future state,
which would seem to be the birthright and aliment of every rational
mind, rarely attract his attention or excite his curiosity.[72]

Mute humans could never attain full humanity because they were
excluded from knowledge of God. It was an argument identical to
that used by missionaries faced with the godlessness of 'savages': in
both cases, the acquisition of European languages was a crucial step in
the conversion process.

The second assumption was just as important. The idea that reason
could not exist without language was at the heart of all debates about
who was fully human, semi-human, and nonhuman. As Immanuel Kant
wrote in *Anthropology from a Pragmatic Point of View* (1798),

Thinking is *speaking* with oneself (the Indians of Tahiti call thinking 'speech in the belly'); consequently it is also *listening* to oneself inwardly (by means of the reproductive power of imagination).

As a result, the mute 'can never arrive at anything more than an *analogue* of reason'. Even if deaf people were taught to produce sounds, this 'speaking' would be nothing more than

a feeling of the play of his lips, tongue, and jaw; and it is hardly possible to imagine that he does anything more by his speaking than carry on a play with physical features, without having and thinking real concepts.[73]

Mute people were, by definition, excluded from the chief trait that set 'mankind' apart from other animals. Lacking rationality, they were excluded from voting, along with 'idiots', infants and criminals. And, of course, women.[74] As the *Saturday Magazine* put it in 1844, speech 'loudly proclaims the fact, that man [sic] possesses the superior powers of reason and judgment'.[75] Or, in the words of the principal of the West of England Institute for the Education of the Deaf and Dumb in 1870,

Without the means of communicating his thoughts, man [sic] must have roamed over the earth a solitary savage, without no power of develope [sic] those instincts of his nature which prompt him to become the being of social and civilized life.[76]

Did their faces resemble that of 'hares or monkeys'? A doctor in 1896 complained that many people thought so. Were the mute 'little better than brute beasts'?[77] An article in 'Our Medical Corner', published in an 1855 edition of *Reynolds's Miscellany of Romance, General Literature, Science, and Art*, explicitly claimed that deaf-mutes were nothing less (or more) than animals. The author noted that managers of institutions for deaf-mutes were fond of boasting that their inmates were

very mild in their temper, willing to do anything they are told, pleased with any attention paid to them, express delight at a future happiness after death, and express their dreams to their teachers.

How does this differ from the lower animals, he cynically asked. Tame animals are temperamentally gentle. Kindness and tuition make many

animals keen to submit to orders, especially when lavished with attention. As to expressing 'delight at a future happiness after death', even
a horse can be trained to 'get up on his hind legs and fight with his fore
legs' when asked what he would do in battle. It is clear that animals also
dream: 'The spaniel dog when asleep often exhibits the usual peculiar
sounds of different kinds of game being present.' None of these characteristics make deaf-mutes human. These 'proficiencies' are
'diminutive in comparison to the knowledge of the sound of the human
voice, by which we laud and sing to the glory of our Creator, and converse with our fellow creatures!' Indeed, even lower animals converse
with each other, unlike mute humans.[78] A teacher at the Pennsylvania
Institution for Deaf-Mutes was equally blunt; mute-people were 'little
above that of the more intelligent brutes, and lower than the most
unenlightened savages'.[79] Mute humans were slotted into a position
very far down the great Chain of Being.

In other words, the main explanation for downgrading the humanity of mutes was because language was assumed to be inseparable from
the faculty of reason. Deaf-mutes 'cannot carry on a train of reasoning
any more than a brute', according to Archbishop Whately, eminent
theologian, logician and economist.[80] Or, as Max Müller put it, deaf-
mutes 'have never shown any signs of reasoning', an argument
consistent with his views on the significance of language.[81] In the words
of an author writing in *North British Review* in 1847,

> The want of hearing, simply, is in fact a defect of comparatively easy
> endurance: it is the want of *language* that creates the immense chasm
> between the uneducated deaf-mute, and the uneducated hearing
> person . . . The uneducated deaf-mute – a being destitute of that
> which forms the most striking distinction between man and brute,
> separated from the rest of his species, and remaining alone in the
> midst of millions.

Deaf-muteness was much worse than blindness because

> the darkness of the deaf-mute is a mental and moral darkness; and
> though he can gaze abroad upon creation, yet it is little more than
> mere animal gratification that he feels; he looks not 'through nature
> up to nature's God', nor does he participate in that high communion
> which, through the sublimity of her visible language, she holds with
> the soul of an enlightened being.[82]

'L. N. S.', writing in the *British Mother's Journal*, went even further, linking muteness not only with animality but also with lack of manliness. In her 'Plea for the Speechless', this author lamented the mute person's dependency and inability to 'exercise those manly functions'. They were truly 'helpless', like animals and lesser humans such as women.[83]

Is Sign Language a Language?

Even early champions of mutes accepted that there was an essential link between language and reason. They differed, however, in drawing a distinction between language and *speech*. If it could be shown that, although incapable of vocal articulation, mutes were capable of conducting reasoned communication in a *silent* language, then surely they should be welcomed as fully human.

Edwin John Mann was a prominent proponent of this view. Mann had lost his hearing and ability to speak at the age of two, and had been raised at the Hartford Asylum for the Deaf and Dumb in Connecticut. In his remarkable account, published in the 1830s, he attacked 'crafty' reformers who were attempting to teach deaf-mutes to speak through manipulating their lips, palate, tongue, and throat (the 'oral approach'). This was 'as unnatural as to teach a parrot' to speak: the 'all-wide Providence never intended them to speak'.

Indeed, Mann went on, the ability to reason was not integral to being able to vocalize. If ignorance could be eradicated simply by teaching mutes to speak, then, he quipped, 'how is it that some men who can speak are so ignorant as to attempt to prove that, by teaching the deaf and dumb to speak, they immediately become rational beings?' Crucially, speech was not language. Mann accepted that 'without a language the deaf and dumb must forever remain little better than the brute creation'. However, the solution was to teach them a *language*, in order to render them 'rational beings'. In other words, what deaf-mutes need to become human, as opposed to degraded members of the 'brute creation', was not *vocal* speech but the '*language* of signs', the 'natural' language of mutes.[84]

Edward Meyrick Goulburn (the theologian mentioned earlier, who argued that speech distinguished humans from 'the inferior animals' and allied people with God) agreed. In 1855, he insisted that mutes possess language but 'some imperfection in their organs prevents their exercising it *vocally*'. If the 'essence' of language was mere sound, then 'a machine might be made to speak'. Goulburn did not want to align mutes with Descartes' animals: that is, mere 'automata' or moving machines, driven by instinct alone. It was obvious to Goulburn that a mute person

> can not only arrange his ideas in an orderly and methodological manner, can not only throw them mentally into consecutive words and proposition, – but can convey them, so arranged, to another person, by talking on the fingers.[85]

Even more radically, the president of the Deaf and Dumb College in Washington alleged that the 'sign and gesture language' was 'in many respects *superior* to articulate speech, as a means of communicating ideas'.[86]

Proponents of signing were faced with formidable foes, however. I have already mentioned Mann's criticism of 'crafty' reformers who used the 'oral method' (manipulating lips, palate, tongue, and throat) to teach mutes how to vocalize, and many other historians have written extensively on the disputes between oralists and signers.[87] Briefly, for oralists such as Evan Yellon, writing in the first decade of the twentieth century, sign language was an inferior form of communication (it wasn't even a 'language' at all) and its use was 'greatly to the detriment of the deaf-mute mental development'. In attempting to 'lift . . . the deaf-mute's mental plane', she had to be taught language, not mere mime. Signing would 'retard the child's advance' and condemn her to a life as a 'savage' or lesser human.[88] In the words of Elisabeth Blackburn in 'Our Deaf and Dumb' (1884), the oral system was best because it 'removes the barriers which kept the deaf-mute from mingling freely with his fellow-creatures', and was, therefore, an 'incalculable blessing to him [sic]'.[89] It was a view strongly influenced by an evolutionary model of human progress. For oralists, signing was primitive. It was a lesser form of language in evolutionary time and its promotion was likely to lead to degeneration.

In contrast, promoters of sign language tended to see signing as a gift of God: it bypassed the problems caused by the proliferation of spoken languages (the Tower of Babel) and their inherent tendency to dissimulate. Signing was, therefore, 'natural' to all humans, mute or not.

Nevertheless, from the late nineteenth century to the 1950s, oralists prevailed. Professional organisations representing teachers of deaf children increasingly promoted vocalisation, coupled with lip-reading, as the superior form of communication for deaf-mutes. In 1880, the Second International Congress of Teachers of the Deaf passed a resolution promoting oral educational methods. Signed languages (at least in schools and asylums) were spurned. As Helmer Myklebust observes in *The Psychology of Deafness* (1960), signed languages lacked 'precision, subtlety, and flexibility', making it 'likely that Man cannot achieve his ultimate potential through an Ideographic language . . . The manual sign system must be viewed as being inferior to the verbal as a language'.[90] Negative views about sign language only started to change after William C. Stokoe joined Gallaudet University (which educated deaf students) in 1955. He quickly concluded that signed languages were 'truly and equally languages' and in 1960 published *Sign Language Structure*, which showed that sign languages possessed systematic structures.[91] This work was followed up in the 1970s by researchers at the Salk Institute for Biological Studies in La Jolla, California.[92]

Teaching Sign Language to Apes

These controversies concerning how speechless humans could (and should) communicate were being replayed within primate laboratories. As we have seen, even before the eighteenth century the importance of teaching apes to communicate with humans has been recognised. In the twentieth century, scientists sought practical ways of making the dream of 'making the mute-ape speak' into a reality. Crucially, they turned to studies on *Homo ferus* for inspiration. Were these 'feral' children (who typically lacked speech) truly human, or were they closer to the animals who had brought them up?

One of the earliest studies was conducted by psychologist Winthrop Niles Kellogg who, in the 1920s, became interested in the history of feral children. Perhaps the most famous of these children were Peter of Hanover (was he an inspiration for Kafka's Red Peter?) and Victor of Aveyron. In 1724 and 1797, respectively, these boys had been captured in forests in northern Germany and France, having clearly been brought up outside human communities. Neither could speak and, although they learned many 'civilized' ways, they never acquired a language. In Victor's case, he failed to learn to speak despite the efforts of Dr Jean-Marc-Gaspard Itard of the National Institute for Deaf-Mutes. Kellogg also became fascinated by the 'wolf children' of India, particularly Amala and Kamala (aged four and nine years respectively), who had been found in a cave inhabited by wolves and acted like animals, including their inability to speak.[93]

Kellogg immediately recognised that these children posed interesting questions about the role of environment in creating the human. He noted that commentators in the past had tended to dismiss the problems faced by these children, claiming that they must be feeble-minded or 'congenitally lacking in the ability to learn'. Instead, he asked, might environment play a key role in explaining why they failed to become fully human? Perhaps, the 'wild' children

> had made natural and adequate adjustments to their environment . . .
> Those placed with animals may actually have learned, in a literal sense of
> the word, to be wild themselves, in the same way that a Caucasian child
> reared among Chinese grows into the Chinese customs and language.

In other words, the 'Caucasian child' would become wolf or Chinese depending upon her environment.

Unfortunately, he mused, it would be 'legally dangerous and morally outrageous' to test his proposition by placing a normal human baby in 'uncivilized surroundings' in order to observe her development.[94] It was possible, however, to treat a non-human infant in an equivalent fashion. Species differences allowed certain forms of cruelty to take place in the name of 'science', while making other forms 'outrageous'.

Kellogg's experimental subject was a seven-month-old chimpanzee called Gua, who had been forcibly removed from her family at the Anthropoid Experimental Station of Yale University, at Orange Park, Florida. In line with thinking of the time, the ideal environment for human education was the nuclear family. In June 1931, Kellogg set up home with his wife Luella, their ten-month-old son Donald and Gua (see Figure 6).[96] The only difference from any other family was that both infants faced a daily range of tests, including of their physiological state (blood pressure and weight, for example) and language comprehension, problem solving and obedience behaviour. It was an intensive programme, which consumed every moment of the Kelloggs' time and grew increasingly difficult as Gua matured.

The results were fascinating. While not disputing that heredity played an important role in infant learning, the Kelloggs concluded that environment was also crucial: just as the 'African aboriginal who is raised in the United States becomes civilized as a result of his removal to the civilized environment', so too Gua adopted aspects of his 'civilized environment'.[97] In some aspects, Gua became 'more humanized' than Donald: she was better able to skip, she was more cooperative and

Figure 6. Sister and brother: Gua and Donald. This image was published in W. N. Kellogg and L. A. Kellogg, *The Ape and the Child*. From the first time they were introduced to each other, Donald and Gua were raised as though they were both human infants. In the words of the Kelloggs, Gua was made 'a thoroughly humanized member of the family of the experimenters, who would serve respectively in the capacities of adopted "father" and "mother".'[95]

Kellogg, *The Ape and the Child*

obedient, she was more skilful in opening doors and had a 'superior anticipation of the bladder and bowel reactions'. Most important, she was a faster learner.[98]

The main problem the Kelloggs faced was that Donald began to copy Gua. At fourteen months, Donald could be heard imitating Gua's food bark. Most worryingly, Donald was not acquiring human language. Although both Donald and Gua responded to vocal stimulus (increasingly, Donald surpassed Gua), 'neither subject really learned to talk during the interval of the research'.[99] The experiment continued until March 1932, when Gua was returned to the primate colony in Orange Park.

The Kelloggs had not attempted to force either Gua or Donald to speak, hoping that language would arise 'naturally' out of normal familial interactions. The failure of their experiment (at least in terms of language) inspired other researchers to look more closely at language acquisition of mute humans. If the 'oral method' could be used to teach mute humans to speak, why not use it with apes and monkeys? This was the view of Cathy Hayes. Like the Kelloggs, she prioritized the home as the locus where language was acquired. In 1947, she removed a chimpanzee called Viki from her mother. Viki would live with Cathy and her husband Keith (a research psychologist from the Yerkes Laboratories of Primate Biology in Orange Park, Florida). It was a highly gendered experiment. As Cathy Hayes admitted, 'the pattern of our family was formed. Viki did it. I observed it. Keith explained it.'[100]

They quickly discovered that Viki seemed not to be acquiring language, so the Hayeses set out to teach her using the method employed by teachers of speech-handicapped humans, by 'shaping her lips and tongue with our fingers to form the various syllables'.[101] They had little success. According to Keith and Cathy Hayes, Viki

> bears little resemblance to those [speechless humans] whose trouble is caused by feeble-mindedness or by abnormality of the speech organs; but she does quite closely resemble those cases, known as aphasics, whose deficiency is caused by abnormal brain structure, congenital or acquired. Like many aphasics, Viki is deficient in language comprehension, as well as in speech, though here the deficit is less striking.[102]

They concluded that 'man's superior ability to use language may be his only important *genetic* advantage', but it was a significant advantage because it was a means of sharing knowledge. As a consequence, humans were 'less dependent on individual abilities', thus possessing a 'group intelligence'.[103] The experiment was short-lived: Viki died in 1954 after a sudden illness. She had only learned four words, which she said with great difficulty and in a hoarse whisper: mama, papa, up and cup.

The failure of these attempts led scientists to consider whether apes could be trained in two other kinds of human languages, sign language and artificial languages. From the 1960s, a large number of experiments were carried out. Examples include Koko the gorilla (Francine Patterson), Sarah the chimpanzee (David and Ann Premack), Lana the chimpanzee (Duane Rumbaugh), Kanzi the bonobo (Sue Savage-Rumbaugh), and Chantek the orang-utan (Lyn Miles). This literature can be reviewed elsewhere.[104] The two most important animals, who I will introduce as illustrative, were Washoe and Nim Chimpsky.

Washoe was the first chimpanzee to be taught human sign language.

This option had been considered as early as the 1920s. In 1927, primatologist Robert M. Yerkes wondered whether the 'chief reason for the ape's failure to develop speech is the absence of a tendency to imitate sounds . . . Seeing strongly stimulates [them] to imitation, but hearing seems to have no such effect'.[105] In *Almost Human* (1925), he concluded that the great apes

> have plenty to talk about, but no gift for the use of sounds to represent individual, as contrasted with racial, feelings or ideas. Perhaps they can be taught to use their fingers, somewhat as does the deaf and dumb person.[106]

However, as we saw earlier in the context of human deaf-mutes, the oralist method was the dominant one until Stokoe's radical defence of signing in the mid-1950s. By 1966 signing had moved into animal studies. If mute people could become more fully human by being taught (sign) language, then what was to stop other primates entering more fully the 'human family' through similar methods?

The first major experiment was carried out at the University of Nevada at Reno, when Allen and Beatrice Gardner set out to teach American Sign Language to Washoe, a ten-month-old female chimpanzee. They believed that the problem other scientists experienced in trying to teach apes to speak was not due to a deficiency in the apes' cognitive ability, but rather 'the unsuitability of the vocal tract configuration of the chimpanzee to the articulation of human language'.[107] Like their predecessors, they taught Washoe within a human child's environment. After fifty months, Washoe had learned 132 signs, which she was able to use both singly and in combinations. She understood what she was communicating, frequently correcting herself when she made a mistake: for instance, faced with an advertisement for a drink, she signed 'THAT FOOD', before changing it to 'THAT DRINK'.[108] In her later life, Washoe adopted a year-old chimpanzee called Loulis and taught him sign language. This has been seen as proof of cultural transmission between chimpanzees.

While the Washoe experiment has been regarded by many scientists to be a success,[109] attempts to replicate the results with a chimpanzee called Nim Chimpsky failed. Nim had been born in 1973 in Norman, Oklahoma, and taken by the primatologist Herbert S. Terrace to New York at the age of two weeks. Like Kafka's Red Peter, whose name had been cobbled together from the identity of another well-known ape and the red scar on his cheek, Nim Chimpsky's name was replete with meaning. His surname was a play on Noam Chomsky, the linguist who believed that language was 'hard-wired' in humans alone, while 'Nim' was given to him because (Terrace said) it 'had a jungle quality'.[110] It was also important for Terrace that Nim was a male. The other animals in the language projects had been female and, as Terrace put it, 'I thought it would be of value to investigate linguistic competence in a male'. Terrace also believed that female chimpanzees were 'more sensitive to depression than males'.[111]

Like Washoe, Nim was enculturated into human society, including being taught to use cutlery to eat and to sit on the toilet (see Figure 7).

Figure 7. Nim Chimpsky sitting on the toilet. Herbert Terrace described how a partially hidden camera was set up in Nim's bedroom: 'What I thought would be a difficult photographical challenge yielded clear pictures of Nim getting up and greeting Joyce Butler [one of his carers] as she entered his bedroom. Nim's docile mood continued when he was taken to the bathroom. There I was able to photograph him using the toilet and brushing his teeth. A few moments later he completed his morning ritual downstairs by dressing himself.' Unfortunately, that evening Nim (temporarily) escaped. Terrace tersely noted that 'Apparently Nim had been more concerned about the events of the day than we thought.' From Herbert S. Terrace, *Nim.*
Terrace, *Nim*

However, unlike Washoe, who was trained in a nurturing environment and encouraged to interact on intimate terms with her human family, Nim was taught in a more rigorous, laboratory environment, using food-reinforcement techniques. In the end, Terrace proclaimed the attempts a failure, claiming that Nim was simply a successful mimic.[112] Nim died of cardiac occlusion on 10 March 2000, at the young age of twenty-six.

The contrasting results that emerged from research with Washoe and Nim Chimpsky demonstrate the potential and difficulty of teaching human languages to primates. Three major issues emerge: the cost of such experiments to the animals themselves; the fluidity of arguments about similarities between humans and other animals; and, finally, the nature of language.

First, the cost to the animals is significant. When very young, both Washoe and Nim had been forcibly removed from their families and communities. Terrace described the moment when Stephanie Lee (who was to look after Nim) and William Lemmon (the Director of the Institute for Primate Studies at Norman) took Nim from his mother and flew him to New York:

> When she [Stephanie Lee] first saw Nim he was still with his mother Carolyn. Having had other babies removed from her, Carolyn seemed apprehensive when Stephanie and Dr Lemmon approached her. Carolyn must have communicated her fear to the chimps in the neighboring cages, for they soon began to act in an agitated manner and hooted loudly as Dr Lemmon fired a tranquilizer dart at Carolyn. A short time later Carolyn fell over, briefly asleep, and Dr Lemmon and Stephanie rushed into the cage to make sure Nim wouldn't be accidentally crushed by his mother. Stephanie gathered Nim up in a blanket and took him to her hotel room, where she diapered him and gave him a bottle. A few days later she and Nim flew to New York. Project Nim had begun.[113]

Nim's fate was sealed from the very beginning. After less than four years from the start of the experiment, Terrace struggled to gain funding to continue the research, and employing appropriate caretakers became progressively difficult. As a result, Nim was returned to the Institute for Primate Studies in Oklahoma, where he spent most of the remainder of his life confined in a cage. Even Terrace admitted that he would 'never forget Nim's incessant, ear-piercing screams and his look of fear and anger' when he 'abandoned him in his cage'.[114]

Second, the research illustrates the volatility of perceptions of 'likeness'. Take Washoe's reaction when, five years after she was forcibly taken from her mother and 'adopted' by human carers, she was abruptly returned to a primate colony at the University of Oklahoma. Washoe had been raised around humans since she was an infant, and so when placed with other chimpanzees she did not recognize her new companions as resembling her. The other chimpanzees, she signed, were 'BLACK CATS' and 'BLACK BUGS' – very derogatory terms for her. Washoe was convinced, from being brought up in a human environment, that she was more like humans than chimpanzees.

Finally, this research is interesting for what it can tell us about the nature of language itself. It suggests that language is not innate to either humans or apes. Apes in the wild do not acquire language. They only do so as human children do: that is, as a social process. This is widely regarded as one of the reasons why Washoe flourished in the Gardners' home, in contrast to Nim Chimpsky in the laboratory. Language is social practice. As Sue Savage-Rumbaugh, Stuart G. Shanker, and Talbot J. Taylor express it in *Apes, Language, and the Human Mind* (1998),

> The formalisms of language are constructed anew by each individual in the process of becoming a competent social being who engages in communication with other social beings for the purpose of coordinating complex patterns of behaviour.

This is why language can only be usefully studied in the 'messy real world that it naturally inhabits', rather than in the scientist's laboratory.[115] Language 'cannot be abstracted from culture'.[116]

Conclusion to Part 1.
Can an Ape Say 'Hallo!'?

L anguage is frequently defined in ways that automatically exclude non-humans. This can be seen in a number of diverse traditions, including that of biology and linguistics. Thus, in a typical statement, a member of the Work Group in the Biology of Language at the Massachusetts Institute of Technology in the late 1970s insisted that language ought to be understood 'in its ordinary sense': it was the 'spoken or written language that human beings use'.[1] By definition, then, language belongs exclusively to the human. Similarly, critics who argue from the tradition of Saussurian structuralism insist that language enables meaning to be found in the world. Language (*dialéktos*), and not mere sound (*psophos*) or voice (*phone*), is what creates the world. In the words of Chris Weedon,

> Feminist poststructuralism makes the primary assumption that it is language which enables us to think, speak and give meaning to the world around us. Meaning and consciousness do not exist outside language.[2]

But if there can be no meaning or consciousness outside of language, what is the world for languageless creatures? If we believe that language is what gives meaning to the world, then once again non-humans are automatically excluded.

These restrictive views not only underestimate the gestural dimensions of *human* as well as animal languages, but also the complexity of animal languages. Instead of teaching animals to communicate using human languages, what would happen if we learnt theirs?

Take, for example, the dance-language of bees. Ethologist Karl von Frisch had first discovered the dance in the 1920s. In 1973, he was awarded the Nobel Prize for his part in delineating the linguistic system of the bees' dance. Their language possesses rules and symbols, has clear structures and conveys performative meaning. In other words, the dances are effectively utterances that convey information, report situations or order action. The dance is not merely a 'behavioural pattern rigidly emitted', but is contextually flexible.[3] Crucially, the dance's code could be translated into human language, enabling researchers to understand what was being communicated and therefore able to predict the bees' responses. Thus, in *Communication Among Social Bees* (1961), Martin Lindaver explained how researchers tested whether or not they were truly understanding the dance:

> The nesting place was completely unknown to us beforehand for the scouting bees had chosen it themselves. We were able only to observe the dancing bees in the swarm and to decide from their behavior the location of what they had found. We did not follow the swarm as it moved into its new dwelling; we were there at the future nesting place hours before its arrival.[4]

In this way, as animal behavioural scientist Eileen Crist observes, honey bees have been

> incorporated into the scientific process as full-fledged actors, partners in the generation of scientific knowledge, who are not simply *spoken for* by scientists but are granted a reliable, independent voice to *speak to* scientists.[5]

This is not to make the act of translating the bees' dance into human language straightforward. After all, it is not possible to know if the

> force of the dance is an order, or an entreaty, or, for that matter, something that no human word exactly translates. If honeybees do speak, it is also the case that we do not fully understand them: the et cetera clauses of their dancing are, for the most part, an obscure affair.[6]

I will be returning to this in the conclusion to this book, when I discuss the fundamental incommensurability between worlds, whether human or nonhuman.

Finally, though, what is at stake in these debates about language? For the fictional Red Peter and the all-too-sentient Gua, Viki, Washoe and Nim Chimpsky, a great deal. Red Peter put a 'brave front' on it but, by being catapulted into the 'community of men' by his inebriated 'Hallo!', he forfeited his 'apeness'. Red Peter recognises this at the end of the story, when he cannot stand coming face-to-face with the 'little half-trained chimpanzee' in daylight, 'for she has that wild, confused look of the trained animal in her eye; no one but me can recognize it, and it is more than I can bear'.[7] His wounds – the one that named him as well as that which gave him his limp – turn out to be the stigmata of his exile. The wound might even be seen as punishment for his hubris: Red Peter not only pretended to be someone else, but he pretended to be a superior sort of animal. As Jacques Derrida wondered aloud,

> It would not be a matter of 'giving speech back' to animals, but perhaps of acceding to a thinking, however fabulous and chimerical it might be, that thinks the absence of the name and of the word otherwise, as something other than a privation.[8]

Rather than asking Red Peter to imitate human language, we might respect the non-human speech of his pre-capture days. Imposing human language on non-human animals is inevitably damaging. Red Peter had no choice but to submit permanently to 'this yoke' of being human.[9]

The Politics of Pain

CHAPTER FOUR

An Earnest Englishwoman

Let's return to the remarkable 'Earnest Englishwoman' with whom I started this book. She was writing in the establishment British newspaper, *The Times*, in April 1872. Charles Darwin's *The Descent of Man* had been published the year before, but the Earnest Englishwoman was not reflecting on the evolutionary history of humanity (and, if she were, the answer would have been straightforward: yes, women *are* animals). Neither was she railing against misogynist clichés, characterizing women as cooing nightingales, docile cows or soft-purring kittens. Instead, she was protesting against the fact that women were not being treated as fully human.

Who, she asked, are entitled to the social and political rights assigned to 'mankind'? How could it be just that animals had been granted more rights under law than women? She sounded exasperated. 'Whether women are the equals of men has been endlessly debated', she admitted, adding that it was a 'moot point' whether women even possessed souls. But, she pleaded, 'can it be too much to ask [for] a definitive acknowledgement that they are at least animals?' If women were allowed to become animal in law, then their status and wellbeing would improve. Surely, all people who respected the female sex must answer an unequivocal 'yes' to the question 'Are Women Animals?'

The Earnest Englishwoman's ire had been fuelled by three court cases that week. In the first, a man had punched another man on the mouth and stolen his watch ring. The 'scoundrel' had been sentenced to seven years' penal servitude, with forty lashes of the 'cat'. In contrast, when a husband killed his wife by throwing her under the wheels of a passing dray, the judge in this second case sentenced him to just three months' hard labour. When another man 'coolly knocked out' the eye of his mistress, and later assaulted her after she left hospital, he was sentenced to four months' hard labour.

Clearly, the Earnest Englishwoman reflected, women were not fully 'persons' in the eyes of the law. Furthermore, marriage diminished their rights even further. A criminal who attacked another *man*, instead of 'merely' assaulting his wife, could have been 'claimed' by the hangman. If the victim 'was only his wife – a degree lower than being only a woman' and 'as he had thus prudently fulfilled that formula of vowing to cherish and protect which converts a woman into a man's private property', hard labour was believed sufficient to settle the score.

In fact, the situation was worse: women's legal status was lower than that of animals. The Earnest Englishwoman had 'read of heavier sentences being inflicted for cruelty towards that – may I venture to say? – lower creation'. The Society for the Prevention of Cruelty to *Animals* had been founded in 1824, nearly half a century earlier: wasn't it about time that Englishmen ensured that legal provisions against cruelty were 'extended to *all* who need them in this country'?

The Earnest Englishwoman acknowledged that many MPs were opposed to granting women the right to vote in general elections. In the 1870s there had been strong opposition to a Bill that proposed that 'wherever words occur which impart the masculine gender they shall be held to include woman'. But the Earnest Englishwoman claimed to be making a much more modest proposition. Who could object, she asked, to the suggestion that 'whenever the word "animal" occurs it shall be held to include women?' She pleaded with parliamentarians to introduce 'at least an equal interdict on wanton barbarity to cat, dog, or woman (even if the latter should happen to be the wife of a barbarian)'.

For the Earnest Englishwoman it was ignominious that animals were granted more legal consideration not to be deliberately harmed or tortured than were women. Because both women and animals have *feelings* – they have interests, including an interest in not being harmed, tortured or killed – they should be treated in certain ways. Exactly a century later, in the 1970s, this approach would be promulgated by philosopher Peter Singer. As he put it in *Rethinking Life and Death* (1994),

> Whether or not dogs and pigs are persons, they can certainly feel pain and suffer in a variety of ways, and our concern for their suffering should not depend on how rational and self-aware they might be.[1]

This philosophical approach is called 'preference utilitarianism'. Ethical behaviour must arise from a consideration of the greatest satisfaction of desires or preferences. The morally correct action is that which produces the most favourable consequences for those involved.

This is not the only way to frame questions about duties of care and respect. Another approach to morality emphasizes possessing certain 'rights' (including the 'rights of man', 'human rights' and 'animal rights'). According to the 'rights' formulation, respect is owed to those given legal personalities: to being a 'person in law'. Most famously, in the *Vindication of the Rights of Woman* (1792), Mary Wollstonecraft responded to the French Assembly's Declaration of the Rights of *Man* and Citizen of 1789 by demanding that *women* should be entitled to rights on the same grounds as men.

In contrast, the Earnest Englishwoman explicitly conceded that she was not (in this letter, at least) fighting for women's right to vote at parliamentary elections. From the mid-nineteenth century, feminists had been demanding that women be given the vote, in the face of immense parliamentary hostility. In the short term, at least, the Earnest Englishwoman recognized that the rights approach was strategically impractical.

Rather, the Earnest Englishwoman was taking up the feminist campaign on different grounds to Wollstonecraft and other rights-orientated thinkers. Rather than appealing to the 'rights of man', she based her argument on the principle that women should be treated at least as well as animals due to their shared ability to feel pain.

The Earnest Englishwoman was appealing to a moral tradition that placed emphasis on the fact that all God's creatures possess the capacity to suffer. As Jeremy Bentham famously contended in *An Introduction to the Principles of Morals and Legislation* (1789),

> The day has been, I grieve to say in many places it is not yet past, in which the greater part of the species, under the denomination of slaves, have been treated by the law exactly upon the same footing as, in England for example, the inferior races of animals are still. The day *may* come, when the rest of the animal creation may acquire those rights which never could have been withholden from them but by the hand of tyranny. The French have discovered that the blackness of the skin is no reason why a human being should be abandoned without redress to the caprice of a tormentor. It may come one day to be recognized, that the number of legs, the villosity of the skin, or the

termination of the *os sacrum*, are reasons equally insufficient for abandoning a sensitive being to the same fate? What else is it that should trace the insuperable line? Is it the faculty of reason, or, perhaps, the faculty of discourse? But a full-grown horse, or dog, is beyond comparison a more rational, as well as a more conversable animal, than an infant of a day, or a week, or even a month, old. But suppose the case were otherwise, what would it avail? The question is not, Can they *reason*? Nor, Can they *talk*, but Can they *suffer*?[2]

Writing more than eighty years later, the Earnest Englishwoman agreed, extrapolating from animals to women. She deplored the fact that the man who stole a watch ring and punched its owner was given a significantly harsher sentence than the men who severely assaulted or murdered women. Although some people might believe that a watch ring was an 'object of greater value than the eye of a mistress or the life of a wife', the Earnest Englishwoman asked her readers to remember that 'the inanimate watch does not suffer'. It must cause 'acute agony' for any 'living creature, endowed with nerves and muscles, to be blinded or crushed to death'. Being 'such a creature, is not woman entitled to a fair amount of that protection accorded by law to other *domestic feræ* subject to man'? Women were 'living creatures' like other animals: should they not be given the same consideration and protection as other animals?

The Earnest Englishwoman's heartfelt cry was for women to be allowed to 'become-animal' (at least in law) in order to reap protections that they were being denied on the grounds that they were not part of 'mankind'. In her view, debased groups of humans could benefit by 'becoming-animal', or at least appealing to broader sentient life.[3] The next two chapters explore this radical proposition.

CHAPTER FIVE

Sentience and Welfare

The Earnest Englishwoman's appeal drew from a tradition of respect and consideration that laid emphasis on the fact that all God's creatures possessed the capacity to suffer. Writing in the 1870s, she argued that as women were 'living creatures' like other animals, why shouldn't they be given the same rights and protections?

Her choice of language was deliberate, feeding into a powerful rhetoric about 'sympathy' that had emerged in the eighteenth century and had come to dominate popular thinking. Ethical thinking in the eighteenth century placed an emphasis on states of *feeling*. It encouraged the cultivation of a new sensibility with stress on the importance of empathetic identification. Increased respect for the bodily integrity of other people both forged and advanced a sentimental sympathy for the human lot. Thus, in *Characteristics of Men, Manners, Opinions, Times* (1711), the third Earl of Shaftesbury developed a theory of ethics that emerged not from religion but from natural affection. Imagination was the home of the 'Divine Presence' in each person. Right and wrong, Shaftesbury argued, could be understood through the application of the imaginative powers of sympathy, allowing one person to experience another's pain.

Shaftesbury's ethics were radical. They posited a new image of humanity as sympathetic and innately moral. Adam Smith developed the idea further in his *The Theory of Moral Sentiments* of 1759. Man may seem selfish, he admitted in the book's first sentence, but there were 'some principles in his nature, which interest him in the fortune of others, and render their happiness necessary to him, though he derives nothing from it except the pleasure of seeing it.' Through acts of imagination, other people's 'agonies' are made manifest, 'and we then tremble and shudder at the thought of what he feels'.[1] Thomas Jefferson expressed it more succinctly: 'Nature hath implanted in our breasts a love of others, a sense of duty to them, a moral instinct . . . which prompts us irresistibly to feel and to succour their distresses', he famously observed in 1814.[2] This belief in a moral instinct – compassion, sympathy or empathy (although each are subtly different) – enabled people to see other human beings as creatures like themselves, opening up a space for talk of rights. It encouraged the view that the other being – human or nonhuman animal – shares certain characteristics 'with me' and so deserves to be treated with consideration.

The Pain of Animals

Jeremy Bentham has famously been cited as applying the argument about sentience and sympathy to animals. In a footnote in *An Introduction to the Principles of Morals and Legislation* (1789), he correctly observed that an adult dog or horse was 'a more rational, as well as a more conversable animal, than an infant of a day, or a week, or even a month, old'. The important ethical question, therefore, was not whether a creature could reason or talk, which have often been regarded as the crucial faculties distinguishing humans from other animals, but 'Can they *suffer?*'[3]

Although Bentham had not used the phrase 'rights of animals' (and, indeed, would have found the idea repellent), other philosophers did so. The first English use of the term occurred in Thomas Young's *Essay on Humanity to Animals* (1798), in which he argued against cruelty to animals on three grounds. The first two concerned scriptural prohibitions against cruelty and the belief that mistreating animals encouraged callous attitudes towards humans. The third reason, however, appealed to sentience. Animals, he pointed out, were

> endued with a capacity of perceiving pleasure and pain . . . We must conclude that the Creator wills the happiness of these his creatures, and consequently that humanity towards them is agreeable to him, and cruelty the contrary. This, I take it, is the foundation of the *Rights of Animals*, as far as they can be traced independently of scripture.

Humans and animals have been created with an equal capacity to experience pleasure or pain: on that basis, God had clearly ordained that both had a right to be treated with respect and consideration.[4]

Bentham and Young insisted that animals *did*, in fact, feel. They were responding, in part, to René Descartes, who insisted that animals were mere 'automata' or moving machines, driven by instinct alone. For Descartes, animals' screams of pain were mechanical responses that functioned simply as a form of human moral edification.[5]

Descartes' view was highly controversial, and much disputed. As Richard Dean put it in *An Essay on the Future Life of Brutes* (1768),

> is it possible for any Person alive really to think, that a Log of Wood, and a Brute Animal are alike, as to Sensibility? That this has no more Feeling under the Blows of a Whip or a Stick, than that has under the Strokes of a Carpenter's Ax?

Animals feel

> every Bang, and Cut, and Stab, as much as he himself does, some of them perhaps more, and therefore he must not treat them as Stocks, or Stones, or Things that cannot feel.[6]

Eight years later, the theologian Humphry Primatt reiterated the point, noting that 'a *Brute* is an animal no less sensible of pain than a Man', since they possess 'similar nerves and organs of sensation'. Although a suffering animal 'cannot utter his complaints by speech or human voice', his 'cries and groans . . . are as strong indications to us of his sensibility of pain, as the cries and groans of a *human* being, whose language we do not understand'.[7]

Evidence of animal suffering was the stock-in-trade of anti-animal cruelty campaigners of the nineteenth century. In the words of one physician giving evidence before a Senate Hearing on Vivisection in 1900, 'Without sensibility there is no right. A being without sensibility can suffer no wrong.' The 'endowment of sensibility is the endowment of rights'.[8] Time and again, evidence was presented of animals crying or laughing.[9] Bizarrely, a long-standing advertisement for the meat extract Bovril featured a crying bull (see Figure 1). Animal sensitivity was such that, in extreme distress, they would even commit suicide.[10]

Animal sensitivity to pain and humiliation was there for all to see in everyday life, and the evidence became overwhelming in the crucible of war. During the First World War, animals were reported to be prone to 'shell shock' just like their human counterparts. In 1918, a milk dealer accused of selling milk that was not of 'orthodox purity' defended

Figure 1. Bovril advertisement, 'Alas! my poor Brother', from the late 1890s. As historian Geoffrey Sumner points out, the text alludes to Shakespeare's *Hamlet*: the bull is the prince while the jar is Yorick's skull.
Mary Evans Picture Library

himself by claiming that the milk had been 'drawn at a time when there was an air raid and the animals were suffering from shell shock'. The judge was sceptical and fined him, but the *Lancet* took it seriously, noting that 'It is well-known that a cow through restlessness or nervousness holds back her milk, and the quality is unfavourably affected.' The authors also noted that *human* women were similarly affected.[11]

In combat zones, too, animals experienced psychological reactions that were identical to those of men. For both, the terror of modern artillery fire damaged their nervous systems, wiping out the higher and more evolved centres of their brains. In battle, frightened men, dogs and horses regressed to primitive fight-or-flight responses. An unnamed officer in the Royal Army Medical Corps put the situation most clearly in a 1917 article entitled 'Animal Sufferers from Shell Shock'. He informed readers that horses in the front lines 'suffer as the men do and have done'. When shelled, they responded as soldiers would: 'Never again would this gun team [of horses] approach that wall without shaking and quivering and falling down', nor would they ever be able to 'hear the sound of a near approaching shell without showing these same symptoms as a soldier might'. As with people on the front line,[12] the quality of an individual's 'blood' and 'breed' mattered. Indeed, the officer insisted, there was a 'vast difference between Australian and English horses, and the spirit with which they take up guns or shells', when compared to horses from Argentina and Canada who 'lie down and flounder in any shell-hole that gives them excuse for rest'. He argued that although 'well-bred horses – like well-bred, or, shall I say, highly organized men – suffer from shell shock more than the low-bred ones', they were also 'infinitely more gallant than his low-bred companion'. In other words, this officer was making a comparison between ranks and, therefore, class. Men of the officer class and well-bred horses were 'infinitely more gallant' than ordinary privates and horses bred for hard labour, although their superior 'nerves' was precisely what made them more sensitive to the terrors and responsibilities of war. He reminded readers that the Blue Cross Fund, launched in 1912, during the Balkan War, to assist animals injured in war, was as important to the warring enterprise as the assistance given to gallant people. The fund to care for animals was not womanish sentimentality because 'you cannot be too careful of a good trained war horse'.[13] It was precisely the sensitivity of certain animals to painful and frightening stimuli that obliged people to treat them compassionately.

Important theological arguments were also canvassed for the sentience of animals. From the late eighteenth century onwards, movements opposed to cruelty towards animals included an extremely broad range of people, but evangelicals and nonconformists were particularly vocal. For these advocates, the ability to experience pain was crucial because of its function within religious discourses about redemption.

Two contradictory perspectives were argued, however. According to one account, animals only have 'this life', so it is worse to be cruel to them than to humans who would at least be rewarded for their fortitude in the next life. In contrast, others argued that animal suffering in this world is evidence that they *would* join good Christians on the heavenly plane.

The first argument can be illustrated by the writings of Humphry Primatt. In 1776 he pointed out that 'the cruelty of Men to Brutes is *more* heinous (in point of injustice) than the cruelty of Men unto Men'. The main reason he gave for this startling statement concerned access to language, explaining that

The oppressed Man has a tongue that can plead his own case, and a finger to point out the aggressors: All Men that hear of it shudder with horror; and, by applying the case to themselves, pronounce it *cruelty* with the common Voice of Humanity, and unanimously join in demanding the punishment of the offender, and brand him with infamy.

In contrast, the 'dumb beast' was afflicted with literal 'dumbness': she was speechless. Animals could neither 'utter . . . complaints' nor avenge all the wrongs done to them. Cruelty to animals caused '*irreparable injury*' because they could hope for nothing more than 'temporary happiness' in their lives. To anyone who challenged that statement, claiming that 'some MEN in the world' were 'as unfortunately circumstanced' as the 'unhappy Brutes', Primatt was dismissive. He reminded them that

a Day will come, when all the injuries which an *innocent* Man can suffer from the hand of violence and oppression will be overbalanced in a future and happy state, where 'our light affliction', which in comparison of eternity 'is but for a moment', shall work for us a far more exceeding and eternal weight of glory.

But for animals there could be no hope of eternal justice because 'His present *life* . . . is the Whole of his existence'. Like children, animals were innocent and helpless, and had 'as much right to happiness in this world as a child can have: nay, more right, if this world be his only inheritance'.[14]

Primatt's views were eloquently argued, but others equally devoted to animal welfare refuted his belief that animals would not share in the afterlife. This theological position was also adamant about the importance of recognizing animal sentience, but argued that suffering fulfilled a positive function in promoting the future salvation of *all* living creatures. For these animal defenders the capacity to suffer entitled living creatures not only to consideration in this world, but also to eternal life in the next. Animal guardians, as they liked to be called, constantly repeated the mantra that, since animals 'share in the punishment and work and suffer with their higher brothers', then they must also be rewarded by an 'after-life of perfect happiness', as the author of 'The Non-Human Races and Continued Existence' insisted in a letter to the editor of the *Animals' Guardian* in 1916.[15] Writing to the same journal a year later, 'F. G. N.' agreed that 'nothing less than some future

compensation can atone for the awful sufferings [animals] are permitted to undergo here'. If God 'permits them to suffer through man's
carelessness and sin, He will repay them somehow and somewhere'.[16]
This point of view often tipped over into sentimentalism, as in another
letter, published in 1915. The author stated that she could not accept
that 'any one believing in the Divine Love' could possibly

> think there is no compensation [in the afterlife] for the weary old cab-
> horse standing so meekly in the rain and bitter cold; the little
> unwanted stray looking up into the faces of the passers-by, dumbly
> asking for a little love and pity, and receiving none; the encaged lark,
> beating its wings in hopeless misery against the bars of the cage that
> imprison it; the quivering, wingless fly – the victim of the cruelty of
> some thoughtless child or any of the suffering animal-life of the uni-
> verse.[17]

Another proponent of animal welfare put it in less florid terms: the suffering of animals 'in this life' was as 'needful for them for their
perfection, as it is for man'.[18]

Central to this perspective was an assumption that animals actually
possess souls.[19] While some authors sought to make subtle distinctions between the souls of male humans, female humans and animals,[20]
others were less equivocal. In 1909, for instance, the Reverend
William Weekes Fowler reminded readers of the *Animals' Guardian* that
anyone who doubted that 'natural immortality of beasts' should
remember that 'there was once, prior to experience, as great presumption against [certain] human creatures' possessing eternal life 'as
there is against the brute creatures'.[21] As one headline quipped in the
same year, 'Have Animals Souls? Yes: But Some Men Have None!'[22]

In this view, as much as in Primatt's, the animal in pain might be *more*
deserving of sympathy than a suffering person. In the 1894 edition of
the *Animals' Guardian*, the author of 'Destiny in the Lower Animals'
stated that,

> The sinless One was made perfect by suffering (I speak with all rev-
> erence) and so may the unsinning animals. Those who suffer most
> here will probably be raised to a higher state hereafter.

He denied that this implied that he had jettisoned the view that 'man
[sic] is the lord of creation', but encouraged his congregation 'in all

humility' to admit that 'in some sense the lower animals are better than man' because they 'have never fallen as man has'. He claimed to have found some significance in the fact that, in the biblical account of creation,

> it is stated that the beasts were made 'out of the ground', but man, 'of the dust of the ground' . . . the worn out particles as it were, the very refuse left over after the other works of God had been formed.[23]

In such a way, the suffering animal could possess a direct link to the divine, even to the bleeding body of Christ. Indeed, in contrast to human suffering, which was the consequence of sin, the suffering animal was even more to be honoured because she was without moral blemish.

The Great Chain of Feeling

Those who advocated that people should treat animals compassionately because animals were sentient creatures faced formidable opponents. Simply put, not everyone agreed that animals experienced pain in a way comparable to humans. As we have already seen, this was certainly the view of Descartes in the seventeenth century.

More commonly, scientists and philosophers pointed to the existence of a hierarchy of sentience. After all, they insisted, isn't it the case that not all *humans* are equally sensitive? The ability to feel, both in terms of physical sensation as well as inner sensibilities, was ranked hierarchically. Belief in a great Chain of Being, according to which everything in the universe was ranked from the highest to the lowest, is one of the most fundamental tenets of Western philosophy. One aspect of this Chain of Being involved the perception of sensation. Put differently, there was a parallel great Chain of *Feeling*, which placed male Europeans at one end and slaves and animals at the other.

Certainly, advocates of slavery and believers in the superiority of the European 'races' adhered to this idea. According to the author of a 1876 tract on vivisection,

> What would be torture to one creature is barely felt by the other. Even amongst the lower types of man feeling is less acute, and blows and cuts are treated with indifference by the aboriginal Australian which would lay a European in hospital.[24]

James Peter Warbasse, surgeon to the German Hospital in Brooklyn, New York, expressed the same incredible belief in 1910. 'Primitive peoples', he avowed,

> have an insensibility to pain which is beyond our comprehension. Their self-mutilations are made possible not by bravery but by this low degree of pain-sense. The savage who chops off his hand and presents it to the king has displayed a stoicism which is comparable to that of the fox who gnaws off his leg to get out of a trap. Neither one is much hurt. We must not interpret these things in terms of our own pain-sense.[25]

A practical consequence of such opinions was that they legitimated giving certain patients minimal (if any) anaesthesia during childbirth or serious operations.[26]

Given claims that lesser humans (including, incidentally, newborn infants[27] and deaf-mutes[28]) were not sensitive to pain, it is hardly surprising to hear people arguing that animals, too, lacked the ability to truly hurt.[29] Again, both theological and scientific explanations were proffered. Joseph Rickaby, a Jesuit priest and author of *Moral Philosophy or Ethics and Natural Law* (1888), clearly believed that the Creator had fashioned animals to act as slaves to humans: 'Brute beasts, not having understanding and therefore not being persons, cannot have any rights ... They are of a number of *things*.' There was 'no shadow of evil resting on the practice of causing pain to brutes *in sport*, where the pain is not the sport itself, but an incidental concomitant of it'. Equally, pain could be caused to animals 'in the pursuit of science'. In case his readers needed greater reassurance, he reminded them that humans were not required 'to any anxious care to make this pain as little as it may be. Brutes are *things* in our regard'.[30]

Intriguingly, in an edition of this book published forty years later, Rickaby was a little more restrained. 'Beasts' became 'animals' and 'brute beasts' became 'dumb animals'. He not only claimed that animals did not possess 'understanding', but also that they did not have 'reflex consciousness nor any power of abstraction'. He also silently excised his opinion that animals were 'things' and that there was therefore 'no shadow of evil' in causing pain to them.

Rickaby may have toned down his rhetoric, but not his overall outlook. His views were not only the preserve of conservative theologians. As we have already seen, the Brooklyn surgeon Warbasse argued that pain was a 'psychic phenomenon, and lower man and animals have but little appreciation of it'. He admitted that certain animals – dogs, cats, sheep, cows and horses, for instance – *seem* to have facial expressions that are 'strikingly similar to the expression assumed by the human face' when in pain, but this was nothing more than 'one of the accidents of anatomical structure'. Part of his proof that these animals were not communicating pain was the fact that elephants and simians, 'though far superior' in intelligence, 'have not this pitiful expression'. Animals have 'no conception of pity . . . and probably no idea that it [sic] is threatened with danger or pain'. Struggles 'under experimentation without anaesthetics' are simply reflexes.[31]

Briggs Carlille, writing in 1886, agreed. For him, the important factor influencing sensation was whether the organism's 'nervous organisation' was 'coarsely-grained' or not. A wolf would 'give no cry of pain' even if her leg was severed, while a 'humanised dog cries if his toe is trodden on'. A 'corresponding difference', he went on,

> can readily be observed in man himself. Between the European and North American Indian, or between civilised man in his drawing-room and the same man reducing himself to a semi-savage state on the field of battle. It needs not to go very far down the scale of existence before coming to creatures to whom, quite obviously, the loss of a limb is a matter of very small concern. . . from this point there is, no doubt, a gradual, very gradual increase in susceptibility, until we reach the apes, or even, we might say, until we reach savage man, and then there is a wide gulf.[32]

Some socialists agreed. In the 1880s, Edward Deacon Girdlestone boldly insisted that the '*facts*' suggested to him that animals were relatively insensitive to pain. For him, 'Movement, Gesture and Outcry do not necessarily connote pain'. After all, 'Brutes, like children, are in the habit of crying out *before they are hurt!*' His basic point was that '*Cries . . .* do not prove pain'. For instance, pigs squealed prior to being killed, but their laments were a protest again their loss of liberty rather than having anything to do with either pain or fear of pain. If released (even if already 'stuck'), pigs stopped squealing and would quietly bleed to death. He denied that animals suffered 'from the *Psychical* side' either. Although animals did experience fear and could remember events,

> their fear and memory appear only in the actual presence or recurrence of the cause of apprehension. They don't lie for hours

pondering on their sorrows; there is little of the Representative faculty about them.

In other words, the exclusively human capacity for abstract thinking greatly exacerbated human sensibility to pain.[33]

Perhaps more surprisingly (since pain clearly has a function in promoting survival), some evolutionists joined conservative theologians and socialists in asserting animal insensibility to pain. A year after founding the British Naturalists' Association, Edward Kay Robinson published *The Religion of Nature* (1906), in which he argued that, because animals lacked 'mental consciousness', they could not be conscious of pain. Indeed, in evolutionary terms, it would have been a 'serious drawback' for animals to be conscious of suffering: 'in the hard struggle of natural existence', he proclaimed, awareness of states of feeling would have made animals 'too "soft"', thus making them extinct.[34]

That indefatigable reformer Henry Salt was not amused by Robinson's proclamations. His poem 'The Modern Descartes' (1906) was addressed to Robinson:

Did ye think the tortured animals could feel?

Nay, be comforted, and know that these seeming signs of woe
Are illusions of a pre-Darwinian age:
Call them 'instinct', 'reflex action' – blessed terms of satisfaction
The uneasy pangs of Conscience to assuage!

To Man, to Man alone, is the sense of suffering known;
The Beast in blank unfeeling torpor lies:
Tho he wince, and cry, and strain, no twinge has he of pain –
On the word of E. Kay Robinson the wise.[35]

In fact, Robinson's insistence that animals lacked the consciousness necessary to register pain did not assume that 'To Man, to Man alone, is the sense of suffering known': according to Robinson, 'lesser humans' were also barely sensitive. His argument began by insisting on that great Chain of Feeling:

[In] the whole range of life from the lowest vegetable up to the highest animal there is no point, until we come to man himself, at which we can pause and say, 'Here consciousness begins'; and without consciousness there can be no personal valuation of happiness or unhappiness.

He then conjured up some opponents, who might wish to contend that if 'we follow the human scale down to savages and cannibals, we find creatures with very slight sensibility to pain'. He imagined his critics telling him that 'there was no evidence to show that these very low human beings are more self-conscious than the higher animals of other classes'. Robinson admitted that countering this argument was difficult because 'questioning horses and dogs on the point' was impossible and 'in the case of savages, the more you interrogate them the more you are impelled to regard them as mere animals'. In his words,

> When you come across a tribe of islanders who have half a dozen words to describe different methods of putting a captive to death, but not a single word to express mercy, gratitude, or any moral virtue, it is not easy to hold to the faith that man alone is made in the likeness of God. In so many respects your faithful dog seems superior to the debased human savage that you are reluctant to erect between them a mental barrier which shuts off the dog among the lower animals, and admits the savage into the select company of beings with a likeness of God in their consciousness.

Nevertheless, Robinson went on to insist, humans were the only beings with consciousness, as was proven by their possession of language, their propensity to 'decorate' their bodies (a trait he regarded as necessary because it was the first step towards literature, art, industry and the other aspects of civilization), and their possession of a religious sense. Even 'savages' possessed these three 'germs of civilisation'. Animals were unconscious and thus felt no pain; 'savages', at least, possessed a kernel of sensitivity.[36]

It would require a book of its own to trace beliefs about the insensitivity of animals to painful sensations from men like Robinson to the present. Suffice to say, advocates of this position can be found in every decade. Let me just take one more recent example. In 1991 Peter Harrison published an article in the influential journal *Philosophy*, entitled 'Do Animals Feel Pain?' He answered 'no' on three grounds. First, he argued that evidence of sensitivity is often drawn from observations of organisms crying out or making attempts to avoid noxious substances. But even single-celled organisms, he reminded readers, withdraw from harmful stimuli and complex animals can be observed engaging in what looks like 'pain behaviour' in the absence of *any* stimuli whatsoever. More important, animals may 'sustain considerable tissue damage' without responding, while robots can be programmed to exhibit 'pain behaviour' even though they have no sensation. In other words, the 'pain behaviour' of animals simply demonstrates 'how well natural selection had fitted them for encounters with unfriendly aspects of their environment'.

Second, he attempted to demolish the idea that animals must feel pain because they possess similar physiological and nervous structures as humans. On the one hand, he argued that, except for some primates, humans possessed much more complex structures than other animals. On the other, it was 'rash' to 'predict the mental states of individuals on the basis of the presence or absence of certain structures'. After all, 'what is painful for one individual is not much for another', and psychological states can make a huge difference to pain perception.

Finally, he addressed the argument that evolutionary processes suggest no radical discontinuity between humans and other animals. According to this theory, not only would similar species experience similar mental events but they would also possess similar adaptive mechanisms (pain helps living organisms avoid danger and thus increases their chances of survival and reproduction, for instance). Here, Harrison's casuistry becomes even more pronounced. He reminds readers that it is not pain that is the adaptation, 'but the *behaviour* which is elicited when the damaging stimulus is applied'. He illustrated his point by comparing the reactions of wildebeests and chimpanzees to being attacked. When a wildebeest is being 'torn apart by dogs', she

> will die in silence, while a chimpanzee will screech out in response to some trivial hurt like a thorn puncturing its [sic] foot . . . Yet neither expresses its pain. Rather, each behaves in a way likely to enhance the survival of the species. The chimpanzee communicates to warn its conspecifics, or to summon aid. The wildebeest remains silent so that others will not be lured to their deaths. It is the behaviour, rather than some hypothetical mental state, which adapts the organism.

Furthermore, pain can be bearable if there are '*reasons*' for it. But 'an animal never has reason to either bear pain, or to succumb to pain. And if pain never needed to be brought into the sphere of reasons – the mind – then there is no need for it'. In other words, he believes that only creatures who can '*think*' can have consciousness of pain. It is an approach that Descartes would have wholly agreed with. Unfortunately, all three of Harrison's arguments could, indeed, be used to argue that it would be wrong to assume that all *humans* experience pain.[37] And, I would wager, that is not his point.

What are the ethical implications of such views? How should animals be treated? Harrison dismisses the idea that we should pay attention to the 'preferences' of animals, since he questions whether animals even possess 'preferences'. Indeed, he seems to dismiss this argument altogether, on the grounds that 'we are in little doubt as to what human beings prefer, and yet so many of them exist in conditions little different from those of battery hens'. Rather, he points to important 'aesthetic, ecological, sentimental, psychological, pedagogical' considerations. It would be 'morally wrong' to attack Michelangelo's *Pietà* with a hammer, even though the sculpture does not feel pain. Similarly, 'If animals are mere machines, they are, for all that, intricate and beautiful machines (most of them), which like old buildings, trees and works of art, can greatly enrich our lives.'[38]

Given such reasoning, it will not come as any surprise to observe that many contemporary arguments *for* animal sensitivity are made precisely to *allow* experimentation on non-human animals. In 2005, for instance, Gary Bennett published an article on the 'clinical relevance of animal models of pain'. Was animal pain identical to human pain, he asks. He notes that, in clinical trials and reports, the word 'painful' has generally been replaced by concepts such as 'nociception' (a 'fancy neologism that few understand') or 'noxious' ('a useful word'). He believes that there is 'good reason to banish "painful"'. It is 'sloppy language' to write of 'painful stimulus' because 'a stimulus may cause pain, but pain is not a property of the stimulus – it is a property of the organism that responds to the stimulus'. He goes on to argue that

> the evidence that animals feel pain is of precisely the same kind as the evidence that you feel pain; of course, the evidence that I feel pain is of an essentially different kind. We can have no direct knowledge of the subjective sensations of others, neither of another person nor of any other kind of animal. We assume that other people have subjective experiences like ours.

In other words, it is impossible to categorically know whether the 'subjective sensation of pain' in humans and animals is identical but 'the neural mechanisms that produce them are sufficiently similar for experiments on one to be relevant to the other'. Precisely because we can assume that animals *do* feel pain, it is legitimate to experiment upon them in order to advance our knowledge about pain.[39] They can be used as 'things' – albeit, 'things' that approximate human 'subjects'.

Cruelty to Animals

Even those who argue that animals are not susceptible to pain-sensations might still be appalled by cruelty to animals (unless 'necessary', as pro-vivisectionists would add *sotto voce*). This only makes sense once we realize that the most important reason animals needed to be treated well was to safeguard *humans*. It was taken for granted by practically everyone – whether an animal-lover or not – that allowing cruelty to animals would open the way to cruelty towards people. Immanuel Kant famously argued in 1797 that behaving kindly towards animals was 'always only a duty of man to himself'. As he elaborated:

> With regard to the animate but nonrational part of creation violent and cruel treatment of animals is far more intimately apposed [sic] to man's duty to himself, and he has a duty to refrain from this; for it dulls his shared feeling of their pain and so weakens and gradually uproots a natural predisposition that is very serviceable to morality in one's relations with other men.[40]

In the early 1790s, the passionate anti-slavery reformer Granville Sharp made the point slightly differently, arguing that witnessing how a person treated 'inferior animals' was an '*unsuspected test of moral character*, by which he might safely ascertain the worth of every man's heart, and the grounds of his action towards his own species'.[41] Even Joseph Rickaby (that Jesuit priest who insisted that 'Brute beasts . . . are *things*') admitted that 'wanton cruelty' to animals was, nevertheless, 'especially deplorable, because it disposes the perpetrators to be cruel also to men'.[42] Routinely, animal advocates repeated the mantra that 'A man who would ill-treat a dumb animal would ill-use a human being'.[43] George Bernard Shaw commented that vivisection was a 'social evil' because 'if it advances human knowledge, it does so at the expense of human character'[44] (see Figure 2).

Figure 2. A physiological demonstration with the vivisection of a dog. This 1832 painting, by Emile-Edouard Mouchy, valorizes physiological experiments as being at the core of scientific progress. British physiologists, such as Sir Charles Bell, were much more likely to emphasize the value of dissection, as opposed to the more French tradition of vivisection.
Wellcome Library, London

Indeed, in the eighteenth century and throughout the nineteenth, arguments against cruelty towards animals were not, in fact, about 'cruelty' as it is understood today. The emphasis was only rarely on the experience of pain. It was almost wholly on the *effect* that inflicting pain on animals would subsequently have on behaviour towards humans. For those religiously inclined, it was also about that terrifying face-to-face encounter with God: when standing before the Almighty God in the afterlife, how would cruel people be able to reconcile animal torture with their divinely ordained guardianship of the lower animals? Soame Jenyns's *Disquisitions on Several Subjects* (1782) made the argument particularly eloquently. Jenyns used the 'wonderful chain of Being' to differentiate between the faces of shellfish, through to insects, fishes, birds, and beasts, then to dogs and apes. After the latter, came the 'brutal Hottentot', until 'in a Bacon, or a Newton, it attains the summit'. Since, he continued, the happiness of creatures beneath humans was 'dependent on our wills', it was reasonable to conclude 'that our lives, and happiness, are equally dependent on the wills of those above us'. After death, people would have to justify their treatment of animals in front of 'their common Father'.

This was certainly not an argument for treating animals equally with people. Jenyns remarked upon the 'agreeable flavour of their [animals'] flesh to our palate'. For him, there was no contradiction between arguing that animals needed to be treated compassionately if people were to be able to hold their heads' high before the Throne of Judgement and killing them for an evening's repast. Indeed, one of the chief reason why animals had to be killed with 'tenderness and compassion' was because Providence had created them in such a way that animals who experienced a 'painful and lingering death' would taste 'rancid and unpalatable'. Jenyns bluntly argued that this was God's way of 'compel[ling] us to be merciful' and 'cautious of [animal] suffering, for the sake of ourselves'.[45]

Legislation against animal cruelty, which started to be passed from 1800 onwards, was not, in fact, much about animals at all, but about the way that many abuses of animals took place in disorderly contexts – bull- and bear-baiting being infamous examples. Cruelty to animals encouraged disorderly conduct that was unworthy of civilized decorum. Protesters against animal cruelty were concerned primarily with the need to control and reform 'lower' classes of *humans*. This helps explain why the Royal Society for the Prevention of Cruelty to Animals had no problem admitting members who were enthusiastic foxhunters, a 'sport' for the decorous affluent classes.

This argument that opposition to cruelty towards animals was, in fact, less about animals and more concerned with encouraging a new middle-class sensibility can also be illustrated by looking at anti-cruelty books directed at children. Such books proliferated in the nineteenth century. *The Child's Ark* (1848), for instance, was structured around twelve animals, each of which was meant to provide lessons to children on why cruelty to animals was abhorrent: animals had been created to bring children to an awareness of Christ. The author praised God for 'causing even the beasts of the field to instruct us'.[46]

It is significant that the role of animals in these books was to illustrate the great Chain of Feeling, with humanity at its pinnacle. Thomas Jackson's book is illustrative here. He posed the question whether animals possessed souls and, after answering in the negative, insisted that this was precisely why children had a duty to treat animals with utmost consideration. According to this view, all life forms were arranged in a 'sort of ladder', comparable to 'a scale of music beginning with the simplest note of melody, and ending with the most ravishing harmonies'. In the words of Edith, one of the book's main characters:

> That the Creator is pleased to begin with minute atoms of animated life; that He proceeds upwards from there through all the ranges of the living, breathing, busy family, bound together by the ties of a common creature-hood, which we call the animal creation. At the summit of the scale stands man, made in the image of God, made a little lower than the angels. May we not then be said to stand before animals as the representatives of Divine providence and care?[47]

Edith echoed, in more plain terms, the arguments of Humphry Primatt, which I quoted earlier in this chapter. Precisely because animals did not possess souls (and, therefore, '*this* life is the final existence of my dog and my horse'), children had a

> duty to make it as much like heaven and as little like hell as lies in my power – remembering that the Supreme Governor of the universe will exact from every one of us, his vicegerents, a strict account of our stewardship?[48]

In 1845, Charlotte Elizabeth Tonna put it even more starkly when she rallied against people who were cruel to monkeys and sheep. 'I can tell you one thing', she informed her readers:

> That it is impossible for a cruel man to be happy: it is entirely IMPOS-SIBLE. He may laugh and shout, and sing, and dance, and tell you that he is very happy; but it is not so. There is in his heart something always whispering, 'Your turn will come. The great God, the holy, just, merciful God, whose creatures you now torment, sees it all, knows it all; and he will punish you . . . HE SHALL HAVE JUDG-MENT WITHOUT MERCY WHO HATH SHOWN NO MERCY!' . . . I could not help thinking how awful would be the state of those boys, if they were cut off by death in such wickedness. Alas! The agonies of one hour hereafter, would be worse than all the tortures that could be inflicted on God's creatures during their whole lives. But instead of an hour, it is for ever and ever that all who go to that dreadful place of punishment must remain.[49]

The irony, therefore, about the great Chain of Feeling is that those creatures ordained by the Almighty God to stand proudly at its pinnacle, acutely sensitive to the least prick of pain, were also those to be tortured for eternity for crimes committed against lesser animals. The 'gift' of supreme sentience was the most outrageous curse imaginable.

Cruelty to People

Callousness towards animals, then, was a grievous sin, in part because it would eventually infect human interactions. As George Bernard Shaw predicted, physicians who practised vivisection would naturally welcome the chance to vivisect humans. After all, human beings were 'nothing to the vivisector but a more highly developed, and consequently more interesting-to-experiment-on vertebrate than the dog'.[50]

The upward seepage of callousness (to adopt, for now, the metaphor of a hierarchy of feeling) affected humans placed at the lower end of the scale more than their superiors. Thus it was suggested that men and women on the border of full personhood ought to be wary of being treated by physicians who practised vivisection, as those who experimented on mute animals would inevitably turn their scalpels on those next in the hierarchy. As one commentator warned in 1891, scientists were doing nothing less than attempting to 'wrench the secrets of life' from sentient beings. Beware, he cautioned: today, they tormented the flesh of 'the cat or the rabbit, the dog or the monkey' but one day they would demand the living flesh of the 'pauper or the condemned prisoner'.[51] Or, in the words of the poem 'The Vivisector', after the physician 'mangles living flesh' of a dog he

> Then seeks the hospital,
> An oft frequented place,
> With knife in hand and knitted brow,
> He scans each anguish'd face,
> With hopes in some poor waif to find,
> An 'interesting case'!
>
> No pity born of human love,
> No sympathy with pain,
> . . . But reader can you – *would* you call,
> This *soulless* thing a *Man*?[52]

'Tender-hearted women', innocent children and paupers would be the first to be vivisected. In the words of the anonymous author 'Mercy's Voice', 'Vindicate humanity; give no countenance to the Vivisector, who would carve your child or yourself as readily as he would little pussy on the hearth'.[53]

Hadn't that day already come? Henry Salt wondered how scientists could justify the vivisection of animals but not humans. He observed that

> It is from the scientists themselves that we have the clearest assurance that men are an animal, and that the great gulf which has been supposed to yawn between the human and the non-human has existed only in imagination.

Therefore, where was the 'ethical warrant for the infliction of prolonged and exquisite torture on sentient beings who, by their own showing, are closely akin to mankind?' To those scientists who argued that there was a difference in '*degree* of sensitivity and intelligence' between humans and animals, why then didn't they vivisect 'the savage or a criminal'?[54]

Salt was perhaps not observant enough. After all, many critics spread rumours (some of which were correct) that human vivisection was already alive and well.[55] In the words of the author of 'Cancer Experiments on Human Beings' (c. 1880), some doctors could be found grafting cancer into the 'breasts of poor patients who were unconscious from chloroform and helpless in their hands'. The author went on to alert readers to the fact that 'the pretence of using (or *mis*-using) animals for experiments "instead of human beings", is only one more of the deceptions practised by this merciless gang on the public'.[56]

For such commentators, it was self-evident that scientists trained in vivisection would develop a callous attitude towards other vulnerable life forms. As one anti-vivisectionist lamented, 'idiot children, paralysed and imperfectly developed infants' were regarded as being of 'no more intrinsic value than rabbits'.[57] Feminist physician Anna Kingsford made a similar protest after observing pauper patients being operated on without any form of anaesthetic:

> Paupers were thus classed with animals as fitting subjects for painful experiments, and since no regard is shown for the feelings of either, it is not surprising that the use of anaesthetics for the benefit of the

patient is wholly rejected. Even the excruciating operation of cautery with a red-hot iron is performed without the alleviation of an anaesthetic.[58]

Within public hospitals, one self-identified 'zoophilist' complained, patients were being treated as though they were nothing more than living 'material'. Everything was subordinated to 'science, considered as an end in itself'. In the midwifery department of a teaching hospital, this critic went on, there was a 'craving' among trainee-doctors to be present during abnormal cases of women giving birth. Students expressed 'disgust . . . if the process proceeded naturally'. This was expressed even though

> chloroform was only given exceptionally, [so] an abnormal and scientifically interesting case meant protracted agony to the patient. The students do not realize how cruel their wish was; they only yielded to a desire for increased knowledge in itself praiseworthy, and overlooked the fact that the patient was not merely what she was often called, 'teaching material' . . . but a sentient, suffering, agonised, human creature.[59]

Finally, a few voices could be heard openly defending the moral legitimacy of human vivisection. Let me take two examples, exactly a century apart. Richard Holt Hutton was a Unitarian minister and member of the 1875 Royal Commission on Vivisection. In 1883 he argued that if physiologists were willing to torture animals in accordance with higher goals, then 'it becomes a duty to root out of our hearts that sickly compassion which interferes with physiological investigations' and allow experimentation on humans. At the very least, physiologists should be allowed to use the bodies of 'all those convicts under sentence of death' since these men and women had 'forfeited their moral claim on the respect and sympathy of man'. It was 'idle to say that the torture of man in the true interests of science is always wicked, if the torture of inferior creatures in the true interests of science is always right'.[60]

A hundred years later, in 1983, R. G. Frey published a similar defence of human vivisection in the *Journal of Medical Ethics*. He confessed that he was unable to categorically state that 'a human life of any quality, however low, is more valuable than an animal life of any quality, however high'. He would, therefore, support vivisection on 'humans whose quality of life is exceeded by or equal to animals'. He only stipulated that the experiments had to benefit human life. Medical research involving vivisection had already conferred great benefits on human society, making it impossible to 'make the choice in favour of antivivisection'. Therefore,

> we are left with human experiments. I think this is how I would choose, not with great glee and rejoicing, and with great reluctance; but if this is the price we must pay to hold the appeal to benefit and to enjoy the benefits which that appeal licenses, then we must, I think, pay it.[61]

Need I add that Frey and his ilk (white, wealthy men in the West) would not be the ones who would be expected or required to 'pay the price'? These are the arguments to which I turn in the next chapter. As we shall see, basing political and ethical behaviour on sentience turns out to be a deeply disquieting politics indeed.

CHAPTER SIX

Humanitarianism and the
Limits of Sympathy

In the last chapter, I explored hierarchies of pain. Theologians and scientists came into dialogue about the sensitivity of animals – human and nonhuman – to painful sensation. Their conclusions had an immense impact on the ways people treated other creatures, influencing sympathetic or spiteful practices and informing assumptions of respectfulness or serviceability.

This chapter follows through these arguments in the context of political campaigns. The Earnest Englishwoman was not the only activist to claim that 'becoming-animal' was a step towards the *humanization* of certain groups who had been designated lesser humans. In the twenty-first century, a campaign on behalf of African-American men adopted a similar rhetoric. Certain radical American lawyers cast a dispassionate eye over the Endangered Species Act (passed in 1973) and argued that African-American men would benefit from being labelled 'endangered animals'. After all, one-quarter of young African-American men in the United States are imprisoned or are on probation or parole. The homicide rate for African-American males is six times higher than that of African-American females, more than seven times higher than that of white men, and twenty-one times higher than for white females. In the words of Joseph Lubinski, writing in the *Journal of Law in Society* in 2002,

> While characterizing humans as animals traditionally was meant to
> degrade racial minorities, animal advocates now attempt to use the

same analogy for the benefit of those they seek to protect. The hope
is that by giving animals human characteristics and relating their experience to that of people, public sympathy can be aroused and their
movement bestowed popular legitimacy.[1]

I would like to think that the Earnest Englishwoman would have been
sympathetic to a rhetoric that seeks to raise awareness of injustice by
consigning an under-privileged male minority to the legislative pen of
'the animal'. According to both the Earnest Englishwoman and radical
lawyers, the human is not 'other' to the animal; rather, the human is
defined as a being 'in sympathy' with the animal. The politics of sentience gestures towards an ethics of care and responsibility for all
creatures but, as we shall see, is inadequate to the task.

This chapter draws attention to a problem faced by advocates of
humanitarianism. Is the economy of sympathy limited? Should we be
worried about zero-sum calculations? If sympathy is allotted to one
group – animals, for instance – isn't there a risk that it will be removed
from another group – such as women, racial minorities, children or the
poor? It also renders problematic the term 'humanitarian' itself. There
are two ways of understanding humanitarianism. The first emphasizes
feeling and acting in ways that protect the integrity and interests of
those placed within the 'human' category. The second expands the
concept by referring to 'humane' traits (allegedly those held by the
supreme representatives of humanity) which should condition behaviour towards all life forms. If we disrupt 'human' – as I attempt to do
throughout this book – both definitions become problematic.

Women are Animals

When the Earnest Englishwoman pleaded for women to be recognized
as animals, she was satirizing a long tradition of treating women as less
than fully human. Rather than arguing against the injustice of devaluing
animals, she railed against the unfairness of reducing women to animal
status. In the end, her point was one of solidarity with animals without
disrupting fundamental hierarchies. Both women and animals are sentient creatures: they *feel*, and therefore should not be harmed, tortured
or killed.

Valorizing states of feeling was not without its own problems. As we
have seen, the most influential way of distinguishing humans from the
rest of the animal kingdom was to point to the possession of reason. In

positing reason and higher than the emotions, full humanity could be conferred on adult, European men, while women, denigrated 'races', children and animals were charged with an excess of 'feeling'. It was a common accusation. In the late nineteenth and early twentieth centuries, 'excessive' female emotions were put forward as evidence of their closeness to animals, particularly to other mammals. Indeed, some texts that purport to be about the emotions of animals shift with subtle ease to human women. An example would be *Protection of Animals* (1874), written by George T. Angell, President of the Massachusetts Society for the Prevention of Cruelty to Animals. In the section entitled 'Milch Cows', Angell moves effortless from cows to lactating women. The milk of both cows and women was 'liable to produce sickness, and may produce death' if either had been 'worried by dogs or frightened or cold or improperly fed'.[2] Equating women and animals also arose casually in late nineteenth-century critiques of the growing number of female-dominated philanthropic societies (including those established on behalf of animals). As the author of 'The Woman About Town' (1871) sneered, he would not be surprised if he were asked to contribute to a 'Fund for Supplying Destitute Old Maids with New Metal Teapots'. He then accused female activists of 'chattering, like female baboons, on the rights of women, and that sort of thing'.[3] A distinguished Professor of Physiology at the University of Cambridge was even blunter when he grumbled that women's 'mawkish sentimentalism' was 'curtailing the good effects of increased enlightenment' and leading to a 'lessening of manliness'.[4] Female emotionalism and 'sentimental' love of animals was dangerous to a humanity that distinguished itself by (manly) reasonableness.

It is no coincidence that a significant proportion of the men engaged in such sniping were opponents of organizations devoted to preventing vivisection, many of which were dominated by women. In a typical example, one supporter of vivisection (who admitted that he had become 'odious to women') mocked women for being over-emotional, sentimental and superstitious. He had received a letter from a woman signing herself 'The Animals' Champion', in which she not only blamed the 'Horrors of our Railway accidents' on the 'sin of Vivisection' but also went on to say that her 'daily prayer [was] that our just God may send some fiery judgment upon all those who perpetrate, support, and even advocate these horrible practices'. This vivisectionist railed against women who believed that vivisection 'should be referred for decision to the tribunal of *Feeling* and *not* that of Reason'. What nonsense! he snarled. 'Of course, our "Feelings" cannot but be interested and called out by such a subject', he began, 'but the practical question in dispute between us is: *Which is to lead the other*: Reason? or Feeling? *We* say: It is the function of "Reason" *to lead*; and of "Feeling" *to follow!*'[5]

He was not alone in positioning women as the sex who valued feelings more than reason. Even *opponents* of vivisection agreed that women were the emotional sex; the only difference was that they sought to invert the respective value assigned to emotion and reason. For them, emotionality was proof of female superiority, rather than inferiority. In other words, anti-vivisectionists routinely argued that emotions should be valorized, not disdained. In Charles Selby Oakley's *On Vivisection. Can It Advance Mankind?* (1895), he rounded on people who 'sneered' at women on the ground that their opposition to vivisection was 'sentimental' and based on 'mere feeling', as if there were something 'better'. Oakley reminded readers, that 'if a feeling be genuine and sensible, it has its cause, that is its intellectual basis. It is only a momentary way of giving effect to a train of reasoning'. He appealed to women to get involved in the anti-vivisection movement, a movement that was 'more within the region of sweet and gracious attractiveness than the questions of costumes and votes, and clubs and smoking carriages'.[6]

Although well-meaning, Oakley's defence of women was patronizing and contradictory. He sought to valorize emotion as constitutive of a highly esteemed female humanity, but at the same time set clear limits: women could not be considered *fully* human since they were not entitled to the vote and a host of other freedoms. In Oakley's view, the 'natural' emotionality of women rendered them suited to the politics of animal guardianship, rather than more radical campaigns for the right to full citizenship or equality within the public sphere. Ultimately, Oakley's vision relegated women to the status of animals.

We must not imagine that such sentiments are a quaint relic of less enlightened times. Unfortunately, some leading spokesmen in the animal rights movements in the late twentieth century have also felt the need to repudiate 'womanish' emotionality. Notoriously, Peter Singer complained that animal rights had traditionally been associated with trivial sentiment. 'The portrayal of those who protest against cruelty to animals as sentimental, emotional "animal lovers",' he complained, has diverted discussion from 'serious, political and moral discussion'.[7] In *The Case for Animal Rights* (1983), Tom Regan similarly protested against the assumption that people (he did not stipulate gender) who were concerned with animal welfare were 'irrational', 'sentimental' and 'emotional'. He urged his fellow liberationists to make a 'concerted effort not to indulge our emotions or parade our sentiments. And that requires making a sustained commitment to rational enquiry.'[8] In this way, even the proponents of animals remained committed to a Cartesian distinction between reason and emotion.

Protest

Female resistance was inevitable. How could they effectively contest the purported relationship between human femininity and animality? Feminists developed a threefold strategy for convincing men that women are fully human in their own right, and not just to the extent to which they approximate men. First, they had to convince their opponents that they were being treated as animals (or worse); secondly, they had to assert female superiority to animals, and, finally, they had to persuade their opponents that this injustice needed to be remedied.

The first of these (that women were being treated as animals) was empirically demonstrable, and not simply in the (objectively true) Darwinian sense. Practically every feminist cause from the mid-nineteenth century onwards expressed fury about being equated with lower animals. In particular, they pointed to one of the most prominent examples: the passing of the Contagious Diseases Acts (CDAs) in 1864, 1866 and 1869. These Acts allowed policemen in certain designated towns to take any woman they suspected of prostitution before a magistrate and have her intimately examined for venereal disease. If infected, she could be forcibly detained.

The legislation had passed through Parliament with very little discussion. Indeed, some Members later admitted that they had assumed that the Acts only applied to animals.[9] It was not an unreasonable assumption, since advocates of the legislation routinely compared the Acts favourably with attempts to deal with cattle plague.[10] For instance, in a speech in the House of Commons in 1870, Lyon Playfair (Liberal politician and a chemist who endorsed the use of poisonous gas against the Russians during the Crimean War) argued for *extending* the CDAs, explicitly comparing the regulations with the Animal Contagious Diseases Act. He lamented that 'stamping out' animal diseases was much easier than human diseases, since in the former case it was 'easy to prevent the movement of cattle, or even kill the infected animals'.

This would be unacceptable behaviour towards women. He considered women who worked as prostitutes as possessing 'the habits of beasts'. They were 'poor creatures' and 'fallen creatures' who needed to be 'redeemed from savagery to something approaching civilization'. They needed the 'humanizing influences' of the reforms.[11]

Feminists – both male and female – actively opposed such stigmatization, forming societies such as the Association for the Repeal of the Contagious Diseases Acts. As the main repeal journal, the *Shield*, explained, the Association was the equivalent to the Society for the Prevention of Cruelty to Animals: both were required to 'interfere for the protection of dumb creatures who cannot protect themselves'.[12] In other words, these reformers sought to repeal the CDAs on the grounds that the legislation treated women as a whole as nothing more than contagious animals, while at the same time they identified the real 'mute creatures' in class terms. *Poor* women were mute beasts; middle-class women reformers had a voice and were the humanity to which working-class women should aspire.

Indeed, these 'creatures' were portrayed as 'dumb' not only in the sense of lacking voice. In *The Ride of Death* (1883), feminist and social purity campaigner J. Ellice Hopkins wrote about women in terms of their resemblance to kittens and birds. She described a 'young girl, full of animal spirits, with plenty of what I call the "black kitten" in her', who longed to 'jump about in ways often anything but discreet'. Hopkins observed that it was 'a bit hard that men should have dug by the side of her foolish, dancing feet a bottomless pit' so that she might 'put on her fine features like the silly bird-witted thing she is' and be pushed 'over the brink . . . leaving her with the very womanhood smashed out of her'.[13] In a speech given to the Medical Society of London in 1870, Charles Bell Taylor added an orientalist twist to this rhetoric, claiming that the Act 'reduced' women 'to the condition of mere animals', allowing them to be treated 'with less consideration than an oriental despot would show to the slaves of his harem'.[14] It is no wonder that author and anti-vaccination activist Mary Catherine Hume-Rothery queried whether 'humanity includes women at all', and railed against those who claimed that 'these poor wretches . . . are not women – not worthy of the name!' No, she cried:

> They *are* women,
> 'As God made them, and as man
> Must fail to unmake them'.[15]

In the furore, women were typically characterized as a particular *kind* of animal: female dogs or bitches. This identification was most explicit in the debates over the Dog Bill of 1871, which allowed police to 'take into custody' any dog 'found out walking by itself' and, if not claimed, sell or destroy it. The establishment *Pall Mall Gazette* protested: 'Is this a free country?' its headlines enquired, adding that the clause was 'a gross infringement on the liberty of the dog'. Feminists writing in the *Shield* were not impressed. The Contagious Diseases Acts, they noted, treated women seen walking at night in a similar fashion. The Acts 'enact that any woman considered "dangerous" . . . "may be brought before a summary jurisdiction, and, if the court thinks it fit *destroyed*" – so far as all sense of decency is concerned'.

This was even more unfair on women because, unlike stray dogs who might bite people, women 'might be injured through no fault of their own' but as a result of the actions of 'licentious men'.[16] At the very least, women would never be treated with respect if men continued to valorize power and sensuality over morality and sensitivity. This was the view of 'Vanessa', writing in the *Woman's Penny Paper* in 1890. She ended her impassioned plea against the denigration of animals by acknowledging that readers were primarily interested in the welfare of women, rather than animals. However, she reiterated, the wellbeing of women and animals were inseparable. If women wanted to 'save' their 'sisters from degradation at the hands of men', they 'must raise the standard of morality' among men and 'must make them more, not less, sensitive to the sufferings of their fellow creatures'. Remember, she exhorted her readers, that

> the recognition of women's rights implies the recognition of animals' rights, for both proclaim a higher law than 'Might is right'; both appeal to the human, and not to the brute instincts in man.

This was necessary not only as 'a *means* to *this* end' (that is, female empowerment) but also 'for pure humanity's sake'.[17] In this way, the rights of dogs benefited women as the *true* exemplars of humanity.

The argument that nineteenth-century feminists routinely drew parallels between animals and women would be incomplete without mentioning Josephine Butler, the leading activist in the movement to repeal the CDAs. A speech she gave in October 1874 contains some typical components of repeal rhetoric. Underprivileged women, she claimed, were forced into prostitution because they had been denied full employment opportunities and would not otherwise be able to feed their families. Criminalizing these women, without reforming employment practices, could only do harm to them and their dependents. In order to persuade her listeners, she equated the treatment of women with the way 'sentimental naturalists' treated dogs. Dogs also had powerful maternal instincts, she averred, and on a freezing winter's night those 'maternal instincts' would have 'prompted it [sic] to tear off its own fur for the protection of its young'. Being 'distressed' at the sight of the self-destructive maternal dog, a 'sentimental naturalist' might muzzle her, 'so as effectually to prevent her denuding her own breast in order to protect her nest'. However, the sentimentalist

> neglects to furnish her with any material in place of her own coat; and she, poor creature, cannot tell him 'If I do not tear off my own fur, my offspring will perish'. She can only inarticulately fret and rage against the restraint put upon her, and her young *do* perish.

In other words, by simply adopting punitive measures against prostitution legislators risked causing greater distress to the women's children and other dependents: instead, they must direct their indignation at the cause of women's poverty – that is, discriminatory employment practices. Butler and other middle-class reformers fervently believed that they had been charged with speaking up for pauper women who, like dogs, could not do so for themselves.

Butler's speech did make a distinction between human mothers and maternal dogs. Like many commentators in the last chapter, she believed that degrading people was worse than doing the same to animals because humans had been 'made in God's image'. The 'humble animal' could suffer in the interests of the '*physical* salvation of her offspring'. Women, however, suffered the additional 'horror' of *moral* dishonour. Most importantly, Butler informed listeners, women's moral ruin was 'forced . . . by the stronger portion of humanity, for the weaker to embrace and be wrecked by it'. In this one speech, then, Butler alludes to a number of the concerns of this book, particularly the idea that (certain) women are animals and, like other animals, are mute. As she reminded her listeners time and again, the 'poor creature, cannot tell'.[18]

Limited Economy of Sympathy

These feminists faced a major stumbling block, however. Many people found it easier to sympathize with animal suffering than that of (certain) people. In other words, people were more empathetic to non-human animals than to lesser humans.

This propensity to sympathize with animals rather than with other people was a common refrain in contemporary critiques of slavery and of aristocratic privilege. In the late eighteenth century, for instance, men and women fighting for the abolition of slavery were cautioned against 'affecting too much pity for the stranger', since 'we have abuses at home'.[19] In other words, the 'stranger' was the slave: a creature set outside those white-skinned humans 'at home'.

In the animal-versus-human stakes, however, the chief offenders tended to be women themselves – particularly those of the upper classes. Thus, in 1761, 'A Gentleman of the Partie' admitted that he could appreciate why a 'woman of sense might extend a DEGREE of affection for a BRUTE', but found it impossible to understand why the same woman would order 'the costly chicken' for her cat or dog but 'never thinks of giving a morsel of bread to relieve the hunger of a MAN'. The problem, he believed, was 'the MANNER in which we express our humanity' towards animals. He observed that a 'fine lady' might

> act as if she thought the DOG, which happens to be under her pre-
> cious care, is incomparably of more value, in her eyes, than a
> HUMAN creature, which is under the care of any other person, or
> peradventure, under no care at all.

From this, he concluded that 'an immoderate love of a brute animal, tho' it may not destroy a charitable disposition, yet it often weakens the force of it'.[20]

Fanny Burney made a similar point in The Wanderer; or, Female Difficulties (1814). In the novel, Mrs Ireton indulged her lapdog with tasty treats but when her black servant offended her she threatened him with being 'shipped back to the West Indies'. 'And there', she contin-ued, 'that your joy may be complete, I shall issue orders that you may be striped, till you jump, and that you may jump, – you little black imp! – between every stripe!'. So, while the spoilt dog was being pampered, 'poor Mungo . . . dropt upon his knees to implore forgive-ness'.[21] In these critiques, it is notable that the people lambasted for their exquisite sensibilities towards animal life were aristocratic *women*, who denied the humanity of pauper and enslaved *men*. It was an attack on gender that was masked as a critique of class privilege.

Such complains about the limits of sympathy for human suffering faced an even more acute problem in the late nineteenth century, when increasing groups of people (including women, workers and children) started to demand political and civil rights. Although feminists, socialists and other radicals theorized connections between different constituents of 'suffering subjects', they also observed that many people found it easier to sympathize with animals. It was very convenient that animals were incapable of uniting together in, say, political parties, trade unions or lobbying organizations. As a consequence, animals could be subjected to a degree of practically unbounded projection, and made to serve a universe of diverse, but exclusively human, interests.

Certain humans are much more difficult to sympathize with than many animals. People are noisy and belligerent in defence of their own authority and wellbeing. Their demands can be financially costly and could require radical shifts in status ranking. Take the plight of children, for instance. Were they truly sentient? Could they feel pain? If so, should they be shielded from violent attacks by their parents, or were they simply forms of property for these selfsame parents? The answer given to these questions could have radical implications. Intervention into the lives of children could rapidly set in motion demands for political action that might be seen to violate the principle of (male) familial governance. The Society for the Prevention of Cruelty to Children was continually forced to defend itself against critics who objected to the ways in which it intruded into the inner sanctum of plebeian families. In a society intensely anxious about the ideological implications of interfering in areas within the domain of paternal authority, this was a grave accusation indeed. The Society conceded that 'No one doubts the sacredness of parental rights', while at the same time appealing to the higher authority of the 'law of parental duty imposed by Him who has constituted the law'.[22] They also had to counter the other 'problem' posed by abused children (as well as women): working-class children were widely regarded as unruly, not innocent; they certainly knew how to answer back. Against great odds, the Society had to emphasize the redeemability of the abused child; her innocence, rather than savagery. The abused child might be (mis)treated as little more than an animal, but 'deep down' she retained a spark of that divinely inspired humanity.

Reformers who were keen to demonstrate their 'civilized sensibility' to suffering creatures of the human variety might be equally zealous about avoiding the fiscal and political consequences that would arise from demonstrating concern for the plight of abused underlings. As the historian James Turner observed in *Reckoning with the Beast* (1980), in comparison to arguments for the rights of slaves and factory children,

> Kindness to animals profaned no social taboos and upset no economic applecarts, either in the theoretical systems of political economists or in the harsh daily encounter of capital and labor.[23]

People active in movements to alleviate the suffering of animals tended to share a wide range of humanitarian concerns. It remained the case, however, that the animal's claim to sentience and, therefore, considerate treatment was an easier one for many people to follow. Kindness to animals did not even require any commitment to vegetarianism. Believing that cows, pigs and chickens were *feeling* creatures did not mean that they could not be eaten: it was possible to 'eat well' so long as the animal was butchered with tenderness.

Radical groups, including socialists as well as feminists, frequently mentioned the conflicts that arose out of the competing demands made by different 'sentient beings'. In the 1890s, for instance, Tom Mann (the first secretary of the Independent Labour Party) adopted a vegetarian lifestyle out of compassion for animal suffering, but confessed that his increasing involvement in the socialist movement 'weakened my ardour'. 'However widely food reform might be diffused,' he admitted, 'it would never prove a cure for the economic evils I deplored'.[24] The point was made even more strongly by Henry Hyndman, leader of the Social Democratic Foundation. He had been invited, along with George Bernard Shaw, to the home of Henry and Kate Salt. Hyndman was not impressed by the Salts' frugality, teetotalism and passion for animal rights. He turned to Shaw and complained that he did not want the socialist movement to become

> a depository of odd cranks: humanitarians, vegetarians, anti-vivisectionists and anti-vaccinationists, arty-crafties and all the rest of them. We are scientific socialists and have no room for sentimentalists. They confuse the issue.

Hyndman accused humanitarians and vegetarians of putting the socialist movement 'back twenty years at least'. Henry Salt replied with indignation, asking, 'Do you expect us . . . to stop feeling until the social revolution comes?' The pain animals were experiencing on a daily basis 'is now and has to be alleviated now. The animals cannot wait as the unemployed cannot wait. Wherever there is preventable suffering we must see to it'.[25] Salt was not a complete idealist, however, since he recognized that there were practical constraints to freedom. As he argued on another occasion, it was

> the fate not only of countless animals, but also of countless men, to be born into a life of unremitting, ill-requited drudgery; and it is the duty of the ethical reformer not to complain that either man or animal should thus be doomed to labor, but rather to quicken the sense of responsibility on the part of society as a whole towards its individual workers, with a view to the gradual humanizing of their lot.[26]

Salt was committed to the gradual humanization of animal and human life, and did not see why one (the poor) should take precedence over another (the animals).

Unfortunately, his was a minority view. Concern about the limited economy of sympathy (which required the elaboration of hierarchies of sentience) was a common mantra among opponents of animal guardians. The socialist Edward Deacon Girdlestone was a vocal supporter of vivisection (albeit, regulated by the state). In 1884, he accused animal guardians of 'thinking more of the sorrows of his pug or puss than of his wife or child!' He insisted that there was 'nothing wicked' in 'Race-selfishness'. Indeed, he continued,

> There is more sacredness, surely, about one Human being than about all the other Animal Species put together! . . . I cannot pay in full my dues of love and kindness to my neighbour and myself, without at times being unkind to Brutes. It is a sad requirement . . . The cry of the Brute from the torture-trough is in my ear, – and grieves me; but the 'Cry of the Human' from his bed of sickness is a louder one.[27]

Even some animal advocates agreed that there was a limited economy of sympathy, but drew the lesson that it was necessary to demote the status of certain *humans*. This could be achieved in two ways: first, by espousing a hierarchy based on aesthetics or, secondly, by ranking people and animals according to moral codes.

First, then, might animals be more beautiful than humans? Many commentators who sought to elevate the aesthetic standing of animals did so by denigrating certain human bodies. This can be illustrated at a number of levels. In an article entitled 'On the Notion of the Souls of Beasts', published in *Bell's Court and Fashionable Magazine* in 1806, the author admitted that it was difficult to categorically declare whether *any* animal (human or non-human) was beautiful. This was not surprisingly, he lectured, since even in human communities 'we are not agreed what [beauty] consists'. What some nations call beauty might be 'considered as deformity among others'. However, it was 'certain, that in cleanness, smoothness, colour, proportion, and disposition of parts, many animals excel us'. He went further, claiming that 'whoever imagines a man stark naked, will judge a covering more proper for him' than for all other animals.[28]

The author of 'On the Notion of the Souls of Beasts' was at least discreet in registering the comparative aesthetics of 'smoothness, colour, proportion' that distinguished white Europeans from other human 'races' and animals. Robert Hartmann, writing in *Anthropoid Apes* (1885), was less so. He reminded his readers that although people were 'sometimes disposed to see the true likeness of anthropoid apes in dark-skinned, naked savages', in reality 'physical beauty, and especially the beauty of feature' was not a feature of the white 'races' either. In his words, 'Among all nations we find individuals whose ugliness is little inferior to that of anthropoids, and which sometimes even exceeds it.' Whose ugliness exceeded that of anthropoids? Predictably, he pointed to people who did not look like himself: 'Mongols, the majority of negroes, Papuans, Guaranis, and Malays'.[29]

Beauty was not the only way to rank sentient life. Another was according to ideas of morality, which tended to be the approach of those feminists discussed earlier. These middle-class reformers believed that the oppression of women and animals was due to the double standard of morality and the 'brute instincts in man' (as 'Vanessa' put it in the *Woman's Penny Paper*).[30] As a result, they abhorred the 'bestiality' of working-class men. This was the predicament for J. Ellice Hopkins. She was not convinced that men of the 'lower orders' could claim to be superior to animals. In her book, entitled *Is it Natural?* (1885), Hopkins admitted that although she had 'spoken very much . . . of my love for working men', she 'couldn't help making an exception' when she spied their 'bestial behaviour in the public house'. That was 'one place where I did not like working men at all'. She was 'extremely annoyed' to hear them begging for 'two-pence for a pot of beer . . . Just like . . . a pig beginning to grunt for his wash the moment you approach his sty!' She claimed that when she made this confession at a public meeting in front of working men, a 'hoary-headed doctor' stood up and said 'I think that's rather hard . . . Hard, I mean, on the *pigs*.' Hopkins agreed, reflecting that

> I have often thought that we are very hard, not only on the pig, but on the whole animal creation in the way we have got into speaking especially of the sins of the flesh as animal, brutal, bestial, and of using the common rough expression of the man who gets drunk or sins against his own manhood, that 'he makes a beast of himself'.[31]

After all, she insisted, a pig did not 'go home and knock about his sow'. Both the Earnest Englishwoman and Hopkins recognized that it was lesser humans – in both cases, working-class husbands and lovers – and not animals who had a tendency to 'go home and knock about' other sentient creatures. How unfair, then, that sows had greater legal protection from cruelty than female spouses (the fact that sows could be eaten was conveniently ignored).

Opponents of animal advocates were quick to accuse women like Hopkins of hypocrisy for feeling sympathetic towards only 'worthy' humans. One of the most ardent responses came from physiologist E. De Cyon, writing in 1883. The focus of De Cyon's attack was an anti-vivisectionist pamphlet that had been endorsed by men 'belonging to the staff of the Prussian army'. How could it be, De Cyon mocked, that people who refuse to allow scientists to 'sacrifice some few animals to the progress of science and the cure of innumerable human sufferers' could 'find it easy to squander thousands of human lives in colonial wars – which means, in fact, in the interests of commercial enterprise'? It was morally disingenuous to view the 'life of the frog and the rabbit' as 'sacred' while supporting wars that 'immolate soldiers by tens of thousands' and 'cause the tears of widows and orphans and bereaved mothers to flow'.[32]

De Cyon went much further. Anti-vivisectionists were not only hypocrites, they were also – greatest insult of all – mere 'women'. He taunted readers to 'show among the leaders of the [anti-vivisectionist] agitation one young girl, beautiful, and beloved, or one young wife who has found in her home the full satisfaction of her affections!' Determined not to dilute his misogyny, he reiterated his belief that animal advocates were 'old maids whose tenderness, despised by man, has flung itself in despair at the feet of cats and parrots'. It was no coincidence, he believed, that such societies flourished in Protestant,

rather than Catholic, countries. Protestant women were irrational spir-
itualists, 'addicted' to 'calling up spirits from the vasty deep'. In contrast,
Catholicism promised 'old maids of excited imagination a refuge in its
convents'. The 'ecstatic adoration of the Heart of Jesus or of the Blessed
Virgin offers sufficient food for the mysticism of these disordered minds'
while the 'cold formalism and rigid creed' of Protestantism left 'old
maids' vulnerable to the 'mysteries of Spiritism' and 'fantastic charity' as
in the animal welfare movement.[33]

The feminist response to De Cyon's diatribe was, relatively speaking, mild. One anonymous respondent agreed that women played a
significant role in protesting against vivisection. She recalled a recent
instance when Charles-Édouard Brown-Séquard (the prominent
animal-experimenter) was vivisecting a monkey, 'without any pretence of anaesthetic'. When the 'poor little thing shrieked with agony',
Brown-Séquard decided to 'stop this vexatious interruption' by cutting
the monkey's vocal cords. At that point, a 'young lady in the audience . . . sprang forward and hit the professor across the face with her
parasol'. For this anonymous respondent, this action was evidence not
of women's tendency to hysteria but their possession of superior sensibilities. Refusing to accept De Cyon's disdainful verdict, the
respondent claimed that women's role in the British pro-animal movement 'affords us the liveliest satisfaction' both as women and as
Protestants. She was proud that Protestantism did not 'invite the with-
drawal of the charitable and sympathetic instincts from objects of
practical utility' to the narrow confines of nunneries. British culture
allowed women a 'healthier, fuller life', so much so that 'even the
despised old maid is now no longer despised'. Responding to the accusation that 'sick folk and women' were those 'whom the passions
sway', she defended the separate nature of female sensibility:

> It may be sentimental to side with the weak rather than with the
> strong, to deal blows with a parasol rather than applaud a skillfully
> conducted experiment, to prefer humanity to science . . . But the fact
> remains. The English public is largely composed of men and women
> with warm hearts and tender consciences, and both, and particularly
> of late, the women are beginning to think and act, and form their own
> judgments on matters they hitherto took for granted.

She judiciously admitted that not 'every step they take is wise', but the
'general cause of justice and humanity will gain in proportion as

women get free scope for the exercise of mercy and charity, and other inexpedient but feminine qualities'.[34] It was a reasoned response to De Cyon's hysteria.

Children are Animals

The 'Three Ws' – women, workers, and non-whites – were not the only ones whose welfare was ranked beneath that of middle-class European men and closer to the animal world. As already implied, children were also slotted into a lowly position in the hierarchy of sentience and of creatures deserving of sympathy.

Evolutionists were particularly keen on characterizing children as animals. From the 1880s, they could be heard arguing that 'ontogeny recapitulated phylogeny': that is, the development of the foetus to old age followed the biological continuum of the species. Children represented a 'phyletic past', and as a result it was important that children had contact with animals. In the words of psychologist C. F. Hodge, writing in 1902,

> The pet animal is thus for the child, as it was for the race, the key to the door into knowledge and dominion over all animal life . . . Its fundamental character and value for education are evinced in the passion of children for pets; and as in the race, so in the life of the child, it should be made the most of as a step toward civilization.[35]

Children were, literally, animals in the process of evolving into full humans. The 'acquisition of dominion over animals', stated the author of a 1909 article in the *Pedagogic Seminary*, was of 'fundamental importance to the development of the [human] race'. If

> the child is to epitomize the race's experiences, the pet becomes the cardinal factor at a certain stage in the child's development . . . To deprive a child of association with animals is to deprive him of his phyletic inheritance.[36]

Philosopher James Sully, in his *Studies of Childhood* (1895), was even more direct. Children belonged 'to the animal community', having 'more in common with the dog and cat, the pet rabbit or dormouse, than with that grown-up human community'. This was not surprising, he went on, if evolutionary principles were understood. After all, if the order of development of the individual follows and summarises that of the race, we should expect the child to show a germ at least of the passionateness, the quarrelsomeness of the brute and of the savage before he shows the moral qualities distinctive of civilised man. That he often shows so close a resemblance to the savage and to the brute suggests how little ages of civilised life with its suppression of these furious impulses have done to tone down the ancient and carefully transmitted instincts. The child at birth, and for a long while after, may then be said to be the representative of wild untamed nature.[37]

Children needed educating in order to evolve higher than animals and 'savages', finally becoming a full member of 'mankind'. It was a sentiment that echoed Sigmund Freud's view that children 'feel themselves more akin to animals than to their elders'.[38]

Earlier in this chapter, though, I pointed out that many people were concerned that if too much sympathy was directed towards suffering children, then highly valued (especially by the male half of the species) principles of family governance might be violated. Children might be animals but, in terms of the morality of outsiders intervening into the family to protect children from abuse, they could be ranked lower than those other sentient creatures dubbed 'animal'.

It was a grading that infuriated child reformers of the late nineteenth century. They were particularly aware that industrialization was dependent on cheap labour, including that of children. As Charles Shaw complained when writing about his childhood spent working in the potteries of Staffordshire, nine-year-old children would be required to work seventy or eighty hours a week, being paid only 'one-and-six or two shillings'. The employer's

carriage-horses would eat as much food at one meal as such sums would buy. But they were 'carriage' horses, and I and others were only work children. Any one can see the difference . . . Human nature was cheaper than beast nature.[39]

Echoing such concerns, Archbishop Manning and the Reverend Benjamin Waugh (founder of the London Society for the Prevention of Cruelty to Children) were appalled to discover that many 'English savages' brought meat for their cats while allowing their own children to starve to death. Interestingly, they insisted that these were often not the poorest members of society: the 'true English savage', they lamented, was in fact 'quiet, and is generally the earner of good wages'.[40] If only 'rich Christians' were 'as interested in the prevention of cruelty to children as they [were] in the prevention of cruelty to animals', lamented Waugh in the *Child's Guardian* in 1890. Only then could reformers effectively tackle 'the vilest, blackest shame of our land, the famine and the pain of tiny staggerers to the grave'.[41]

Ironically, the Earnest Englishwoman's satire came true, but for children not adult women. Her plea that 'whenever the word "animal" occurs it shall be held to include women' was what happened for oppressed children. The Society for the Prevention of Cruelty to Animals had been founded in 1823. From the 1840s to the 1890s, commentators regularly urged the Society to 'turn their attention' to the sufferings of 'helpless children', as well as working men and women forced to toil long hours in mines or factories.[42] As the author of 'A Word for Children' put it in the *Home Journal* in 1866, 'It is for the relief of these "animals" that all would desire to see founded a "Society for the Prevention of Cruelty".'[43] The *New York Ledger* was equally direct, stating in 'Cruelty to Animals: Also to Wives and Children' on 3 August 1867 that it 'would not be amiss to suggest' that the Society for the Prevention of Cruelty to Animals

> should extend the sphere of its labors so as to include a few classes of ill-used bipeds – such as children who are unmercifully whipped and starved by their brutal parents; poor sewing girls who are swindled out of their hard earnings by soulless employers; broken-spirited wives who are habitually cuffed and kicked by drunken husbands, and the like. Nobody interferes to prevent such cruelties as these; and except in a few flagrant cases that force themselves upon the attention of the authorities, they are perpetrated with entire impunity.

They were sentiments that the Earnest Englishwoman would echo less than five years later. The 'cudgeled woman, or a flayed and starving child, or a seamstress swindled out of her daily bread', the anonymous *New York Ledger* correspondent went on, 'deserves commiseration as much as a horse with a sore back, or a leveret in a boa's cage'.[44] In the words of 'A Lady Who is Deeply Interested', writing in the *New York Times* on 27 January 1872,

> In protecting your work of mercy for dumb creatures, do not forget the creature whom God made in his own image, and to whom He has

given a soul that may be saved by saving his body. These dumb creatures will not meet you in the life to come, but if you rescue but one human being, angels will envy you your reward.[45]

'A Lady Who Is Deeply Interested' even made the argument that children suffered *more* than animals. 'Can you not prevent the cruelty used toward the little children in our streets?' she asked, since children were 'as powerless to help themselves as the dumb brutes, and yet with a far greater capacity for suffering'[46] (see Figure 1).

Indeed, the first successful court case against child cruelty in America was brought by the Society for the Prevention of Cruelty to *Animals*. In 1873, Marietta (Etta) Angell Wheeler, a church visitor from St Luke's Mission in New York City, complained about the treatment of a young

A CASE FOR THE SOCIETY FOR PREVENTION OF CRUELTY TO ANIMALS.

Figure 1. 'A Case for the Society for the Prevention of Cruelty to Animals', from *Moonshine* (1896). Note the markings of class, in terms of the men's clothing, height and comportment, and physiognomy.

Moonshine (19 September 1896)

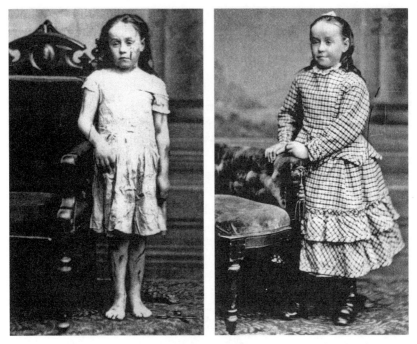

Figure 2. Mary Ellen Wilson photographed in 1873, shortly after being 'rescued', and then a year later. The original images are held by the New York Society for the Prevention of Cruelty to Children.

The George Sim Johnston Archives of The New York Society for the Prevention of Cruelty to Children

girl called Mary Ellen Wilson (see Figure 2).[47] She had found Mary chained to a bedpost with clear signs of having been badly beaten. Mary had been indentured to Mrs Mary Connolly when she was just two years of age. When Wheeler found her, she looked about five, but was actually nine. After failing to persuade the police to intervene, Wheeler approached Henry Bergh, the President of the American Society for the Prevention of Cruelty to Animals, and persuaded him that 'a little animal' was being abused, so the society for animals brought charges. The court found Mary Connolly guilty of felonious assault.

Such individual efforts could only have a minimal effect. Their attempts to give children the same protections against cruelty as animals were dramatically enhanced when, in 1884, Benjamin Waugh founded the Society for the Prevention of Cruelty to Children.[48] Like their predecessors, Manning and Waugh explicitly set out to 'place the child of the [English] savage on the same level as his dog'. 'Already', they noted,

the English savage has learnt that it is not safe nor decent to knock his
cattle about, but he has all sorts of maxims as to parental rights – his
house being his castle, and the like – which make it both safe and
decent and altogether as it ought to be, to knock his child about . . .
At present the law explicitly forbids 'ill-treating, abusing, torturing
and insufficient feeding' of dogs, allowing the Court to construe the
meaning of these simple words. What the Society [for the Prevention
of Cruelty to Children] will submit to Parliament is a proposal to do
the same for children.

Like the Earnest Englishwoman, Manning and Waugh proposed that a
wife should be allowed to give evidence on behalf of her child against
a 'cruel husband': 'At present she counts for nobody in the case,
though she is as good a witness as anybody else in the case of the
dog'.[49] Or, as Waugh, writing in the *Child's Guardian* in May 1889,
exclaimed, 'If wretched children were only dogs, what sunlight would
fall into their doomed and dismal lives!'[50] Indeed, linking the Society
for the Prevention of Cruelty to Animal to that of one for humans had
a pedagogic aspect: cruel parents could be taught valuable lessons by
observing animals. In the words of Henry Ricketts, the Rector of
Landcross, in 1898, 'What lessons such inhuman beings may learn
from the dumb creation, and the touching affection they show for
their offspring. What dangers, too, they will brave for to rescue them
from harm.'[51]

As this implies, the links between the societies for protecting animals
and children were not simply rhetorical. In Britain, it was over sixty
years after the establishment of the Society for the Prevention of
Cruelty to Animals that the London Society for the Prevention of
Cruelty to *Children* was established.[52] The London SPCC actually
shared facilities in Jermyn Street with the RSPCA for a time, and there
was a significant overlap in membership. The London SPCC adopted
the same organizational and propaganda structures as the RSPCA and
their journal, the *Child's Guardian*, was explicitly modelled on *Animal
World*. Increasingly, however, the two movements drew apart, with
the child protection societies recognizing that animals were in fact
generating more sympathy than children. 'We are not a little amazed',
complained Waugh, 'that we receive so little from the wills of benevolent persons. It is not the dogs but the children to whom fall the
crumbs from these tables.'[53] Compassion was a limited resource: many
people possessed a 'feeling for animals that was of a higher nature than

that possessed by those who may love animals only, but who dislike what they call "gutter children",' observed the head of the London Metropolitan Police.[54]

What Will We Lose If We Win?

According to feminists like the Earnest Englishwomen, as well as people fighting to shield children from cruelty, less than fully human persons could be accorded status by claiming a sentience that was shared by the animal world. It was a deeply problematic politics. As political philosopher Hannah Arendt jotted down in a note during a discussion of women's liberation in 1972, 'the real question to ask is, what will we lose if we win?'[55]

Indeed, a politics based around shared states of *feeling* is greatly flawed, for at least six reasons. The first is the least important, since it simply points to a problem of attribution. However, it still needs to be said: the Benthamite mantra that all animal rights activists cite – that is, Bentham's statement that 'The question is not, Can they *reason*? Nor, Can they *talk*?, but Can they *suffer*?' – has been decontextualized, seriously misleading readers about Bentham's philosophy.[56] Bentham was a great lover of animals,[57] but he was no vegetarian. Immediately before the quote in which Bentham asks 'Do they *feel*?', he wrote:

> If the being eaten were all, there is very good reason why we should be suffered to eat such of them as we like to eat: we are the better for it, and they are never the worse. They have none of those long-protracted anticipations of future misery which we have. The death they suffer in our hands commonly is, and may always be, a speedier, and by that means a less painful one, than that which would await them in the inevitable course of nature.[58]

People could even have a *duty* to kill animals for food, because 'Nature' was far crueler than humans. Vivisection was also acceptable to Bentham. In the *Morning Chronicle* on 13 March 1825, he noted that he had 'never seen, nor ever can see, any objection to the putting of dogs and other inferior animals to pain, in the way of medical experimentation'. He only stipulated that the experiments have 'a determinable object, beneficial to mankind, accompanied with a fair prospect of the accomplishment of it'.[59]

More to the point, Bentham was a fervent *opponent* of natural rights for humans, let alone animals. As he expressed it in 'Anarchical Fallacies; Being an Examination of the Declaration of Rights Issued During the French Revolution' (1843), the men who issued the French declaration were sowing 'seeds of anarchy'. Their declaration was nothing more than 'Shallow and reckless vanity! . . . a perpetual vein of nonsense, flowing from a perpetual abuse of words . . . execrable trash . . . nonsense upon stilts'. He exhorted readers to 'Look to the letter, you find nonsense – look beyond the letter, you find nothing'. It was ridiculous to state that all men are born free. On the contrary, Bentham insisted,

> All men . . . are born in subjection, and the most absolute subjec-
> tion – the subjection of a helpless child to the parents on whom he
> depends every moment for his existence . . . All men born free?
> Absurd and miserable nonsense!

This was the case when you looked at the relationship of apprentices to their masters, or of wives to husbands. Indeed, 'without subjection and inequality' the institution of marriage could not exist, 'for of two contra-dictory wills, both cannot take effect at the same time'. Bentham ridiculed the idea that rights belonged to 'all human creatures'. In his words, this would mean that women would have to be included, as well as 'children – children of every age', because, his sarcastic analysis con-tinued, 'if women and children are not part of the nation, what are they? Cattle?' For him, this was nothing more than 'smack-smooth equality, which rolls so glibly out of the lips of the rhetorician'.[60] Given such strong views against human rights, it is highly distorting to claim that Bentham was on the side of animal rights, even those based on sentience.

There are much more substantive reasons, however, why basing pol-itics around shared states of *feeling* is mistaken. The second reason is very basic: it hasn't worked. Despite centuries of ardent pleading, the pass-ing of a voluminous amount of legislation and the pervasive demonization of even subtle forms of cruelty, the fact remains that inflicting pain on human and non-human animals is routine. Western society professes to be exquisitely sensitive to the sufferings of animals, but animals – including beloved pets – continue to live despised lives. In 2009, over sixty thousand animals were killed by the RSPCA, they investigated 140,575 complaints of animal cruelty, and seized or 'res-cued' over 143,500 animals.[61] Around one-third of all pet dogs in America ended their lives in an animal shelter and, each year, ten to twelve million pets are classified as 'surplus' and 'put to sleep' – most commonly by carbon monoxide poisoning or a lethal injection of sodium pentobarbital.[62] As an investigator into human bereavement after the death of a pet dryly observed, 'the grief experienced by some people associated with pet loss is not the typical response of animal owners'. For many, pets are simply a 'trivial part of our consumer orientated society'.[63]

The politics of sentience has also not managed to translate into legislation. Legal protections of animals are very narrowly defined. In law, it turns out that the definition of 'animal' is very flexible. For instance, the US Animal Welfare Act and the Animal Enterprises Protection Act have different definitions of what is an 'animal'. Rats used in medical experimentation are not animals for the purposes of the welfare laws but they are animals for the purposes of the Protection Act.[64] Chickens are not animals under the Humane Slaughter Act, but they are under legislation dealing with cockfighting. And I haven't even mentioned chicken fillets. For all the talk of sentience of animals, the fact is that we remain incredibly cruel towards them.

The acceptance of cruelty towards other humans – who we all admit are exquisitely sensitive to painful stimuli – is also commonplace. No one needs to be reminded of this. Even torture has once again become ethically acceptable. Thus, a *Washington Post*/ABC News poll in May 2004 found that one-third of Americans supported the use of torture.[65] A *Newsweek* poll four years later found that 44 per cent were willing to endorse torture against terrorist suspects.[66] The practice of waterboarding was condoned by half of Americans polled by the CNN/Opinion Research Corporation in April 2009.[67] The broader carceral tendencies of American legal culture in particular, which condones acts of extreme cruelty towards 'ordinary' criminal suspects and convicts,[68] seems to have made torture of suspected terrorists – especially if they could be designated 'foreign' – humdrum to many Americans.

The third reason for being sceptical about the efficacy of sentience in driving ethical behaviour is that the rhetoric can easily be counterproductive, further cementing prejudices about the nature of subordinate groups. An example might be the dilemma faced by proponents of Négritude, a black liberationist movement that was greatly stimulated by Haitian thinkers, who sought to reclaim a positive identity in the face of racial oppression, yet ended up reinforcing prejudices about 'Black spirit' against 'European rationality'.[69]

Similarly, when the Earnest Englishwoman and other feminists bound together female and animal sentience, they played into the hands of powerful figures who were claiming exactly the same thing – but as evidence of women's inferiority and incapacity as political subjects. Both femininity and animality could be posited as 'natural', arising out of emotional ('bestial') rather than rational ('mankind') ways of being. The politics of sentience allows all the oppressive hierarchies to remain intact: wo/man, animal/human, colonized/er, emotion/reason, and so on are simply further reified and solidified. It is a politics perfectly consistent with the Reverend Hamilton Morgan's sermon in 1895, in which he told his congregation that

> The horse is more sensitive in nerves than you are . . . The whip stings him more than it would you. Many a time you call him ugly, when he is hysterical or frightened: and instead of soothing him, as you would your wife under the same circumstances, you shout and beat him.[70]

Implicit in this is not only the exquisite sensitivity of the horse over that of the wife, but also the notion that both are hysterics. Both horse and wife are 'under the whip' and are to be coddled and their resistance calmed in the interests of a conflict-free master–slave relation.

Fourth, it simply is not the case that sympathy for animals translates into sympathy for human sentient beings. Empathetic identification is not transferable. As I will be arguing in more detail in the next Part, within the *animal* rights movement some *humans* were classified as lesser beings, on whose bodies pain might legitimately be inflicted. Many philosophers and activists working for animal rights find within its liberal discourse an endorsement for harming certain people (those who are cruel to animals, for instance). Some even sanction torture. Thus, animal liberationist Peter Singer proved unable to repudiate torture:

> It will not do to say 'Never!' . . . in extreme circumstances, such absolutist answers always break down. Torturing a human being is almost always wrong, but it is not absolutely wrong. If torture were the only way in which we could discover the location of a nuclear bomb hidden in a New York City basement and timed to go off within the hour, then torture would be justifiable.

Although Singer does admit that 'in actual life the benefits are always more remote, and more often than not they are nonexistent', he leaves the argument open for the torture of sentient humans. Indeed (and he is at least consistent), Singer also does not repudiate torturing animals. His utilitarianism allows him to legitimize inflicting pain on animals in laboratories if it can be shown to result in significant improvements to human welfare.[71]

Fifth, the link between the sentience of women and animals is dependent on a construction of the 'body in pain' that can be profoundly seductive. Fully human persons willing to 'concede' that their lesser cousins are sensitive can take a 'savage delight' in witnessing the suffering body. Suffering can be turned into exquisite spectacle. Indeed, reports published by societies dedicated to the prevention of cruelty to both animals and humans are swollen with lurid accounts of suffering flesh, with readers expected to bear their humane witness to it. Sympathetic witness to cruelty *requires* the suffering body. As Edmund Burke observed as long ago as 1757, people 'have a degree of delight . . . in the real misfortunes and pains of others'. Terror could be 'a passion which always produces delight when it does not press too close'.[72] It was a sentiment lamented in the 1870s by Lewis Carroll, an ardent anti-vivisectionist. 'It is a humiliation but an undeniable fact', he argued, that

> man has something of the wild beast in him, that a thirst for blood can be aroused in him by witnessing a scene of carnage, and that the infliction of torture, when the first instincts of horror have been deadened by familiarity, may become, first, a matter of indifference, then a subject of morbid interest, then a positive pleasure, then a ghastly and ferocious delight.[73]

The lurid accounts of suffering as expounded in lingering detail by self-designated 'guardians' of animals and children in the late nineteenth- and early twentieth-century accounts explored in this chapter provided a spectacle that was inherently part of a broader politics of consumption (in the 'yellow' or popular press, for example) and class power (the proliferation of institutions dedicated to aspects of 'the problem' of the 'lower orders', both animal and human).

Finally, the politics of suffering is sensitive to gradations. Once it is accepted that creatures vary in their susceptibility to pain and suffering, it is easy to argue that inequity may actually be a form of kindness. In other words, languages of sentience and humanitarianism can be effortlessly co-opted to *defend* cruelty to living beings – human and non-human animals. They were, for instance, employed to defend slavery. Thus, Maria Edgeworth's 1804 story 'The Grateful Negro' acknowledged that the slave's humanity was crucial for the *reform*, but not the *overthrow*, of slavery. The 'humane' slave owner in her tale 'wished that there was no such thing as slavery in the world' but was equally convinced that the emancipation of slaves 'would rather increase than diminish their miseries'.[74] Indeed, supporters of slavery and animal servitude candidly employed the language of sympathy to argue that it was their humanitarian duty to maintain slaves and animals in servitude. They only admitted the need to manage these slaves more effectively, as employers would supervise any other worker.

This outcome of the politics of sentience was addressed in 1895, when philosopher David Ritchie published *Natural Rights. A Criticism of Some Political and Ethical Conceptions*. According to utilitarian theory, he observed, rights were linked to sentience. Obviously, then, animals must possess rights. But would not this create 'very difficult questions of casuistry', he asked. If differences in 'grades of sentience' were to be recognized in animals, then it should also be recognized in people. As he put it,

> If the recognition of Animal Rights is compatible with the kindly use of a horse as a beast of burden, would not a kindly negro-slavery be also perfectly compatible with the recognition of Natural Rights generally? And if we discriminate between what may be rightly done to the mollusc from what may be rightly done to the mammal, on the grounds of different grades of sentience, should we not also . . . discriminate between what may be rightly done to lower and higher races among mankind – the lower and less civilized being undoubtedly less capable of acute feeling?[75]

In recent decades, the problem with 'grades of sentience' has gained new prominence because of debates about the rights of infants and foetuses. If it can be shown (and it can) that human infants are less rational, less sensitive and less self-conscious than some (indeed, many) animals, what does this mean in terms of our ethical obligations? Peter Singer, as the most prominent 'preference utilitarian', tackles the issue head-on, contending that the life of a newborn baby possesses less value than that of a pig, a dog or a chimpanzee. Killing a newborn infant does not carry the same weight as killing an adult. He proposes 'a breathing space of 28 days should be allowed' after the birth of a severely impaired infant. In consultation, parents and doctors 'should have discretion to make life and death decisions about a newborn child'.[76] It is a point of view endorsed by the philosopher Michael Tooley, who asked 'what properties a thing must possess in order to have a serious right to live?' His conclusion was that while some 'adult animals belonging to species other than *Homo sapiens*' might possess a 'serious' right to life, infants lacked the self-consciousness to have a similar right.[77] The capacity for suffering is not enough: the sentient being (whether dog or infant) could simply be sedated before being killed.

According to utilitarian principles, then, ethics is reduced to a form of moral accountancy, an empirical calculation that could in fact lead to great suffering of humans and animals. They are simply a set of rules to be applied; the only considerations become consistency and accountability. An ethics based merely on a 'calculable process', as Derrida argued in 'Force of Law' (1992), is no ethics at all.[78]

Tying ethics to 'gradations of pain' is not only problematic because of the way it ranks *victims* in a pecking order that goes from lesser to more deserving: it is also premised on a distance between those victims of suffering and the empathetic observer. While sympathy claims to reduce social distance, it is in fact dependent upon it. It is dependent on a wide gulf between specific classes of sentient beings and their imagined underlings, on whom they are able to generously bestow sympathy. As on Josiah Wedgwood's anti-slavery medal, which was embossed with the words 'Am I Not a Man and a Brother?' (see Figure 1 in Chapter Nine, p. 165), the slave must be kneeling. The humanitarian is 'naturally' superior to the oppressed person or animal on whose behalf she is petitioning. As the historian Howard Malchow put it, 'the idealized black [slave], though a "man and a brother", is inevitably still on his knees as a grateful man and a younger brother'.[79] It is not simply that empathetic languages can be manipulated by the barbarians, but that sympathy for the sufferer is infused with symbolic violence.

It doesn't help matters to attempt to break down these graduations. If we repudiate the hierarchy of pain and try to empathize with all 'bodies in pain', the result is either unbearable or banal. With respect to human suffering, such a politics leads to fear and avoidance more often than to responsibility and attempts at alleviation. In terms of animals it is even more problematic. What Derrida called the 'discourse of carnophallogocentrism' (that is, the ideas, values, and practices that

are used to justify humanity's total sovereignty over animals) was precisely what enabled humans to believe that they possess a thorough
knowledge of 'the animal'. For animal advocates, animals can be understood (and empathized with) precisely because suffering is conceived of
as universal in *all* sentient beings. However, this is a deeply flawed logic.
The allegedly universal capacity to suffer turns out to be profoundly
localized: pain is defined through literary tropes and scientific discourses
based entirely in knowledges developed within human societies. When
animal suffering is acknowledged,[80] it is not individuated, not unique: it
is made in the likeness of the human. I will return to the problem of
sameness and difference – absolute alterity versus the politics of similarity – in my concluding remarks to this book.

Conclusion to Part 2:
'Should We "Become-Animal"?'

The ability to *feel* led people to extend compassion to (certain) animals, if only on the grounds that displays of sympathy would inevitably influence human-to-human interactions. Perhaps this would even promote sympathy towards women, children and the poor. That was the hope of the Earnest Englishwoman, feminists fighting against the Contagious Diseases Acts and for the vote, members of organizations set up to protect children, and many socialists. They all assumed, however, that there was a limited economy of sympathy, and they lacked confidence about the potentialities of 'their side' to win the battle for hearts, minds and stomachs. If anything, empathy proved easier to bestow on non-human animals, upon whom a universe of states and feelings could be safely projected, than on (certain) human animals whose pain was understood to be absolutely unique, shattering worlds, and terrifyingly beyond adequate empathetic response.

The excluded cry out to 'at least' be acknowledged to be animals. The frantic tracing of the Möbius strip, attempting to identify where 'the human' starts and 'the animal' stops, is fundamentally governed by the need to set the limits and expand the possibilities of violence to sentient creatures. This was what the Earnest Englishwoman recognized when she pleaded that the violence of men against women should be treated as violence of men against female animals. Ironically, her satirical question 'Are Women Animals?' was a plea to allow for the *humanization* of women. She was a 'speciesist' who professed no hope in abstract definitions of 'being human'. Attributes such as possessing a soul, or language, or being entitled to certain essential 'rights' were too intangible and unstable. Instead, activists like the Earnest Englishwoman sought to shift emphasis towards material conditions. She drew attention to the experience of visceral pain among a *range* of sentient bodies, human and non-human. To be 'human' was to be 'humane' to sentient life. It was not lost on these reformers that the true human in this politics was female; she was the person who valorized emotions over reason.

The Legal Construction of Humanity

CHAPTER SEVEN

Mr Heathcliff

A quarter of a century before the Earnest Englishwoman posed the question 'Are Women Animals?', another Englishwoman had also hidden behind a pseudonym, but her question was exactly the opposite. Are men really human? she asked.

Ellis Bell – in reality, the shy twenty-nine-year-old Emily Brontë – published *Wuthering Heights* in 1847. In that novel, Isabella tragically wants to know if her husband is fully human: 'Is Mr Heathcliff a man?', she begs.[1] Unimaginative readers might quip: Heathcliff is a creation of Brontë's imagination so, of course, he is neither a real man nor a bloody-minded husband. But most of us willingly entering Brontë's moorlands around Wuthering Heights and Thrushcross Grange might wonder whether (as Isabella feared) Heathcliff is really a devil in human form.[2] Brontë proffers two other possibilities, however: Heathcliff is either an anthropomorphic animal (in other words, although he *looks* like a human animal he is really a non-human one), or he is a racial outsider, excluded from the rights allocated to fully integrated persons. In either case, Heathcliff is not completely human.

In this Part, Isabella's question – 'Is Mr Heathcliff a Man?' – will be broadened. As I do throughout this book, I will critique the basic tenet of humanism, showing that there is no essential, uncomplicated 'human', no unambiguous correspondence between physically resembling other humans and being culturally and morally 'a person'. Who has a right to full personhood? Do women or slaves? Should animals be included? What legal and political processes enable powerful groups within society to drive other creatures into precarious states of being? The process of distinguishing between different kinds of animals involves violence (most obviously when deciding which animals can be eaten). Processes of defining humanity by excluding non- and lesser humans have a similar effect in eliciting violence and – crucially – resistance.

Wuthering Heights is a novel perfectly suited to this exploration. It is set in a period dominated by revolution and counter-revolution. Emily Brontë's story takes place between 1771 and 1802, that is, at a time when many oppressed groups – women and slaves, for instance – were forcefully protesting against their subjugation. It was a time of violent revolutions in France and Haiti. In both countries, men and women demanded the 'rights of man', confronting tyrants with 'liberté, égalité, fraternité' on their lips. The French Assembly's Declaration of the Rights of Man and Citizen of 1789 not only claimed that 'Men are born free and remain free and equal in rights', but also promised rights of 'resistance to oppression'.[3] There was no guarantee that armed struggle would triumph, though. Starting in August 1791 and ending with the Declaration of Independence thirteen years later, rebels on the island of Saint-Domingue (renamed Haiti) launched the first victorious slave revolt. In 1804 Haitians waged the first successful anti-colonial revolution, to found the first black republic. Their armed struggle won them a nation to call their own at a colossal cost. The fury of the entire Western world turned against the new nation, ostracizing them and even insisting that former slaves pay compensation to their owners. Well into the twentieth century, the poorest country in the Western hemisphere was paying this financial debt to one of the world's strongest economies, France. The struggle for political independence turned into a phantom triumph when not accompanied by social and economic rights.

Brontë was familiar with these revolutions. Although she spent much of her life in a protected West Yorkshire parsonage, the existence of slavery, and resistance to it, was very much a part of her world. Her father had been financed during his studies for the evangelical ministry by William Wilberforce,[4] and for Patrick Brontë, Wilberforce was one of the 'friends of the human race'.[5] In 1830, when Emily Brontë was twelve years of age, her father helped organize a petition to both Houses of Parliament demanding that slavery be abolished in the British Empire.[6] Within three years, they were successful (it took another thirty-two years and a civil war for the United States to follow suit).

References to slavery can be seen throughout *Wuthering Heights*.

Heathcliff explicitly compares his degradation to that of slaves.[7] He had been found wandering the streets of Liverpool, 'starving, and houseless, and as good as dumb'.[8] In 1771, when Mr Earnshaw picked 'it' up and 'inquired for its owner' (but 'Not a soul knew to whom it belonged'),[9] Liverpool was the slave capital of Europe. Ships sailed from the city's harbours to the Guinea Coast, loaded slaves and then continued to the New World to sell them. They would then return to Liverpool bearing cargoes of rum and molasses. They would also bring back 'left-overs', slaves who had not been sold. Some critics have speculated that Heathcliff was in fact one of these. Whether or not this was Brontë's intention, at the time that she had Mr Earnshaw find Heathcliff, slave merchants in Liverpool dispatched over six hundred slave ships a year, a figure that represented 60 per cent of all slave ventures from Britain.[10] As the actor George Cooke allegedly quipped when hissed for being drunk on stage at the opening of Liverpool's Theatre Royal in June 1772, 'there is not a brick in your dirty town but what is cemented by the blood of a negro'.[11]

Even if Heathcliff was not literally an enslaved 'left-over', he was a racial outsider. He is described 'as dark almost as if it [sic] came from the devil', a 'gypsy', a 'little Lascar, or an American or Spanish castaway' and 'a dark little thing'.[12] 'Why, how very black and cross you look!' Catherine exclaims when she returns to Wuthering Heights after staying with Edgar and Isabella Linton at Thrushcross Grange. His 'dusky fingers' are contrasted to her 'wonderfully whitened' hands.[13] Throughout the novel, Heathcliff is an 'it': he is a 'stupid little thing', a 'strange acquisition'.[14] Like slaves, Heathcliff is dependent on the will of his owners. As a consequence, his precarious position in the household deteriorates significantly after Mr Earnshaw dies. Hindley, as the new master at Wuthering Heights, drives Heathcliff 'from their company to the servants', terminates his education and forces him to 'labour out of doors'.[15]

Heathcliff is not only set outside full personhood on account of his identity as a dark-skinned, abandoned slave-child (when I first read this book as a child growing up in Haiti, I always imagined him as Haitian). He is treated as nothing more than a debased kind of property for another reason: from the start of the novel, Heathcliff is described as an animal. When he first arrived at Wuthering Heights the housekeeper Nelly Dean attempted to get rid of the young child by setting him on 'the landing of the stairs, hoping it [sic] might be gone on the morrow'.[16] In the presence of Heathcliff, Dean does not feel as if she is 'in the company of a creature of my own species'. Heathcliff is a 'dog'.[17] He is beaten 'like a dog' and when in agony he 'gnashed . . . and foamed like a mad dog'.[18] He 'howled, not like a man, but like a savage beast getting goaded to death with knives and spears'.[19] His 'sharp cannibal teeth' mark him out as a 'fierce, pitiless, wolfish man', an 'unreclaimed creature', an 'evil beast'.[20] Even his wife calls him 'a monster, and not a human being!'[21]

In many ways, then, Brontë is appealing to certain prejudices of her time. She assumes that describing someone in animal terms means that they are brutish. By making Heathcliff dark-skinned, she implicitly endorses an epidermic hierarchy. But there are hints also that she is critical of these judgments. Brontë seems to be implying that cruel people are *made*, not *born*. As her sister observed, if 'the black gipsy-cub' (as Charlotte dubbed Heathcliff) had been 'carefully trained and kindly treated', he 'might possibly have been reared into a human-being, but tyranny and ignorance made of him a mere demon'.[22] Emily Brontë intimates that people who are debased as slaves or 'mere' animals will gradually become brutalized. They will eventually fantasize (as Heathcliff does) about being 'born where laws are less strict, and tastes less dainty', so that they can indulge in torturing or vivisecting other people 'as an evening's amusement'.[23] 'The tyrant grinds down his slaves and they don't turn against him', he informs Cathy, but those slaves then 'crush those beneath them – You are welcome to torture me to death for your amusement, only, allow me to amuse myself a little in the same style.'[24] Brontë goes further, suggesting that people can gain extraordinary pleasure in inflicting pain on other sentient creatures. Indeed, this pleasure increases when the victim is seen to be particularly sensitive. As she put it near the start of the novel, Wuthering Heights is the 'perfect misanthropist's Heaven'.[25]

The ability of living creatures to truly *feel* – to have emotions based on an interest not to be harmed, tortured or killed – is one reason why they should be treated with care and respect (see the last three chapters). Isabella's sensitivity means that she has a right not to be tortured by Heathcliff: he is her husband, but she is not his property. Charlotte Brontë makes the point even more starkly in *Jane Eyre* (1847), where her heroine argues that 'women feel just as men feel'.[26] Ethical behaviour requires that people act in ways that maximize the pleasures (and minimize the pains) experienced by sentient beings. Today, 'preference utilitarianism', or the view that the morally correct action is the action that satisfies the desires or preferences of those involved, has been endorsed by philosophers like Peter Singer in their defence of animals.

There is another line of argument, however – and this will be the theme of the next two chapters. Instead of focusing on utility or welfare, this approach draws attention to universal 'rights'. Historically, this position has been conceived of in terms of the 'rights of man' (in the eighteenth century) and 'human rights' (from the mid-twentieth century). 'Animal rights' have always been in dialogue with both these traditions, a dialogue that has become intense from the late twentieth century. Who is a 'man', and what are 'his' rights? Is Heathcliff a 'person' who possesses certain inalienable rights? If Heathcliff possessed the face and form of *Canis lupis familiaris* (domestic dog) or, even better, *Pan troglodytes* (chimpanzee), could he still be a 'person'?

The answers we give to these questions have important implications. There is no neat fit between being physically a 'human' and being culturally and morally 'a person'. Not every member of *Homo sapiens* is a 'person'. Some are property; many are consigned to a status of less consequence than animals. Indeed, as I shall show, some animals attain personhood well in advance of certain humans.

The question 'who is truly human?' depends largely on the power of the law and judicial practice. Although, in common parlance, it is often assumed that all humans are 'persons', in fact, this is not the case. In law, a person is a subject of legal rights and duties. It is law that distinguishes between the most basic existence shared by people and animals (life or *zoe*) and full personhood within the polis or political community (meaningful life or *bios*). Often, the distinction is based on nothing more than contingencies of birth. Thus, a black-skinned child born in Haiti could be accorded less status than the dog born into a middle-class home in California. 'It is not so much that humans have rights,' explains philosopher Costas Douzinas, 'but that rights make humans.' Furthermore, 'law's participation in the making of the human is highly volatile: legal subjectivity can be given and taken away and there is no guarantee that the "natural" and the legal human will coincide'.[27]

The next two chapters, therefore, explore conflicting notions of personhood. Whenever commentators attempt to unravel the ever-twisting Möbius strip of human/animal life, crying 'There is the demarcation! I recognize the Person!', they are met with counter-claims. Personhood may include many, although not all, adult humans and, in law, it also includes corporations and ships. Rights are what create the person; they are not what belong to people. Who are given 'rights'? How did marginalized groups such as women and slaves contest this narrow construction? Are animals 'persons'? Racist and sexist beliefs have been crucial in excluding certain members of Homo sapiens from full personhood; but is 'speciesism', or discrimination based on membership of a species, just or unjust? Is 'anti-speciesism' as necessary to justice as is anti-racism and anti-sexism? Is it legitimate to harm 'speciesists' who exploit, kill, or eat animals? Who should do the harming – God (as in nineteenth-century accounts) or His representatives here on earth (the dominant executioners from the 1970s)? If it is legitimate to assassinate a Nazi dignitary at Auschwitz, then why not a worker at the local bacon factory? When does the freedom fighter become the terrorist?

Crucially the authority of the law rests on the threat of its suspension, suddenly throwing certain former persons into zoe. Legal theorist Carl Schmitt declared in Political Theology (1922) that 'Sovereign is he who decides on the exception'.[28] The philosopher Giorgio Agamben has most productively interpreted and radicalized Schmitt's concept.[29] A 'state of exception' occurs when the sovereign power suspends the law in order to save it from challenges. This leads to a suspension of legal protections and guarantees, and the abandonment of people to the arbitrary diktat of the state. They become literally nameless, unclassifiable and subject to the omnipresent will of the sovereign power. When the law is suspended, there is a reversion to bare life, or simple zoe. As Agamben explained, although the suspension of the norm is supposed to be provisional and temporary, it often instead becomes the norm. As we shall see, torture begins as an exceptional measure, introduced in an emergency, but rapidly acquires legitimacy through the elaboration of rules and regulations. In this way, certain physical humans are set outside full humanity. Indeed, I will argue, animal rights can actually trump human ones.

CHAPTER EIGHT

Human Rights

Emily Brontë set *Wuthering Heights* between 1771 and 1802, the time when the idea of the inalienable 'rights of man' first became widely publicized. In 1776, Thomas Jefferson's Declaration of Independence proclaimed to the world that

> We hold these truths to be self-evident, that all men are created equal, that they are endowed by their Creator with certain unalienable Rights, that among these are Life, Liberty and the pursuit of Happiness.

Central to Jefferson's conception of rights was the relationship of the executive to the citizens. He insisted that 'Governments are instituted among Men' in order to 'secure these rights'. Since governments derived 'their just powers from the consent of the governed', if that government acted contrary to the 'Life, Liberty and the pursuit of Happiness' of its people, 'it is the Right of the People to alter or to abolish it'. They were entitled to 'institute [a] new Government', most likely 'to effect their Safety and Happiness'.[1]

The French Assembly's Declaration of the Rights of Man and of the Citizen of 1789 was equally radical. The Assembly 'determined to set forth in a solemn declaration the natural, inalienable, and sacred rights of man'. The first Article broadcast the revolutionary principle that 'Men are born free and remain free and equal in rights'. The second Article promised rights not only of 'liberty, property, [and] security', but also of 'resistance to oppression'.[2] As already mentioned, the grand Declaration saw its first trial by fire, sword and rifle on a small island in the Caribbean. As Frederick Douglass (a former slave who was deeply involved in struggles for the rights of slaves and women and who was the US ambassador to Haiti between 1889 and 1891) observed,

> Until Haiti struck for freedom, the conscience of the Christian world slept profoundly over slavery . . . The Negro was in its estimation a sheep-like creature, having no rights which white men were bound to respect, a docile animal, a kind of ass, capable of bearing burdens, and receiving stripes from a white master without resentment, and without resistance.

Haitian slaves proved the 'Christian world' wrong. They set out to 'dispel this degradation and dangerous delusion, and give to the world a new and true revelation of the blackman's character'. The Haitian revolution of 1791 'taught the world the danger of slavery and the value of liberty'.[3]

From the time of the establishment of the new Haitian republic in 1804 to the 1940s, however, the rhetoric of *universal*, 'natural' rights was fanciful. The enlightenment hopes of revolutionaries were purposefully crushed from the moment they were articulated. After all, although slavery was abolished in metropolitan France in 1792 (and in 1794 for France's colonies, like Haiti), it was rapidly reinstated in 1802 – a situation that lasted forty-six years.

Rights discourse rapidly contracted after its initial revolutionary declamation. They became restricted to the rights of citizens of bounded (albeit frequently shifting) nation-states. In part, this was due to the extreme hostility towards natural rights by the powerful monarchies of the nineteenth century. Rights were dangerous, socialist, abstract and indeterminate. With nationalism and the spread of democracy, universalist notions of rights were increasingly viewed as irrelevant: what was important was the individual rights of citizens within their own nations. Rights were not eternal, absolute and inalienable, but invented and contingent on geography and nationality.[4]

The idea of universal human rights returned to the political agenda in the aftermath of the genocide of Jews in Nazi-occupied Europe, and the enslavement and mass slaughter of Roma peoples, homosexuals, the physically and mentally disabled, and religious and political dissidents. This revival was strengthened by the war-crime trials in Nuremberg and Tokyo, the signing of the Charter of the United Nations and the adoption of the Universal Declaration of Human

Rights. Notably, the first article of the 1945 Charter of the United Nations promised that the UN would promote 'respect for human rights and for fundamental freedoms for all without distinction as to race, sex, language, or religion' while Article 55 dedicated itself to encouraging 'universal respect for, and observance of, human rights and fundamental freedoms for all without distinction as to race, sex, language, or religion'.[5]

Three years later, the Universal Declaration of Human Rights was adopted by the General Assembly of the United Nations. The Declaration was modelled, to some degree, on the earlier French one, although substituting 'human' for 'man'. In its preamble, it reaffirmed their faith in 'fundamental human rights' and recognized that the 'equal and inalienable rights of all members of the human family is the foundation of freedom, justice and peace in the world'. Indeed, it stated, the 'disregard and contempt for human rights have resulted in barbarous acts which have outraged the conscience of mankind'. Article 1, therefore, stated that 'All human beings are born free and equal in dignity and rights. They are endowed with reason and conscience and should act towards one another in a spirit of brotherhood', while Article 2 claimed that 'Everyone is entitled to all the rights and freedoms set forth in this Declaration, without distinction of any kind'. In what followed were rights to 'life, liberty and security of person', the right not to be 'held in slavery or servitude' and the right not to be tortured. The entire human race was given the right to be recognized 'as a person before the law' and not to face discrimination. There were thirty articles in total, giving political, social and cultural rights, on a universal and inalienable basis.[6]

Since 1948, international human rights legislation has proliferated. The Universal Declaration of Human Rights was followed by the Convention Relating to the Status of Refugees (1951), the Discrimination (Employment and Occupation) Convention (1958), the Declaration on the Rights of the Child (1959), the International Convention on the Elimination of All Forms of Racial Discrimination (1965), the International Covenant on Economic, Social and Cultural Rights (1966), the International Covenant on Civil and Political Rights (1966), the Protocol Relating to the Status of Refugees (1967), the Declaration of the Rights of Mentally Retarded Persons (1971), the Declaration on the Rights of Disabled Persons (1975), the Convention on the Elimination of All Forms of Discrimination Against Women (1979), the Declaration on the Elimination of All Forms of Intolerance and of Discrimination Based on Religion or Belief (1981), the

Convention Against Torture and Other Cruel, Inhuman and Degrading Treatment or Punishment (1984) and the Convention on the Rights of the Child (1989), to name just a few[7] Indeed, as legal philosopher Tom Campbell noted,

> The discourse of rights is pervasive and popular in politics, law and morality. There is scarcely any position, opinion, claim, criticism or aspiration relating to social and political life that is not asserted and affirmed using the term 'rights'.[8]

Although Campbell is correct, it is nevertheless true that these grand, sweeping declarations of the 'rights of man' and then 'human rights' have always been less than universal. 'Mankind' never included all humans. At various times, slaves, women, religious minorities, Jews and actors (on the grounds that they pretended to be someone else) were set outside of the 'rights of man'. Before the human rights declarations, 'mankind' tended to refer to well-off heterosexual men. They claimed citizenship of a sovereign state. They were swathed in white skins, Western bodies. The 'human' part of human rights has always been unstable, variable in scope and inclusiveness.

Are Women 'Persons'?

From the start of the human-rights age, people barred from 'mankind' (with its inalienable rights) protested against their exclusion. Women were particularly vocal from the start. Just a couple of years after the French Assembly's Declaration of the Rights of Man and of the Citizen, playwright, feminist and anti-slavery activist Olympe de Gouges (born Marie Gouze) issued her *Declaration of the Rights of Woman and the Female Citizen* (1791). De Gouges exhorted the French National Assembly in these words:

> Man, are you capable of being just? It is a woman who poses the question; you will not deprive her of that right at least. Tell me, what gives you sovereign empire to oppress my sex? Your strength? Your talents?

She argued that it was impossible to find in 'Nature' any examples of a 'tyrannical empire'. She urged the French Deputies to 'Go back to animals, consult the elements, study plants, finally glance at all the modifications of organic matter', and observe that the sexes are 'mingled; everywhere they cooperate in harmonious togetherness in this immortal masterpiece'. The first Article in de Gouges's declaration insisted that 'Woman is born free and lives equal to man in her rights'. While the original French declaration had simply proclaimed the right to resist oppression, Article 2 of de Gouges's version proclaimed a right '*especially* [of] resistance to oppression'.[9] She also added rights specific to women, such as the right of unmarried women to the 'name and property of the father of her children'.[10] De Gouges was also vocal against the slavery of Haitians, accusing the colonists of being '*inhumains*' and, in her play *L'Esclavage des noirs*, explicitly linking the sexual exploitation of women with slavery.[11]

Olympe de Gouges was vilified, not only for her feminist and anti-slavery views but also for being a supporter of the Girondists (a political faction in the French Legislative Assembly), which made her an enemy of Robespierre. De Gouges had her head chopped off by the guillotine (incidentally, by an executioner who would also have been set outside the 'rights of man' for engaging in a dishonourable profession). Revolutionary politician Pierre-Gaspard Chaumette urged republican women to 'remember that virago, that woman-man'. The 'impudent' de Gouges, he continued, had 'abandoned all the cares of her household

Figure 1. A portrait of Mary Wollstonecraft, c.1792, by her friend John Opie.
Granger Collection/Topfoto

because she wanted to engage in politics . . . This forgetfulness of the virtues of her sex led her to the scaffold'.[12] De Gouges had been set outside the human because of her politics as well as her sex.

In demanding women's rights as members of 'mankind', she was far from alone. A year after de Gouges's execution, Mary Wollstonecraft published *A Vindication of the Rights of Woman* (1792). Wollstonecraft also insisted that women are entitled to rights on the same grounds as men, but her argument was more sophisticated than that of de Gouges. For Wollstonecraft, the 'Rights of Woman' must be granted: womanhood 'loudly demands JUSTICE for one half of the human race'. Women 'may be convenient slaves, but slavery will have its constant effect, degrading the master and the abject dependant'. Treating woman as fully human would promote morality and virtue in society, make for securer families and promote the greatest happiness. The denial of a proper education to women and their constraint in a limited sphere stifled female reason, strength and morality. Because women had not been allowed to develop reasoning abilities (the trait that, Wollstonecraft agreed, 'raises men above the brute creation') they could be 'treated as a kind of subordinate beings, and not as a part of the human species'. She acknowledged that women had 'different duties to fulfil', but insisted that 'they are *human* duties'. In rousing rhetoric, she insisted: 'Let woman share the rights and she will emulate the virtues of man; for she must grow more perfect when emancipated'.[13]

Wollstonecraft's book created an immense stir, and has continued to be read throughout the centuries. In 1848, Charles Darwin listed the 'Life of M. Wollstonecraft & Rights of Women' in his 'reading notebooks'.[14] At the time of the writing, however, her critics worried about the impact that 'rights-talk' might have on conventional gender hierarchies. In the words of an anonymous review of the *Vindication of the Rights of Woman*, if Wollstonecraft had her way,

> The female Plato will find it unsuitable to 'the dignity of her virtue' to dress the child, and descend to the disgusting offices of a nurse: the new Archimedes will measure the shirts by means of the altitude taken by a quadrant; and the young lady instead of studying the softer and more amiable arts of pleasure, must contend with her lover for superiority of mind.[15]

Reason, politics, and autonomy – those characteristics of humanity – were unsuitable for the 'female Plato'.

The nature of Wollstonecraft's death, five years later, was also proffered as evidence against her. Wollstonecraft was to be forever linked to mammalian functions because she died of puerperal fever caused by the manual removal of the placenta shortly after giving birth to her daughter Mary (who would later write *Frankenstein*). On the day of her daughter's birth, Wollstonecraft had excitedly told her husband William Godwin that 'I have no doubt of seeing the animal to day'.[16] The birth was to be a tragedy, though. Owing to her puerperal fever, Godwin recalled in *Memoirs of the Author of 'A Vindication of the Rights of Woman'* (1798), her physician 'forbad the child's having the breast, and we therefore procured puppies to draw off the milk'.[17] It is difficult to know for certain why puppies would have been used in this way. It was a popular, although increasingly discredited, cure for puerperal fever because it was believed to extract the 'milk gone astray'. More likely, the puppies were being used as a kind of breast pump. However, this image of Wollstonecraft suckling puppies on her deathbed was regarded by her critics as proof of a grossly disordered female body and mind.[18] Clergyman and poet Richard Polwhele was ruthless in his *The Unsex'd Females: A Poem* (1798). Wollstonecraft was guilty of 'licentious love', for 'whom no decorum checks', he declaimed. Her inglorious death in childbirth was further evidence that she was 'unsexed' and was being punished for 'despising NATURE'S law'.[19]

Polwhele was particularly vicious. More commonly, Wollstonecraft and talk of 'rights' were simply lampooned. My favourite was published in the same year as the *Vindication of the Rights of Woman*. Richard Graves entitled his satire 'Maternal Despotism; or, The Rights of Infants'. Its infant narrator exhorted his nurse to 'unhand me! . . . Thou saucy queen!' Despite the 'Rights of human kind', he complained, a 'female tyrant' had bound him from 'head and foot' and stretched him 'Like a poor culprit on the rack'. The infant continued:

> An infant, like thyself, born free,
> And independent, slut! on thee.
> Have I not right to kick and sprawl,
> To laugh and cry, to squeak and squall!
> Has ever by my act and deed,
> Thy *right* to rule me been decreed?
> How dar'st thou, despot! then control
> Th' exertions of a free-born soul?

The infant promises that

Though now an infant, when I can,
I'll rise and seize 'The Rights of Man';
Nor make my haughty nurse alone,
But monarchs tremble, on their throne;
And boys and Kings henceforth you'll see
Enjoy complete *Equality*.[20]

In other words, Wollstonecraft's vision of female equality was as ridiculous as giving rights to squalling infants. As will be explored in the next chapter, you might as well give rights to animals.

In a more scornful vein, 'Lætitia Lookabout' sneered at 'Mrs Mary with the hard German name'. She quibbled that, with the assistance of Wollstonecraft's work,

Figure 2. 'Woman, the Slave of Man', from *Judy*, 1872. This cartoon lampoons the idea that women in their domestic environment are in bondage, while their suffragist sisters are truly free. The woman in the kitchen is tranquil and attractive ('marriageable'), compared with the disturbing and discontented physiognomies of those demanding women's rights. The suffragists are portrayed as deranged spinsters, while the man on the platform is clearly eccentric. The poster contains the name 'Jacob Brich' is probably a coded reference to radical politician Jacob Bright who was a keen supporter of female suffrage. The reference to Exeter Hall is not coincidental: the Anti-Slavery Society regularly convened their meetings there. Indeed, Exeter Hall became synonymous with the anti-slavery lobby. Both women and slaves were fighting for recognition of their full humanity.

Judy (25 September 1872)

mankind, womankind I mean, [will] be aided by a plain and simple code of instruction; in which all foolish prejudices are overturned; and in which women are taught to regard with becoming scorn the means by which they have till now captivated, namely, softness of beauty, grace and elegance of manner, and the pursuit of more delicate employments.[21]

Friedrich Nietzsche put these fears in a misogynist political context when he bluntly stated that 'the influence of woman in Europe has *declined* in proportion as she has increased her rights and claims'. It has led to a 'disintegration of womanly instincts, a defeminising' which was nothing less than '*stupidity*'[22] (see Figure 2). For all their efforts, then, Wollstonecraft and de Gouges failed to convince their governments and critics of the need to expand the rights of 'man' to women. It wasn't until 1928 and 1944 respectively that the British and French parliaments conceded voting rights to women on the same grounds as men.

All aspects of women's lives were affected by their exclusion from the rights given to those who were fully human. In their novels, the Brontë sisters remonstrated about the vast array of injustices women were forced to accept. The eponymous heroine of *Jane Eyre* (1847) was particularly frank, pointing out that women

> need exercise for their faculties, and a field for their efforts, as much as their brothers do; they suffer from too rigid a restraint, too absolute a stagnation, precisely as men would suffer; and it is narrow-minded in their more privileged fellow-creatures to say that they ought to confine themselves to making puddings and knitting stockings, to playing on the piano and embroidering bags. It is thoughtless to condemn them, or laugh at them, if they seek to do more or learn more than custom has pronounced necessary for the sex.[23]

Emily Brontë also engaged in a withering critique of masculinist norms in *Wuthering Heights*. In that novel, Catherine Earnshaw was unable to marry Heathcliff because, as she put it, 'if Heathcliff and I married, we should be beggars'.[24] When Catherine's father died, all his property was inherited by the oldest son, leaving her with nothing in her own right. Brontë's ire was also provoked by the same injustice that annoyed the Earnest Englishwoman: women became 'property' on marriage. Not only did Heathcliff callously admit to thrashing his wife, but he even bragged about keeping 'strictly within the limits of the law – I have avoided, up to this period, giving her the slightest right to claim a separation'.[25] At the time at which Brontë was writing, it was extremely difficult for a wife to divorce her husband. Indeed, it required an Act of Parliament. It wasn't until 1857 – that is, a decade after *Wuthering Heights* appeared – that a wife could claim a divorce though the courts, and even then she had to prove both cruelty and adultery (a husband only had to prove adultery). It took another seventy-two years for women to be able to claim a divorce on the same terms as men. This state of affairs led Grant Allen (a science writer and novelist) to quip in 1889 that women were not really human: they were simply creatures who '"produced" the human race'.[26]

Feminists retaliated. One, enraged by Allen's comment, asserted that 'revolt has set in among the "reproducers of the human race"'.[27] Many activists continued to use arguments based on sentience but, increasingly, they began appealing to notions of inalienable, innate 'rights'. The fact that women were not fully 'persons' in law – while 'the wife-beater', as well as the male 'drunkard, and the illiterate' *were* – was condemned by all factions of the women's movement.[28] An anonymous poet writing in a pamphlet published by the radical suffragists echoed the Earnest Englishwoman's sentiments. She was furious that suffragettes who had aggressively demonstrated outside the Prime Minister's residence were convicted and incarcerated in Holloway Prison. The second stanza read:

> We went before a magistrate; who would not hear us speak;
> To a drunken brute who beat his wife he only gave a week;
> But we were sent to Holloway a calendar month or more
> Because we dared, against his will, to knock at Asquith's door.[29]

As Teresa Billington-Greig (co-founder of the Women's Freedom League) complained, in her grandmother's time women 'were regarded as little lower than the angels in the poet's Song, yet in the hard world of fact they were treated as little higher than domestic animals'. As late as 1913, when Billington-Greig was writing, men continued to regard women as 'less human' than themselves: it was 'against this incapacity of man to consider his mother as human that the woman's fight has to be waged', she complained.[30] Thomas J. Haslam, speaking to the Irish Women's Suffrage and Local Government Association in 1906, was even blunter: 'I have it on the highest authority,' he started, 'that the men generally have no more conception of the rights of women than of the rights of dogs'.[31]

The battles of women in Britain and the United States to be included in the 'rights of man' have been told elsewhere and are not relevant to this chapter, which sets out to show some of the ways that 'being human' or a 'person' contracted to explicitly exclude women. The designation of full humanity and personhood did, however, gradually expand to admit certain female members of the human species. Significant, albeit piecemeal, victories included the right to own property, to vote, to sit in national assemblies, to divorce, to be educated and to be employed in a full range of jobs. In all these cases, however, 'humanity' continued to be defined as male. Against that standard women were measured and found to be wanting: the reforms did no more than *accommodate* women within a model based on male personhood. It took until the twenty-first century for this to change. In 2001, the Statute of the International Criminal Tribunal for the former Yugoslavia and the Statute of the International Criminal Tribunal for Rwanda recognized rape as a crime against *humanity*, as opposed to 'merely' being a crime against women. For the first time, instead of men being the norm for 'human', women constituted humanity.[32]

Can Slaves be 'Persons'?

Women were not the only group excluded from full legal personhood. As many feminists recognized, there was a strong connection between the denial of full humanity to women and the even more brutal refusal to admit male and female slaves into the 'human family'.[33] The injustice was most marked for female slaves, the most abject and abused of all their co-sufferers.

Feminists identified their own travails with those of slaves of both sexes. As early as the 1790s, Wollstonecraft was drawing an analogy between female disenfranchisement and the subjection of slaves labouring in the sugar plantations of Haiti and Jamaica. 'Is sugar always to be produced by vital blood?' she asked in *A Vindication of the Rights of Woman*. Wollstonecraft wondered whether 'one half of the human species, like the poor African slaves' were 'to be subject to the prejudices that brutalize them . . . only to sweeten the cup of man?'[34] Emily Brontë implicitly endorsed this critique in *Wuthering Heights*, modelling Thrushcross Grange on Harewood, the home of Henry Lascelles, later second Earl of Harewood, who owned a plantation in Barbados. When Lascelles sought to become the Member of Parliament for Yorkshire, he faced opposition from Charles Wentworth Fitzwilliam (Viscount

Milton), a passionate abolitionist who had the support of William Wilberforce. Viscount Milton won the seat and was instrumental in helping to pass the Abolition of the Slave Trade Act of 1807.[35] It was no coincidence that Brontë depicted the detestable Linton Heathcliff sucking on sugar-candy. Every teaspoon of sugar, abolitionists reminded readers, was 'steeped in the blood of our fellow-creatures'.[36]

Just as the 'property' rather than 'personhood' status of women met with resistance, so too was the tyranny of slaves challenged. We will never know whether it was intentional or not, but Emily Brontë chose 1771 as the year when the young Heathcliff was found wandering the streets of Liverpool. In that year, over fourteen thousand slaves resided in the British Isles.[37] More importantly, it was the year the famous Somerset v. Steuart case began. James Somerset had been sold into slavery in Virginia in 1749. Twenty years later, when his master (Steuart) travelled to England, he brought his slave with him. Somerset escaped, only to be recaptured and imprisoned. The abolitionist Granville Sharp took up his case, petitioning for a writ of habeas corpus declaring slavery illegal on English soil. Standing before the King's Bench in 1772, Francis Hargrave argued that slavery

> corrupts the morals of the master, by freeing him from those restraints with respect to his slave, so necessary for controul [sic] of the human passions, so beneficial in promoting the practice and confirming the habit of virtue.

Slavery did not only undermine the morals of their masters. Hargrave insisted that it also 'excites implacable resentment and hatred in the slave' and was 'dangerous to the State' because it gave rise to a group of people who were 'interested in scheming its destruction'. For all these reasons, it was important that slaves not only

> become free on being brought into this country, but . . . the law of England confers the *gift of liberty, intire* [sic] *and unencumbered*; not in *name* only, but *really* and *substantially*; and consequently, that Mr. Steuart cannot have the least rights over Sommersett the negro.

Serjeant John Glynn put the case even more succinctly, asking the court the rhetorical question, 'Can a Man become a Dog for another Man?'[38] In other words, the slave Sommersett was not Stuart's property, like a dog might be: he was a person.

Chief Justice Mansfield of the King's Bench agreed: he decided that a slave who accompanied his or her master to England could not be forcibly returned to the colonies for resale. 'The slave-holder will know, then, when they introduce a slave into this country *as a slave*, this air is too free for him to breathe in'.[39] It was too poetic a line to languish even in a grand court. As William Cowper enthused in *The Task* (1825):

> We have no slaves at home – Then why abroad?
> And they themselves once ferried o'er the waves
> That parts us are emancipated and loosed.
> Slaves cannot breathe in England; if their lungs
> Receive our air, that moment they are free;
> They touch our country, and their shackles fall.[40]

Cowper might be excused some poetic licence, of course. The ruling did not actually abolish slavery. Slave masters found ways around the prohibition, including forcing slaves to sign or mark an indenture under which they would be rendered 'servants' for the duration of the trip. Nevertheless, masters were henceforth no longer allowed to remove slaves from Britain against the slave's will. It took another sixty-one years for human enslavement to be absolutely abolished in Britain.

Benjamin Franklin (himself a slave-owner) was in London at the time of Somerset v. Steuart. He criticized

> the hypocrisy of this country, which encourages such a detestable commerce by laws for promoting the Guinea trade; while it piqued itself on its virtue, love of liberty, and the equity of its courts, in setting free a single negro.[41]

In Franklin's America, the question of whether slaves were 'persons' or simply 'property' was significantly more fraught. Slave labour was a much larger factor in the economy of many US states. At the time of Somerset v. Steuart, between 30 and 40 per cent of the population of Georgia, Maryland, Virginia and South Carolina were slaves.[42] Many feared that abolishing slavery would wreak havoc on the southern states. From the slave masters' perspective, the slave was like the monster of Frankenstein, a novel (as we have already observed) written by Wollstonecraft's daughter Mary Shelley. As one politician warned when arguing against the abolition of slavery in March 1824,

> We must remember that we are dealing with a being [a slave] possessing the form and strength of a man, but the intellect only of a child. To turn him loose in the manhood of his physical passions, but in the infancy of his uninstructed reason, would be to raise up a creature resembling the splendid fiction of a recent romance [*Frankenstein*]; the hero of which constructs a human form with all the physical capacities of man, and with the thews and sinews of a giant, but being unable to impart to the work of his hands a perception of right and wrong, he finds too late that he has only created a more than mortal power of doing mischief, and himself recoils from the monster which he has made.[43]

Canning clearly had not read *Frankenstein*, or he would know that the problem posed by that novel was precisely the fact that the monster keenly felt a sense of right and wrong. However, his belief that slaves, like monsters, were childish, sexually voracious and lacking in moral judgment effectively placed slaves outside the area ring-fenced for humans, let alone legal persons.

This construction of slaves as inhuman monsters or 'things' allowed significant degrees of violence to be directed against them. In the supposedly idyllic New World, brutality was covertly legitimated in law – often by permitting 'necessary' or 'ordinary' cruelty. For instance, John Haywood's *A Manual for the Laws of North-Carolina* (1808) allowed masters to kill slaves if the slaves resisted them or when slaves died 'under moderate correction'.[44] Similarly, the *Black Code of Georgia* (1732–1899) only outlawed 'unnecessary and excessive whipping' and 'cruelly and unnecessarily biting and tearing with dogs'. In other words, whipping and 'tearing with dogs' was legitimate, so long as it was not done cruelly, excessively and unnecessarily. To quote the distinguished Caribbean scholar Colin Dayan,

> This commitment to protection thus becomes a guarantee of tyranny, and the attempt to set limits to brutality, to curb tortures, not only allowed masters to hide behind the law but also ensured that the guise of care would remain a 'humane' fiction.[45]

So were slaves in the American South nothing more than 'property', like animals? It certainly seemed that way to slaves. Ex-slave Charles Moses from Brookhaven, Mississippi, recalled that slaves were 'worked to death'. His master would 'beat, knock, kick, kill. He done ever' thing he could 'cept eat us'. He insisted that 'God Almighty never meant for human beings to be like animals. Us Niggers has a soul an' a heart an' a min'. We aint like a dog or a horse.'[46]

In 1850, Frederick Douglass also claimed that masters had unlimited power over the bodies of slaves. Slaves' names were 'impiously inserted in a *master's leger* with horses, sheep and swine' and that master could

> work him, flog him, hire him out, sell him, and, in certain circum-stances, *kill* him, with perfect impunity. The slave is a human being, divested of all rights – reduced to the level of a brute – a mere 'chat-tel' in the eyes of the law – placed beyond the circle of human brotherhood [sic].[47]

This was not strictly accurate. Slaves were not simply 'things' in law. Rather, they were carefully constructed quasi-legal persons. Because they were 'property', they could be harshly punished by their masters. But they were categorized as 'persons' when it came to serious crimes. They could not be murdered ('unnecessarily') and they could be indicted and punished for murder. Thus, in Cresswell's Executor v. Walker (1861), slaves were held to have 'no legal mind, no will which the law can recognize' so far as civil acts were con-cerned. As soon as they committed a crime, however, they were ascribed personhood.[48] A similar point was intriguingly argued in 1857, the first time a slave stood as a defendant in a US court. This was the federal prosecution of 'Amy', who had been convicted for stealing a letter from the post office in violation of federal law. Her defence attorney argued that she was not a legal person. Because she was a slave, she could not be indicted under an Act of Congress that forbade 'any person' to steal a letter from the United States mail. The prosecutor's response to this ingenious defence was blunt: 'I cannot prove more plainly that the prisoner is a person, a natural person,' he exclaimed, 'than to ask your honors to look at her. There she is.'[49]

Of course, personhood was not straightforwardly located in an identifiably 'human' face and figure. For one thing, both were highly racialized. Indeed, the prosecutor could just as easily have gestured towards Amy to illustrate the point that she was *not* a 'natural person'. This was exactly what racists did, on a routine basis. Pro-slavery argu-ments often introduced the idea of polygeny, or the view that Africans and Europeans had evolved from two entirely different species. As physician Josiah Nott put it in a lecture given in 1844, the 'Caucasian and Negro differ in their Anatomical and Physiological character' and these differences 'could not be produced by climate and other physical causes'. There were, he insisted, 'several species of the human race'; these 'species differ in perfection of their moral and intellectual endowments'; and 'a law of nature' was 'opposed to the mingling of white and black races'. He ended his lecture by quoting Alexander Pope's *Essay on Man*: 'One truth is clear, WHATEVER *IS*, IS RIGHT'.[50] In other words, slavery was 'natural': the 'black races' were 'naturally' property, like many other species. Or, as William Harper put it in the mid-nineteenth century, just as it was right and proper for humans to 'exercise dominion over the beasts of the field', so too, it was 'as much in the order of nature, that men should enslave each other'.[51]

This naturalization of the European (and masculine) body has been a central theme of Western culture. American businessman and author George Francis Train, in a London speech a few years after the decision of US v. Amy, argued that African inferiority was based on his belief that black people were incapable of blushing (a view heavily debated by scientists such as Sir Charles Bell, Charles Darwin and others expert in physiognomy). In Train's typically flamboyant fashion, he harangued his audience to

> explain why, in His wisdom, He [God] made one mountain over top another mountain – formed one ocean larger than another ocean – planned one valley wider than another valley . . . when you would tell me the reason that Providence ordained that the fair Saxon should be permitted to express, in the blush upon her face, all the emotions of her soul, while the African knows not the signification of the word – (*applause*) – when these things are made clear to me, I will tell you how and why he has made the African the servant of the Anglo-Saxon race, but not till then. (*Cheers.*) They were born and bred servants, they cannot be masters.[52]

In this way, slaves were reduced to bare life, to little more than beasts of burden.

The increased political acknowledgement that particular creatures – whether animal or slave – possessed self-consciousness and could therefore 'truly *feel*' was an important element of reform rhetoric. In the case of animals, arguments against cruelty were aimed at safeguarding humanity from the effects of its actions on other humans rather than being concerned with the intrinsic pain caused to animals. In the case of slaves, the same argument was dominant. Some claimed that slavery was evil because it brutalized slaves (it was common, for instance, to insist that the extreme violence of the rebelling slaves in Haiti was due to the fact that they were 'savage by reason of the many years of cruel slavery').[53] But greater concern was expressed about the effect of slavery on slave-owners and their communities.

There was one notable exception. Some commentators argued that the institution of slavery was actually *necessary* for the invention of 'rights'. In 1895, a philosopher from the University of St Andrews made this argument most cogently. According to him, slavery was a 'necessary step in the progress of humanity'. The 'horrors of primitive warfare' stemmed from the fact that the captured enemies were slaughtered: in contrast, enslaving the enemy 'gave some scope for the growth however feeble, of kindlier sentiments towards the alien and the weak'. Having slaves to undertake the lowly jobs in society

> gave to the free population sufficient leisure for the pursuit of science and art and, above all, for the development of political liberty; and in this way slavery may be said to have produced the idea of self-government.

By observing the lives of slaves, free men 'discovered the worth of freedom'. Thus, this philosopher concluded, 'slavery made possible the growth of the very ideas which in the course of time came to make slavery appear wrong'.[54]

As with the history of resistance to female oppression, the struggle to abolish slavery and thus admit that slaves were truly persons rather than merely property has been told elsewhere. Although not fought primarily because of slavery, the role of African-Americans in the American Civil War of 1861–5 was significant (see Figure 3). In 1865, when approximately four million slaves still existed in the United States, the Thirteenth Amendment to the American Constitution declared that

> Neither slavery nor involuntary servitude, except as a punishment for a crime where the party shall have been duly convicted, shall exist within the US, or any place subject to their jurisdiction.

To be sure, slavery did not simply vanish from the American continent. Industrialists found ingenious ways to ensure that certain humans retained the designation of lesser beings. At the very least, they were

CUTTING HIS OLD ASSOCIATES.
MAN OF COLOR. "Ugh! Get out. I ain't one ob you no more. *I'se a Man, I is!*"

Figure 3. Published on 17 January 1863 in *Harper's Weekly*, this cartoon takes its inspiration from Wedgwood's famous medallion. It links African-Americans with animals, while seeking to undermine the connection. The cartoon appeared during the American Civil War, in which approximately 180,000 black men fought, the vast majority of whom had been recruited from slave plantations or contraband camps.

New York Public Library

denied full personhood. Notoriously, peonage was introduced as a way of evading the Thirteenth Amendment. Under peonage, employees were required to accept a 'loan' or an 'advance of wages' from their employers. Being in debt, they were therefore forced to work for their employer for as long as that employer required their labour (see Figure 4).[55] Peonage was not, however, identical to slavery. In slavery, owners used the law to enforce their *property* rights: they owned the slave. In contrast, under the system of peonage, a fiction of 'free choice' was maintained. Employers used the law to enforce *creditor* rights, or the right of creditors to be repaid their debt. In 1900, according to one estimate, one-third of all croppers in Alabama, Mississippi and Georgia were working against their will.[56] As an expert from Florida noted seven years later, slavery was 'just as much an "institution" now as it was before the [civil] war'.[57]

Figure 4. 'Caught!' from Richard Barry, 'Slavery in the South To-day', *Cosmopolitan Magazine*, 1907. The picture shows dogs being used to track fleeing white and black peons in Florida, just as happened to black slaves prior to 1865. The preface to Barry's article read, 'The Standard Oil Clique, H. M. Flagler's Florida East Coast Railway Co., the turpentine trust, the umber trust, and other trusts have put in force a system of peonage which is actual slavery.' The exposé created a sensation.
<small>Cosmopolitan Magazine (1907)</small>

The question of who is truly human – and who is merely 'property' to be relentlessly exploited – remains relevant to modern debates on slavery. Every war of the twentieth century has resulted in the enslavement of thousands of people and in the case of the Second World War, many millions.

Furthermore, in the twenty-first century, the claim that some humans are property rather than true 'persons' is still rampant. At the end of 2006, there were 28.4 million slaves in the world.[58] Indeed, there are more slaves in the world today than at any time in the past (although they are a smaller *proportion* of the world's population).[59] In

Haiti, for instance, restavèks (from the French *reste avec*) or 'stay-withs' are child slaves to wealthier families. Each year around 34,000 adult Haitians labour in the cane fields of the Dominican Republic in conditions that closely resemble slavery or, at the very least, forced labour: they are unable to terminate their employment or leave, for instance.[60] According to one estimate, Haiti has more slaves than any country outside Asia. Indeed, Haiti currently has more slaves 'than toiled on the entire island of Hispaniola (including Haiti and the Dominican Republic) when the [1791–1804] revolution began'.[61]

Importantly, the USA and Britain continue to be implicated in the modern-day slave trade, designating certain humans as not entitled to the rights and consideration due to fully human persons. A major example is the trafficking of girls and women to serve as sex slaves. In 2006 there were around 1.2 million young women and children who had been abducted or sold into prostitution.[62]

Anglo-American businesses remain major users of labour-slaves, albeit offshore. As the president of the organization Free the Slaves explained in 2004,

> In the past, slavery entailed one person legally owning another person, but modern slavery is different. Today slavery is illegal everywhere, and there is no more *legal* ownership of human beings. When people buy slaves today they don't ask for a receipt or ownership papers, but they do gain *control* – and they use violence to maintain this control. Slaveholders have all of the benefits of ownership without the legalities. Indeed, for the slaveholders, not having legal ownership is an improvement because they get total control without any responsibility for what they own.[63]

In other words, the cheap, unregulated and desperate workforces in other countries are exploited as slave labourers for consumer-orientated economies in the affluent West. In this way, the full humanity of Westerners has become dependent upon the exploitation of incomplete persons outside their borders.

The Rhetoric of 'Rights' and Torture

The persistence of slavery (and, indeed, the limited breakthroughs made by the women's movement) might be seen to dampen hope in the revolutionary promise of the political philosophy of human rights. Despite this, the language of rights has become the political slogan of our times. The legal philosopher Tom Campbell is not exaggerating when he states that 'there is little chance that any cause will be taken seriously in the contemporary world that cannot be expressed as a demand for the recognition or enforcement of rights of one sort or another'. It is no longer 'enough to hold that a proposal will lead to an improvement in wellbeing or a reduction in suffering'. Every cause must also 'be presented as a recognition of someone's rights, preferably their human rights'.[64]

And that is one of the problems: even malevolent causes can be advanced using the language of rights. This is because debates about rights often involve a form of moral accountancy, balancing *this* creature's happiness against *that* creature's suffering, and judging one to be greater.

Why should it be surprising, then, to hear prominent figures within the human-rights community defending torture, an act most calculated (after murder) to set a being outside the 'human'? In *The Lesser Evil: Political Ethics in an Age of Terror* (2004) Michael Ignatieff, former Director of the Harvard University Carr Center for Human Rights, publicly accepts torture for political-realist reasons; it is the 'lesser evil'. The first sentences of his book declare that

> When democracies fight terrorism, they are defending the proposition that their political life should be free of violence. But defeating terror requires violence. It may also require coercion, deception, secrecy, and violation of rights.

Although Ignatieff does not want torture to become a 'general practice' within democracies, he argues that 'permissible duress might include forms of sleep deprivation that do not result in harm to mental or physical health, and disinformation that causes stress'.[65]

Jean Bethke Elshtain, Professor of Social and Political Ethics at the University of Chicago's Divinity School and former member of President George W. Bush's Council on Bioethics, has also spoken publicly in favour of 'torture lite': that is, exposure to heat and cold, use of drugs, forcing prisoners to stand for days and 'rough treatment'.[66] Elshtain argues for an uncompromising, absolute condemnation of extreme forms of physical torment but turns into a utilitarian when it comes to 'lighter' forms, similar to atrocities committed by Americans in order to gain intelligence from terrorists.

Most famously, though, Alan Dershowitz (a professor of law at

Harvard University) defends the use of torture using the patois of human rights. In his words, 'we cannot reason with them [terrorists] . . . but we can – if we work at it – outsmart them, set traps for them, cage them, or kill them'. It is no coincidence that he uses a language more typically used to refer to the abuse of animals: the tortured are no longer fully human. Dershowitz is an experienced lawyer, and the full flavour of his argumentation needs to be appreciated. He argues that

> Constitutional democracies are, of course, constrained in the choices they may lawfully make. The Fifth Amendment prohibits compelled self-incrimination, which means that statements elicited by means of torture may not be introduced into evidence against the defendant who has been tortured. But if a suspect is given immunity and *then* tortured into providing information about a future terrorist act, his privilege against self-incrimination has not been violated . . . Nor has his right to be free from 'cruel and unusual punishment' since that provision of the Eighth Amendment has been interpreted to apply solely to punishment *after* conviction.

He proposes allowing judges to issue 'torture warrants' licensing authorities to torture individuals (he calls them 'cunning beasts of prey') suspected of concealing information about terrorist acts.[67] What he is, in effect, proposing is ways to turn an exceptional *practice* (torture in a 'ticking bomb' scenario) into a legalized and therefore justifiable *principle*.

Intellectual justifications for overriding the right of people not to be tortured are even more common in the fields of international relations and 'conflict resolution'. Yale University academics Leonard Wantchekon and Andrew Healy titled their justification of torture 'The "Game" of Torture'. It was published in the *Journal of Conflict Resolution* in 1999, and seeks to remove 'emotions' (something that, as we have seen elsewhere in this book, has been coded and denigrated as 'feminine') from the discussion of torture. 'The appalling practice of torture is contrary to the foundations of human dignity and naturally clouds judgment with anger', they write, pleading for the return of 'objective reasoning'. They develop an equilibrium analysis of a theoretical model based on three 'players' – the state, the torturer and the victim – each with their 'strategies and payoffs'. They conclude that 'when all parties act rationally to maximize their utilities, the state might be able to torture to gain useful information that exceeds any incurred cost'. After a lengthy series of calculi, they conclude that the most effective way to stop torture is to 'eventually achieve a situation in which most victims act in a strong manner, thereby altering the state's utility, so that torture no longer is a rational decision'. They advise the state to screen potential torturers so that they will get the very best for the task at hand: 'Entrance examinations to the military and police, as well as interviews and psychological evaluations, can help to target the correct candidates' for the job of torturer, they coolly conclude.[68]

Wantchekon and Healy were writing before the ethical schism prompted by 9/11. The organizers of the 'Torture: When, If Ever, Is It Permissible' symposium hosted by the University of San Francisco had no such excuse. They even invited Janis Karpinski, the former commander of the military police brigade that oversaw Abu Ghraib while torture was taking place in its cells, to give the keynote lecture. Two speakers from the Deakin University School of Law in Melbourne, Australia, garnered the headlines, though, when they insisted that torture was not only legitimate, but necessary. Mirko Bagaric and Julie Clarke's justification for torture was eventually published in the *University of San Francisco Law Review* (2004–5), under the provocative title, 'Not Enough Official Torture in the World? The Circumstances in which Torture is Morally Justifiable'. For them, Dershowitz's proposal to issue 'torture warrants' on the pragmatic grounds of 'harm minimization' does not go far enough. Rather, they point out that 'torture is indeed morally defensible, not just pragmatically desirable'. Like Wantchekon and Healy, they plead for 'dispassionate analysis'. If the 'propriety of torture' is to be seriously considered, its 'pejorative connotation' must be ignored. For them, the relevant variables include the number of lives at risk, the immediacy of the harm, the availability of other means to acquire information, the level of wrongdoing of the agent and the likelihood that the agent actually possesses the relevant information. They sneer at those who declared that all persons have a right not to be tortured. 'How can we distinguish real from fanciful rights?' they asked. If rights are in conflict, which should take priority? For them, even the right to life is not sacrosanct.

Bagaric and Clarke argue for 'hedonistic act utilitarianism' in which the morally right action is 'that which produces the greatest amount of happiness or pleasure at the least amount of pain or unhappiness'. They tackle head-on one of the most famous objections to utilitarianism –

that of Henry John McCloskey in *Meta-Ethics and Normative Ethics* (1969). McCloskey set up a hypothetical situation in which a US sheriff is faced with the choice of either framing an African-American man for rape or risking loss of life as a result of serious race riots that the sheriff predicted would occur if the African-American is not framed. For McCloskey, this case demonstrates what is wrong with utilitarianism: it justifies framing the innocent man. Significantly, McCloskey was an Australian atheist writing at the time of the US Civil Rights Movement. He assumes that his readers will accept that it is wrong to frame a man simply because of the colour of his skin.[69] Bagaric and Clarke were writing in a very different sociopolitical context – that of war in Afghanistan and Iraq, and President George W. Bush's first term in office. 'Bad as it seems', they write,

> framing the African-American, imprisoning the innocent, and torturing the terrorist are certainly no more horrendous than the decision history has shown we have made in circumstances of monumental crisis . . . The decisions we do actually make in a real life crisis are the best evidence of the way we actually do prioritize important, competing principles and interests. Matters such as rights and justice are important, but, in the end, are subservient to and make way for the ultimate matter of significance: general happiness.

Furthermore, they continue, 'punishing the innocent and torturing the culpable is, in fact, no worse than other activities we condone'. To squeamish people who fret about 'slippery slopes', they calmly remark that the 'floodgates are already open'. The lawful use of torture will not necessarily lead to its propagation, and 'promulgating the message that the "means justifies the end" [sometimes] [sic] is not inherently undesirable. Debate can then focus on the precise means and ends that are justifiable.'[70] Critics of such an approach might observe that, in this line of argument, the 'state of exception', or the temporary suspension of the law, has become the law.

My examples have been academic: lawyers, ethicists, philosophers and political scientists have provided justifications to allow torture. The consequences have not been 'merely academic'. The legitimation of torture has had practical consequences, most obviously for the men, women and children who found themselves incarcerated as suspected terrorists in the American-occupied territory of Guantánamo Bay after the 11 September 2001 attacks. By April 2002, around five hundred 'terrorist' detainees were being housed there. Contrary to the Fifth Amendment, that 'no person shall be . . . deprived of life, liberty, or property, without due process of law', the detention facility at Guantánamo Bay forcibly detained 'unlawful combatants' outside the law of the United States. What was new about the category 'unlawful combatant' was that it 'radically erases any legal status of the individual, thus producing a legally unnameable and unclassifiable being', as Giorgio Agamben explained in *State of Exception* (2005). He clarified their position:

> Not only do the Taliban captured in Afghanistan not enjoy the status of POWs as defined by the Geneva Convention, they do not even have the status of persons charged with a crime according to American laws. Neither prisoners nor persons accused, but simply 'detainees', they are objects of a pure de facto rule, of a definition that is indefinite not only in the temporal sense but in its very nature as well, since it is entirely removed from the law and from judicial oversight.[71]

The shift in legal discussions from state obligations towards 'rights' was an important factor in the deterioration of life for the prisoners. As in prisons on the American homeland, 'evil' people forfeit their rights.

These new inmates were stripped of those rights based on belonging to (or residing in) a sovereign state. They clung desperately on to one of the only liberationist languages they possessed: *universal* (as opposed to sovereign, or nation-based) rights. Like the Earnest Englishwoman, they appealed to both human and animal rights. Thus, British detainee Jamal Al Harith fearfully noted that his guards told him, 'You have no rights here'. After a while, he confessed,

> we stopped asking for human rights – we wanted animal rights. In Camp X-Ray my cage was right next to a kennel housing an Alsatian dog. He had a wooden house with air conditioning and green grass to exercise on. I said to the guards, 'I want his rights' and they replied, 'that dog is member of the US army'.[72]

The relationship between animal and human rights was made even more explicit during the court hearings about whether prisoners at Guantánamo were entitled to file a habeas corpus petition under the US Constitution. In the autumn of 2003 Thomas Wilner, a lawyer for one of the prisoners, noted that when an iguana crossed the border from

Cuba into Guantánamo, the animal was protected under American law, so surely human beings were 'entitled to the same protection as a Cuban iguana'.[73] At the Supreme Court hearings of Shafiq in 2004, Justice David Sowter also recognized that American law had been applied to 'all aspects of life' in Guantánamo Bay for over a century: 'We even protect Cuban iguana,' he bragged. But the British lawyer Clive Stafford Smith told a more sinister story. He described visiting the detention centre and observed that

> The motel sign also trumpets the base's motto, 'Honour Bound to Defend Freedom', but freedom is a relative term here. Iguanas are free enough, and if my escort accidentally runs one over it's a $10,000 fine, as US environmental laws apply in Guantanamo [sic]. On the other hand, if you feel the need to hit one of the 500 prisoners who are now four years into their captivity it is called 'mild non-injurious contact' and there are no consequences. Two years ago in the Supreme Court, we argued that it would be a huge step for mankind if the judges gave our clients the same rights as the animals.[74]

Justice Ruth Bader Ginsburg put it more succinctly: 'I think Guantanamo [sic], everyone agrees, is an animal, there is no other like it'.[75]

Ironically, at Guantánamo Bay there was a detention facility called Camp Iguana, which housed prisoners aged between thirteen and fifteen years of age.[76] We are back to the discussions about patriarchal power and the lesser humanity of children, as examined in earlier chapters. As the Earnest Englishwoman observed 133 years earlier, animal rights once again trumped those of children, as well as women and other lesser humans.

What's Wrong With Rights?

Something must be wrong with rights if proponents of torture can so easily employ its concepts and rhetoric. I have already mentioned a number of problems with 'rights talk', including its ability to be appropriated by any cause, moral or immoral, and its tendency to degenerate into a form of accountancy in which some people's desire to avoid pain (that is, the desire of rich Western people) trumps other people's pleasures (the comforts of a home life for thousands of people picked up on the streets of Baghdad, Dahor and Kabul and incarcerated as suspected terrorists).

There are other reasons, though, why we should hesitate from proclaiming human rights the emancipatory politics of late and post-modernity. The first thing to observe is that, for all the talk of universality, rights remain essentially individualistic and litigious. 'Genuine issues of justice and injustice', as philosopher Simone Weil complained, become trivialized because, in the final reckoning the issue is not the 'evil done to a person, but with how much he or she gets compared to other participants in the system'.[77] Tom Campbell also addressed this problem. 'Claiming and demanding rights', he explained,

> often go with a narrow selfishness and egoism that emphasises the personal rather than the social aspects of our lives. In other words, rights can be seen as essentially self-centred and *egotistical*. Further, rights often lead us into litigious modes of argument that get in the way of sensible compromise and common humanity. People 'stand on' their rights, often to the detriment of others. Rights can be excessively adversarial and *legalistic* . . . Finally, despite their egalitarian appearance often rights contribute to injustice and inequality through the entrenchment of the power of those who are in a position to control and manipulate their content and operation to exclude and control others.[78]

Campbell believed that these limitations could be overcome. I am much more sceptical, because I believe that there are even more fundamental problems with the rights agenda.

The universality of post-1948 human rights slogans was always a hopeless aspiration. Rights only operate within societal contexts: 'they do not belong to abstract men but to particular people in concrete societies', as philosopher Costas Douzinas insists.[79] This was what Karl Marx meant when, in the 1850s, he wrote that 'Man is in the most literal sense of the word a *zoon politikon*, not only a social animal, but an animal which can develop into an individual only in society'.[80] In other words, the concepts of 'man' or 'human' are merely metaphysical generalities: they do not exist without the substance conferred by specific societies, legal systems and their concrete protections.

Abstract equality is inadequate to deal with problems of social justice. Rights – such as the right to property – mean nothing if they cannot be realized. As philosopher Anatole France put it, the law in its majesty punishes both the rich and the poor for stealing bread and sleeping under bridges.[81] The philosopher Wendy Brown was even more decisive when she reminded readers that rights not only depoliti-cize the 'social power of institutions such as private property or the family', but they actually 'organised mass populations for exploitation and regulation, thus functioning as a modality of what Foucault termed "biopower"'.[82]

Ironically, human rights exclude the most vulnerable people in our society. In particular, people who are stateless have found themselves set outside the 'human' of human-rights discourse. As Hannah Arendt astutely observed, human rights are inextricably tied to nation states. In *The Origins of Totalitarianism* (1973), Arendt noted that personhood was both conferred and revoked by sovereign leaders.[83] By becoming refugees, people lost any entitlement to claim rights:

> The conception of human rights, based upon the assumed existence of a human being as such, broke down at the very moment when those who professed to believe in it were for the first time confronted with people who had indeed lost all other qualities and specific relation-ships – except that they were still human. The world found nothing sacred in the abstract nakedness of being human.

Arendt registered the fact that 'in view of objective political condi-tions', it was

> hard to say how the concepts of man upon which human rights are based – that he is created in the image of God (in the American for-mula), or that he is the representative of mankind, or that he harbors within himself the sacred demands of natural law (in the French for-mula) – could have helped to find a solution to the problem.[84]

It was a view echoed by Agamben when he noted that 'the so-called sacred and inalienable rights of man show themselves to lack every pro-tection and reality at the moment in which they can no longer take the form of rights belonging to citizens of a state'.[85] This is implicit in the title of the 1789 *French* Declaration of the Rights of Man and of the Citizen. Paradoxically, by becoming profoundly vulnerable (and there-fore requiring rights more than ever) stateless people become liminal subjects. They could be relentlessly exploited as lesser humans, not due full consideration under the 'human' part of human rights.

These arguments can be illustrated by looking briefly at American policy towards the plight of Haitian refugees fleeing political repression from the 1980s (see Figure 5).[86] They were eventually picked up on the high seas and incarcerated in Guantánamo Bay (before being evicted to make way for suspected terrorists after 9/11). At its height, the base at Guantánamo held over 45,000 Haitians. Like their successors, they were stripped of the 'human' designation essential to any 'human

Figure 5. Cartoon by Archie Asberry, Jr. The Statue of Liberty, dedicated in 1886, was a gift from the people of France to the US. Engraved (in 1903) on a bronze plaque inside the statue is a poem by Emma Lazarus entitled 'The New Colossus'. It contains the lines,

> *'Give me your tired, your poor,*
> *Your huddled masses yearning to breathe free,*
> *The wretched refuse of your teeming shore.*
> *Send these, the homeless, tempest-tost to me,*
> *I lift my lamp beside the golden door!'*

At the time she wrote the sonnet, Lazarus was involved in helping refugees fleeing anti-Semitic pogroms in Europe.

In this cartoon, Libertas (the Roman goddess of freedom) is depicted letting some refugees into sanctuary, but telling Haitian's fleeing persecution that there are 'No Vacancies'.

Cartoon by Archie Asberry, Jr. From *Stanford Law Review* (February 1993) rights'. Guantánamo Bay was a camp under a 'state of exception'. Because the bay was not US territory, people housed there were not constitutionally entitled to protection. Refugees were effectively reduced to the status of animals. In the words of Milot, a twenty-eight-year-old dentist and asylum seeker from Haiti who was imprisoned in 'Gitmo' after making the 'mistake' of supporting Fanmi Lavalas, Aristide's populist leftist party,

> This conflict is older than me and you. We've just inherited what was begun by Toussaint and Dessaline . . . [sic] really even before that, when our ancestors, like wild animals, were lassoed from *Ginen* and brought to *Ayiti*.

Lawyers questioning Haitian refugees such as Milot adopted a paternalistic tone. Typically, a US representative would talk to the refugees like 'a trainer who, afraid of the ferocity of the animal before him, disguised his commands in calm requests, all the while having a clear agenda'. The language of human rights served to camouflage abuse. 'Are you not embarrassed?', Milot asked,

> You pretend to be lovers of law and order when you are the leading destroyers of peace. Destroyers who use law not to uphold fairness and equality, but to manipulate and take advantage of helpless people whom you have brought to their knees before you, so that they might behold and worship you.

Like the abolitionists discussed earlier, Milot believed that cruelty would inevitably 'leave a mark on the oppressors. It had to.' As he sarcastically exclaimed to his translator: 'And [you say] *we're* savages?'[87]

As the treatment of stateless persons implies, the rhetoric of rights does little to address the causes of oppression, such as material inequality and exploitative practices. The central problem is the refusal of wealthy countries to provide meaningful assistance, let alone adopt policies of redistribution. Indeed, protective rights can bring increased surveillance. As Wendy Brown put it,

> While rights may operate in an indisputable force of emancipation at one moment in history – the American Civil Rights movement, or the struggle for rights by subjects of colonial domination such as black South Africans or Palestinians – they may become at another time a

regulatory discourse, a means of obstructing or coopting more radical political demands, or simply the most hollow of empty promises.[88]

This is especially the case when rights are claimed on behalf of someone else who is *not* claiming them. Homi K. Bhabha, in 'On Minorities: Cultural Rights', posits that to be human is to be

> identified not with a *given* essence . . . but with a *practice*, a task . . .
> and the value of human agency arises from the fact that no one can be
> liberated by others, although no one can liberate herself or himself
> without others.[89]

Rights are historically contingent; they lack any inherent link to justice. They tie ethics to *law*, rather than *justice*. In the words of Simone Weil, 'rights can work for justice or for injustice'. They are 'a kind of moral noncommitment to the good'.[90]

Why should the failure of 'human rights' to radically transform the world be disturbing? Surely, it may be argued, the emancipatory *language* of rights is the only language we have today to assert claims to full personhood. We will turn to these questions next, in exploring whether other sentient creatures should be given 'rights'. Can animals be 'persons'? What violence is involved in giving, and taking away, legal rights?

CHAPTER NINE

Animal Rights and 'Speciesism'

In the last chapter, I looked at two groups of people who were explicitly excluded from the 'rights of man' – women and slaves – showing how the rhetoric of these two groups was, to a large extent, shared: feminists petitioned to abolish slavery; former slaves (such as Frederick Douglass) lobbied in favour of female suffrage. For both Emily Brontë in *Wuthering Heights* and Mary Wollstonecraft in *Vindication of the Rights of Woman*, arguments for the rights of women and slaves were regarded as mutually reinforcing. Fears about the 'limited economy of sympathy' turn out – at least in the case of these women – to be unfounded.

The chapter then turned to problematic uses of human rights ideology and rhetoric. The 'human' of human rights is not self-evident. Proponents of torture in the late twentieth century, for example, clearly set some individuals outside the rights bestowed on the fully human. Although the language of human rights is the most important one we can currently use when gesturing towards an equitable world, it is not unambiguously liberationist.

What does all this mean for animal rights? Unlike women, slaves and refugees, animals are not agents in their own liberationist struggle. As I shall show, the rights of animals have always been implicated in debates about the rights of women and slaves. For many of the same reasons mentioned at the end of the last chapter, the language of 'rights' comes at a high price for animals as well as humans.

Are Animals Persons, Like Slaves?

On a commemorative medal for the Society for the Abolition of the Slave Trade, Josiah Wedgwood (Charles Darwin's father-in-law) etched the words: 'Am I Not a Man and a Brother?' Clearly, Wedgwood's answer was yes, slaves were kin. But what about animals? Could certain animals be 'men and brothers'?

Figure 1. Commemorative medal by Josiah Wedgwood for the Society for the Abolition of the Slave Trade in 1787.

Wedgwood jasper medallion decorated with a slave in chains and inscribed with 'Am I not a Man and a Brother', 1790s (ceramic), English School (18th century)/© Wilberforce House, Hull City Museums and Art Galleries, UK/The Bridgeman Art Library

The cartoonist who drew 'Monkeyan'a' (see Figure 2) implied that the kinship between slaves and monkeys was close enough to be worthy of satire. At the time *Punch* printed the cartoon, in 1861, it was actively supporting the emancipation of slaves in the American Civil War. Would the movement to free human slaves eventually spread to humans' other relatives, the cartoonist seems to be asking.

It was a common alliance. From the very birth of the language of 'rights', and a century before Darwin published *The Descent of Man*, the enslavement of people was associated with concerns about the status of animals. Theological, literary and political arguments were canvassed to this end.

Theological comparisons were the most influential. In the words of the Anglican clergyman Humphry Primatt, in *A Dissertation on the Duty of Mercy and Sin of Cruelty to Brute Animals* (1776),

> It has pleased GOD, the Father of all men, to cover some men with white skins and others with black skins: but as there is neither merit not demerit in complexion, the *white* man (notwithstanding the barbarity of custom and prejudice) can have no right by virtue of his *colour*, to enslave and tyrannize over a *black* man . . . For the same reason, a man can have no natural right to abuse and torment a beast, merely because a beast has not the *mental* powers of a man.

Figure 2. 'Monkeyan'a', *Punch* (18 May 1861). The first stanza of the poem accompanying this cartoon was signed 'GORILLA' of the Zoological Gardens, and reads:

> *Am I satyr or man?*
> *Pray tell me who can,*
> *And settle my place in the scale.*
> *A man in ape's shape*
> *An anthropoid ape,*
> *Or monkey deprived of his tail?*

After all, he continued, all living creatures exist according to 'GOD's appointment' and so neither humans nor animals

> can lay claim to any intrinsic *merit*, for being such as they are; for before they were created, it was impossible that either of them could deserve; and at their creation, their shapes, perfections, or defects were invariably fixed, and their bounds set which they cannot pass. And being such, neither more nor less than GOD made them, there is no more demerit in a beast's [sic] being a beast, than there is in a man's being a man.[1]

In 1802, poet, reformer and deacon Percival Stockdale took up some of these themes in *A Remonstrance Against Inhumanity to Animals*. If readers were expecting the tract to begin by discussing 'inhumanity to animals', as promised in the title, they would have been disappointed. Stockdale introduced his argument with a statement about human slaves. He began by craving indulgence from his readers: before turning to his 'main subject', Stockdale 'beg[ged] leave to turn my mind, for a moment, to the iniquitous and hitherto irremediable fate, of a very numerous part of our own species'. He warned that 'If liberty, the sacred and inalienable right of every human being, is not restored to the AFRICANS by a prudent policy, and by true religion', slaves would be forced to use 'irresistible and desolating force'. 'Humanity' was owed to slaves; only then could it be 'extend[ed] to the animal creation'.[2]

Writers of fiction, especially stories in which the narrator purported to be an animal, also drew attention to similarities between the abuse of animals and slaves. For instance, the spotted terrier who claimed to be the author of *The Dog of Knowledge; or, Memoirs of Bob* (1801) pointed out that the abuses he faced were akin to those inflicted on slaves. He concluded that it was better to have been 'born a dog, and not a Negro'.[3] *Black Beauty* made a comparable point. When Anna Sewell's novel, which is replete with descriptions of animal suffering, was first advertised in the United States, it was billed as 'The Uncle Tom's Cabin of the Horse'.

All these genres were motivated by political concerns but, in other cases, political lobbying was explicitly the issue. William Wilberforce, leader of the anti-slavery movement, was also active in legislating against animal cruelty, introducing in 1800 the first British parliamentary bill in against bull-baiting. Humanitarians and anti-vivisectionists took up the mantle later in the century. As a prominent opponent of animal cruelty put it in *Appeal to British Humanity* (1877), we are as much bound to protest against [vivisection], by 'Petition', and through our Representatives, as we were bound to protest against NEGRO SLAVERY until at last the Nation's voice, like the trumpets of JOSHUA, shook and laid low that accursed system.[4]

Or, in the words of Charles Selby Oakley, author of *Vivisection. Can It Advance Mankind?* (1895), it took the American Civil War to

> open the doors of pity in the human heart, and to admit into the human family a man whose skin was differently coloured to our own . . . To-day I say that where the negro was then the dog and the monkey should be now.

Oakley claimed that the main reason some people believed that animals could be treated cruelly was 'selfishness'. The slave-owner recognized that he 'held a valuable asset for nothing in the negro, and he meant to keep it'. Bigotry was legitimized by 'specious arguments about inferiority of race and the intentions of God'. Similarly, Oakley contended, 'to-day we know that we hold a valuable asset for nothing in the monkey and the dog; and we mean to keep it'. Identical arguments about 'the inferiority of species, and the intentions of God' were used to oppress animals. Indeed, it was 'much baser' to abuse animals 'because there is not the slightest chance of combination or therefore of retaliation'.[5] It is important to note that Oakley also argued *against* admitting women to Parliament, on the grounds that women's influence over men was 'so incessant, so egregious and so unescapable [sic] that man in self defense and in order to secure freedom of discussion, is compelled to shut her out'.[6] He was willing to grant certain rights to dogs, monkeys and slaves, but baulked at conceding women's right to parliamentary representation. Women, after all, were eminently capable of 'combination [and] therefore of retaliation' against their oppressors.

The relationship that Oakley and others made between the rights of slaves and animals has been rekindled in recent times by animal rights proponents. Steven M. Wise is the author of a 2006 book subtitled *The Landmark Trial that Led to the End of Human Slavery*, which illuminates the legal history of Somerset v. Steuart (1771–2), the case I discussed in the last chapter. The book concludes by informing readers that '*Somerset*'s principles have begun to radiate beyond humanity' since 'some lawyers are insisting today that at least the most cognitively complex non-human animals should no longer be treated as slaves'.[7] He is one of those lawyers, drawing connections between the enslavement of African-Americans, the slaughter of Native Americans and the 'war on pigs', and dubs these three forms of violence the 'American trilogy'. Wise concludes his 2009 book of that name by stating that people's 'absolute power over hogs has corrupted us'. He continues, employing the language of American Protestantism and harking back to a mythical world (before European invasion, perhaps?) when humans and animals conversed together in some kind of Garden of Eden:

> Experience has taught us that only fundamental rights can stand between any of us and cruel despotism. The day may come when Christians recognize that the only way they can fulfil their duty as Creation's stewards is to robe some animals with the legal rights necessary to protect them from our unangelic, thoroughly corrupted selves. Then perhaps men and animals can begin talking with one another on this continent again.[8]

Wise is writing as part of a much broader community of activists. In their introduction to *Terrorists or Freedom Fighters? Reflections on the Liberation of Animals* (2004), leading animal liberationists Steven Best and Anthony J. Nocella also make the connection between the abolitionist movement and the rights of animals. 'Although human slavery has been outlawed in liberal democracies', they pointed out,

> animal slavery in many ways has become worse than ever. This is the case in the sheer number of animals killed, the degree of violation of their natural lives (culminating in the technological manipulations of genetic engineering and cloning), and often in the intensity and prolonged nature of their suffering (as evident in the horrors of vivisection, fur farming, factory farming, mechanized slaughter, puppy mills, and so on) . . . Just as the nineteenth-century white abolitionists in the US worked across racial lines to create new forms of solidarity, so the new freedom fighters reach across *species* lines to help our fellow beings in the animal world.[9]

Marjorie Spiegel's book, *The Dreaded Comparison. Human and Animal Slavery* (1988), is even more contentious. She asks her readers to ponder 'Why is it an insult for anyone to be compared to an animal?' Although she admits that there are some differences between systems of oppression against animals and slaves, they 'share the same basic essence, they are built around the same basic relationship – that between oppressor and oppressed'. Both animals and slaves are treated as property of their masters, who have almost limitless power over them: masters can torture, sell, or kill their property. Spiegel insists that

> Comparing the suffering of animals to that of blacks (or any other oppressed group) is offensive only to the speciesist . . . To deny our similarities to animals is to deny and undermine our own power. It is to continue actively struggling to prove to our oppressors, past or present, that we are *similar to our oppressors*, rather than those whom our oppressors have also victimized. It is to say that we would rather be more like those who have victimized us, rather than like those who have also been victims.[10]

In other words, it was essential for the liberationist struggle to identify with the slave and animal, rather than with the slave-owner and speciesist. Spiegel maintains that it is an honour not 'an insult for anyone to be compared to an animal'.

From the early slave abolitionists to current animal liberationists, then, allocating rights to slaves and animals have been linked. Early abolitionists recognised the logic of extending the allocation of rights from one oppressed group (slaves) downwards to yet another oppressed group (animals): their rhetoric either assumed a Chain of Being or paid homage to a philosophy of difference. In contrast, their twenty-first century successors are more concerned with equating the experiences of these two oppressed groups. They adhere to a rhetoric of similarity. This tension between difference and similarity is one that I allude to throughout much of this book. I return to it in the conclusion.

Are Animals Persons, Like Women?

What about the comparison between women and animals? From the eighteenth century, their rights were also enmeshed. In the last chapter, I discussed Mary Wollstonecraft's response to the exclusion of women in the French Assembly's Declaration of the Rights of Man and of the Citizen. Philosopher Thomas Taylor published an anonymous, and highly sarcastic, retort. His *A Vindication of the Rights of Brutes* was a satire in which he attempted to take Wollstonecraft's proposition to what he considered its logical, and absurd, conclusion.

Who was Thomas Taylor? He was not (as many have claimed) a Cambridge professor. Instead, he was a self-taught philosopher, dependent upon wealthy patrons to support his writings and translations. He was a Platonist (that is, an adherent of the philosophy of Plato and related philosophical traditions) and served as assistant secretary to the Society of Arts and Sciences between 1797 and 1806. He was the first person to translate the complete works of Plato and Aristotle into English, including, in 1809, Aristotle's *History of Animals*. He was also a fanatical lover of animals.[11]

Taylor was personally acquainted with Wollstonecraft. When she was young, Wollstonecraft had lodged with Thomas and Mary Taylor. At that time he observed that, although Wollstonecraft 'confessed herself more inclined to an active than a contemplative life', she was 'a very modest, sensible, and agreeable young lady'. Taylor claimed that she told him that 'one of the conditions she should make previous to marriage, with the man intended for her husband, would be this – that he should never presume to enter the room in which she was sitting till he had first knocked at the door'.[12] He seemed to disapprove of such independence.

So what was *A Vindication of the Rights of Brutes* about? The tract veered from acute philosophical satire to vulgarity. At one point, Taylor called Wollstonecraft a 'virgin', following this comment with a snide remark about the 'prodigious size' of elephants and their 'amorous' nature, which made them 'very well calculated to become the darling of our modern virgins'. Because these 'virgins' had 'wisely laid aside the foolish veils of antiquity', they were 'seldom intimidated by any thing uncommonly large'. He also poked fun at Wollstonecraft's suggestion in her *Elements of Morality for Children* that parents and educators should speak openly to their children about sex in order to cure them of the 'detestable vice' of 'self-pollution' (that is, masturbation). Taylor suggested that dogs would be the best instructors because 'these sagacious animals . . . would not only be well calculated to explain the noble use for which the [genital] parts were designed but would be very willing at any time, and in any place, to give them specimens of the operation of the parts in the natural way'. Dogs would also encourage children to set aside the 'foolish habits' of 'decency and shame'.

In a more decorous manner, Taylor purported to argue for 'the perfect equality of what is called the irrational species, to the human'. He claimed that he was 'well aware' that, 'even in these luminous days', some people still adhered to the Aristotelian principle that 'some men are naturally born slaves, the others free'. Such a principle 'will surely be ridiculed by every genuine modern'. After all, the trend was clear: 'an approximation to equality' was already 'taking place among the different orders of mankind'. Female servants

> so happily rival their mistresses in dress, that excepting a little awkwardness in their carriage, and roughness in their hands, occasioned by untwisting the wide-bespattering radii of the mop, and strenuously grasping the scrubbing brush, there is no difference between my lady and her house-maid.

If the 'most consummate wisdom and wit' of writers like Wollstonecraft insisted that women possess reason and were thus entitled to rights, Taylor sneered, then the rest of the animal kingdom must also be reasoning creatures and given rights:

> Brutes possess reason in common with men, though not in quite so exquisite a degree; and hence, the deficiency of reason, combined with superiority of strength, renders the lion an animal equally excellent with man; in like manner, the swiftness of a hare united with hare-like reason, puts the hare upon an equality both with the lion and the man; the advantages of flying in a bird, united with the reason of a bird; the subtilty [sic] of spinning in a spider with spider-like reason; and the microscopic eye of a fly, with the reason of a fly, will severally be found to be equal to each other, and of equal dignity with the reason and bodily advantages of man.

He even promised to write a treatise 'on the rights of *vegetables* and *minerals*' at a later date.

Parodying Wollstonecraft's emphasis on the importance of education in raising women to men's equal, Taylor argued that people had to learn the language of animals, enabling them to educate animals, and eventually restoring them 'to their natural equality with mankind'. When that happened,

> We may expect to see physicians equal to the most illustrious among men, in the persons of bears, dragons and weasels; and till all distinctions among mankind are levelled (an event which it is to be

hoped will shortly happen) I do not see why an elephant may not become the king's principal Surgeon.

He derisively praised Thomas Paine (author in 1791 of *Rights of Man*, which defended the French Revolution) for 'convincing thousands of the equality of men to each other', and Wollstonecraft for having 'indisputably proved, that women are in every respect naturally equal to men, not only in mental abilities, but likewise in bodily strength, boldness, and the like'. It was only a matter of time, he stated, before 'mankind' will 'universally join in vindicating the rights of brutes'.[13] Taylor's *reductio ad absurdum* highlights widely shared fears about what would happen if the 'rights of man' were extended to other sentient beings. Once rights began to 'trickle down' the Chain of Being, where would it end? The day might indeed come when the 'rights of vegetables and minerals' reached the top of the agenda.

Current Debates: Should Animals Have Rights?

What does this mean when we turn to the rights of animals today? In this next section, historical disputations will have to take second place to the political positioning currently engaging a daunting array of activists, philosophers, lawyers, social scientists and literary figures. Their arguments for and against animals rights cannot comprehensively be dealt with in these few pages, so I seek only to set out the most prominent debates. What Taylor regarded as patently absurd, worthy only of satire and sneer, was taken up in the late twentieth century as a serous proposition: why *not* give rights to animals, and even to 'vegetables and minerals'?

In the last quarter of the twentieth century, arguments about the status of animal came to the attention of philosophers and activists enthused by the 'rise and rise' of human rights.[14] Rights-speak had become both incredibly popular in deliberations by and about oppressed human groups, so might it not be applied to animals?

An influential proponent of animal rights is philosopher Tom Regan. He claims that, as 'possessors of intrinsic value', all 'moral agents' (which includes some animals) and all 'moral patients' (people who are severely mentally handicapped, for example) possess basic rights. He asks: might moral behaviour be based on conferring certain 'rights' on sentient beings? For Regan, all 'moral agents and patients' possess rights, and these rights are universal. In other words, they exist 'independently of anyone's voluntary acts . . . and independently of the position they happen to occupy in any given institutional arrangement'. The basic right is 'the right to respectful treatment'. According to Regan, Peter Singer's emphasis on pleasure or preference satisfaction is irrelevant because all beings are 'possessors of *inherent* value', and are not 'mere receptacles of *intrinsic* values'.[15] Regan argues that people have a 'prima facie duty not to harm, by killing, animals and those human moral patients like those animals in the relevant respects'. Crucially, Regan is concerned as much with 'moral patients' as he is with animals. He criticizes Singer's insistence on the 'preference to go on living' as the central criterion for ethical behaviour, since moral patients and animals might not possess the 'intellectual wherewithal to conceive of their own death' or to make a decision about whether they prefer to 'continue to live in preference to dying'. He reminds readers that Singer's position would justify killing a conscious being, so long as 'this brought about the optimal aggregate balance of pleasure over pain for those affected by the outcome'. As Regan rebukes proponents of utilitarianism: '*that* makes killing too easy to justify'.[16]

In a society in which 'rights' had become the dominant ideology on both the political left and right, equating human and animal rights was an inspired one. The proposition was eagerly taken up by the Great Ape Project of the early 1990s, which argued that chimpanzees, orang-utans and gorillas should be welcomed into the 'community of equals'. These animals are entitled to certain basic rights, including an entitlement to life, the protection of their individual liberty and the right not to be tortured. Human guardians would be assigned to safeguard their interests and rights. In the words of their 'Declaration on Great Apes' (1993), 'We have not forgotten that we live in a world in which, for at least three-quarters of the human population, the idea of human rights is no more than rhetoric, and not a reality in everyday life'. Nevertheless,

> The denial of the basic rights of particular other species will not . . . assist the world's poor and oppressed to win their just struggles. Nor is it reasonable to ask that the members of these other species should wait until all humans have achieved their rights first. That suggestion itself assumes that beings belonging to other species are of lesser moral significance than human beings.[17]

The implication that 'poor and oppressed' humans might indeed be of 'less moral significance' than chimpanzees, orang-utans and gorillas has exasperated many subjugated peoples.

Tom Regan and the authors of *The Great Ape Project* (who include Peter Singer and Paolo Cavalieri) are joined by a vast range of supporters. Steven M. Wise, author of *Rattling the Cage: Toward Legal Rights for Animals* (2000) and *Unlocking the Cage. Science and the Case for Animal Rights* (2002), is a prominent spokesperson,[18] who focuses on the capacity of certain animals for 'practical autonomy'. As he points out, many animals are functionally like children: indeed, some function at a higher level than many children. Many animals are self-conscious, capable of using tools and clearly experience and express emotions. Wise proposes that animals should be categorized in terms of such abilities. Category One animals, such as chimpanzees, bonobos, orang-utans, gorillas and dolphins, possess practical autonomy. They are self-conscious, can plan ahead and some may even be capable of learning human languages (such as sign language). Therefore, these animals are 'entitled to the basic liberty rights of bodily integrity and bodily liberty'. Categories Two and Three have progressively fewer abilities and fewer rights. By the time Wise reaches Category Four, the animals there lack autonomy and, as a result, are not entitled to rights.[19]

It is important to note that these animal proponents are not arguing that animal rights should be *identical* to human rights. It is nonsense to provide them with the right to marry or to become a member of parliament, for instance. In addition, assigning personhood on any creature involves making decisions about 'thresholds'. Arachnids are not apes. They also acknowledge that there are clear differences between members of *Homo sapiens*. Many people do not show the ability to make moral judgments: infants, those with dementia, severely brain-damaged patients and psychopaths, to name a few.[20]

Rather, proponents of animal rights insist that animals should be given rights in harmony with their interests and dignity. This position has generated lively debates about exactly what 'interests' any particular animal may possess, in line with their practical skills, emotional intensity, cognitive abilities, creative flair and self-consciousness. Typically, these proponents become frustrated at the continual shifting of this threshold. For instance, when they are able to prove that animals suffer, opponents of animal rights shift the debate to questions of language; then, when that is breached, opponents develop even more ingenious ways of defining and delimiting self-consciousness. Taimie L. Bryant, distinguished animal-rights lawyer, points to what is probably the main hurdle encountered by advocates of animal rights. 'The problem is not failure to recognize that animals have some degree of moral standing,' she begins. After all, anti-cruelty laws are proof that 'we already recognize that sentient animals are morally entitled to be protected from suffering'. Rather, she correctly observes, the issue is that many people 'ignore or override that moral standing when our human interests conflict with those of animals because we assign lesser moral standing to animals than to ourselves'.[21]

Opposition to Animal Rights: Pragmatism and the Law

Bestowing rights on animals has met with impassioned opposition from certain quarters. As Bryant notes, much opposition arises from conflicts of interest. It is not surprising to hear hostility from businesses that benefit from the exploitation of animals. The list is vast, but includes certain sports societies, biomedical research institutes, consumer-defence coalitions and cosmetic associations. Given the incalculable number of products and services dependent upon the exploitation of animals, it is hardly surprising that opposition to animal rights is fierce.

Other opponents of animal rights include right-wing commentators and libertarians. At times, their views are bizarre in their extremity. Thus, the founder of the Libertarian Alliance called environmentalism 'a fundamentally wicked and inhumane movement . . . and a far more sinister threat to human freedom than communism ever was'.[22] Kathleen Marquardt, co-founder of Putting People First and author of *Animalscam. The Beastly Abuse of Human Rights* (1993), also believes that animal rights pose the greatest risk to human civilization. Animal liberationism is 'not just left-wing; it is against productive people and for political agitation'. And she points her finger of blame at women in particular:

> The typical animal rights activist is a white woman making about $30,000 a year. She is most likely a schoolteacher, nurse, or government worker. She usually has a college degree or even an advanced degree, is in her thirties or forties, and lives in a city. She has five pets but no children . . . Animal rights groups can draw on the support of women who don't have to devote their energies to children.

According to Marquardt, not only do animal rights activists harbour a 'bias against Western civilization and its Judeo-Christian foundations', but they also pose a risk to human rights. Importantly, her definition of rights is drawn from the American constitution, rather than the French

Declaration of the Rights of Man and of the Citizen, or the Universal Declaration of Human Rights. Marquardt regards rights as

> the linchpin of a free society. Without them, people would not be able to go about their business free from arbitrary interference by government. Rights offer a people freedom to convince others of different points of view without having to resort to violence and the resulting breakdown of civilization. The animal rights movement would allow people no more rights than rats or cockroaches.

For Marquardt, it is no coincidence that Nazi Germany introduced laws protecting animals from cruelty while slaughtering millions of people.[23]

Few people will be convinced by such rants. There are some good reasons to be sceptical about the emancipatory potential of animal rights, however. Serious concerns can be divided into, first, the pragmatic and legal implications of extending rights so dramatically, and, second, philosophical disquiet.

Pragmatic and legal concerns come in many forms. Fundamentally, taking animal rights seriously would require people to adopt a vegetarian, if not vegan, lifestyle – an impossibly utopian dream in the current context of Western culture. After all, the most direct evidence that animals are not regarded as 'persons' lies in the fact that they can be killed and eaten. This is what Jacques Derrida meant when he coined the concept of 'carno-phallogocentrism': that is, a society that is founded on the principle that some sentient beings – those designated 'animal' – can be killed for food and other forms of consumption. Animals are 'things'. The author of *The Right to Torture* (1905) put it this way:

> Man, because the stronger, is the arbiter of their [animals'] fate. Everyone acknowledges this when he stamps on a black-beetle. When we ask ourselves, therefore, 'have we the right to kill animals?' we mean merely, is it expedient, does it make for the good of the race, to do this? The common-sense of humanity has long answered this question on the affirmative. The right may be limited, defined, guarded from abuse; but we cannot negative [sic] its existence.[24]

Perhaps no one argued this point more succinctly than Henry Salt when, in 1914, he sneered at the 'lively argument' that was 'lately raging between 200 philosophers and Jesuits, as to whether animals are "persons"'. He dismissed their casuistry with these words:

> Is not the battle an unreal one, so long as the 'persons' in question are by common agreement handed over to the tender mercies of the butcher, who will make exceedingly short work of their 'personality'?[25]

Clearly, humans are 'heavily invested' in defining themselves in opposition to animals.[26]

There has also been unease about the way some of the arguments for the rights of animals have been framed. In particular, proponents of the Great Ape Project routinely compare apes with severely disabled people. This is dangerous, according to advocates of rights for the disabled. Isn't it reminiscent of the eugenics movement? In the past, disabled people have been routinely dehumanized and compared with animals and 'lower races'. For instance, in one of the earliest systematic investigations of the deaf (1858), Laura Redden claimed that

> The deaf and dumb are guided almost wholly by instinct and their animal passions. They have no more opportunity for cultivating the intellect and reasoning faculties than the savages of Patagonia or the North American Indians.[27]

Or, in the words of the late nineteenth-century linguist Max Müller, 'deaf-mutes left to themselves, would rise no higher than orangoutangs'.[28] The longevity of such bigotry caused the authors of an article published in the *American Anthropologist* in 2000 to worry that contemporary defenders of the rights of the great apes were actually appealing to wider prejudices that denigrated the disabled. They were concerned that comparing apes with the severely disabled would 'justify less care' and lead to a diversion of medical and other resources.[29] There were people – such as R. G. Frey and Peter Singer – who were willing to vivisect human beings whose quality of life was as low as certain animals'.[30] This isn't simply a problem of a 'limited economy of sympathy', but a purposeful attempt to draw up a hierarchy of rights in which members of the human species are most definitely not at the head. Minority groups and the economically disadvantaged are probably right to be less than enthusiastic with the idea of animal rights as commonly proposed.

Many of these pragmatic concerns have legal aspects to them. An excellent summary of the legal difficulties of bestowing limited personhood on animals was composed by law professor Richard Cupp in 2007. He warns that 'rights are not absolute, and do not exist in a vacuum. Assigning rights to one party creates obligations for other parties.'[31] In other words, there will be costs involved in giving certain animals even limited rights. He admits that corporations and ships have been awarded personhood, but this legal fiction did not provoke major societal upheavals for the simple reason that assigning this personhood is nothing more than 'a device to indirectly facilitate and control the combined efforts of humans'. There is no question of giving them 'dignity rights', such as the right not to be enslaved.[32] Similarly, giving infants, incompetent adults and those in a vegetative state certain rights as 'persons' is also not revolutionary because these beings are closely allied to adult persons on emotional and ideological levels. In contrast, he warns, giving rights to animals will have even wider implications than did giving 'personhood' to slaves (an act that had been extremely expensive because it involved compensating slave owners). In particular, Cupp frets about what would happen to medical advances if scientists were no longer able to use animals. He raises the spectre of removing HIV research laboratories' 'property' interest in its chimpanzees. If animals are given the same rights under tort law as plaintiffs, the legal system could be pushed into chaos. Cupp conjures up the spectre of opening the floodgates of litigation. 'The potential number of tort plaintiffs in the United States would instantly grow from our current 300 million human citizens,' he cautioned, 'to well over 25 billion.' And the animal rights proponents who will be employed to represent animals would be particularly litigious, less willing to settle out of court and less concerned with the expense of attorney's fees and expert witnesses.[33] Practically and legally, then, the carno-phallogocentric nature of Western societies would make bestowing legal personhood on animals a very costly proposal indeed.

Opposition to Animal Rights: Philosophical Concerns

These practical and legal misgivings about giving certain rights to animals are not insurmountable. However, philosophical critiques are much more significant. These criticisms may conveniently be divided into three categories. The first was anticipated by the 'Declaration on Great Apes', when its drafters admitted that they had been criticized for focusing on animal rights when 'we live in a world in which, for at least three-quarters of the human population, the idea of human rights is no more than rhetoric'.[34] There are dangers in giving rights to certain animals when so many humans lack them. This is a concern that has appeared throughout the century: there is a limited economy of sympathy and if it is given to one group (animals) it will inevitably be subtracted from others (certain humans). As in *Wuthering Heights* (1847), Heathcliff's concern for his horse leads him to prioritize the horse's welfare over that of his lodger Lockwood.[35] This limited economy of sympathy was not inevitable (Mary Wollstonecraft and Frederick Douglass are evidence that it could be overcome). Nevertheless, it is a concern that needs attention, particularly as it involves many millions of oppressed and poor people throughout the world. I will return to this argument later in this chapter.

The second concern is about the role of humans as 'guardians of the rights of animals'. This is not new, and can be seen in David Ritchie's *Natural Rights. A Criticism of Some Political and Ethical Conceptions* (1895). If animals are to be given rights, he reasoned, then these rights will have to be protected by humans. 'Must we not protect the weak among them', he asked, 'against the strong?'

> Must we not put to death blackbirds and thrushes because they feed on worms, or (if capital punishment offends our humanitarianism) starve them slowly by permanent captivity and vegetarian diet? What becomes of the 'return to nature' if we must prevent the cat's nocturnal wanderings, lest she wickedly slay a mouse?[36]

Those of us fond of Jean de La Fontaine's 'The Cat Metamorphosed into a Woman' (described in the Introduction) might ponder about the indeterminacy of any 'return to nature' when the woman-turned-cat wickedly 'leapt upon and, in a trice, done in' the mice.

By the twenty-first century, the basic tenet of Ritchie's critique can still be heard, but with a twist. Instead of worrying about human responsibility for protecting 'lesser' animals like mice against 'higher' ones such as the peripatetic cat, some critics point out that if certain animals (great apes, for instance) are given rights then this would legitimate those apes exploiting other animals. As Bryant put it,

> even if some animals gain entrance to the exalted community of those with moral standing, the result will be simply the entitlement of

these animals, through their human representatives, to participate in the oppression of other animal species that have not yet gained entrance to the moral community.[37]

Put more bluntly, the Great Ape Project only protects apes from human cruelty and oppression. It not only refuses to protect other animals from apes, but it actually encourages such exploitation by admitting apes into a category of 'higher species'. The Great Ape Project turns out to be extremely speciesist.

The final criticism of animal rights – and I believe this is the most important one – addresses the fact that any scheme that distinguishes between animals (as does the Great Ape Project and categories one to four in Wise's scheme) judges animals according to human character-istics and priorities. As Wise explicitly states, rights can be given to animals according to the degree to which 'the behaviour of any non-human resembles ours'.[38] Admitting a few animal species to 'personhood' will simply cement the view that places humans in an exalted category, above all other members of the animal community. It does not challenge 'the presumption that humans are morally entitled to do whatever they please'.[39]

This is what concerns some radical philosophers. Donna Haraway, for instance, observes that the 'last thing' animals need 'is human subject status . . . The best animals could get out of that approach is the "right" to be permanently represented, as lesser humans, in human discourse, such as the law – animals would get the right to be permanently "orientalised".'[40] Similarly, Rosi Braidotti is concerned by the dependence of animal rights advocacy on liberal ideals that have been shown to be damaging. The 'becoming-human' of animals cannot be 'generated by or at the centre, or in a dominant position'. She objects to the 'humanization' of animals 'on the grounds of bio-centred egalitarianism':

> We need to move beyond anthropocentrism altogether, rather than to extend humanism to the formerly exploited others. Humanism in this context is only the prelude to possessive individualism and the exten-sion of individual rights to non-human actors. As such it also leads to commercialization and commodification.[41]

Costas Douzinas is also sceptical, albeit on slightly different grounds. In *The End of Human Rights* (2000), he forcefully argues that rights are what create the person; they are not what belong to persons.[42] The chief problem with conferring rights, then, is a fundamental one for post-humanists: it merely shores up a specific notion of 'the human'. This is exactly the point Jacques Derrida was making in his critique of the Great Ape Project. He argued that it is 'a fault or a weakness' to extend to animals a 'certain concept of the juridical, that of human rights'. The advocates of the Great Ape Project seek to reaffirm the particular 'concept of the human subject, of post-Cartesian human subjectivity' which is 'at the foundation of the concept of human rights'. Such a position is 'naïve'. Derrida goes on to clarify his position by pointing out that

> To confer or to recognize rights for 'animals' is a surreptitious or implicit way of confirming a certain interpretation of the human subject, which itself will have been the very lever of the worst violence carried out against nonhuman living beings . . . Consequently, to want absolutely to grant, not to animals but to a certain category of animals, rights equivalent to human rights would be a disastrous contradiction. It would reproduce the philosophical and juridical machine thanks to which the exploitation of animal material for food, work, experimentation, etc, has been practiced (and tyrannically so, that is, through an abuse of power).[43]

Granting rights to a certain category of animals will simply reinforce the human/animal distinction; it will solidify a particular conception of what it means to be human. In fact, it simply reifies the distinction between animals and humans. Furthermore, since the project can implicitly *exclude* certain humans from rights – the neurologically impaired, for instance – it (in Derrida's words) 'amounts to reintroducing, in effect, a properly racial and "geneticist" hierarchy'.[44] This is the strongest reason for being wary of animal rights: it is a modern humanist politics for a world that has already gone post-human.

Animals and the 'Holocaust'

The first philosophical objection to animal rights focused on fears of a limited economy of sympathy. If we give rights to one group (certain animals), we risk having them taken away from other groups (the mentally impaired or the poor). In my view, it is important to acknowledge this risk, but it is not inevitable.

Nevertheless, it was an argument that emerged time and again after the genocidal violence of the Nazi regime. Just three years after the defeat of Nazi Germany, Aristotelian philosopher A. M. MacIver published 'Ethics and the Beetle'. His initial concern was with those animal proponents who did not distinguish between 'dogs, cats or horses, or stags, foxes and hares, and that of tsetse-flies or tape-worms, or the bacteria in our own blood-stream'. This could lead people to conclude that 'there is so much wrong that we cannot help doing to the brute creation that it is best not to trouble ourselves about it any more at all'. In such a case, he went on,

> The ultimate sufferers are likely to be our fellow men, because the final conclusion is likely to be, not that we ought to treat the brutes like human beings, but that there is no good reason why we should not treat human beings like brutes.

Indeed, he argued, extension of the principle of rights to the animals 'leads straight to Belsen and Buchenwald, Dachau and Auschwitz, where the German and the Jew or Pole only took the place of the human being and the Colorado beetle'.[45]

Animal liberationists refuse to be cowed, regarding such arguments as yet further examples of speciesism. In fact, some animal advocates co-opt the Holocaust motif for their own purposes. They take speciesism to its logical end. If there is no significant difference between people and animals, they argue, then the exploitation of animal labour and killing them becomes hard to distinguish from the enforced labour of people, and their murder, during the Holocaust. This analogy was first made in 1949, when Martin Heidegger maintained that the 'materialized food industry' was 'in essence the same as the manufacture of corpses in gas chambers and extermination camps'.[46]

Heidegger's support for the Nazi cause dampened enthusiasm for his ideas. In 1972, however, a leading Jewish author seemed to endorse the view that 'in their behaviour towards creatures, all men were Nazis'. It was a comment made by the main character (Herman Broder) of Isaac Bashevis Singer's novel *Enemies, A Love Story*. Broder railed against the 'smugness with which man could do with another species as he pleased', claiming that it 'exemplified the most extreme racist theories, the principle that might is right'. Herman Broder was a fictional character, but his comment is usually cited as though it was unambiguously Isaac Bashevis

Figure 3. Roger (Ben) Panaman, 'How to Do Animal Rights – and Win the War on Animals'. The original caption reads: 'Every week people kill two million pigs in the US and twelve million pigs in China. The human holocaust is over but the animal holocaust is ongoing and Man's [sic] inhumanity continues.'

http://www.animalethics.org.uk/i-ch1-3-animalholocaust.html

Singer's view. In fact, in the novel, Herman is a disagreeable character and his wife, a Polish converted Jew, would not agree to vegetarianism on two grounds: first, 'they had starved enough in the village and later in the camp' and, second, 'ritual slaughter and kashruth were the roots of Judaism'.[47] Unfortunately, the statement that 'what the Nazis had done to the Jews, man was doing to animals' has been taken out of its complex, fictive context and become central to animal-liberationist rhetoric.[48]

From the late 1970s, when the animal liberation movement was becoming increasingly radicalized, their publications and websites frequently juxtaposed images of the mass slaughter of people in Nazi camps and of animals in factories (see Figure 3).[49] In a typical example, the magazine *Arkangel for Animal Liberation* (founded by Ronnie Lee, of whom we will be hearing more, in 1989) published an article by prominent activist David Lane, which asked readers to imagine if the crimes carried out against animals were being carried out on humans. 'I suggest', Lane began,

> that if we were truly to reject speciesism . . . then we would see no difference at *all* between the imaginary human internment camp scenario and the very real non-human one. We would react in a similar way because both situations would stir similar feelings within us.

He accused people who condemned liberationists' attacks on people involved in animal-exploitation of being 'as guilty of speciesism as the wearer of a fur coat'. 'Would they also have condemned the sabotage of gas chambers in Nazi Germany?', he asked.[50]

The point was made even more strongly by the controversial activist Ward Churchill. In 2004, Churchill also argued that attacking the 'grotesqueries' of medical experimentations on simians would

> seriously undermine the pseudointellectual foundation upon which the Nazi doctors stood when using dehumanized humans to the same purpose at Dachau and elsewhere (and upon which the Nazis' American counterparts stand when undertaking projects like the Tuskegee Experiment, MK-ULTRA, and so on). By the same token, to assault the meatpacking industry is to mount a challenge to the mentality that allowed well over a million dehumanized humans to be systematically slaughtered by the SS Einsatzgruppen in eastern Europe during the early 1940s, and in the Nazis' simultaneous development of truly industrial killing techniques in places like Auschwitz, Sobibor and Treblinka.[51]

The following year, activist Karen Davis set out to make a systematic attempt to compare the two atrocities. Davis is the president of United

Poultry Concerns ('Promoting the Compassionate and Respectful Treatment of Domestic Fowl') and promotes the view that 'Chickens are People Too'.[52] Her book *The Holocaust and the Henmaid's Tale* brazenly equates the treatment of the Jews during the Holocaust with chicken farming. The first sentence in her preface even reminds readers that Heinrich Himmler, the administrator of the Nazi death camps, 'was initially a chicken farmer'.[53] She urges people to reduce their 'cognitive distance' from chickens: 'Vicarious suffering is possible with respect to the members of not just one's own species but also other animal species, to whom we are linked through evolution.' (Humans evolved from chickens?) She exhorts readers to imagine themselves

> placed helplessly in the hands of an overpowering extraterrestial species, to whom our pleas for mercy sound like nothing more than bleats and squeals and clucks – mere 'noise' to the master race in whose 'superior' minds we are 'only animals'.[54]

She quotes Albert Kaplan's rebuke to Holocaust survivors that they were 'no more concerned about animals' suffering than were the Germans concerned about Jews' suffering'.[55] Davis claims not to expect Jews to 'rise above the rest of humankind' but she observes that 'the Jewish response raises questions about our species no less than does Nazism'.[56]

It is important to observe that these animal advocates are not uniquely invested in the business of comparing genocides. The 'Holocaustizing' of terrible events arose in the late 1970s in the context of rising awareness of the Holocaust within American society, encouraged by the media frenzy over Mossad's abduction of Adolf Eichmann and television series such as *Holocaust: The Story of the Family Weiss*. Anti-war activists and humanitarians have found it a useful rhetorical trope in drawing Western attention to the atrocities endured by American Indians over five hundred years, or the Maoris in New Zealand during colonization, as well as the Khmer Rouge violence in Cambodia during the late 1970s, Bosnia in 1992 and the genocide in Rwanda two years later.[57] People like Lilian Friedberg argue in favour of 'Americanizing the holocaust', explicitly stating that there are three reasons to insist that the genocide of American Indians was worse than the assaults on Jews by the Nazis. First, because Jews today are no longer threatened and are, in fact, one of the wealthiest groups within society while American Indians continue to suffer extreme privations.

Secondly, American Indians, unlike Jews, continue to be persecuted: in other words, 'their experience of persecution is not a vicarious one', like that of American Jews. Finally, Holocaust denial is widely regarded as offensive, but many people continue to dispute the horrors of the American Indian holocaust.[58] To suggest that such arguments are highly problematic is an understatement.

Admittedly, the Holocaust analogy is used to attract attention to tragedies, in the hope that this knowledge will galvanize citizens and governments to respond to protect or compensate victims. It prompts many questions, most pertinently: should the Jewish holocaust be regarded as a unique case of evil? Of course, all events are distinctive. The question is, are there any *important* distinctions?

Despite honourable motives, making analogies between the Holocaust and other conflicts is lazy, inappropriate and probably counter-productive. It is even more problematic when the comparison is with animal cruelty and slaughter. One may be passionately against the maltreatment of animals and yet still assert that there are simply too many differences between the slaughter of Jews in the 'Final Solution' and that of animals today for a valid comparison to be made. It is not 'speciesist' to argue that the Holocaust and animal cruelty occupy different universes. Heidegger's focus on the similarities of the industrialized techniques of slaughter of animals and Jews has generally been seen to be beside the point, on the grounds that the relevant comparison is motivational. This was the point being made by Raphael Lemkin when, in 1944, he coined the term 'genocide'. 'Geno' is Greek for 'people' and 'cide' is Latin for killing. Lemkin's argument was that the numbers killed were not relevant: what was important was the perpetrator's *intent*. The comparison between human and animal genocides neither helps us comprehend the full horror of what happened to Jews during those years (because they were not battery hens), nor does not it encourage empathy with the fate of battery hens (because they were not Jews). The analogy erases all that is relevant about the Holocaust: anti-Semitism, racism, war, an ideology of totalitarianism, systematic dehumanization and the attempt to destroy an entire culture. It pretends that there is nothing relevant in the widespread need to humiliate Jewish victims before killing them: to turn them into 'vermin', force them to wear yellow stars, tattoo their arms and shave their heads. The complete absence of any utilitarian motives to the slaughter is rendered naught. It ignores the powerful trans-generation legacy of the Holocaust, which is now an inextricable part of the history of what it means to be (in)human. The analogy also ignores all that is relevant in any critique of the farming industry, including a philosophical tradition of asserting human superiority to all animals that has lasted more than a millennium, the carnivorous appetites of most people in the West, the fixation on the profit calculus of intensive animal husbandry and human dependency upon the labour and love of a large number of animal species.

The analogy is not sensible strategically. As anti-war activists have long realized, drawing parallels with the Holocaust has become so widespread that there is a very serious risk of it having already lost its shock value. Pragmatically, people arguing on behalf of oppressed animals are faced with the fact that the vast majority of people they wish to convince are simply not willing to accept a moral equivalence between the crematoria of Nazi Germany and a chicken roasting in the oven.

Politically, the analogy is potentially dangerous. For many Jews, even the term 'Holocaust' is offensive since it is a reference to the religious sacrifice of animals to Yahweh. As psychologist Bruno Bettelheim explained, the term is a 'linguistic circumlocution'. Calling 'these most wretched victims of a murderous delusion . . . martyrs or a burnt offering is a distortion invented for our comfort'.[59] Applying the concept to animals is doubly distasteful. Furthermore, comparing animal slaughter with the Final Solution threatens to normalize the Holocaust. Just as bad, it could lead to a relativization of the event. An extreme anti-speciesist might logically ask: 'What? Only *six* million Jews, compared with the *billions* of animals eaten each year?' Neo-fascist websites have appropriated the comparison between animal and human killing, using it as one plank in their denigration of Jews.[60] Making murdered Jews metaphors not only for all humanity, but also for all abused animality, is to denigrate the experience of millions of people (and not only Jews, but Roma peoples, homosexuals and religious and political dissidents as well) during the Holocaust. It would make future atrocities to both humans *and* animals easier for perpetrators. In 'The End(s) of Human Rights' (2002), Douzinas wisely contended that

> History does not teach anything; it is historians and journalists, intellectuals and politicians, academics and ideologues who turn historical events into stories and myths, and in so doing, construct ways of seeing the present through the lens of the past.

It is the duty of these history-makers to pay attention to the 'unique, singular' being 'who has place and time, gender and history, needs and desires'.[61] The reductive, ahistorical and non-contextual tendencies of those who seek to equate animal and human suffering display a murderous indifference to difference.

Legitimating Violence

Within radical animal activist circles, however, the analogy between violence towards people during the Holocaust and towards animals today is regarded as strategically important because it is one of their chief rationales for physically attacking *people* involved in acts they regard as abusive towards animals. In other words, *refusing* to tie a knot in the Möbius strip defining animals/humans can also lead to violence.

The vast majority of animal activists simply point out that an abhorrence of speciesism requires people to compare the treatment of humans (at Auschwitz, for instance) with that of animals (in factory farms). A minority, however, draw a moral lesson from it: people who are cruel to animals deserve to be treated nastily themselves. In the first instance, the moral equivalence of harming animals and people engenders a sense of outrage about atrocities; in the second, moral equivalence excuses further violence.

Post-1970s radical animal liberationists did not invent the notion that it was legitimate to inflict vengeance on these abusers. There are significant differences, however, between recent and more historical rationales. As I will show, in earlier periods retributive violence was *Heaven-sent* while, from the 1970s, it was all too human.

Perhaps I can best illustrate this shift by turning to a nineteenth-century periodical. In the early part of that century, the *Children's Friend* was keen to depict the wrath of God towards people who harmed animals. In April 1826, for instance, children were informed that God 'often makes his ill-used animals his instruments of vengeance to punish those who abuse him' (see Figure 4 for the image accompanying this story). To illustrate the threat, the *Children's Friend* recalled how one ten-year-old boy left his parents' home 'in health and spirits', only to return 'a stiff, cold corpse'. What caused this tragedy? The boy had stuck a pin into a horse and the 'poor animal plunged with pain, and darted suddenly and quickly round a corner', throwing the boy out and crushing him to death between the wheel and a wall. Young readers were advised: 'Now, children, be warned by this that God observes your sins, and sometimes punishes them the instant they are committed.'[62]

Figure 4. Illustration accompanying 'Cruelty to Animals', *Children's Friend* (1 April 1826). The article begins by stating that 'Children are very apt to be cruel. They cannot surely remember, that the poor animals they torment, feel pain as keenly as they do themselves. Children do not like to have their hair pulled, or their ears pinched, or to fall and hurt themselves.' The last words of the article threaten that

> '*God is love, and never can,*
> *Love or bless a cruel man . . .*
>
> *The merciless in mind,*
> *Shall themselves no mercy find.'*
>
> The Children's Friend (1 June 1826)

In the 1840s, the *Children's Friend* continued to alert children to God's wrath towards animal abusers. They reported on a 'distressed father' whose seven sons were all unable to speak. An old man, whose own sons were 'blooming and healthy', was asked to explain why 'God [had] visited him so dreadfully'. 'Do you not remember', the old man told him, that when a boy, how you laid snares for the birds, and, when caught, tore their tongues out of their mouths, and then, with malignant joy, let them fly again? How often have I not warned you! Oh! The birds under the heavens, who cannot praise God with their tongues have accused you, and you shall never hear the sweet name of father from the lips of your children.[63]

This story gives an additional inflection to the debates about people who cannot speak: the lesser humanity of mutes may, in fact, have been the result of their inhumanity to animals.

The argument about God's vindictiveness was not a speciality of the *Children's Friend*, but can be found in a wide range of nineteenth-century literature addressed to young children. In *Kindness to Animals* (1845), for instance, Charlotte Elizabeth Tonna described the horrible death of a butcher-boy. On his deathbed, this boy was tormented by the memory of being 'cruel to God's dumb creatures'. The boy 'died shrieking out that he must go to hell'. Tonna reminded readers that

> the agonies of one hour hereafter, would be worse than all the tortures that could be inflicted on God's creatures during their whole lives. But instead of an hour, it is for ever and ever that all who go to that dreadful place of punishment must remain . . . It is impossible for a cruel man to be happy: it is entirely IMPOSSIBLE . . . HE SHALL HAVE JUDGMENT WITHOUT MERCY WHO HATH SHOWN NO MERCY.[64]

A sermon on 'Behalf of Dumb Animals', preached in 1898, concurred. 'A terrible retribution will overtake those who have inflicted pain on the defenceless dumb creation,' argued the Rector of Landcross, adding

> Call it hell or what you like, I believe they will in the life to come undergo severe chastisement, for it is only by enduring pain themselves that they will ever be brought to realise the depth of their own brutality.[65]

(It is unclear how sinners punished in the afterlife could go on to prove that they had realized the depth of their transgression.) (See Figure 5).[66]

A VIVISECTOR'S NIGHTMARE.

Figure 5. 'A Vivisector's Nightmare', *Animals' Guardian* (August 1911). The image accompanies a graphic list of 'Some Recent British Experiments', meaning vivisections. The original caption reads:

> CAT: You remember. Two years ago you divided the spinal cord of
> a cat to produce convulsions?
> VIVISECTOR: Too true – alas, I did!
> CAT: I am that cat!

The Animals' Guardian (August 1911)

This emphasis on Divine retribution continued until late in the century, but the nemesis increasingly took on a human form. For example, in 1888, the Toronto Humane Society published a poem as part of their 'Aims and Objects'. The poem was prefaced with the assertion that 'divine truth' decreed that 'With what measure ye mete, it *shall* be measured to you again'. After this bow to theology, the Society identified the actual punisher as God's human agent. The poem introduced readers to a young boy called Tom, who had a habit of plucking off flies' legs and wings. Tom's father decided to 'give him a lesson'. Tom's father,

catching his son of a sudden,
And giving his [Tom's] elbow a twist,
He pulled his ears till he halloed,
Then doubled him up with his fist.

And didn't he twist on the carpet!
And didn't he cry out with pain!
But whenever he cried, 'Oh, you hurt me!'
His father would punch him again.[67]

The message was clear: retributive violence – whether inflicted by God the Father or His paternal representative here on earth – was justified.

So far, all these examples of retributive violence come from polemical works against animal cruelty. From the 1970s, reprisals against animal abusers became literal, rather than literary. The increased willingness of some animal liberationist groups to use violence reflected a general radicalization within advocacy groups in the aftermath of the Vietnam War and the anti-establishment tendencies of the 60s generation, but it also arose from widespread disillusionment at the lack of progress being made through lawful campaigning. Some of the original agitators included the Sea Shepherd Conservation Society, Earth First! and the Hunt Saboteurs Association. Arguably more influential, the Band of Mercy (a name borrowed from the early nineteenth-century juvenile wing of the animals' guardian movement) initiated a spate of violence after setting fire to an animal experimentation laboratory being built in Milton Keynes on 10 November 1973. In 1976 the Band of Mercy became the Animal Liberation Front (ALF). In the words of Ronnie Lee, its founder, 'Animal liberation is a fierce struggle that demands total commitment. There will be injuries and possibly deaths on both sides. That is sad, but certain.'[68] Even more radical groups included Animal Rights Militia (established in 1982), Hunt Retribution Squad (1984), the Justice Department (1993) and Stop Huntingdon Animal Cruelty (1999). As one unnamed activist explained, one of the principles of the ALF included the requirement to 'take every reasonable precaution not to harm or endanger life, either human or non-human', but 'if someone wishes to act as the Animal Rights Militia or the Justice Department? Simply put, the third policy of the ALF no longer applies'.[69] For law enforcement agencies, this slipperiness was exacerbated by a number of other characteristics, including the fact that these groups were leaderless and had no formal membership registers. Members were generally white and middle-class and, having not been engaged in prior criminal activity, their fingerprints would probably not be on record. Furthermore, as one counter-terrorism manual blandly observed, members easily vanished from view within university settings where policemen and potential informants were 'unlikely to have their suspicions aroused by young people dressed casually – or even sloppily – hanging around university office and research buildings'.[70]

What forms of activism did these groups engage in? Most commonly, they rescued animals from farms or laboratories, released wild animals from captivity and damaged property, particularly research facilities, factory farms, meat-processing plants and fur shops. Accurate statistics about the frequency and cost of their attacks are impossible to determine.[71] What no one disputes, though, is that the financial cost (in terms of damage to property or increased security for laboratories and their employees, for instance) was small in contrast to the psychological impact on people accused of animal cruelty, as well as on their families, friends and neighbours.

More controversially, they threatened people with assault, arson and bombs.[72] After an explosion caused by animal activists injured a child, Ronnie Lee asked, 'how many innocent animals have been injured (and tortured and slaughtered) by the human race?' Although innocent people should not be put at risk, the issue of 'whether or not it is right to kill a vivisector is a question for debate'.[73] Dr Jerry Vlasak, a trauma surgeon in Los Angeles and press officer for the North American Animal Liberation Press Office, insisted that the time for debate was over: the moment had arrived to consider assassinating people who use animals in experiments. 'I think for five lives, 10 lives, 15 lives, we could save a million, 2 million, 10 million non-human lives,' he said.[74] Vlasak informed participants at an animal rights conference in 2003 that

> there is a use for violence in our movement. And I think it can be an effective strategy. Not only is it morally acceptable, I think that there are places where it could be used quite effectively from a pragmatic standpoint. For instance, if vivisectors were routinely being killed, I think it would give other vivisectors pause in what they were doing in their work.[75]

Not surprisingly, sponsoring violence was controversial, even within the movement. Some opponents of the shift towards violent action wondered where the line would be drawn. Might violence towards people and property inadvertently kill animals? What about the spiders killed during arsonist attacks on factories? Jim Hepburn, writing in *Arkangel for Animal Liberation* in 1991, sneered at the image of

> your average hunt sab [saboteurs] van tearing across the countryside with sabs inside (no speciesists they) quite as concerned about the snakes, toads, spiders, and worms they are killing as the foxes they are saving!

He believed that condoning violence ignored the possibility that speciesists – even vivisectionists – might change their minds. He recalled that he only became a vegetarian when he was aged sixty and it took another six years for him to adopt a vegan lifestyle. 'Lucky me that in my meat-eating days some virtuous AR [animal rights] extremist didn't decide that I deserved to die,' he quipped. The 'price of violence' was to cause the 'hardening of hearts'. It was a price too high.[76] Others admitted that they were 'appalled by the suggestion that we would actually learn from the IRA.' Had activists forgotten 'the horror of Hyde Park', he asked.[77] Richard D. Ryder put the issue within the debate about sentience. 'I am against violence done to humans on the same grounds that I am against violence done to nonhumans; it causes suffering,' he began, adding, however, that he believed that 'Causing suffering to humans in order to prevent suffering to nonhumans is as wrong as causing suffering to nonhumans allegedly to prevent suffering to humans. *Both* are speciesist.'[78]

Not everyone opposed physical aggression. There was vocal support for retributive violence: after all, the movement for animal rights was 'not a game of cricket'.[79] *Arkangel for Animal Liberation* led the debates. In the spring of 1990 'Neil from Shrewsbury' strenuously defended violence against humans in the interests of non-human animals. It was 'hard to see', he insisted, 'how even an equal amount of violence used against an animal abuser could be unacceptable'. He exhorted his readers to imagine being present when an elderly person was being attacked on the street. What was the correct action: turning a blind eye, adopting a stance of pacific reasoning or physically retaliating against the attacker? 'Neil from Shrewsbury' believed the third option was the ethically correct one. The cartoon in Figure 6 accompanied Neil's article.

Indeed, 'Neil from Shrewsbury' was also prepared to justify harming people who were not directly guilty of cruelty to animals. Shortly

Figure 6. The illustration accompanying 'Speaking Out' by 'Neil from Shrewsbury', *Arkangel for Animal Liberation* (1990). The chicken is pictured killing 'Colonel' Harold David Sanders, the founder of Kentucky Fried Chicken.

Arkangel for Animal Liberation (1990)

after the ALF torched the fur-selling Dingles department store in Plymouth, he challenged 'anyone to come up with a logical argument against the use of incendiary devices in department stores'. As he reasoned:

> We often hear poorly thought out comments that life is in danger. A very emotive argument as life is sacrosanct to most people (as long as its human life), but really if the unfortunate did happen, would the blame really lie with the people who planted the device? As I understand it, these incendiary devices create a short but intense amount of heat in order to activate the premises' inbuilt sprinkler system. At Dingles the system didn't work – what would have happened if a legitimate fire had started there during a busy Saturday afternoon? Hundreds of dead need not be an overstatement. Therefore, by logical deduction, the incendiary campaign has two major features which would seem to make it an 'acceptable' form of attack.[80]

According to Neil's bizarre logic, the attack not only was a defence of animals, but it also highlighted Dingles' defective sprinkler system.

In a later issue of *Arkangel*, Neil went further. He defended poisoning food, claiming that activists who employed this form of violence were careful to 'minimize the risk to the consumer', if only because of 'the state's desire that someone dies just to discredit the movement'. 'Morals change with time', he lectured, and 'as long as the ends that these people are hoping to achieve can remain justifiable, the means of achieving those ends must also be just'.[81]

Not surprisingly, appealing to Holocaust resistance was a prominent legitimizing strategy. The link between Holocaust resistance and activism against animal cruelty was systematically addressed in a book edited by Steven Best, co-founder of the North American Animal Liberation Press Office, and Anthony J. Nocella, who describes himself as a 'peace activist'.[82] Entitled *Terrorists or Freedom Fighters? Reflections on the Liberation of Animals* (2004), Best and Nocella firmly align themselves with the 'freedom fighters' side of the equation. They claim that their movement modelled itself after the 'Jewish anti-Nazi resistance movement and the Underground Railroad' (which helped fugitive slaves reach free states and Canada),[83] and the book includes a lengthy exposition of the link between resistance movements. The chapter 'At the Gates of Hell: The ALF and the Legacy of Holocaust Resistance' written by Maxwell Schnurer claims that

> Much like the system of meaning that allows genocide to 'make sense' to a community, speciesism is a system that makes sense not only to those who benefit from that system, but also those who simply live within that system . . . Functioning like the Holocaust resistance fighters, the ALF makes a pointed rebuttal to the ideas of speciesism.

He boasts that the ALF 'elevates a previously non-considered group [animals] to the level of humanity'.[84]

State authorities disagree. As a result of activist violence, animal rights groups have frequently been castigated as terrorist organizations. President George W. Bush's 'Patriot Act' of 26 October 2001 gives the government and law enforcement agencies unprecedented powers to 'deter and punish terrorist acts in the United States and around the world' and 'to enhance law enforcement investigatory tools'. The definition of 'terrorist' used in that Act covers many animal liberation movements.[85]

Conclusion to Part 3:
Being Human, Becoming Animal

Radical animal groups justify acting in violent ways on the grounds that they are taking revenge on behalf of suffering animals. They hope that their counter-aggression will discourage other people from abusing animals. They appeal to great struggles in the past. The aggressive exploits of abolitionists during the slave era and anti-Nazi resistance warriors during the Holocaust had been vindicated: so, too, will theirs.

Identical arguments have been propounded by entire nations to legitimate torturing people. Since 11 September 2001, prominent spokesmen and women can be heard justifying acting in extremely violent ways towards people designated 'terrorists' on the grounds that they are taking revenge on behalf of suffering co-patriots. 'Security' requires the introduction of 'extraordinary measures'. They also anticipate that this counter-aggression will act as a deterrent. Given the perceived failure of pacific forms of politics, they argue that retributive violence is not only justified, but essential. They are confident that 'History' will show that they are right.

There are three significant differences between the radical animal liberationists and those espousing violence against people accused of being terrorists. First, the relative power of the two groups is starkly disparate: animal liberationists are absent from those corridors of sovereign power within which the anti-terrorists confidently stride. Second, animal liberationists claim to be identifying and punishing *specific* acts of violence towards animals, while anti-terrorist militants brazenly claim that they are involved in *pre-emptive* counter-violence. In other words, they justify torturing people who *may* become serious criminals. Third, because the agent is a sovereign power, it can erase the legal status of a group of people with great ease, suspending the law.

As Giorgio Agamben explained, although the suspension of the norm is supposed to be provisional and temporary, it often instead becomes the norm. In this way, torture – officially ended in France in the 1780s and Europe in the nineteenth century, but remaining 'widespread and persistent' in more than seventy countries worldwide – has made a comeback as an instrument of state policy in Britain and America.

In *The Politics of Atrocity and Reconciliation* (2002), sociologist Michael Humphrey contends that

> The politics of atrocity challenges the very basis of modern political life: the belief in the sacredness of human life, of bodily inviolability in law, and that our humanity confers rights which stand in opposition to the political sovereignty of the state.[1]

On the contrary, it makes more sense to me to argue that the politics of atrocity has been situated firmly within liberal mores, including its emphasis on the dispensability of human life, most obviously in state-legitimized war, innumerable colonial 'encounters' and the death penalty. Western democracies are characterized by an excess of bodily violation in law, particularly in the cases of the legitimation of torture and the introduction of biopolitics (that is, the application of political power on all aspects of biological life). Finally, humanist liberalism demonstrates the incapacity of the 'human' part of 'human rights' to have any meaning outside the political sovereignty of the state: refugees and other people who have been rendered stateless become nothing more than *Homo sacer*, creatures stripped of the designation 'human' with its accompanying 'rights'. Humphrey's 'politics of atrocity' also entirely ignores other forms of sentient life, such as that of 'the animal'. Clearly, in dominant Western politics, there is no belief in the sacredness of 'animal life'; the law legislates for the bodily violation of animals; animal rights are as flawed as those bestowed on humans.

Humphrey is entirely entitled to focus only on the political life of *Homo sapiens* (the ideologue-police who insist that everyone must deal equally with human and non-human animals are much too dogmatic and unhelpfully rigid in their thinking). His belief in the foundational 'goodness' of modern political humanism is much too optimistic, however.

In Emily Brontë's *Wuthering Heights*, Isabella wants to know if her husband is fully human: 'Is Mr Heathcliff a man?', she asks. Enslavement and torture, human rights and the assignation of personhood, have all been used to dictate behaviour towards *Homo sapiens* and other animals.

Wuthering Heights is strewn with tortured and dead animals, reiterating the point that torturers of animals become torturers of people.[2] As I contended in the Introduction to this book, debates about the respective territories of 'the human' and 'the animal' not only involve violence but also inspire it.

This chapter has emphasized one side of this equation: the violence of people who seek to untie the knot in the Möbius strip and tie it elsewhere in order to protect animals. I could equally have pointed to the violence instigated by people demanding a position within full humanity who, given the gross inequalities in the world today, baulk at the idea of giving animals rights that they do possess. In the case of Haitians, attempting to free themselves from slavery and tyranny led to profuse bloodshed.

Rights are a volatile principle upon which to base ethics. The law giveth, but it also taketh away. As we have seen in this chapter, 'rights' can be bestowed on people who did not have them earlier: slaves or women, for instance. It is also possible to extend rights to animals: there is nothing in their essence that stops them from being given rights. But rights can also be taken away, as happened for Haitian refugees and alleged terrorists. In Douzinas's words, 'Humanity's mastery, like God's omnipotence, includes the ability to re-define who or what counts as human . . . [But] what history has taught us is that there is nothing sacred about any definition of humanity and nothing eternal about its scope.'[3] It was a point made by an unidentified man speaking to American journalist Philip Gourevitch in 1995, in the aftermath of a genocide that killed around one-fifth of people in Rwanda. In Gikongoro, a town in the south-west of the country, Gourevitch started a conversation with a man he simply labelled 'a pygmy'. This 'pygmy' was keen to tell him about his 'principle of *Homo sapiens*', or the notion that all of humanity is one. However, his universalist principle turned out to be very particular indeed. The 'pygmy' explained that he was sad, because he believed that he must marry a white woman because 'Only a white woman can understand my universal principle of *Homo sapiens*'. The chances of this happening were very poor. Warming to his theme, the 'pygmy' asked Gourevitch if he had read a novel entitled *Wuthering Heights*. The 'pygmy' then explained:

> It doesn't matter if you are white or yellow or green or a black African Negro. The concept is *Homo sapiens*. The European is at an advanced technological state, and the African is at a stage of technology that is

more primitive. But all humanity must unite together in the struggle against nature. This is the principle of *Wuthering Heights*. This is the mission of *Homo sapiens* . . . It is the only way for peace and reconciliation – all humanity one against nature.

After some silence, Gourevitch ventured: 'But humanity is part of nature, too'. The 'pygmy's' response was melancholic: 'That is exactly the problem.'[4]

PART 4. SEEING

Ethics and the Face

CHAPTER TEN

Bobby the Dog

Bobby was a dog. Like Jacques Derrida's cat, who made a brief appearance in the Introduction, he was not a substitute for a person; he was not the 'other' against whom 'the human' is constituted. He was a real dog.

For a few weeks during the Second World War Bobby lived with seventy slave labourers in Camp 1492 just outside Hanover. Each morning and evening Bobby would greet the prisoners by 'jumping up and down and barking with delight'. One of those interned in Camp 1492 – Emmanuel Levinas – was entranced by Bobby: wasn't it remarkable that, a time when millions of *Homo sapiens* were being classified as sub-human or even non-human, Bobby had 'no doubt that we were "men"', Levinas mused. The dog bore witness to the humanity of slaves.

Nearly half a century later, Levinas sat down to tell the story of Bobby and he immediately faced a problem. In the decades since the war, Levinas had espoused a philosophy premised on the belief that ethics, or the correct way to act, was always predicated upon a '*face-to-face*' encounter between a human subject and an 'Other'.[1] 'Can an animal enter into an ethical relationship with a human being?', Levinas asked. Crucially: '*Does a dog have a face?*'

The question, which appeared in his essay 'The Name of a Dog; or, Natural Rights' (1975), emerged out of the horrors of the Holocaust, an event that radically questioned what it means to be human. The six members of Levinas's family who had remained in Lithuania during the war were killed by the Nazi *Einsatzgruppen* and pro-Nazi Lithuanian anti-Semites. Levinas, as a naturalized French citizen, was shielded from the worst of what he dubbed 'Hitlerian violence'. Instead, he was forced to work as a slave labourer in a forestry unit. It was there that Levinas asked his second question: are slaves truly 'human'?

Bobby certainly thought so. This dog looked up into the faces of slaves and recognized them as human. In contrast, Levinas noted, people who 'had dealings with us or gave us work or orders or even a smile' simply 'stripped us of our human skin'. To these onlookers, the prisoners were 'subhuman, a gang of apes'. As persecuted peoples, slaves might utter 'a small inner murmur', a defiant reminder of their 'essence as thinking creatures', but, in reality, they were 'no longer part of the world'. They were even denied language, which, as we saw in Chapter Three, was often regarded as the feature distinguishing humans from animals. Slaves had been rendered 'beings without language'. They had been rendered mute: 'dumb', in the sense of both speechless and stupid. Their world had been crushed under the weight of Nazi vocabulary, whose systems of classification were inescapable. Racism was the archetype form of 'social aggression', Levinas observed, because it 'shuts people away in a class, deprives them of expression'. In the dehumanizing environment of the camp, slaves might legitimately ask: 'How can we deliver a message about our humanity which, from behind the bars of quotation marks, will come across as anything other than monkey talk?' Were they condemned for ever to communicate like Red Peter, Kafka's confused ape?

Only Bobby recognized the slave labourers of Camp 1492 as neither Jew nor Gentile, but human. Eighteenth-century philosopher Immanuel Kant had argued that, as rational and free agents, humans were enti-tled to be treated as 'ends in themselves', not simply as a 'means to an end':

Humanity itself is a dignity; for a man cannot be used merely as a means by any man . . . but must always be used at the same time as an end. It is just in this that his dignity (personality) consists, by which he raises himself above all other beings in the world that are not men and yet can be used, and so over all *things*.[2]

As a dog, was Bobby one of those 'things', lacking dignity and able to 'be used'? Even Levinas failed to surmount the belief that animals like Bobby were 'without the brain needed to universalize maxims and drives'. Bobby was therefore bereft of what many philosophers believed promoted ethical understanding. The puzzle for Levinas was this: although Bobby could not universalize from basic principles, it seemed as if the dog *did* treat humans as 'ends in themselves'. In this respect, asked Levinas, might not the dog Bobby be 'the last Kantian in Nazi Germany'?[3]

If Levinas was to remain committed to his attachment to the centrality of witnessing the other's face in all ethical encounters, it was obviously important to know if Bobby actually possessed a face. As Peter Steeves, a philosopher at DePaul University in Chicago, quipped, what in the world could Bobby be missing? Was 'his snout too pointy to constitute a face?' Was 'his nose too wet?' Did 'his ears hang long; do they wobble to and fro?'[4] Clearly Bobby had a mouth, nose, eyes and ears. So what was the 'face' for Levinas? Was there anything that distinguished the face of 'the human' from that of other animals? Levinas admitted that it was not possible to 'entirely refuse the face of an animal', yet he insisted that 'the priority here is not found in the animal, but in the human face' since the 'phenomenon of the face is not in its purest form in the dog'. The face of the animal was what Levinas called 'in accordance with *Dasein*' – that is, the animal's face was nothing more (or less) than 'pure vitality', a being in the world.

Although Levinas believed that humans had evolved from other animals, his experience with Nazism confirmed his rejection of any suggestion that the 'ethical is biological', a 'question of might'. For Darwinians, the animal was engaged in a constant struggle for life: it was a 'struggle of life without ethics' in which the strongest triumphed. In contrast, Levinas insisted that, for the human, there was 'something more important than my life, and that is the life of the Other. That is unreasonable. Man is an unreasonable animal.'[5] Unlike animals, whose entire being was a struggle for existence, humans transcended Nature in face-to-face relations, which enabled them to act ethically. Thus, Levinas drew a distinction between 'human desire', 'animal needs' and 'vegetable dependency'. Animal needs were 'inseparable from struggle and fear'. In contrast, humans were subjects capable of surmounting material needs and wants and thus attaining something metaphysical: an openness to others. This was a radical act that required cooperation with other people.[6]

For Levinas, therefore, ethics requires the transcendence of animality to the human. Intriguingly, he argued that what makes a sentient animal 'human' is not the possession of reason but the possession of an urge to 'unreason'. From an evolutionary standpoint, it is unreasonable to put the 'life of the other' first. This is what makes human beings 'a new phenomenon'. Through the 'face-to-face encounter', humans are able to transcend the self, giving themselves up to the 'other'. Ethics arises when the 'other' faces oneself, revealing his- or her self in all its vulnerability and difference. In the face-to-face encounter, and irrespective of the capacities or motives of the other person, humans have an ethical obligation to consider the desires of strangers. In 'The Name of a Dog; or, Natural Rights', Levinas insists on the 'humanness' of the ethical imperative of transcending nature by becoming a 'new phenomenon', an 'unreasonable animal'. That is ethical behaviour for Levinas.

So, that was Levinas's view, forged on his experiences as a slave in a labour camp, where he came face to face with Nazi guards who dehumanized him, and a dog named Bobby who was delighted to cavort among 'men' like himself. What happens, then, when we look at other stories that philosophers and scientists have told about faces, and the ethical demands that are made in face-to-face encounters? When these storytellers come face to face with dogs like Bobby, how do they respond? It turns out that the 'face' has no literal, corporeal existence. Our gaze assembles it. The eighteenth- and nineteenth-century 'art of physiognomy' (which purported to teach people how to read character from the contours and lines of human and animal faces), the Darwinian revolution in understandings of facial expressions (which stressed continuity in the evolution of facial musculature of all animal life) and the more blunt instruments of the surgical knife (which claimed to be able to reveal a 'true, inner self' by sculpturing the outer body) were all ways in which the 'face' has been constructed. In seeking to distinguish animals and humans according to their corporeal, and specifically facial, contours, we are always making ethical statements.

Of course, the surface of the body has, since time immemorial, been used to distinguish the animal from the human. According to philosophers like Aristotle and Kant, the external frame reveals – indeed, unintentionally exposes – inner characteristics. It must be possible, people have insisted time and again, to draw precise links between the corporeal materiality of bodies (human or animal) and certain personal traits. Indeed, might an exploration of flesh – as opposed to spirit or soul – reveal the essential, innate truth about a person or animal? Is the body a mirror of the soul?

Philosophers and scientists have frequently sought to illuminate ways of 'reading' the body that would uncover 'natural' hierarchies of superiority and inferiority, as well as revealing intrinsic personality traits and intellectual propensities. These sciences have been crucial not only to political processes of drawing boundaries between animals and humans, but also of distinguishing between different kinds of humans. Indeed, as a writer in 1806 admitted, there may be 'more differences between man and man, than between man and some species of brutes'.[7] Distinguishing 'them' from 'us' has always been an ethical project.

Admittedly, the face has not been the only part of the body considered crucial in distinguishing the human from non-human. For example, some commentators argued that the evolution of the human-shaped toe gave fully human persons their physiological advantage. They claimed that animals, 'lesser races', prostitutes and criminals only possessed prehensile toes.[8] More frequently, the human hand, with its opposable thumbs, has been viewed as decisive. Thus, when the anonymous author of 'Our Simian Cousins' (1895) wanted to claim that 'lower races' were not fully human but more closely resembled apes, he began by drawing attention to faces ('the negro profile – his protuberant jaws, retreating forehead, and flat nose'), but quickly moved to consideration of thumbs and toes. As he insisted,

> Similarly to apes, the lower races of mankind are unable to oppose their thumbs and forefingers . . . Polynesians, Malays, and other inferior races make use of their outstretched great toes in climbing trees, after the manner of monkeys.[9]

In more measured, but equally derogatory terms, Sir Charles Bell (a scientist discussed in the next chapter) declared in the 1830s that the hand belonged 'exclusively to man'. Its 'sensibility and motion' enabled the creature that was 'the weakest in natural defence' to become 'the ruler over animate and inanimate nature'.[10] Similarly, a contributor to the *Anthropological Review* declared in 1869 that 'Man alone has a true hand' and 'he alone uses this admirable instrument for creating thousands of industrial and artistic masterpieces'.[11] As this author implied, the hand was more than just a physical appendage to the body: it gained meaning from the way it was employed within ethical contexts. Therefore, when philosophers were forced to admit that some animals possessed appendages that seemed to *resemble* hands, they quickly added that these could not be 'true hands' because animals lacked reason. This was the view of Sylvester Graham, dietary reformer and tireless warrior against all manifestations of lust. Writing in 1839, he reluctantly admitted that the 'monkey has a hand and an arm like man'. However,

> without the reason of man, his hand serves in no degree to elevate him above many other animals . . . The human hand, as the instrument of human reason, has elevated man to the heavens, and plunged him into the deepest hell.

Used to worship God or create music, for instance, rather than to masturbate (Graham was obsessed with this vice), the human hand was 'second [only] to the omnific power of God'.[12]

Despite these other physical features that have been seen as important in distinguishing 'man' from 'beast', the next three chapters focus on the face because, more than any other part of the Western body, it has been the central sign of individuality and interiority. What happens if we take Levinas's question literally? Who has a face? Does a dog have a face? Do all *Homo sapiens*?

Faces – or, more accurately, the way the various cultural meanings given to faces have been chiselled out of the blunt materiality of bone and tissue – turn out to be at the centre of hierarchical schemas. Not all *Homo sapiens* were thought to possess faces, or, at least, faces that demanded equal consideration. Levinas based his ethics on the view that humans are 'unreasonable animals' because they can act ethically – that is, they are capable of putting the needs and desires of other people before their own. But in the following chapters I show that people can gaze deeply into the eyes of other sentient beings and deny the ethical claims being made by that face. Put another way, the face is always an artifice, a creation, and, as such, it asks something from the viewer. The face always makes moral claims. And that is why certain animals and humans have been denied true faces. Instead of recognizing the desire expressed in the Other's face, the chief impulse of the 'unreasonable animal' confronting another sentient being might be more akin to Nietzschean cruelty or Darwinian struggle.

CHAPTER ELEVEN

Physiognomic Arts

Faces matter. To be human was to possess a certain *kind* of face: a face that differs from that of Levinas's dog Bobby or, for that matter, from that of the Gua, Washoe, Koko, Nim Chimpsky, Sarah, Lana, Kanzi, Chantek or Red Peter. To be fully human requires even more subtle graduations in contours of skull, muscle and tissue.

From ancient times, facial anatomy was used to distinguish humans from other animals. It was believed to provide insights into that creature's character and, as such, made ethical demands on the viewer. This was why it was so important that faces were 'read' correctly: it guided people's treatment of other sentient beings. The art of physiognomy, therefore, offered people a set of rules for this all-important task. According to *Physiognomonics* (attributed to Aristotle), physiognomy attempted to posit 'for each genus a particular animal form, and a peculiar mental character appropriate to such a body'. It followed that 'if a man resembles such and such a genus in *body* he will resemble it also in *soul*'.[1] Since sportsmen were able to 'judge the character' of their dogs by observing their 'bodily form', why shouldn't people be able to do the same with each other, Aristotle asked.[2] (See Figure 1).

Johann Kaspar Lavater

It was in the late eighteenth and early nineteenth century, however, that physiognomic ideas became widely employed in the West. The decisive influences were the works of two pious men, Johann Kaspar Lavater and Sir Charles Bell. They were as obsessed with the face as Levinas,

Figure 1. Human physiognomies next to animal physiognomies, c.1820, after Charles Le Brun, an influential seventeenth-century French painter who sought to breathe life – literally, a soul – into his portraits, and who established a connection between animal passions and the human visage.
Wellcome Library, London

although on entirely different grounds. What did Lavater and Bell believe was the relationship between the faces of animals and humans? What role did the Deity play in creating the human face as irrevocably distinct from sentient beings lower in the Chain of Being? Does a dog (or indeed any other animal) even possess a face?

Lavater was a Swiss poet and Protestant pastor, as well as physiognomist. By the time of his death in 1801, his *Essays on Physiognomy* (1775–8) had been published in more than fourteen editions in English.[3] Like his ancient predecessors, Lavater's theories emerged from a kind of zoological physiognomics. According to the art of physiognomy, the facial anatomy of animals was a reflection of that species' character. Humans who resembled these animals shared their temperament. In other words, animals were first anthropomorphized: based on their appearance, they would be assigned traits appropriate only to humans, such as being licentious, greedy or malevolent. Then, that particular trait was applied back to the original *anthropos* who possessed similar physical features. In this way, people trained in the art of physiognomy would know how they ought to respond to the other person or animal. Put another way: face-to-face encounters with animals enabled people to see human traits in the animal; face-to-face encounters with humans then enabled people to read back those animal traits in the human. These acts of seeing laid the foundations for ethical behaviour.

What Lavater sought to do, therefore, was to 'systematize and define' the 'gradations of form in men and animals' in order to enable people to *accurately* mark out

> the transition from brutal deformity to ideal beauty, from satanical hideousness and malignity to divine exaltation; from the animality of the frog or the monkey, to the beginning humanity of the Samoiede [inhabitants of Siberia], and thence to that of a Newton and a Kant.[4]

In this way, in any face-to-face encounter people would immediately understand the nature of their ethical responsibilities. They would know whether they were dealing with someone who was fully human or sub-human, a rogue or a beast. And the hierarchy was unambiguous: for Lavater, Immanuel Kant represented what it meant to be truly human. Monkeys and Samoiedes did not.

How did Lavater link faces with personality? His theory of the face was composed in opposition – albeit respectful – to both pathognomy and craniological approaches to facial beauty. Pathognomy focused on the gestural features of the face, or those expressive movements of the facial muscles that were in flux depending upon a person's emotional state. In contrast, Lavater sought to uncover something more innate: he was less concerned with passing passions than with an individual's essential nature. This was why silhouettes were so important for Lavater's science. Physiognomy was intended to indicate character rather than emotion.

Lavater was also responding to the craniological-based 'facial line' schema devised by Petrus Camper, an eighteenth-century Dutch naturalist. Camper's comparative anatomy was primarily about defining beauty in a systematic way (see Figure 2).[5] His classification involved drawing two lines against a facial profile. The ideal angle was 90° – a measurement conveniently approximating that of European humans. In contrast, dogs like Bobby could be expected to have an angle of only 25°, and as such were not deemed to truly possess faces. Significantly, orang-utans and Africans had 'inferior' facial angles (60° and 70° respectively). Fully human faces belonged to the classical Greeks.

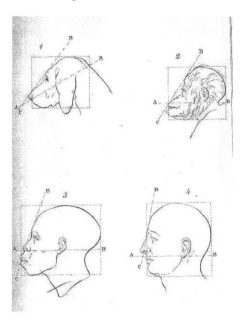

Figure 2. Petrus Camper's 'facial line', from Robert Henri Joseph Scoutetten, *Eléments de Philosophie Phrénologique*. To calculate the facial profile, two lines needed to be drawn: one horizontally, from the nostril to the ear, and the other perpendicularly from the upper jawbone to the forehead. The more vertical this second line, the close the face came to resemble the 'human'.

Scoutetten, *Eléments de Philosophie Phrénologique*

Lavater believed that his reading of the human face was more scientific, more nuanced and more accurate than that of Camper. His philosophy was summarized in a poem that appeared in the 1804 edition of his *Essays on Physiognomy* – that is, three years after his death.[6] The poet clearly adhered to the great Chain of Being, which, as we saw in the introduction, Alexander Pope extolled in his *Essay on Man* (1732–34). The poem paid homage to the Creator's 'wond'rous power', in creating 'one great law' that united even the 'smallest link of the great chain' to that of 'beings endless'. The poet continued:

> All things by regular degrees arise
> From mere existence unto life, from life
> To intellectual power; and each degree,
> Has its peculiar necessary stamp,
> Cognizable in forms distinct and lines.

In God's wisdom, humans were placed at the pinnacle of life on earth. To be human, a creature has to possess

> the face erect, the nose,
> The mouth minute, the eye with acute angle,
> The oval regular, encircled round
> With tender, flowing, and luxuriant hair.
> In him alone are wisdom and beneficence:
> He is of measure and of fair proportion
> Alone the original. He can enjoy
> The great reward of action and enquiry;
> The sense refined, the feeling exquisite
> Of the high rank and worth of human nature![7]

If this was the face of the human, enabling 'man' to act in accordance with reason, refinement and sensitivity, what about the animal? Does a dog have a face? In the great Chain of Being, it would be surprising if Lavater believed that dogs possessed that 'necessary stamp'. Lavater exhorted his readers to observe the 'astonishing difference' between 'men and brutes'. It was sufficient to simply gaze into the eyes of dogs to determine the vast 'difference in character'. Their eyes resembled something 'between that of man and the wildest animals', but the balance between their forehead, mouth and cheeks confirmed the 'brutality of the creature'.[8] As *Lavater's Looking Glass* (1800) put it, the 'brutish shape' of the dog's snout and his 'fallen chops' were evidence enough of his lowliness, but most indicative were the dog's ears: a 'dog's dangling ears' were 'characteristic sign of his slavery'.[9] It would seem that philosopher Peter Steeves's question to Levinas (discussed in the last chapter) about what was lacking in the face of the dog Bobby was apropos here as well: the dog does not possess a face because 'his ears hang long . . . they wobble to and fro'.[10] Dogs possessed radically inferior faces, and so could be treated with as little consideration as other radically inferior beings.

Sir Charles Bell

In 1806, five years after Lavater was shot dead during the siege of Zurich, another influential author set out to define the human through an analysis of the faces of humans and animals. Sir Charles Bell (see Figure 3) was even more concerned with the faces of animals than

Figure 3. Sir Charles Bell lecturing at the Royal College of Surgeons. Note the symbols of majesty (the sceptre), the frailties of the human body (the bone and skull), time (the watch) and science.
Wellcome Library, London

Lavater had been. Narcissistic adoration of the human form soared to new heights under his pen. For Bell, as with Lavater, dogs did not truly possess faces. Neither did any other sentient being, except humans. The reason? Facial expressions were part of God's design.

Bell's *The Anatomy and Philosophy of the Expression as Connected with the Fine Arts* (1806) was the most influential exploration of anatomy and the emotions in the first half of the nineteenth century. It went through seven editions and was much more widely read at the time than Charles Darwin's *Expressions of the Emotions in Man and Animals* would be later in the century. Bell's argument was elegant and transcendental: for him, anatomy bore a divine stamp. God had designed the human body differently from that of the animal. According to Bell, a 'character of nobleness' could be observed in human faces, pointing to 'the prevalence of the higher qualities allied to thought and therefore human'.[11] Specifically, the human body was created to be capable of emotional expression, thus allowing all humans (but not the rest of the animal world) to communicate with each other. Bell's principle was based on the premise that only humans had proper faces.

He claimed to be placing comparative anatomy on a more systematic basis. Like Lavater, Bell was critical of Camper, rebuking him for his dependency on a very small number of skulls and, more importantly, his failure to take into consideration the full complexity of the character of the human countenance.

However, Bell also distanced himself from Lavater. Bell drew an inviolable line between 'man and beast', a line that the physiognomists crossed when they connected the appearance of animals and corresponding traits in people. In other words, Bell chided physiognomists for drawing too direct a link between the facial architecture of animals and humans, failing to acknowledge the radical uniqueness of the *function* of human organs. A 'fully developed nose', for instance, did not necessarily indicate 'groveling propensities' (like a pig's snout), nor did an 'extended mouth' suggest that the person possessed 'the ferocity of the lower animals'. Comparative anatomy could not ignore the fact that human organs served a different function from those of animals. Thus, while both animals and humans used the mouth for eating, only humans also used it for speech. 'Look at the antique head', Bell exclaimed, and ask yourself: 'is the mouth for masticating, or for speech and expression of sentiment?' Similarly, the 'nose on a man's face has nothing in common with the snout of a beast'. It, too, was designed to aid speech, a capacity belonging only to humans.[12] For Bell, facial expressions were exclusively human; they were wondrous enablers of speech. Anatomy was the 'instrument of expression', both verbal and facial. Humans were the most glorious living creatures because of their ability to communicate through speech and facial expressions. What was remarkable about Bell's work was his elaboration of the relationship between (God-forged) anatomy and communication.

As an illustration, Bell instructed his readers to imagine a man who was terrified. Upon looking at the object of his fears, his eyes would be staring or 'wildly searching'; his eyebrows would be raised. These expressions were nothing more than responses of his mind to his fears. 'But observe him further', Bell directed:

> There is a spasm on his breast, he cannot breathe freely, the chest is elevated, the muscles of his neck and shoulders are in action, his breathing is short and rapid, there is a gasping and a convulsive motion of his lips, a tremor on his hollow cheek, a gulping and catching of his

throat; and why does his heart knock at his ribs, while there is no force of circulation? – for his lips and cheeks are ashy pale.[13]

Since the mind had no control over these innate corporeal responses, what was their purpose? According to Bell, God had created the human body as an expressive instrument. Unlike the faces of animals, in whom there were no 'expressions', only 'acts of volition or necessary instincts', human muscles enabled both speech and expression.[14] The human face was a 'special apparatus, for the purpose of enabling him to communicate with his fellow-creatures': it was a 'natural language'.[15] Any close investigation of this 'instrument' provided the 'most overwhelming proof of the excellence of design'.[16]

This emphasis on 'design' came from Natural Theology, the most influential proponent of which was William Paley. The title of Paley's enormously popular book says it all: *Natural Theology or, Evidence of the Existence and Attributes of the Deity Collected from the Appearance of Nature* (1802). Paley argued by analogy:

> In crossing a heath, suppose I pitched my foot against a *stone*, and were asked how the stone came to be there, I might possibly answer, that, for any thing I knew to the contrary, it had lain there for ever . . . But suppose I had found a *watch* upon the ground, and it should be enquired how the watch happened to be in that place, I should hardly think of the answer which I had before given, that, for any thing I knew, the watch might have always been there. Yet why should not this answer serve for the watch, as well as for the stone? Why is it not as admissible in the second case, as in the first? For this reason, and for no other, viz. that, when we come to inspect the watch, we perceive . . . that its several parts are framed and put together for a purpose.

This statement was followed by the most important tenet of Natural Theology: 'There cannot be design without a designer; contrivance without a contriver; order without choice; arrangement, without any thing capable of arranging.'[17]

What did this conjunction of anatomy and Natural Theology theory say about animals, then? Does a dog have a face? Bell was clear: the answer was no. The irregular shape and large capacity of the dog's mouth 'could never be adapted to produce articulate sound', nor could she use her paws to write.[18] Speech was not only dependent upon 'certain inward propensities, a conformity of internal organs, and a peculiarity of nervous distribution'. Equally important, it 'implies a particular outward character or physiognomy, a peculiar form of the nostrils, jaws, mouth, and lips. These latter are the visible signs of this high endowment.'[19] Like other animals, dogs neither laughed, nor cried, nor blushed. They did not possess any true 'sensibility':

> Dogs, in their expression of fondness have a slight eversion of the lips, and grin and snuff amidst their frolic and gambols, in a way that resembles laughter; but in all these there is nothing which truly approaches to human expression. That is produced by the relaxation of the orbicular muscles of the lips, and the consequent preponderating action of the elevating muscles; and, of course, it can exist only in a face which possesses both the orbicular and the straight muscles of the lips in perfection.

Lacking human facial muscles, dogs lacked true faces. Admittedly, their countenance changed when they were frightened: for instance, faced with a lash, a dog might 'yelp and howl as if he actually felt the blows'. But this was the 'only kind of fear which brutes know'. The 'higher degrees of fear, in which the mind operates' and which were 'characterized in the countenance by an expression peculiar to mental energy' were absent.[20] The mere movements of animals' faces were not communicative of true, complex emotion. In contrast, humans were unique in that they possessed 'powers of expression varying almost to infinity'.[21] Face to face with other humans, there was communication, which led to an abundance of moral claims. The capacity of expression was the 'bond of the human family'.[22] Animals were set outside this ethical realm. They did not require the same kind of moral consideration.

Bell claimed that there was other evidence that the Creator had specifically designed human physiology differently from that of animals. Even in the 'rudest slave', God had 'implanted' the 'higher intellectual faculties' and the 'foundation of emotions that point to Him, affections by which we are drawn to Him'. Spiritual sentiments 'spring up spontaneously' in humans, 'they are universal, and not to be shaken off'.[23] In this, Bell departed from many commentators who concluded that evidence that deaf-mutes never conceived independently of a God was proof that spirituality could not be innate. In contrast, Bell argued that human eyes had been designed to be 'indicative of the higher and holier emotions' that 'distinguish man from brutes'. Thus, when people were 'wrapt in devotional feelings' their eyes instinctively looked upwards to the heavens 'by an action neither taught nor acquired'. Bell admitted that 'the savage' and the 'idolatrous Negro' might not always believe in God, but even they raised their eyes 'to the canopy of the sky' when 'praying for rice and yams'.[24]

Bell's theologically infused comparative anatomy, with its insistence that each muscle of the human face had been individually 'designed' to facilitate speech and to communicate inner emotional states to other humans, was profoundly influential. It provided a rationale for maintaining the superiority of humans over all other of God's creations. As we shall see next, it also enabled distinctions to be made between different types of humans. The 'rudest slave' and 'savage' might have been made in the image of God, and were therefore human, but they were of a decidedly lesser variety.

Ethics and the Physiognomic Sciences

As will already be obvious, the art of physiognomy was concerned as much with delineating the correct conduct towards animals and humans as it was with defining beauty. The inferior faces of animals justified dominance over them. Physiognomists could admit that the faces of certain animals were less *im*perfect – the faces of dogs and horses, for instance, were appreciated more than those of pigs or hyenas – but this was a limited form of recognition. For instance James W. Redfield, the author of *Comparative Physiognomy or Resemblances Between Men and Animals* (1852), argued that studying 'our relationship to the inferior animals' should make humans more

> disposed to treat them [animals] more kindly. We sympathize with them, for we perceive that the same faculties which warm our hearts animate theirs . . . Our moral and religious inspiration, by which we are distinguished, prompts us to confer happiness on others.

His point was that if people did not act benevolently towards animals, 'we are inhuman – that is, we are neither men nor brutes'.[25] Kindness should be granted to animals precisely because humanity occupies a superior moral and religious status. To do otherwise was to denigrate what it means to be human. Animals were not granted full ethical consideration as beings in their own right.

As has also been briefly alluded to, physiognomic principles also created hierarchies of humans and animals. This was clearly noted in an article entitled 'Knackers, Pork-Sausages, and Virtue', published in 1839. The author noted that the 'misery' of working horses could be seen in their countenances:

> You may see the hacks of London actually weeping, and the mournful expression which the mouth presents is different from that of a well-fed gentleman's horse, or a brewer's nag, as is the smile of a vigorous and young bride, from the deplorable grin of a superannuated debauchee, or a Malthusian pauper.

He claimed to have 'studied keenly the physiognomy of beasts' and could

> see happiness and misery in their very faces – not in their eyes as some stupid sentimentalists imagine. There is no expression in their eyes. Expression is all in the nose and mouth, but especially in the mouth. There is the soul discovered.[26]

In other words, 'virtue' or the proper way to treat other creatures could be read directly from the face. Human facial expressions informed viewers whether they were looking at a healthy young bride or a lewd man and reproductively prolific pauper. Similarly, the expression on a horse's face could tell you whether she was on her way to the knacker's yard or should be gently stroked as a well-fed horse serving a gentleman.

Typically, though, physiognomists were obsessed with *human* expression. In this respect, there were two interesting groups: deaf-mutes and women. The principles of physiognomy were used to denigrate people who could not speak (one of the central traits of humanness). On the one hand, it was admitted that deaf-mutes were forced to become expert physiognomists. As deaf poet Laura C. Redden Searing attested,

> I learned to read in every face
> The deep emotions of the heart;
> For Nature to the stricken one
> Had given this simple art.[27]

Even people suffering from aphasia could communicate via their physiognomy. In the words of Frederic Bateman, writing in 1890,

When all other forms of language are either suspended or perverted, there may still remain one, which is the same in all countries and among all people – the language of physiognomy: the aphasic may still evince pleasurable sensations by a smile, give evidence of shame by the blush on the forehead, and of fear by pallor of the countenance.[28]

On the other hand, a deaf-mute was likely to have 'arrested development', shown in the 'physical expression' of her 'relatively smaller head'.[29] Another commentator put it more harshly: the deaf-mute's 'pitiable' condition meant that 'his countenance wears a blank and almost brutish expression'. It may be doubted whether they were 'but little above the spiritual level of the beasts that perish'.[30]

Physiognomists were less dismissive when turning their gaze to women. Indeed, they both idealized and denigrated women. Lavater was fond of pointing out that the physiognomies of women were 'less bony, less projecting, less strongly delineated, it is not so easily to be defined, as that of strongly-formed, firm-boned men'.[31] Women's faces resembled those of children and the higher animals more than they looked like the faces of exemplary humans; that is, male ones.

Not surprisingly, Lavater attracted a good number of female critics. An anonymous woman, writing in the *Lady's Monthly Museum* in February 1801, protested against Lavater's statement that 'woman knows not to *think*; they perceive, can associate ideas, but can go no further'. She pointed out that reducing women to the level of the 'beasts that perish' was 'derogatory to the sex, himself, and the Deity'. Like the Earnest Englishwoman, she insisted that women were 'thinking, accountable' people. She regarded Lavater's opinion as having emerged from his physiognomic beliefs and his ignorance. Physiognomy was partly to blame, she claimed, because 'intellectual capacity is not so strongly marked upon the countenance as [are] vicious inclinations'. By implication, women were possessed of a high degree of 'intellectual capacity', while men were plagued by 'vicious inclinations'. She went on to say that, as a result, physiognomists were often 'deceived' when judging the quality of a person's *mind*, as opposed to their *character*. She argued that the

operations of vice are violent and severe, leaving marks of desolation and furrows of anxiety in every countenance: reason, on the contrary, moves on silently and calm, giving tranquility within, serenity without; and this serenity may most frequently be mistaken for a mark of incapacity.

It was a brilliant retort to the usual dichotomy of male reason versus female emotion.

This anonymous woman, writing over seventy years before the Earnest Englishwoman threw down her gauntlet, believed that another explanation for Lavater's prejudices could be that he lacked contact with women in the private sphere. She regarded this as a serious handicap since, in public, women's lives were so constrained that they were incapable of fulfilling their full human potential:

> When the determination of the mind is biassed [sic] by custom; where sense is deemed madness, and study called folly; where folly is deified as a virtue, and virtue ridiculed as ignorance, at a time when fashion makes its deepest impression upon our features, and our whole conduct is regulated by its tyrannic [sic] influence, are we to sit for our pictures? – if so, how unreal a likeness will be produced, and how ridiculous an appearance would even the wisest of us exhibit!

I am sure that the Earnest Englishwoman would have approved of these sentiments. If physiologists really wanted to accurately 'read' a woman's character through her face, this anonymous critic continued, then the woman had to be seen within her domestic sphere. It was only within her designated sphere that a woman's 'real character appears' and her rationality and 'capacity of thinking and judging for herself' flourished. A woman's domestic physiognomy would provide proof – if it were needed – that woman was 'not a mere machine' but was 'equally a candidate for Heaven and Eternity!'[32] In other words, physiognomic principles that relegated women to categories of faciality more usually attributed to animals or children were the result of the misogynist assumptions of its founding fathers.

If this anonymous woman writing in the *Lady's Monthly Museum* thought women were being unfairly treated by the art of physiognomy, non-Europeans had even more right to protest. (See another version of 'Camper's Facial Angles' in Figure 4.) Non-European countenances were also relegated to subordinate categories of humanity – if they were human at all. It was physiognomic assumptions that enabled English novelist William Makepeace Thackeray to comment, after observing African-Americans, that those men were 'not my men and brethren, these strange people with retreating foreheads, and with great obtruding lips and jaws . . . Sambo is not my man and brother'.[33]

Excluding certain faces from full humanness was common in both

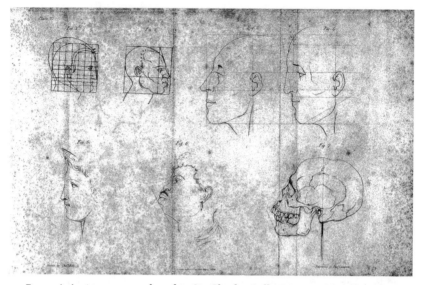

Figure 4. An image reproduced in Sir Charles Bell, *Essays on the Anatomy and Philosophy of Expression.*
Wellcome Library, London

the theological and secular versions of physiognomy. Soame Jenyns's *Disquisitions on Several Subjects* (1782) illustrates this point from the standpoint of natural theology. Jenyns waxed lyrically about the 'wonderful chain of Beings, with which this terrestrial globe is furnished'. His vision not only ranked animals lower than humans, but also carefully differentiated between humans. He traced animal life from the 'low beginning in the shell-fish, thro' innumerable species of insects, fishes, birds, and beasts' and then to 'the dog, the monkey, and the chimpanzee'. At that point, he introduced the 'lowest degree in the brutal Hottentot', from which

> reason, with the assistance of learning and science, advances thro' the various stages of human understanding, which rise above each other, 'till in a Bacon, or a Newton it attains its summit.[34]

This was not simply a matter of calculating the density of muscle and fat or measuring the angles of bones. As a racial science, physiognomy was also founded on principles of whiteness. It was based upon classical models with European visages. This was implicit in practically every discussion of the 'art of reading faces'. For instance, in the early 1880s, the Kansas Academy of Science held a conference to discuss 'Facial Expression and its Psychology'. According to one delegate, as humans evolved, so too their faces were 'humanized', enabling the face to become 'the index of the human soul'. He elaborated his position, explaining that the face of 'the lowest savage man' was 'little above that of animals in expression . . . because the higher mental qualities and emotions are yet dormant'. As this early man emerged 'from savagery into barbarism', however, he began to 'feel somewhat for others, acknowledges that others have some rights, and from this stage the emotions are developed, and his subsequent refinement and elevation assured'. Intelligence alone was not enough to separate the 'refined' man from the savage or the beast. What was needed was the 'birth of the emotions', a 'great step forward' that was literally written on the face.[35]

Popular European culture embraced such views. A fairly representative example would be David Ker's article, 'In a Haytian Village', which appeared in *Good Things. The English Boy's and Girl's Magazine* in 1876. Ker described being given a tour of the village of Jeremie by the captain of his ship. The captain promised him that 'there'll be plenty to see, never fear', adding that Haitian 'niggers' are 'a sight enough for anybody'. 'Hideous old negresses' could be seen lolling about 'with short pipes in their mouths'. For Ker, the 'spirit of the whole race' was 'personified' in the visage of a 'luxurious pig immersed in a pool of muddy water up to the very snout, with half-closed eyes and an occasional thick grunt of lazy beatitude'. With sarcasm, the captain explained that

> This is the first *black* republic you've been in, I fancy . . . and a sweet place you'll find it. Here you have the black man left to his own devices, without anybody to interfere with him; and nice work he's made of it, by jingo! I wish some o' those folks at home, that make such a bother about the 'oppressed negro', would just come and have a look at him as he is at home; I'll be bound, afore a week was out they'd be glad to walk fifty miles to his funeral!

The first black republic alternated 'between monstrous parodies of white civilization and the unredeemed brutalities of the born savage'.[36] It was a status written on Haitian faces.

Others commentators set out highly complex 'racial' categories. Redfield's popular *Comparative Physiognomy* (1852) is a good example of the way physiognomy was applied to specific 'racial' groups. In this

Figure 5. According to James W. Redfield, in *Comparative Physiognomy or Resemblances Between Men and Animals*, anyone who compared an Irishman to a dog would 'be convinced that there is a wonderful resemblance' in respect to 'barking, snarling, howling, begging, fawning, flattering, backbiting, quarrelling, blustering, scenting, seizing, hanging on, teasing [and] rollicking'.
Redfield, *Comparative Physiognomy or Resemblances Between Men and Animals*

lengthy book, he has chapters comparing (among many others) Germans to lions, Prussians to cats, 'Negroes' to elephants, Jews to goats and Chinese to pigs. Does a dog have a face? Yes, Redfield concluded, and it was the face of an Irishman (see Figure 5).[37]

What Redfield called 'bodily hospitalities' were based on such physiognomic evaluations.[38] He reminded readers that in countries where people 'oppress and enslave the bodies and souls of men' and mistreat animals, the 'natural man' resembled 'the ape, [and] is selfish and disgusting in the extreme'.[39] The fully human transcended their beastly — their apish — inheritance, in part by recognizing in the face of other people their own reflection. Physiognomy promoted an ethic of narcissism, at least for white Europeans.

Such commentators were concerned with philosophical generalities. The question of *actual* face-to-face encounters remained. What, after all, should a Christian do when looking upon a man or woman whose physiognomy indicated a corrupt nature? Might physiognomy encourage misanthropy, or the turning away in disgust from other people? This was certainly the view of an unnamed person writing to the author of 'Familiar Lectures on Physiognomy' (1807). Might the 'sole effect of this science . . . be that of increasing the number of misanthropes, who fear and avoid all intercourse with their fellow-creatures, because they dread to fall victim to their unruly passions'?, he asked. Because there were 'more wicked than just men' in the world,

> sorrow is the only harvest we may expect to reap from it [physiog-nomic thought]; for we cannot help being saddened by the reflection, that the immense family to which we belong is composed of such despicable beings.

The author of 'Familiar Lectures on Physiognomy' did not really have a satisfactory answer to this dilemma. He weakly agreed that 'folly is more natural to men than wickedness', so if face-to-face encounters resulted in 'a moderate share of misanthropy, would it not, on the contrary, prove useful to many persons'?[40]

This was not the view of the pastor Lavater. He strongly argued that Christian charity had to be applied, even to men and women whose physiognomy indicated an evil character. If a Christian sensitive to physiognomic principles 'reads the villain in the countenance of the beggar at his door', Lavater insisted, his duty was not to 'turn away' but to address the person with a heart swollen with friendship. Even faced with a face revealing 'an abyss, a chaos of vice', the physiognomist

> sees, prays, turns away his face, and hides a tear which speaks, with elo-quence inexpressible, not to man, but to God alone. He stretches out his friendly hand . . . Man is not to be the judge of man – And who feels this truth more coercively than the physiognomist? . . . He forgave.[41]

Theological precepts thus enabled Lavater to engage in a defence of accepting the stranger, even if his face exposed him as a 'villain'.

There was a more important reason why physiognomy should lead to philanthropy rather than misanthropy: God is just. By His grace, and after human struggle, a person could overcome certain innate traits. In other words, despite the seemingly essentialist rhetoric of physiog-nomic principles, Lavater still insisted that it was a science that allowed men and women to improve – albeit with God's help. Lavater exhorted readers to 'rejoice'. 'In proportion as his heart is ennobled', he pointed out, a man's 'countenance improves'.[42] Admittedly, it was a bounded freedom: 'Man is as free as the bird in the cage', Lavater declared, explaining that each person had 'a determinate space for action and sensation, beyond which he cannot pass'.[43] Nevertheless, 'in proportion as he is morally good, he is handsome; and ugly, in proportion as he is morally bad'.[44] There was to be no improvement of the physiognomies of animals, since they remained 'of this world'. In contrast, humans had been blessed with free will, an immortal soul and the privilege of being able to throw themselves on Christ's mercy.

The Popularity of Physiognomy

The art of physiognomy, with its promise of allowing correct judgments to be made about a person's character, was extremely popular. In a mid-nineteenth-century edition of the *Encyclopedia Britannica*, credulous readers were informed that the publication of Lavater's essays 'created everywhere profound sensation. Admiration, contempt, resentment, and fear were cherished towards the author'. The encyclopedia went on to embellish Lavater's fame by claiming that 'in many places, where the study of human character from the face became an epidemic, the people went masked through the streets'.[45] Clearly, the encyclopedia believed that many people were not convinced that their true faces would elicit their preferred ethical response from strangers they met in the crowded streets of early urbanization.

Some of the keenest debates about the value of physiognomy took place within fiction. For example, the protagonist in *Wuthering Heights* (1847) could have emerged unadulterated from physiognomic musings of the early nineteenth century. Heathcliff's dark face, broad and 'jetty' eyebrows, full nostrils, heavy brow and deep eyes would have been 'read' as betraying a vicious, animalistic nature. As Mr Linton observed when he first saw the young Heathcliff, 'the villain scowls so plainly in his face, would it not be a kindness to the country to hang him at once, before he shows his nature in acts, as well as features?'[46] Even Heathcliff's dogs understood the basic principles of physiognomy, attacking Lockwood because 'some turn of [his] physiognomy so irritated' them.[47]

Other authors reflected physiognomic principles much less favourably. Mary Shelley was one such sceptic. Shelley's mother, Mary Wollstonecraft, had translated Lavater's book 'with the liveliest interest'.[48] Wollstonecraft admitted that she 'love[s] sometimes to view the human face divine, and trace the soul, as well as the heart, in its varying lineaments', even though she accused Lavater of having 'a knack at

[sic] seeing a great character in the countenances of men in exalted stations, who have noticed him, or his works'.[49] Shelley's father, William Godwin, had commissioned a physiognomic reading of his daughter in 1797.[50] But Shelley herself was less impressed. In *Frankenstein*, she deliberately set out to critique physiognomic ideas. In her novel, Victor Frankenstein described how he created his monster:

> How can I describe my emotions at this catastrophe; or how delineate the wretch whom with such infinite pains and care I had endeavoured to form? His limbs were in proportion and I had selected his features as handsome. Handsome; Great God! His yellow skin scarcely covered the work of muscles and arteries beneath; his hair was flowing and his teeth of a pearly whiteness but these luxuriancies only formed a more horrid contrast with his watery eyes that seemed almost of the same colour as the dun white sockets in which they were set, his shrivelled complexion and strait [sic] black lips.[51]

Shelley's monster was thus a parody of Lavater's model human. The monster protested that he possessed 'good dispositions'. He loves 'virtue and knowledge' and insists that his life 'has been hitherto harmless & in some degree beneficial'. Nevertheless, 'a fatal prejudices clouds their eyes and where they ought to see a feeling and kind friend, they behold only a detestable monster.'[52] Frankenstein's monster possessed a face that, according to the physiognomists, should have provided evidence of his less than human, even bestial status. Shelley was chiding her readers, entreating them to remember that outward appearances were not a reflection of inner depths.

Shelley's scepticism about the art of reading faces is less surprising when we reflect that physiognomic predictions must have proved wrong in most instances. Even Lavater could not claim that it was an infallible art. Much to his embarrassment, he was unable to 'read' Kant's face, even though he had claimed that the philosopher had one of the most refined visages. According to an anecdote that Kant used to recount 'with great glee', a traveller showed Lavater two portraits: one was of a highwayman who had been executed by being broken on the wheel and the other was of Kant. Lavater looked at the illustration of the criminal and exclaimed:

> Here . . . we have the true philosopher; here is penetration in the eyes, and reflection in the forehead; here is cause, and there is effect;

here is combination, there is distinction; synthetic [used in the sense of 'combining'] lips!, and analytic nose!

When shown the illustration of Kant, Lavater was briefer: 'The calm, thinking villain is so well expressed, and so strongly marked, in this countenance, that it needs no comment.'[53]

Furthermore, when the lessons of physiognomy were applied to conduct towards people, it could cause considerable disgruntlement. Even Charles Darwin was personally affected. In his autobiography, Darwin recalled that the captain of HMS *Beagle* considered rejecting his application to work on board the ship 'on account of the shape of my nose!' The captain 'was an ardent disciple of Lavater', Darwin sighed,

> and was convinced that he could judge of a man's character by the outline of his features; and he doubted whether any one with my nose could possess sufficient energy and determination for the voyage.

Darwin noted that the captain was eventually 'well satisfied that my nose had spoken falsely'.[54] As we shall see in the next chapter, Darwin's *The Expressions of the Emotions in Man and Animals* (1872) was to revolutionize understandings of facial expression. His conclusions permanently changed the way people thought about human and animal faces. For Darwin, a dog definitely had a face.

Given its inherent unreliability, why was physiognomy so popular? It must be admitted that both Lavater and Bell were energetic in promoting their ideas, often in charismatic and charming ways (as their physiognomies would have predicted, perhaps). Their followers were equally passionate in propagating what were often highly creative versions of physiognomic ideas and marshalling elaborate refutations of critics.

However, there were much more important reasons for its popularity. Rapid urbanization and industrialization, accompanied by dislocation and distress, fundamentally altered face-to-face encounters in nineteenth-century society. Physiognomy promised to give people a way to rapidly assess the character of masses of strangers. Reassuringly, 'No man appears other than he is', argued one adherent.[55] Or, as the author of 'The Descent of Facial Expression' (1891–92) put it, facial expressions were a 'natural sign language'. Because the face 'consists largely of hereditary impulses left over from a primitive state', it could be accurately read in a 'direct and simple' manner.[56] As in the cartoon in Figure 6, this meant that it could be used to naturalize differences according to class (the poor), ethnicity (Irish) and gender (violent men and maternal women).[57] To truly know another creature and to know how they should be treated, a person had only to apply certain physiognomic rules. Incidentally, this was an approach to ethics that would have appalled Levinas: it declared that human responses to other beings should be dependent upon an abstract system of obligations – the rules and laws of physiognomy – as opposed to any idea of absolute justice. Readers of physiognomic works understood that they were being given a technique for the mastery of other

Figure 6. 'On Physiognomy', from *Fun*, 1881. The caption reads:

On Physiognomy.
Enthusiastic Young Lady: What a sweetly pretty little boy of yours, Mrs Finigan! What beautiful black eyes he has! I'm sure he will be both excitable and impulsive; black-eyed people always are, you know.
Mrs Finigan: Shure, Miss, an' perhaps you're right. His father's excitable and impulsive enough, bedad! So loikely it's why he's never widout a black eye, sorra a bit!
National Library of Scotland

people and animals. It was a shorthand way of deciding how other sentient beings should be treated.

In one sense, then, the art of physiognomy was highly democratic. The face was the 'visible record, the map of the heart, advertising the character of the man to all who care to read', insisted one believer. The 'expressive duty of the face to symbolize character' was 'not occult and secret and known only to the initiated' but were 'so open and plain that even a child may read and know plainly and simply the heart of the wearer of them'. It was a power that was 'instinctive in all Men for it is born with them, and is exercised unconsciously from the cradle'. There was nothing accidental about it: 'Nature always works by law.'[58] As the *Anthropological Review* observed in 1868, not only adults but also the 'infant in arms' could be a 'most unprejudicial witness to the truth of physiognomy'. Indeed, the author went on, the human visage even had a 'physiognomical sensation' on 'lower animals': one man's 'fierce glance may make a lion quail', while the 'tender accents' of another 'invite to his bosom the timid and gentle dove'. The 'physiognomical sensation' that the human face 'excites' was 'an important adjunct to his executive over lower forms of life'.[59] Humans had been granted lordship over the animal world because they alone possessed 'true faces'.

This was why the art of physiognomy was crucial for professions such as medicine and forensic criminology.[60] Interpreting facial signs could tell the physician what the person herself might not know. As Sir Alexander Morison of the Royal College of Physicians put it in *The Physiognomy of Mental Disease* (1840), physiognomy is necessary to diagnose mental diseases. 'It not only enables us to distinguish the characteristic features of different varieties', he went on, but also 'gives warning of the approach of the disease'.[61] Because people often simulated insanity, physiognomy was essential. No matter how well a patient might have 'learnt his lesson as to speech, dress, and actions', James Shaw shrewdly observed in *The Physiognomy of Mental Diseases and Degeneracy* (1903), he would be unable to fake 'the facial colouring, the pallor or the flushing, the dry, harsh skin, the lack-lustre or glistening eye, or the infected conjunctivæ presented by the insane patient'.[62]

As this implies, physiognomists also appealed to a concern about the unreliability of language. The art of physiognomy worked 'notwithstanding all the dissimulation which artifice and artificial life heap upon him'. It was a 'language older than the builders of Babel'.[63] Deaf-mutes often celebrated this facility of physiognomy to tell the truth. As one poet put it in the 1890s,

Too much is made of speech alone; we show the wants we feel,
For signs as well as words can speak, and all the heart reveal . . .
You know the saying, 'Words are used when people seek to hide
Wrong thoughts that in their bosoms dwell', their jealousy, or pride.
But feelings, to the deaf and dumb, upon the face are shown;
The eyes are 'windows of the soul', and most folks' thoughts are known.
The born deaf-mutes will closely scan, and read a face as well
As if they from the cradle up had studied Sir Charles Bell.[64]

This awareness that people were liars was particularly strong in Lavater's work (in contrast, Bell argued that human facial musculature functioned to *allow* speech and thus human communication – ignoring often fraudulent uses). Lavater lamented 'the universality, and excess, of dissimulation, among mankind'. As he sadly observed, 'It is possible to carry out the art of dissimulation to an astonishing degree of excess; and by this art the most discerning man may be amazingly deceived.' The face, therefore, promised to bypass the human tendency to lie. Emmanuel Levinas noted in *Entre Nous: On Thinking-of-the-Other* that the 'nakedness of the face is not a figure of speech'.[65]

Given Lavater's dismissive attitude toward women, it comes as no surprise to hear him lambasting them as the chief offenders. It was 'undoubtedly true', Lavater asserted, that women 'are what they are only through men; or, rather, that they assume, in the presence of men, the character which they think most proper to be assumed'.[66] Thankfully, though, there were 'many features, or parts of the body, which are not susceptible of dissimulation; and, indeed, such features as are indubitable marks of internal character'. Even in women, Lavater gloated, there were 'certain firm, unchangeable, undisguisable features, tokens of the internal basis of their character, in which the physiognomist will not easily be deceived'. So long as physiognomists focused upon the 'grand outline and form of the countenance, we shall not greatly err', since it was 'only the moveable features are within the influence of dissimulations'.[67] A person was incapable of altering the 'conformation of his bones, according to his pleasure', Lavater insisted, rhetorically asking,

Can man give himself, instead of a flat [forehead], a bold and arched forehead; or a sharp indented forehead, when nature has given him one arched and round? . . . Can any [person] fashion the fat and short into the well-proportioned and beautiful nose?[68]

Lavater's point would, of course, be demolished with the rise of cosmetic surgery – but that revolution in dissimulation would occur a century after his death.

The ability to 'read faces' accurately, using physiognomic principles, was a reassuring science both within a masculine culture suspicious of women (especially as make-up was increasingly being used by respectable women, and not just those with questionable reputations) as well as within a broader culture affected by the movement of populations within urbanized societies. The tenet that the face never deceived was heartening. As one physiognomist stated, the eyes were the

> chosen abode of the soul ... When our stock of expressions are exhausted, we have recourse to the silent eloquence of the eyes, which, freed from the shackles of grammatical rules, express with one look, what numerous and complicated sentences would have failed to unfold ... They never can betray truth.[69]

More important, though, physiognomy was able to fuse the exciting but risqué reputation of modern science with religious piety. Lavater and Bell were adamant about the scientific nature of their work, while being equally insistent that the human face mirrored that of the Divinity. In Lavater's words, the face was the 'noblest of all the works of the Creator'.[70] Physiognomy was a narcissistic science, loudly proclaiming its admiration for the human species. As Lavater breathlessly declared,

> How exaltedly, how exclusively, honorable to man! Contemplate his exterior; erect, towering, and beauteous ... How does the present though concealed Deity speak, in his human countenance, with a thousand tongues! ... thus the Godhead darkly pourtrays [sic] itself in a rude earthly form ... Survey this soul-beaming, this divine, countenance; the thoughtful brow, the penetrating eye, the spirit breathing lips, the deep intelligence of the assembled features! How they all conspiring speak! What harmony! ... And there he stands in all his divinity![71]

Philosophy and piety, the worship of man and God, were in perfect harmony.

In addition, physiognomy survived so long (it remains popular) because it promised health, wealth and happiness, and at such little economic cost. Thus, late twentieth- and twenty-first-century physiognomic textbooks sport titles such as *Reading People. Secret Tips That Reveal the Truth Behind Body Language* (1998), *Simply Face Reading* (2005), *Secrets of Face Reading. Understanding Your Health and Relationships* (2008), and *Reading the Face. Understanding a Person's Character Through Physiognomy. A Spiritual-Scientific Study* (2008). It turned out to be an immensely flexible art, effortlessly shifting its language to suit prevalent societal concerns.

Finally, in the revolution inspired by evolutionary approaches from the late nineteenth century, physiognomy successfully made the transition from arguments based on design to those based on materialist understandings of the body. As we shall see in the next chapter, arguments based on Natural Theology were being supplanted by those based on Darwinian evolution. Although there was severe opposition to Darwinian ideas in many circles, most physiognomists were able to make the transition relatively easily. As one proponent calmly asserted at the end of the 1880s, in the past, physiognomy had been understood to be part of the Divine plan but now the 'argument of design is . . . superseded by the principle of evolution; the mind and body developed together'.[72] Physiognomy was a flexible science. Lavater and Bell would have turned in their graves but their successors accommodated secular knowledges drawn from evolution of the face and body as easily as their forefathers had espoused Natural Theology.

CHAPTER TWELVE

Darwinian Revolutions

O nly humans truly possessed faces, according to Lavater and Bell. Bobby the dog was an inferior creature, in large part because his facial muscles and tissue were incapable of subtle expressions and speech. Unfortunately, in that great Chain of Being, it was possible to identify lesser humans or people who were decidedly closer to the animal than to God's true creations. A designing Godhead, and the moral claims that being created in *this* and not *that* way was central to physiognomic thought. Although many of Lavater's and Bell's successors wove secular, racial sciences into the art of physiognomy, the theological knowledges underpinning their categorization of what it means to be human continued to be influential throughout the nineteenth century. In the 1870s, however, the most influential scientist of the century – Charles Darwin – changed everything.

Darwin and Evolution

Darwin's *The Expression of the Emotions in Man and Animals* (1872) was published thirteen years after *The Origin of Species*, and he intended it to be read by a wide audience. Like the publications of Lavater and Bell, Darwin's book was a best-seller.[1] There was a vast gulf between the work of Darwin and his predecessors, however. Darwin sneered at the popularization of physiognomy (it did, after all, almost wreck his chance of boarding HMS *Beagle*) and he disagreed with its fundamental premise. A designing Creator would have no place in Darwin's humanist science. Darwin also shifted the debate from the physiognomic meaning of *expressions* to physiological explanations of *emotions*.

Contrary to the Natural Theologians, Darwin argued that emotional behaviour and facial expressions were not unique to humans. Did Darwinian dogs have faces, then? Darwin noted that 'dogs understand expression on man's face'[2] and, more significantly, they could have faces that were more expressive than those of humans. Mere humans, he stated, were incapable of expressing 'love and humility by external signs so plainly as does a dog, when with drooping ears, hanging lips, flexuous body, wagging tail, he meets his beloved master'.[3] Darwin most probably had his beloved terrier Polly in mind: in fact, Polly's photograph was included in the original edition of *The Expression of the Emotions in Man and Animals* 'as an example of the stance dogs often adopt when their attention is roused'.[4] The observation that animals possessed expressive faces was a direct refutation of Bell's belief that the Creator had designed facial muscles specifically for human communication. As Darwin wryly remarked,

> But the simple fact that the anthropoid apes possess the same facial muscles as we do, renders it very improbable that these muscles in our case serve exclusively for expression; for no one, I presume, would be inclined to admit that monkeys have been endowed with special muscles solely for exhibiting their hideous grimaces.[5]

For Darwin, then, the expression of emotions was universal in humans and animals, and so he sought to link *particular* expressions with *particular* emotions. He concluded that expressions were the outcome of three 'principles'. The first was 'serviceable habits', or the idea that an expression that served as a form of communication or signal would eventually become habitual. For instance, if an expression helped to gratify some desire or relieve some sensation, the movement would continue even in situations where the same desire or sensation was extremely weak and thus the movement was no longer 'serviceable'. This helped explain why, when people witnessed a 'horrid sight', they would 'often shut their eyes momentarily and firmly, or shake their heads, as if not to see or drive away something'.[6] The motion was an inherited tendency: in the long-distant past the movement served a 'definite end' but now the expression was simply performed as a kind of habit since it was no longer of any use to the organism.[7]

The second principle was that of 'antithesis':

When a directly opposite state of mind is induced to those serviceable movements, there is a strong and involuntary tendency to the performance of movements of a directly opposite nature, though these are of no use, and such movements are in some cases highly expressive.

For example, when Polly approached another animal or human whom she considered hostile, she lifted her body as she walked, her hair bristled and her ears became rigid. Her teeth might even be bared and her eyes fixed. In contrast, the moment Polly discovered that the person was a friend, 'completely and instantaneously' her whole stance was reversed: her body sank down, her tail was lowered and moved back and forth, her lips and ears hung loose, and her hair became smooth (see Figure 1). Darwin observed that

> Not one of the above movements, so clearly expressive of affection, are of the least direct service to the animal. They are explicable . . . solely from being in complete opposition or antithesis to the attitude and movements which . . . are assumed when the dog intends to fight.[8]

It was not possible to believe that dogs, or indeed humans, would have 'deliberately thought' of adopting these friendly expressions and

Figure 1. The emotions of dogs, as revealed by their face and posture, published in Charles Darwin, *The Expression of the Emotions in Man and Animals.*
Alamy

gestures because they knew that these movements 'stood in direct opposition to those assumed under an opposite and savage frame of mind'.[9] The movements were innate.

The third principle was related to the constitution of the nervous system. When an animal or person was in intense pain, for instance, they gnashed their teeth or perspired profusely. Angry people were incapable of preventing their hearts beating wildly, their chests heaving and their nostrils quivering.[10] These expressions were shared by humans and animals and had nothing to do with learning or imitation, will or habit.

How different was Darwin's interpretation of the face, and what does that tell us about his construction of what it means to be human? Like physiognomists, Darwin believed that facial expressions revealed a truth that was impossible to totally conceal. As he observed in one of his notebooks,

> Seeing how ancient these expressions are, it is no wonder that they are so difficult to conceal. – a man insulted may forgive his enemy & not wish to strike him, but he will find it far more difficult to look tranquil. – He may despise a man & say nothing, but without a most distinct will, he will find it hard to keep his lip from stiffening over his canine teeth.[11]

However, at a more important level, Darwin's three principles were radical refutations of earlier views, and they significantly blurred the distinction between humans and the rest of the animal world.

The immediate ethical implications of Darwinian insights were not as revolutionary. After all, he was certainly not the first to posit human origins in the animal world. James Burnett (Lord Monboddo) had done so in *On the Origin and Progress of Language* (1773–92) and Erasmus Darwin (Charles's grandfather) in *Zoönomia* (1794–96). More to the point, narrowing the species barrier did not necessarily translate into any sense of equality between humans and animals, nor did it necessarily encourage notions of animal rights or even guardianship.[12] Darwin was not totally opposed to vivisection, for instance, believing that it might be necessary in the pursuit of scientific knowledge. In fact, as historian Rod Preece has shown, in the late nineteenth century, Darwinism was more likely to be read as *affirming* the great Chain of Being, with humans at its pinnacle.[13] Darwin had, indeed, shown that humans were more highly evolved than the other animals.

Furthermore, some humans were demonstrably more highly evolved than others. In *The Descent of Man* (1871), written a year before his book on the expressions, Darwin placed the 'barbarous races of mankind' and 'microcephalous idiots' in the same category as monkeys (all three shared a tendency to imitate other creatures, he observed).[14] In his notebook of 1838, Darwin had gone even further, writing,

> Let Man visit Ourang-outang in domestication, hear expressive whine, see its intelligence when spoken [to]; as if it understood every word said – see its affection. – to those it knew. – see its passion & rage, sulkiness, & very actions of despair; let him look at savage, roasting his parent, naked, artless, not improving yet improvable & let him dare to boast of his proud preeminence. – not understanding language of Fuegian, puts on par with Monkeys.[15]

James Watson, a leading Darwin scholar, hypothesized that it was Darwin's meeting with native Fuegians in Tierra del Fuego that made him interested in emotional expressions in the first place: Darwin believed that the 'very signs and expressions' of these people were 'less intelligible to us than those of the domesticated animals'.[16] Even Darwin's critics recognized that Darwin's evolutionary principles could be used to defend human inequality and servitude, with one observing that,

> If man is only a developed ape – What becomes of the Democratic doctrine of the 'equality of mankind?' To be consistent, we must believe in cast, believe that a noble is superior to a peasant, a white man to a negro; just as a thoroughbred is superior to a common cart horse.[17]

With the rise of Social Darwinism, the potentials for using Darwin's science to radically arrange humans along a continuum that went from sub-human, to lesser human, to fully human dramatically increased. Later, this was twisted into two of the most destructive ideas of the twentieth century: imperialist expansionism and Nazism.

Opposition to Darwinian Evolution

Darwinian physiology did more than simply threaten late-nineteenth-century attempts to distinguish 'man' from 'beast': it also denied the belief that humans had been created in the image of God. An anonymous review of Darwin's *The Expression of the Emotions in Man and*

Animals, published in the *Edinburgh Review* in 1872, presented the main criticisms of Darwin's theory, albeit more eloquently than most. We now know that its author was Thomas Spencer Baynes, Professor of Logic and English Literature at St Andrews University.[18]

Baynes began by noting that the book was of 'profoundest disappoint-ment' since Darwin concentrated on the 'lower and more animal' aspects of emotions and seemed 'unwilling to admit that an expression is human at all, unless he can verify its existence in some of the lower animals'. Humanity's 'higher mental powers' were 'passed over'. Moreover, the

> very limited expressive element in the countenances and gestures of animals is habitually overstated, while the enormously higher power of expression possessed by man is systematically understated.

Indeed, Baynes sneered, the 'extent to which Mr Darwin persistently reads his own theory into the ambiguous muscular twitches and spasms of monkeys and other animals is often amusing in a high degree'. Unforgivably, Darwin omitted 'any reference to soul or mind, to rational order, foresight, and adaptation . . . moral order, ordained purpose, formal or final causes in nature'. Darwin's crime was simple: he 'degrades and vulgarizes' human emotion.

Baynes's attack was deeply personal: he criticized Darwin for eschewing theological thought, while simultaneously spawning a sect-like fellowship of likeminded humanists. Darwin 'boldly employs the unverified hypothesis' with

> all the confidence of a theological disputant applying some dogmatic assumption, such as universal depravity or satanic influence, or defending some sectarian symbol, such as Sacramental Efficacy or an Effectual Call.*

Darwin's over-zealous adherents possessed 'facile minds'. They paraded their passion for 'novelty and notoriety' and immaturely wallowed in that 'exhilarating sense of freedom and independence in adopting advanced views . . . against the alarmed remonstrances of acquaintances and friends'. Towards opponents, Darwinians showed 'intolerance'.

Having attacked Darwin's science and sectarian enthusiasm, Baynes

---

* A call by the Holy Spirit that not only invites sinners to salvation, but actually brings them to it.

then turned to his choice of sources. Darwin's evidence had been drawn from observing infants, animals, the 'ruder and more savage races', the insane, people whose facial muscles had been 'galvanized' (made to move through the application of electricity) and images of faces in paintings and sculpture. With the exception of this last category, Baynes pointed out, all other sources were incapable of illustrating anything other than the 'simpler, ruder, and more violent forms of passion'. Indeed, Baynes questioned whether animals possessed emotions at all: were animals 'not always moved by bodily appetites, passions, and desires rather than by purely mental causes and antecedents', he asked. It was a question that was heavily debated at the time. Did animals possess emotions; could they even feel pain? According to Baynes, the only source that would have been of use in interpreting the 'mysteries of human passion' – art – was the one source that Darwin had dismissed as relatively unhelpful.

Prioritizing the emotional expressions of animals and 'savage races' over those revealed in art was ridiculous, Baynes exclaimed. On this point, he sided with Bell, insisting that human expressions of emotion were endowed with 'progressive intelligence' and were integral to what it meant to be human. Human facial expressions were a 'universal language' that 'overrides all local dialects' and was 'universally intelligible alike to the savage and the civilized'. Indeed, it was superior to speech. Facial expressions were not only 'more rapid and direct', they were also 'the truest and most authentic index of emotion – more delicate, diversified, and instantaneous than any other'. By trying to 'extract reason and conscience out of animal elements', Darwin was 'little better than a physiological alchemist', and his discoveries were 'just as barren as those of his chemical predecessors, traditionally connected with the darkest ages and the blackest arts'. With devastating wit, Baynes conjured up an image of Darwin

bending over his slow metaphysical fire mingling animal ingredients in the favourite crucible of natural selection and sexual variation, and announcing with an air of absolute confidence and triumph the anticipated result. He evidently thinks that he has at length secured the 'drop profound', the proto-plasmic globule, which, under skilful distillation, may be evolved, not only into the panorama of animated nature, but into the long phantasmagorial procession of the different races and generations of men. But like the drop profound caught by the witches in its fall from the corner of the moon, and distilled with unholy rites in their seething cauldron, it simply leads on the eager inquirer into the mysteries of nature to his own confusion. The pursuit is a hopeless one . . . The *elixir rationis* is not thus to be obtained.[19]

Even Darwin was forced into grudging praise, describing the review as 'magnificently contemptuous towards myself and many others'.[20]

Darwinian Faces

Darwin's work on the emotions allowed his imitators and disciples to admit that, yes, a dog does have a face, and one that was subject to the same laws of nature as human faces. It also allowed for discrimination between various groups of humans, and therefore prescribing rules of conduct. The two most obvious categories were gender and ethnicity.

Women's facial expressions were routinely portrayed as closer to those of monkeys than those of male humans. As the author of 'Our Simian Cousins' (1895) noted, the expression of surprise was registered on the faces of both humans and monkeys by 'raising the eyebrows, opening wide the eyes, and showing more or less of the whites', but this habit could be observed 'more in women than in men'. Women, this author believed, also shared with monkeys a certain proneness to pout.[21] In more general terms, a poet in the late 1880s admitted that 'the trace of the ape' could be observed over the entire 'poor race of man', but 'women's charms' more than any other were simply 'developed beauties of the baboon!'[22]

Unlike baboons, however, women were particularly prone to dissimulation, thus making reading their faces more difficult than reading the faces of other animals, including male humans. This concern was expressed most wittily in a poem published in the broadsheet *Fun*, in the year that Darwin's *The Expression of the Emotions in Man and Animals* was released. The author of 'The Emotions' had clearly just read Darwin's book, referring to a 'famous lecturer on apes' who devoted his 'frolicsome imagination' to studying emotions and 'their Expression, by the features / Or other lineaments of living creatures!' But Darwin faced a problem, the poet continued, when attempting to analyse the facial expressions of women:

> But, ah, my DARWIN, does it not perplex,
> Puzzle and vex,
> To trace, with even your intense devotion,
> The various expressions of emotion

Employed by what we call the gentle sex?
We think we see a blush –
Why, tush!
'Tis but a flush
Obtained with powder and a brush,
Or coloured lotion!
And so we fail to trace
In woman's face
The real, plain expression of Emotion![23]

In other words, the 'famous lecturer on apes' believed that emotional
expressions could be read from the 'lineaments' of the face and body of
animals, but if he turned to the 'gentle sex' he should be 'perplexed,

THAT TROUBLES OUR MONKEY AGAIN.

Figure 2. 'That Troubles Our Monkey Again'. Darwin's head on a monkey's
body, being admonished by a female descendant of a marine ascidian (a
primitive invertebrate organism, commonly known as a 'sea squirt'). It
was published in *Fun* (16 November 1872). The original caption reads:
Female descendant of Marine Ascidian '—Really, Mr Darwin, say what you like
about man; but I wish you would leave my emotions alone!'
British Library

puzzled and vexed' because 'powder and a brush or coloured lotion' rendered it impossible to trace a woman's emotion. (See Figure 2 for the cartoon accompanying this poem).

These comments were light-hearted and, while they represent a subtle denigration of the 'gentle sex', they were scarcely malicious. Not so when facial architecture was discussed in 'racial' terms. It was typical to assume that evolutionary processes 'developed and humanized' the face. As it 'receded from the animal face and approaches a higher form, it became the index of the human soul'.[24] Certain people, however, were regarded as less highly evolved than others: they had defective, inferior 'human souls'.

In some cases, anatomists went so far as to argue that by dissecting the facial muscles of white Americans and African-Americans they could provide indisputable proof that the latter were developmentally closer to apes than they were to white Americans. Notoriously, Ernst Huber, Associate Professor of Anatomy at Johns Hopkins University and author of *Evolution of Facial Musculature and Facial Expression* (1931), claimed that the facial muscles of African-Americans were 'much coarser', 'darker in colour' and 'more powerfully developed' in comparison to those of white Americans.[25] While white Americans had 'responsive faces' capable of serving as 'an admirable index of character or mental state', African-American faces lacked this capability. Their 'thick skin', densely graded nerve impulses and 'less differentiated, coarsely bundled mimetic musculature' rendered them incapable of expressing sensitive or 'civilised' emotions. Huber's sketches (see Figure 3) show typical 'Negro' and 'White' facial musculature.

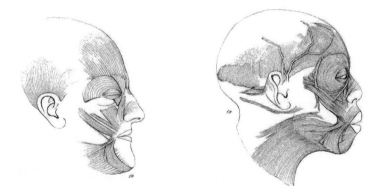

Figure 3. Ernst Huber's 'Adult Male White' and 'Adult American Negro' in his *Evolution of Facial Musculature and Facial Expression*.

Huber, *Evolution of Facial Musculature and Facial Expression*

Huber went even further, claiming that the inability of the muscles in African-American faces to *express* particular emotions meant that they were incapable of *possessing* these emotions. He believed that 'the elaboration of facial expression during the phylogeny of man closely followed the evolution of emotional life'. African-Americans were thus portrayed as possessing basic emotions such as fear, but not more civilized emotional states such as noble reflection.[26] It was precisely such legacies of Darwin that have tarnished evolutionary theory for many non-scientists.

CHAPTER THIRTEEN

Surgical Sciences

Physiognomists and Darwinians reserved a special role for the face in defining human/animal identity. Their rules and techniques for 'reading' faces assumed the existence of a personal identity or self that was somehow natural or intrinsic to the particular life form, on the grounds that it was created by an omnipotent Deity or was the result of evolutionary forces. To a greater or lesser extent, this self was malleable through education (intellectual and moral) and the invisible yet relentless civilizing process. In all cases, though, the perceived status of the face dictated an ethical response from the viewer: the answer to the question of whether a dog, a Fuegian or an Englishwoman truly possesses a face has enormous consequences for that dog, Fuegian and Englishwoman.

Increasingly, however, more blunt ways of ensuring that people making those judgements 'got it right' were devised. Knives and needles became quick-fix devices to ensure that the exterior mask, with all its imperfections, accurately mirrored the beautiful, eternally young, inner self. While Lavater, Bell and Darwin trusted the face because it resisted dissimulation, cosmetic surgery undercut such fancies. In the late eighteenth century, Lavater had intended his question, 'Can any [person] fashion the flat and short into the well-proportioned and beautiful nose?', to be nothing more than rhetorical.[1] In the twentieth century, things were not so certain. Furthermore – and ironically – while cosmetic surgery seemed to imply that the face and its expressions were amazingly malleable, in fact it represented the most extreme form of essentialism that we have explored so far. In the words of an article published in *Clinics in Plastic Surgery* (1995), the face is the vanguard of our aging process, the herald of our fleeting nature. When, as so frequently happens, the inner self remains young and strong while the outer surface is aged, the disparity leads some to seek some form of correction. We as plastic surgeons have taken the role of camouflaging these outer changes, seeking to close the disparity between surface and soul.[2]

Surgery was the instrument for imposing that inner, essential self on a corrupt, crumbling exterior.

Cosmetic Surgery and Physiognomics

Classical ideals and ways of thinking about 'the human' were always part of plastic surgery as a modern craft. Textbooks on cosmetic or aesthetic surgery routinely included images of famous Ancient Greek faces and bodies.[3] As historian Ana Carden-Coyne has persuasively demonstrated in *Reconstructing the Body: Classicism, Modernism, and the First World War* (2009), reconstructive surgeons during and after the First World War were obsessed with the beauty and symmetry of classical forms. They saw themselves as artists, working with living flesh instead of clay. The pioneering plastic surgeon Sir Harold Gilles (who was a painter as well as a surgeon) hoped that at some time in the future his 'strange new art' might actually be able to chisel the faces of men who had been disfigured into forms traditionally reserved for Greek gods. When facial reconstruction failed, the disfigured were given masks of painted tin made by artists. At the 'Tin Noses Shop' – as the Masks for Facial Disfigurement Department at the Third London General Hospital came to be called – the sculptor Francis Derwent Wood admitted that his work began the moment surgeons admitted defeat. His classical training was of greatest help to him. Inspired by the statutes of Apollo, Praxiteles' Hermes and Polycleitos' Doryphoros, Wood went on to design the male nude in the Machine Gun Corps Memorial in Hyde Park (see Figure 1).

After the war, the techniques used to reconstruct the faces of seriously mutilated men were applied to more mundane, cosmetic concerns. By the twenty-first century it had become a leading industry. In 2002, members of the British Association of Aesthetic Plastic Surgeons were carrying out over 10,700 procedures per year. Within five years, this had trebled to over 32,000.[4] A survey for *Grazia* magazine in 2005 showed that more than half of British women expected to

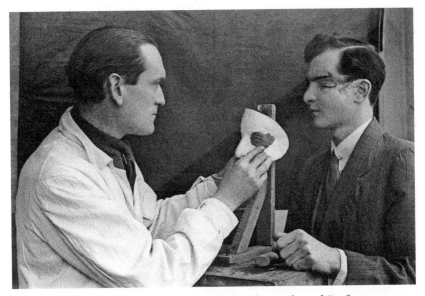

Figure 1. Captain Francis Derwent Wood in the Masks and Disfigurement Department of the Third London General Hospital. He is putting the finishing touches to a cosmetic plate and compares it to the face of a patient. Wood was a sculptor who enlisted in the Royal Army Medical Corps in 1915. At the end of the war, he was appointed Professor of Sculpture at the Royal College of Art.

IWM Q030456

have cosmetic surgery.[5] In the United States, over $9 billion is spent on cosmetic surgery annually.[6] On television, radical reconstructive surgical programmes proliferate, including *Extreme Makeover*, *The Swan*, *I Want A Famous Face*, *Plastic Surgery: Before and After*, *Plastic Surgery Beverly Hills*, *Dr 90210*, *Miami Slice*, *Ten Years Younger*, *Brand New You* and *Bride and Grooming*.

Within this prosperous industry, the classical heritage of physiognomy dominated. Camper's 'facial line' was updated, as were the physiognomics of Lavater and Bell.[7] As the editor of the *Annals of Plastic Surgery* admitted in 1979,

> Aesthetic plastic surgery is an art that must be cultivated. Although some individuals have inherited good taste and instinctively see, know, feel, and enjoy beauty, most need long exposure to art, architecture, music, and dance to create a working schema of beauty. To this end they must visit art collections, and museums.[8]

In this way, ideal forms of beauty would be both consciously adopted and unconsciously absorbed by surgeons, keen to re-forge the human in the image of European, classical sculpture.

While the beauty myths propagated by men like Lavater and Bell directed the movement of the scalpel against skin and tissue, cosmetic surgery was premised around pressures to be successful in the 'workplace, politics, and marriage' (as contemporary evolutionary psychologist Paul Ekman put it).[9] As the editor of the *Annals of Plastic Surgery* in 1979 reminded his fellow surgeons, 'beauty has importance, for just as Mars kneels before Venus, power and wealth kneel before beauty'.[10] Indeed, innumerable surveys have shown that most people believed that 'looking good' was a main route to advancement.[11] The 'search for beauty . . . guided the advance of humanity'.[12]

The beautiful human (and later in this chapter I will explore surgical constructions of the beautiful non-human animal) was first judged by the contours and texture of her face. Nineteenth-century surgery was concerned primarily with removing evidence of social disgrace. For example, in 1887 the *Medical Record* distinguished between Roman, Greek, Jewish, snub and celestial noses. Roman noses indicated strength; Greek noses, refinement; snub (or pug) noses, 'weakness and lack of development'. Since snub noses could be an indication of syphilis (causing the nasal bridge to collapse), it could be corrected, the author promised, by 'a Simple Operation'.[13]

In the twentieth century, facial symmetry took pride of place as unambiguous evidence of a person's wellbeing and reproductive potential. Facial symmetry (in the words of a typical book on the psychological aspects of cosmetic surgery) was evidence of 'pathogen resistance' since 'the ability to develop symmetrically in environmentally harsh conditions will be conferred upon only the healthiest and hardiest of a given population'.[14] The effect of hormones on the face provided another important marker. As the authors of a chapter in *Psychological Aspects of Reconstructive and Cosmetic Plastic Surgery* (2006) explained, the contours of the face were affected, at puberty, by levels of oestrogen and testosterone. In women, oestrogen was associated with the development of prominent cheekbones while, in men, testosterone contributed to the development of the eyebrow ridges as well as the cheekbones.[15] These facial 'markers' attracted sexual mates. If not given 'naturally', or if processes of aging had eradicated the precision of the sign, they could be artificially crafted. As one cosmetic surgeon quipped, facial surgery 'can turn an eyesore into an eyeful. It can turn someone's glance into a gaze.'[16]

Clearly, such thinking demands a radically different face-to-face ethic to that assumed by the scientists of the previous two chapters. Rather than the face being an accurate reflection of the inner self, cosmetic surgery was premised on the assumption that the external representation of the self was somehow distorted: surgery was required to ensure that there was a correct match between the interior and the exterior. Partners, employers and acquaintances risked being fooled by a person's exterior; surgery could set matters right. The face was a commodity. The body was not 'natural', but required 'upgrading' by specialists. There was no such thing as a 'natural' human visage: mismatched interior and exterior selves were an unfortunate part of the human condition.

Excising 'Race'

In one area, however, cosmetic surgeons conformed to the human ideal of previous chapters. Like the other sciences, cosmetic surgery is highly 'raced'. This is most blatantly revealed in the context of surgical practices that seek to make non-white European faces more closely resemble the classical ideal. 'Ethnic cosmetic surgery' is popular, most notoriously including such practices as nose reductions among Jews and Italians.[17] As the author of an article in *Plastic and Reconstructive Surgery* put it in 2003, surgery on the noses of African-American women could correct for where the nose 'deviates from the accepted norm'.[18]

One of the most common examples, though, is the restructuring of the eyelids of Asian women.[19] During 'double-eyelid' surgery, a fold of skin is excised from the upper eyelids to create a crease above each eye. The surgery tells us a lot about status gradations of the human face (see Figure 2).[20] After all, although between one-third and a half of people in Asia have a naturally occurring eyelid crease, it is generally said that the highly sought-after crease is 'European'.[21]

What was the rationale for such a sensitive surgical procedure? The authors of *Cosmetic Surgery of the Asian Face* (1990) claimed that 'traditional Asian cultures' have

a tendency to place great significance on physiognomy that is the relationship of physical traits and characteristics to behavior and personality as well as to prospects for success in business, friendship, marriage, and other relationships.[22]

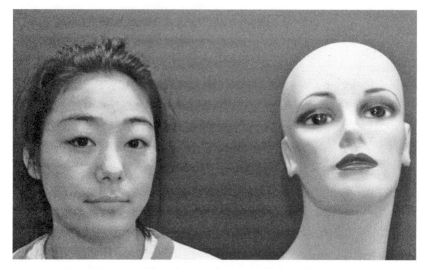

Figure 2. A '19-year-old girl [sic] of Korean descent' who arrived at a cosmetic surgery clinic with a 'dummy model' in order to 'precisely explain her desires'. From Igor Niechajev and Per-Olle Haraldsson, 'Ethnic Profile of Patients Undergoing Aesthetic Rhinoplasty in Stockholm'.

Niechajev and Haraldsson, 'Ethnic Profile of Patients Undergoing Aesthetic Rhinoplasty in Stockholm', *Aesthetic Plastic Surgery* (1997)

Its proponents believed that the absence of the palpebral fold was responsible for producing the 'passive expression' that 'seems to epitomize the stoical and unemotional manner of the Oriental'.[23] To advance in a world that was economically and culturally dominated by the West, facial architecture and expression needed to conform to the dominant power. Asians could 'choose' to improve their prospects by facial resculpturing. Cosmetic surgery became a matter of personal choice rather than racism.

Cosmetic surgeons Richard Aronsohn and Richard Epstein elaborated such arguments in *The Miracle of Cosmetic Plastic Surgery* (1970). According to them, the eyelid of 'Orientals'

> hangs down like a thick curtain, obscuring the eyelid margin. This upper-lip droop conceals a portion of the iris, framing an expressionless eye peeking through a slit, an image that (mostly through fiction) has become associated with mystery, intrigue, and inscrutability.

They went further, arguing that oriental women chose to have the operation in order to satisfy their own esthetic preferences or those of their immediate peer group. Many Chinese, for example, tend to look derisively upon the 'mouse-like eye' (the mouse is not esteemed in Chinese culture) and girls with that feature can encounter romantic difficulties. More familiar to the West is the 'Cio-Cio-san' complex, wherein the pliable Oriental charmer [female] strives for further appeal in the eyes of her Occidental lover.

Who was their typical patient? They discussed the case of 'S. N.', an 'Oriental' who visited their surgery. The surgeons described this twenty-six-year-old married woman as a 'shy, reticent, introverted girl [sic]' who confessed that she wanted to 'be more beautiful'. She had met and married her American husband – a marine lieutenant – in Vietnam three years previously and moved with him to the United States. However,

> her husband's interest in her had declined to the point of rejection. He teased her about her eyes, telling her that she constantly looked sleepy. He had begun comparing her to American girls and she felt the comparison was now based on more than visual perception. The appearance that had been enticingly exotic in Vietnam had become obtrusively foreign on Main Street. To recapture her husband, she wished to have 'big, round, beautiful eyes like American girls'.

The surgeons did not leave their analysis at that point. They described the woman's eyes as 'puffed out with the fatty fullness of the upper lids . . . The typical Mongoloid "single eye"'. They then admitted that 'In the surgeon's judgment, her eyes, brimming with Oriental charm and gentle humility, reflected the simple elegance of a Haiku line'. They fretted that the operation 'might change a butterfly into a moth' but, nevertheless, agreed to operate 'in view of the patient's selfless sincerity'. Readers were not told of the final result, except that the surgery had the effect of 'alleviating the "flat" Mongoloid appearance'. Perhaps 'S. N.' is pictured in Figure 3, a photograph taken from the same pages in Aronsohn's and Epstein's book in which her case is discussed.[24] This was orientalism at its most racist.

Of course, all cosmetic surgery is 'ethnic'. In Britain and America it was always 'raced white': that is, 85 per cent of cosmetic surgery is performed on white-skinned patients.[25] Indeed, the popularity of facelifts among white women in the West can be seen as partly an

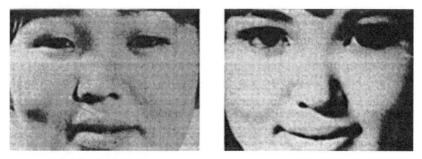

Figure 3. 'Blepharoplasty. Incision technique. Six months postoperative'.
Aronsohn and Epstein, *The Miracle of Cosmetic Plastic Surgery*

attempt to eradicate the effects of an ethnic inheritance that includes the fact that Europeans have thinner facial skin compared with many other 'racial' groups. The surgery always sought to conform to a particular norm of beauty, which, in Britain and the United States, generally meant an ideal drawn from so-called Caucasian models. As the journal *Clinics in Plastic Surgery* insisted in 1995, Agamemnon understood true human beauty: it was cheeks looking like 'roses in milk'.[26] Alas, cosmetic surgeons in journals as diverse as *Plastic and Reconstructive Surgery*, *Archives of Facial Plastic Surgery*, *Aesthetic Plastic Surgery* and *Annals of Plastic Surgery* lamented, the neoclassical face was not typical for *any* Americans, whether white, Asian or African.[27] The nineteen-year-old Korean woman who, in 1997, implored surgeons Niechajev and Haraldsson to make her resemble a 'dummy model' who had 'Occidental' features (see Figure 2) understood that American society valued *certain* human faces over others. Niechajev and Haraldsson actually advised her not to have the surgery, partly because of her unreasonable expectations. Becoming fully human is never going to happen, not for any of us.

Does the Dog Truly Have a Face?

In modern society, cosmetic surgeons have played a central role in drawing up hierarchies of humans. They have ranked humans from those exemplary ones whose faces most closely followed the contours of Greek art to those denied status on the grounds that they possessed a different – 'inferior' – balance of bone, muscle and blood.

However, surgical processes of grading and moulding faces were not only applied to members of *Homo sapiens*. Crucially, the question of 'who *truly* has a face?' has been applied to *all* sentient life forms in that twisting and turning Möbius strip of *zoe*.

To illustrate, let's ask just one question: for cosmetic surgeons, do dogs like Bobby have a face? Certainly, they have faces that are amenable to improvement through surgery. Cosmetic operations on the ears, lips, eyes and cheeks (do these 'parts' constitute a 'face'?) of animals such as dogs has a long history. In Britain and America, the ears of dogs were often cropped. The procedure was relatively simple, although gruesome for those of us unfamiliar with animal surgical practices. To crop the ears of terriers or bulldogs, the author of *Breeding, Training, Management, Diseases, &c. of Dogs* (1857) instructed,

> First . . . cut the top off one ear to the desired length; the piece taken off to be used as a measure, by which to cut the other top. When both tops are off, flatten the ear out with one hand and cut in a straight line from the base of the ear to the farthest point at the top, cutting of course both ears exactly alike. Do not cut too close in at the base, if you do not wish to subject the dog to great discomfort for the sake of fashion . . . Be careful to cut both ears exactly alike, or the beauty of the handsomest animal may be ruined for life.[28]

Increasingly, veterinary associations have become hostile to such operations, and they have been banned in many countries.

Nevertheless, there have been successful face transplants on animals (see Figure 4).[29] Dogs in Brazil are given facelifts and their ears are straightened with Metacril; some vets use Botox to fix inverted eyelashes.[30] These operations were explicitly compared to similar ones for humans. As with humans, the 'laws' of beauty and personality applied. Individual dogs, each with a unique visage, had to be made to resemble their 'true' breed's nature. The external face had to be made to conform to the internal 'natural' self (youthful representatives of a particular breed, or the dog equivalent of young, white neoclassical faces). With these assumptions in mind, the author of the *Atlas of Small Animal Reconstructive Surgery* (1999) followed a sentence proclaiming that 'most owners are aware of the advances in *human* cosmetic surgery' with one about their dogs. Just as people expected to be able to buy their improved humanity through cosmetic surgery, so too they 'expect a higher quality surgical "product" for the money spent on their pet. Owners naturally take great pride in their pets' appearance.'[31]

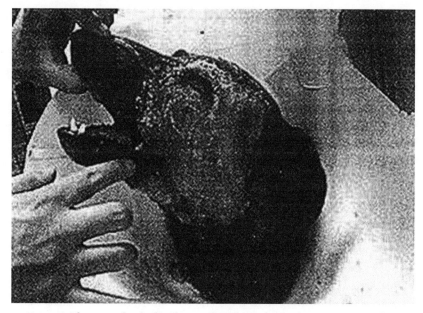

Figure 4. Photograph of a facial transplant from donor dog to recipient dog.
The accompanying text by surgeon Luis Eduardo Bermúdez reads: 'After
facial dissection in rats, rabbits, pigs and dogs, we found that the animal
with a facial vascular anatomy most similar to that of humans was the
dog . . . We performed a hemifacial transplant between two dogs to prove
the viability of a facial transplant . . . The procedure was performed with
the animals under general anesthetic in a veterinary operating room; strict
rules for experimental surgery in animals were followed. We obtained the
dogs from the municipality 10 days before the procedure, and they were
wormed and given nutritional support to improve their general condition
for the operation. The recipient dog received immunosuppressive therapy.'
Bermúdez described transferring the donor's face to that of the recipient,
after which the donor was 'killed by lethal injection while under general
anesthetic'. The dog 'was kept alive for seven days, and the flap perfused
normally for 5 days'. The dog was then killed. From Luis Eduardo
Bermúdez, 'Experimental Model of Facial Transplant'.

Bermúdez, 'Experimental Model of Facial Transplant', *Plastic and Reconstructive Surgery* (October 2002)

Physiognomic principles applied to both humans and animals, and surgery could provide where 'nature' failed.

W. D. Drury, writing in the late 1890s, also made explicit comparisons between cosmetic procedures on people and dogs. 'For every
defect in Nature,' he pointed out, 'we are taught to believe that Art
offers a remedy.' He compared the 'many little artifices that are

indulged in for the beautification of the human subject' with those of dogs. 'Who has not heard', he asked, of the fashionable methods

> for giving, may be the Fox Terrier, the orthodox carriage of ear? Cutting, boring, and weighing have been resorted to in the past to bring about the desired end – a close drop ear . . . As is fairly well known, the ears of the Fox Terrier should be small and well shaped, and, moreover, should drop closely to the head, and it is astonishing what a large percentage of these dogs one meets with that are defective in that respect.

He went on to describe techniques to 'drop' the ear, including 'severing the muscles by an ingenious cut in the inside, or by running a seton in the ear'.[32] It seems that terriers (like Darwin's beloved Polly) with ears that 'hang low' and 'wobble to and fro', needed cosmetic improvement to be true terriers.

Of course, it was often unnecessary to employ radical cosmetic procedures on animals because there was another way of achieving the same result: breeding. Unlike in human populations, where eugenic breeding has often (with some vicious exceptions) been rejected as dangerous, if not evil, in animals it is routine. Dog breeders routinely use genetic selection to obtain desirable facial traits: extremely long and narrow faces for Collies; short noses and bashed-in faces for English Bulldogs; rounded ears for Cardigan Welsh Corgis; pointed ears for Pembroke Welsh Corgis; and so on.[33] They also select to eradicate certain features – the 'large ears' of Fox Terriers, for instance, had to be 'got rid of', insisted the author of *The Breeding of Show Fox Terriers with a Gallery of the Celebrities in the Fox Terrier World* (1897).[34] As the author of a dog-breeding book in 1890 bragged, the 'judicious selection of parents can produce almost anything in the shape of dog-flesh'.[35] At dog shows, judges were encouraged to exclaim, 'What a sweet expression!'[36] This represented an extreme of anthropomorphism: the dog's face elevated to that of a mild-mannered child.

Conclusion to Part 4: Does a Dog Have a Face? Does a Human?

In the last paragraph, I mentioned that although eugenic breeding of *humans* has often been rejected as dangerous, there were some important exceptions. I was thinking, of course, about proposals to prevent certain humans from breeding. In Britain and America this has included attempts to limit or prevent reproduction by criminals, the poor and indigent, 'racial' minorities, the mentally or emotionally deviant, homosexuals and lesbians, and so on. However, some cosmetic surgeons were willing to apply animal breeding techniques to the human population, believing it would lead to a utopia more quickly. What would happen if 'ugliness' was outlawed, for instance? The potential of cosmetic breeding to transform what it means to have a human face was spelt out by Aronsohn and Epstein in *The Miracle of Cosmetic Plastic Surgery* (1970). In the final chapter of their book, 'Future – The Shape of Things to Come', they observed that a 'different attitude toward medical ethics will lead to a different attitude toward the quality of being human'. Through selective breeding, it would be possible to 'produce a race of esthetic people with little more difficulty than that needed to produce cows that yield more milk or horses that run faster'. They modestly admitted that the main problem for this scheme would be the 'lack of agreement on the desired attributes of a superior being'. Given that the title of their book was *The Miracle of Cosmetic Plastic Surgery*, readers might wonder what selective breeding had to do with this miraculous (and lucrative) profession. After all, the authors acknowledged, if ugliness was 'bred out of the population', then cosmetic surgery would become 'superfluous'. But would it? As with dogs, so too with humans: no matter how intricate the breeding, 'nature' makes mistakes. Cosmetic surgeons would always be present to make human faces more human. Aronsohn and Epstein imagined

> a future society where ugliness is deemed an affront to the eyes punishable by solitary incarceration. Billboards in that fanciful future will exhort the motorist:
> KEEP AMERICA BEAUTIFUL
> VISIT YOUR LOCAL PLASTIC SURGEON.[1]

The ethics of the face-to-face encounter just took another nasty turn.

The final chapter of the *Miracle of Cosmetic Plastic Surgery* imagined a utopia where ugliness-of-face would be a crime worthy of 'solitary incarceration'. In the introductory chapter to Part 4 of this book (Chapter Ten), Emmanuel Levinas personally experienced the result of such eugenic ways of thinking (although multiplied a great many times over) when he found himself enslaved during the Holocaust. At that time, it was Jewishness or membership of a number of other denigrated human groups (rather than mere ugliness of visage) that relegated people to 'solitary incarceration' or worse. This was what inspired Levinas to expound a philosophy in which the ethical response to face-to-face encounters would have no reality in (human) biology. He dreamt of a world in which people would transcend the corporeality of the face. Unfortunately, although Bobby the dog inspired his reflections by being the only living creature who recognized him and his fellow slaves as truly human, Levinas remained unclear about whether Bobby himself truly possessed a face.[2] For all his brilliance in writing about his encounter with Bobby, Levinas remained a humanist.

In that chapter, I also implied that an interesting debate could take place if philosophers, dogs and slaves came face to face. Unfortunately, slaves have been too silent in the last three chapters. But, let's remedy this oversight in some concluding words. And what better place to start than with the encounter between slaves and another dog called Bobby, who also happened to be a terrier (like Darwin's dog, immortalized for her facial expressivity)?

More than 170 years before Levinas wrote about his encounter with Bobby, another dog named Bobby (his name had been shortened to just Bob) could be heard musing over the question of 'who is human?' His reflections were published in *The Dog of Knowledge; or, Memoirs of Bob, the Spotted Terrier: Supposed to be Written by Himself* (1801). Unlike the Bobby that Levinas met, this Bob was not a real dog; he was a phantasm

against which human persons could be judged and found wanting.
However, like the real-dog Bobby, this fictional American dog also
acknowledged that slaves were human. He had been taken to a
Caribbean island, where he had encountered some slaves. Bob was
relieved that he had been 'born a dog, and not a Negro, as these poor
creatures are called', and over whom certain humans could 'tyran-
nize . . . without compunction'. The slaves 'had not the complexion of
Europeans, and perhaps possessed none of the same delicate sensibilities', Bob ruminated, 'yet they walked on two legs like the rest of the
species, and seemed to me to differ in nothing but the colour of their
skin and the contour of their face'. Was there some 'fallacy in appearances' that meant that these men were 'born to subjection, the same as
dogs or horses'?[3] Both dogs – Bobby and Bob – turn out to be 'true
Kantians', that is, creatures who recognized that humans are entitled to
be treated as 'ends in themselves', not simply as 'means to an end'.[4]

Unfortunately, the views of dogs are not generally respected. A
'fallacy in appearances' (Bob's phrase) has 'dogged' science and many
popular views in the West. What the spotted terrier Bob recognized in
his 1801 memoir was radical. What Bob's scribe did not mention was
that, at the same time his story was being written, slaves in Haiti were
fighting a war to overturn their enslavement. They succeeded in 1802,
but popular opinion in the West continued (and continues) to denigrate
the Haitian face. The Haitian is defaced as contorted by some inexpli-
cable voodoo mania, ravaged by poverty and (in recent decades) Aids,
and dehumanized by secret poisons that render the human nothing
more than a zombie. These zombies retained a human physiology yet
the evidence of their vacant faces showed that they had been stripped
of any human 'essence' or soul.

This latter characterization of the Haitian face can be illustrated by
exploring the immensely influential writings of American adventurer
William Buehler Seabrook. In *The Magic Island* (1929), Seabrook's
account of travels in Haiti, he observed certain strange, beast-like men
toiling in the cane fields near Gonâve, as African slaves had done under
French whips prior to 1802 and as Haitian labourers continued to do
almost a century later, in 'The Black Demons of Hayti' (this is discussed
in the following chapter). Seabrook recalled that there was something
'unnatural and strange' about these workers, as they 'plodded like
brutes', chopping at the cane with their machetes and dragging the
stalks to the pile a few hundred yards further up the stony slope. When
Seabrook's Haitian guide motioned to one of them to look at them,

Seabrook found himself staring into the eyes of a creature that resembled 'an animal'. 'The eyes were the worst', he wrote, insisting that

> It was not my imagination. They were in truth like the eyes of a dead man, not blind, but staring, unfocused, unseeing. The whole face, for that matter, was bad enough. It was vacant, as if there was nothing behind it.

Like some of the scientists in the previous pages who believed that animals did not have true faces and were thus incapable of expression, Seabrook concluded that the faces of these workers 'seemed not only expressionless, but incapable of expression'. He admitted experiencing

> a sickening, almost panicky lapse in which I thought, or rather felt, 'Great God, maybe this stuff is really true, and if it is true, it is rather awful, for it upsets everything'. By 'everything' I meant the natural fixed laws and processes on which all modern human thought and actions are based.

If, as Levinas would have us believe, the human is the being that possesses a 'face' and all ethics is a response to face-to-face contacts, then Seabrook's horror may be seen as an attempt to grapple with the question: are humans rendered zombies no longer human? Were they beyond humanity, mere beasts, slaves, without truly human faces?

Seabrook's viciously racist assumptions about Haitians led him to other conclusions. A zombie, he observed, was a man who had been reduced to nothing more than 'an animal', possessing a face that was 'incapable of expression'. Such a creature possessed

> the face of a dog I had once seen in the histological laboratory at Columbia. Its entire front brain had been removed in an experimental operation weeks before; it moved about, it was alive, but its eyes were like the eyes I now saw staring.

In other words, these Haitian workers not only had the faces of dogs but, because of their inferior visages, they were legitimate subjects for vivisection. It was, he went on to say, a connection that his mind 'seized . . . as a man sinking in water clutches a solid plank'. Only by identifying the tortured faces of 'zombies' as identical to the nonhuman faces of dogs could he justify their abuse, thus reinstating 'the natural fixed laws and processes on which all modern human thought and actions are based'.[5]

There is a footnote to this story. Eleven years after *The Magic Island* was published to much acclaim, the occultist Aleister Crowley used the metaphor of the dog against Seabrook himself. 'The swine dog W. B. Seabrook', he confided to his diary, 'has killed himself at last, after months of agonized slavery to his final wife.'[6]

And so we return to face dogs and slaves, and what philosophers and scientists tell us about them. The literal human face – whether forged by the hand of God, 'Nature' or, less lofty, surgeons – might be deemed beautiful or ugly, but ethically it was often monstrous. The three named dogs that have appeared in the last three chapters (Levinas's Bobby, Darwin's Polly, and Bob the spotted terrier) have come across as rather agreeable characters, even if their human interlocutors felt the need to project much-lauded, although exceptionally rare, human traits upon them. The dogs have been partly humanized; the mass of unnamed persons in these chapters, partly animalized. Both of these processes have led to the great acts of brutality of our times.

I have emphasized the diverse ways in which the faces of people and animals have been socially constructed, primarily within the sciences of physiognomy, evolution and surgery. These sciences were not neutral. They did not simply reveal Nature; they were implicated in the process of creating classical whiteness as beautiful, and the dog's face as ugly. Love and sympathy turned out to be founded on a narcissistic model: the perfection (or perfectibility) of the human countenance. But the main problem is that shared by all attempts to define 'the human': the 'face', too, has no literal, corporeal existence. It is always constructed by the viewer, who is able to choose how to avoid ethical claims or, more correctly, deny that claims are even being made because they refuse to identify any real face.

The face is not a universal given. Philosophers, scientists, and their loyal followers, sought to find or forge a language that was beyond speech but would enable people to understand their ethical responsibilities in the world. In the end, though, they all ended up recognizing difference. The face they sought simply did not exist. It was like the Möbius strip. Philosophers, scientists and writers attempt to tie a knot in that Möbius strip of faciality, declaring '*this!* and not *that!* is the true face. Here and not there is where we must act ethically.' Human narcissism and violence come face-to-face.

Carnivorous Consumption

CHAPTER FOURTEEN

'The Black Demons of Hayti'

Three months before the start of the twentieth century, *Big Budget*, a magazine addressed to adolescent boys and promising 'to amuse, interest, and, when possible, help its readers', published a tale replete with images of carnivorous sacrifice, both animal and human. Set in the then densely forested mountains of Haiti, 'The Black Demons of Hayti' (see Figure 1) was authored by William Shaw Rae. Its sly pornography, vicious racism and accusations of cannibalism were typical of stories published in the West about Haiti.

As we saw at the end of the last chapter, Haitians were routinely

Figure 1. Title image of William Shaw Rae's 'The Black Demons of Hayti', *Big Budget*, 1899. The original caption reads, 'A roar of ribald revelry resounded; obscene jests were freely bandied; the most depraved and degraded petitions were loudly voiced; while the Mamanloi shook and rattled the snake-box to heighten the frenzy . . .'

Big Budget (7 October 1899)

excluded from humanity. In that chapter, their continued enslavement to systems of labour that required backbreaking work in sugar-cane fields enabled xenophobic Western observers to characterize them as faceless, expressionless zombies. They were creatures able to be endlessly exploited on the grounds that they were nothing more (or less) than dogs. True humans did not owe them any ethics of care because there could be no face-to-face encounter. In this chapter, I take this argument further. The precariousness of being human was also intertwined with debates about eating well. 'The Black Demons of Hayti' introduces some of these arguments: at the very least, the story suggests that the act of eating the flesh of animals – *human* as well as non-human ones – plays an important role in debates about what it means to be human

Stephen Vining was the handsome hero of 'The Black Demons of Hayti'. He was a rich young Englishman and a keen hunter of wild 'beasts'. In this sordid tale, however, it turned out that the white-skinned men were to be hunted for their sweet flesh; the 'beasts' were dark-skinned men rather than wild guinea fowl. Similar to Seabrook in the last chapter, William Shaw Rae made his views clear. For both of them, dark-skinned people simply possessed a veneer of 'humanity'; they were, in fact, crueller and more vicious than the noble animals.

The story proceeded quickly from Stephen mooring his boat off a lonely part of the Haitian coast to the first scene of sexualized bestiality. Stephen had gone ashore in search of new and exotic 'game' to kill where he unexpectedly met another white man, Alan Malcolm, the son of the local planter. Alan persuaded him to enjoy 'Creole hospitality' on his father's plantation, an invitation made more tempting after Stephen was introduced to Alan's attractive younger sister Mona.

All went well until Stephen, wandering into a cane field, heard the 'shriek of agony, dying in a sobbing wail' of a damsel in distress. 'Jove! . . . what mischief is afoot?', Stephen exclaimed. He had stumbled into a scene straight out of any adolescent male's wet dream: a 'comely mulatto girl' was 'crouching' on the ground, her wrists firmly tied to a palm tree. Towering over her stood a 'powerful, full-blooded black, brandishing a heavy stock whip'. The 'light cotton dress' of the 'shrinking maid' had already been torn, displaying her 'shapely shoulder' (see Figure 2).[1] Stephen's 'British blood boil[ed] at the outrage' against a woman who was not only Mona's maid but also a mulatto, or a woman whose 'blood' was partly 'white' (there is no hint given of her parentage, although the only white-skinned residents in this story are the Malcolm family). Stephen 'sprang forward indignantly' and, in a

Figure 2. 'Flagellation of a Female Samboe Slave'. The eroticization of torture is a common element in pro-slave accounts, as in popular magazines like *Big Budget*. In this image, brutality is erased by positioning the viewer in front of the woman's breasts, screening us from the aggression being inflicted on her lacerated back. Her discreetly torn skirt and ballerina-like bearing, as she struggles against the delicate branch to which she is bound, are conventional motifs in pornography.

Flagellation of a Female Samboe Slave, engraved by William Blake (1757–1827), published 1793 (engraving), Stedman, John Gabriel (1744–97) (after)/Private Collection/© Michael Graham-Stewart/The Bridgeman Art Library

series of highly improbable manoeuvres, defeated the 'brute', identified as the plantation's overseer with the villainous name of Sable Gross. The overseer might have been 'Herculean in bulk and muscle' and 'bull-like' but, Rae informed readers, 'not for naught had Stephen practiced assiduously with gloves and foils in the gymnasium' in England. To Stephen's taunting question, 'Is that enough? Want any more, you brute?', Sable Gross replied, as he skulked away, 'Want no more now . . . your turn now, mine comes next, oh, bery soon. You make one mortal enemy ob Sable Gross, he get even wid you, sah, as' more dan even.' And so the scene was set for the main conflict – a life-and-death struggle between a Haitian speaking bastardized English and an exemplar of civilization, a protector of the weaker sex who practised fencing in England and possessed a yacht in a Caribbean harbour. And whose 'blood' was not like many other men's blood: it was 'British'.

Another marker of civilization was also quickly established: carnivorism. Stephen was a keen hunter but he did it for sport, not (like animals) for nourishment. While Stephen tucked into his 'morning coffee and crisp "crackers"' (brought to his bedroom by a 'smiling nigger "boy"'), the Haitians were keen consumers of meat – of all varieties. Although they appeared 'quiet and submissive', at a certain time of the voodoo calendar they turned into 'fiends incarnate', eagerly devouring 'little bodies' as well as adult ones. Indeed, Sable Gross held high office among the cannibal sect, acting as 'loup-garou', translated as 'werewolf' or man who kidnapped people to be sacrificed during cannibalistic festivals. 'No wonder God's curse lies heavily on the Black Republic', simpered the pretty Mona.

A different kind of curse was about to descend on Stephen and the Malcolm family: a few days after Mona's dismissive verdict on Haitian governance, Sable Gross snatched Mona and her young brother Evan. Besides revenge, what was his aim? To rape Mona and sacrifice Evan – the 'little white goat widout de horns' – at a great voodoo ceremony. Desperate to avert these events, the two intrepid heroes went in pursuit, on their way picking up an 'Obeah fetish' in the shape of a little rag doll that had been placed on the path in order to discourage nosy outsiders from gatecrashing the feast. Their sole Haitian guide understood its significance and deserted them. As Alan pompously announced, obeahism was 'a strange compound of tawdryness and savagery, of childish ignorance and fiendish ferocity'. The Haitian guide had proved himself to be as 'ignorant' and 'credulous' as the rest of his race.

In the middle of 'cannibal country', Stephen and Alan finally stumbled into a clearing where a group of Haitians were beginning their festivities in front of a fire on which several joints of meat were roasting. On spying the foreign intruders, the 'convivial carousers' turned into 'furious fanatics . . . mad and drunk with lust'. 'Streaming like a wolf-pack', the revellers attacked the men only to come to a sudden halt when Stephen brandished the fetish. Holding it 'in view of the wolfish pack, [and at] the same time yelling some words of gibberish', Stephen threw it at the 'child minded murderers'. The fetish landed in the 'gaping mouth' of one of the 'savages' who immediately fell down dead. While the terrified revellers fled, Alan spied one of his servants – Yam Pete, the young lover of the mulatto maid who had been whipped by Sable Gross. Yam Pete cordially invited them to share in 'refreshments'. Alan, though, was suspicious: 'Refreshment eh?', he asked, adding, 'What sort of refreshment can you offer? What are these joints cooking before the fire; man-flesh?' The muscle and bone being roasted on the fire turned out to have been cut from (in Yam Pete's words) a 'black fellow; an' he no' kill; him die. Him wery old, an' wery tough'. Alan and Stephen declined the invitation and, discovering that Evan and Mona were being held further up the mountain, continued their rescue mission.

On approaching the 'sanguinary headquarters of the cannibals', they found that the 'hideous revelry was approaching its climax; the sacrifice on the altar of a child-victim'. Haitian men and women, 'excited by drink and lust', were dancing in a state of 'delirious frenzy':

> The 'Chic' and 'Colenda' had been danced, with their voluptuous wantonness; many animals had been slaughtered, the blood drunk warm, yet still large wineskins containing goat's blood freely dashed with rum, passed from mouth to mouth in hideous glee, alternated with jars of fresh, raw spirit-liquid fire . . . 'Twas a living picture of the Inferno.

Although they did not know the 'Mamanloi' (a 'blood-thirsty harangue'), the 'Papaloi' was none other than Sable Gross. While they watched the 'unholy rites', the crowd started baying for the 'little white goat without the horns. Give us the white kid. Let Obeah be gutted.' Preparations were made: Papaloi picked up the sacrificial knife; an assistant seized a tin basin to receive the blood; and another assistant came forth, bearing the child. Alan and Stephen leapt forward 'with one common, instinctive, overmastering impulse', brandishing their revolvers and immediately 'the clamour was stilled . . . to frightened silence' because (at least according to Rae's frenzied imagination) the 'black Haytians believe the fiends to be white' and so the 'crazy crew fancied their unholy incantations had raised up Satan and his imps'.

Sable Gross was not to be so easily overcome. He 'quickly rallied' and began to shout 'Kill, kill, kill! Slay these defilers of the temple. Hew them to pieces . . . then shall Obeah be gutted, and you, his children shall indeed be fed.' His cry roused the 'frantic savages', allaying their 'superstitious fears' and, their 'blood-lust surging', they rushed towards the two men, 'each one thirsting to be first in the slaughter'.

The devil himself could not have predicted what happened next. In the agitation, the cage holding a 'sacred snake', the venomous fer de lance, was overturned and the 'springing devil' leapt out, fastening its fangs on the nearest person, who happened to be Sable Gross. The 'giant black' frantically tried to slice through the neck of the snake with the sacrificial knife, but it was too late and he fell back 'like one in a fit'. In a scene combining cannibalism and vampirism, the Mamanloi uttered a 'loud wail of fear and rage' and

> fastened on the prostrate body like a tigress on a wounded cub . . . Raising the arm of the stricken man, she located the punctures, then deliberately bit out the part, tearing away a considerable portion of the surrounding flesh. Spitting out the disgusting mouthful, the woman next applied her lips to the gaping wound she had made, sucking out the blood in the hope of extracting along with it the venom ere it spread.

While the Haitians were thus distracted, the young men grabbed the child Evan who – showing remarkable aplomb – promptly told them where his sister was being held. Mona was found, 'firmly lashed' to a pole in the middle of a hut. Once freed, she threw herself on her brothers, hugging and kissing them before 'showering gratitude' upon Stephen who, 'in the excitement of the moment, soothed and petted the hysterical maid in more than brotherly fashion'. And Mona, 'far from resenting the endearments, artlessly responded to them'. In the bliss of approaching concupiscence, the young men let down their guard. The 'lawless, lustful' Haitians easily recaptured them. Now, all four found themselves 'helpless in cannibal clutches'.

Readers of the *Big Budget* might fear that all was lost – except that the tale was only halfway through! The four captives now found themselves being 'fattened-up' for slaughter. After ensuring that there was no 'man-flesh' on the plate (the 'cannibals' fed them vegetarian food, perhaps aware of the belief that recently ingested animal meat could make human flesh taste bitter), Stephen encouraged the others to eat with the words, 'these fellows don't mean to starve us anyway'. Recalling his own practices of animal husbandry, Alan groaned, 'Of course not . . . Does the English farmer starve his turkeys before Christmas?'

In case the link between the sacrifice of the flesh of fowl and human was not clear enough, when their enemy reappeared he greeted the captives with the words, 'aha, my birds!'. 'Dis wery night, you two be

led out to stake', he informed them, reassuring them that 'we no torture you' because that would 'spoil um flesh'. Rather, he promised to
them that he would 'kill sharp. Oh, I do it myself, quick, den we eat.
Oh, grand "long-pig"'. Smacking his lips 'lustfully', he added, 'As for
Missy . . . she one dainty piece – mine, mine alone – I deal wid her
myself. She be my queen, yet my slave. Oh, it is grand, grand, grand!
Ho, ho, ho!' 'Throwing back his head', Sable Gross proved himself a
'monster':

> [He] laughed uproariously, opening his mouth gapingly, his gleaming
> white teeth and the horrid redness of his prominent gums and swollen
> tongue contrasting hideously with the ebony-black of his complexion.
> He was no longer man, but demon.

Hardly surprising, Stephen was consumed by a 'fierce, loathing hate',
imagining the likely fate of his 'pure, innocent Mona'.

After these lessons in meat husbandry and the corporeality of evil,
the tale moved swiftly to an improbable escape and retrieval of their
weapons. This miracle, achieved only by the daring assistance of Yam
Pete, is dealt with in a perfunctory manner (indeed, Yam Pete was not
even credited with bravery and the men were said to be happy to 'dispense with the further services of their rather dubious friend and rely
solely on themselves'). Suffice to say, the route back home was not
without its trials. In the final scene, the four young people found themselves cowering inside a cave high up a cliff. Equipped with only a
limited supply of ammunition, they had to deal with a seemingly unlimited number of 'savages' making their way towards them. Mona
confessed her love for Stephen and begged him to

> save your last cartridge for me . . . I must never again fall alive into the
> hands of that terrible man-fiend. Death is far preferable, indeed, I
> shall welcome it at your hands, Stephen, as saving me from that other
> fate.

The fight to the death, though, was about to begin. Perhaps aware
that, during slavery in Haiti, dogs had been especially bred to eat
Haitian flesh, William Shaw Rae has two man-eating bloodhounds
racing toward them. Readers were told – in gruesome detail – how
one of the dogs was killed while the other was seriously crippled.
Although the bloodhounds had been keen to eat them, the men agreed

that the dogs, nevertheless, were 'gallant beasts' who were 'worthy of a better fate'. It would have been charitable to end the suffering of the wounded dog, but prudence dictated that they reserve their ammunition 'for the greater brutes' (who, it must be remembered, had also been keen to dine on their flesh).

This was when (once again) they made a mistake. Focusing all their firepower on the 'human brutes' making their way towards them from the front, they left their back undefended. Once again, it was Yam Pete who observed the sneaky Papaloi coming up from behind. Yam Pete fired his arrow, Sable Gross uttered a 'fierce shrill shriek' and tumbled down the hill, landing (bad luck!) in front of the injured bloodhound. The maddened dog did not hesitate: 'fastening its fangs in his throat', he 'began rending and worrying, snapping and tearing, quickly driving life out of the impious high-priest'. Not a word of pity did the intrepid heroes utter. Moments later, Alan's father, the planter, arrived with a team of 'faithful blacks'. Despite his numerous acts of selfless service and bravery, Yam Pete was neither thanked nor mentioned again.

The customary happy ending was tagged on: Stephen Vining and Mona Malcolm were married at the British Consulate in Port au Prince before setting sail for England 'by the Royal Mail line' (it is unclear why they did not use Stephen's elegant yacht, which was still moored in the harbour). Stephen was 'now quite disposed to settle down in "merrie England"' and the bride was 'happy to leave distracted Hayti under the protecting care of a loved and loving husband'.[2]

What can this vicious little story of 1899 tell us about debates about what it means to be human or, perhaps more correctly, debates about the inhuman? In my view, 'The Black Demons of Hayti' provides us with a space to explore the carnivorous sacrifice that – according to Jacques Derrida – is central to Western thought. The story also complicates the argument about face-to-face encounters discussed in the last three chapters. In those chapters, Levinas argued that responsibility for other people comes before all other considerations. It even comes before responsibility towards oneself. In contrast, he implied, animals are set outside that absolute response because they are unable to 'universalize maxims and drives'. Levinas was a humanist, albeit a radical one.

But what if this humanistic assumption is shattered? Derrida turned his gaze to the violence people inflict on animals as well as on other people. He invented a word for the violence glorified in 'The Black

Demons of Hayti': it was a form of 'carno-phallogocentrism'. There are numerous ways of interpreting this concept but, broken up into its components, it is less daunting. The heroes of 'The Black Demons of Hayti' are the incarnation of a hierarchical ethic that glues status to the masculine ('phallo') and language ('logos'). It also assumes a willingness to sacrifice other sentient beings ('carno'). Carno-phallogocentrism enables – indeed, encourages – violence towards animals and subjugated peoples. Carno-phallogocentrism places those with language above those without, even if this distinction is rather unfair since 'language' is defined in such a way that it is always 'reserved for what we call man'. It privileges the masculine over the feminine (are women part of 'mankind' or are they closer to 'the animal'?).

Carno-phallogocentrism is also founded on the principle that some sentient beings – those designated 'animals' – can legitimately be killed. Animals are sentient yet 'things'; while animals are 'like' humans in that they can feel, they are 'unlike' humans in that they are 'things permitted to be killed', a 'noncriminal putting to death'. 'Eating well', according to this ethic, is not a matter of 'taking in and grasping in itself': if eating is nourishing only for 'me', then one would 'eat badly' since 'it must be shared'. 'Eating well' involved offering 'infinite hospitality'. The next two chapters, then, take up Derrida's provocations, posing questions about the meaning of eating the flesh of Others.

In William Shaw Rae's story, Yam Pete (the Haitian who constantly rescues the Europeans, yet is never even thanked) is hospitable, inviting Alan and Stephen to share in a meal being prepared on an open fire. Alan is suspicious, demanding to know 'What sort of refreshment can you offer?' The consequent refusal of hospitality is at the heart of Derrida's critique of Western philosophy. What is the sociohistorical context for 'eating well', though? In what follows, I will examine narratives that deal with the killing and eating of animals – that is, human as well as non-human ones. Historically, what did it mean to slaughter sentient beings and then eat them? Modern Western subjectivity is founded upon 'executions of ingestion, incorporation, or introjection of the corpse'.[3] Literally and symbolically, the corpse is the animal, rendered 'meat'. And sometimes it is also literally the human. Rae's tale of carnivorous appetites is interesting in the way it explicitly juxtaposes the sacrifice of animals with the attempted sacrifice of people. While 'goat's blood freely dashed with rum, passed from mouth to mouth', the revellers prepared to eat a human child, the 'little white goat widout de horns'. Importantly, Alan was the son of the local sugar-cane plantation owner. In 1899, when William Shaw Rae was writing his story, plantation owners in Haiti were little different from the slave-owners prior to the 1804 revolution. They literally consumed the bodies of their workers: put into the language of the last chapter, they turned Haitian workers into 'zombies', faceless beasts of burden. What do such juxtapositions tell us about the Möbius strip representing concepts of humanity and animality?

Two sentences in 'The Black Demons of Hayti' that will be used to structure the next two chapters. Near the middle of the story, Alan asked Yam Pete, 'What sort of refreshment can you offer? What are these joints cooking before the fire; man-flesh?' These questions raise some important points. First, they assume that the flesh of non-human animals is legitimate 'refreshment'. Second, they acknowledge the difficulty of clearly distinguishing between animal and human flesh. Third, they imply that the consumption of flesh – animal or human – is central to the development of a hierarchy of humans. The fourth and fifth points concern the magical element of flesh-eating. Eating flesh can either 'animalize' consumers or symbolically refresh them. Finally, I will conclude with reflections on the literal consumption of other people. When the master Alan asked the slave Yam Peter 'What sort of refreshment can you offer?', he was alluding to the fact that the bodies of the enslaved could be literally (as well as symbolically) consumed by their masters: that is, Alan's question could be interpreted as asking: 'What can I eat of you to refresh me?' Put in Derrida's language, in Western thought, there is always a 'place left open' for a 'carnivorous virility' that is dependent upon consuming those on the margins of humanity, as well as those designated 'animal'.

CHAPTER FIFTEEN

Eating Animals

Gastronomy has always been one of the ways in which people have distinguished themselves from other animals. Only 'animals' can be legitimately killed; only they can be eaten. Of course, like all generalizations, there are exceptions: in certain jurisdictions and at certain times people (certain criminals and enemy people at war, for instance) are 'fair game' and not all animals can be eaten (humanized animals such as pets are generally forbidden).

Nevertheless, for much of Western history, the mantra that God created animals to grace our tables can be heard. English writer Soame Jenyns put it succinctly in *Disquisitions on Several Subjects* (1782):

> God has been pleased to create numberless animals intended for our sustenance; and that they are so intended, the agreeable flavour of their flesh to our palates, and the wholesome nutrient which it administers to our stomachs, are sufficient proofs: these, as they are formed for our use, propagated by our culture, and fed by our care, we have certainly a right to deprive of life.

He went on to say that the 'disagreeable' task of killing them should not excuse butchers from performing the bloody deed 'with all the tenderness and compassion' possible. Indeed, proof that God intended animals to die at least honourably could be found by noting that providence created animals 'in such a manner that their flesh becomes rancid and unpalatable by a painful and lingering death'. This heaven-inspired 'trick', if you like, compels people to 'be merciful without compassion' and cautions people to be wary of acting cruelly towards those creatures who are destined to become our steak 'for the sake of ourselves'.[1] As the *Children's Friend* put it in 1826,

> If the creatures must be slain,
> Thankless sinners to sustain;
> Such a child, methinks, will cry,
> Treat them gently when they die;
> Spare them while they yield their breath,
> Double not the pangs of death.[2]

Human beings were created as distinct from all other animals by the fact that they alone were at liberty to eat and not be eaten. The only duty people possessed towards animals was to kill them 'humanely', and even this obligation was imposed in the interests of humans, rather than those lesser creatures.

The Consumption of Meat

Jenyns's *Disquisitions* were published in 1782, but his assumption that it is just and necessary to kill and consume animals remains humdrum in Western society, despite the wishes of many vegetarians and vegans. Killing animals is an unavoidable part of everyday life in the affluent West. For instance, the corpse of a single lamb can be used to make textiles, shoes, leather, plastic, rubber, dyes, lubricants, string, adhesives, cosmetics, cleaning products, soap, fertilizer and so on. Non-vegetarians roast, grill, fry, braise and boil the lamb's corpse.

The extent of the slaughter is staggering, as evidenced here by just a few examples. Between twenty-five and fifty billion animals are killed for food each year.[3] In America, forty-five million turkeys are killed in preparation for Thanksgiving Day. Annually, over six billion broiler chickens are raised in sheds. In factories for killing pigs, 'hog stickers' can slit over a thousand throats an hour. In the UK, twenty-eight animals are slaughtered for food every second – a total of over 883 million animals each year.[4] None of these statistics include animals killed for clothing, display or any of those products mentioned above. America, Australia and Ireland are notoriously heavy animal-eating countries (as compared with Indonesia, Pakistan, Ethiopia and some countries in Sub-Saharan Africa), and 95 per cent of people in Britain eat animal flesh.[5] In contrast to the practice of humanizing animals as pets, most animals we have contact with are, in fact, 'animalized animals', that is, animals produced for our consumption. Even if we include pets and animals living in circuses and zoos, 98 per cent of all animals that people in the West have contact with are bred for us to eat.[6] It is no exaggeration to state that Anglo-Americans eat animals more than we do anything else with them.

This was not always the case, and does not always have to be the case. Although only about 3 to 7 per cent of Americans and Britons today are vegetarians (and fewer than 0.2 per cent are vegans),[7] in the recent past many people subsisted primarily on non-animal products. This was largely through necessity. Many animals were more valuable for the labour they performed than for the succulence of their flesh. Rendering their bodies into meat was expensive. Production and transport costs were high. As a result, meat was a high-status food and, except for special occasions, it was beyond the price-range of most people who worked in the fields and factories.

Compared with meat-eaters today, when poor people in the past did eat meat they could choose from a much greater range of animals. For instance, in early America men (primarily) on the west coast ate teal, summer and mallard duck, plover, lark, robin, prairie grouse, quail, snipe, wild geese, swan, wild pigeon, wild turkey, grey and white cranes, white and black tail deer, antelope, beaver, black bear, hare, raccoon, opossum, grey, black and fox squirrels and bison. If especially hungry, they might also tuck into the flesh of blackbirds, bluebirds, buzzards, crows, doves, dippers, eagles, owls, hawks, mockingbirds, ravens, mice, gophers, prairie dogs, panthers, skunks, foxes, wild-cats, coyotes, wolves or mustangs.[8] As army officer Richard Dodge complacently observed in *The Plains of the Great West* (1872), animals such as prairie dogs were 'machine[s] designed by nature to convert grass into flesh, thus providing meat for the carnivore of the plains'.[9]

The great expansion in meat-eating in Britain and America only occurred after the 1860s. There are many ways to track this remarkable shift in eating practices. For instance, the *proportion* of household income spent on meat and meat products has risen dramatically. In the late 1880s the average household spent just over 12 per cent of their income on meat; by the end of the First World War, this had escalated to around 20 per cent.[10]

Another way of illustrating the growth in carnivorous appetites is by calculating the amount of meat actually eaten. According to one estimate, meat consumption in Britain almost doubled between the 1860s

and the 1890s, and had increased still further by 1914.[11] American statistics are equally striking. In 1909, Americans consumed (on average)
51 kilograms of boneless trimmed (edible) meat each year. Although
this dipped slightly in the 1930s, it began to rise again in the 1940s. By
the late 1960s the average person was eating more than 70 kilograms
of such meat a year – or the equivalent in animal flesh of his or her own
body weight. By the 1980s they were eating even more (82 kilograms).[12] Today, the average American consumes a staggering 125
kilograms of meat a year.[13]

What kinds of animals were being eaten? Certainly not black bear,
squirrels, owls or prairie dogs. The range of animals consumed was
generally confined to cows, pigs and poultry. Within this trinity, the
share dedicated to the flesh of cows declined from a high of half in 1910
to just over one-third by 2000. The consumption of pigs was more
stable. It peaked in the 1930s (when half of all meat eaten was pork)
but settled at around 27 per cent by mid-century. In contrast, the
share allocated to poultry increased from only 10 per cent in 1900 to
37 per cent a century later.[14]

What explains this dramatic increase in meat-eating? Rising real
incomes, coinciding with the falling prices of foodstuffs – due, in part,
to improved agricultural productivity and dramatic reductions in the
cost of transporting products from farms to towns and cities – meant
that consumers could actually afford to buy and eat more meat. After
the Second World War, mechanization, innovations in chemical production and breeding techniques and the gradual conversion of
low-yield crops to new, high-yielding ones were important.[15] Higher-
yielding crops were particularly significant because they enabled a
larger proportion of the harvest to be dedicated to animal feed. At the
turn of the century, only around 10 per cent of the world's grain was
fed to animals. This had risen to one-fifth by the middle of the twentieth century and 40 per cent by the century's end. In America today,
around 60 per cent of grain is fed to animals.[16] This shift is even more
remarkable when it is noted that the animals being fed grain in 1900
were primarily those working in the field (draft horses, mules, cattle
and water buffaloes, for instance) as opposed to animals raised to satisfy people's carnivorous appetites.

The rise in the consumption of animal organs, muscles and fat is also
due to ideological reasons: meat has been widely assumed to be healthy.
Meat has been promoted as recuperative, especially for jaded urban
dwellers in industrialized society. In the nineteenth century, reformers

forecast amazing transformations in working-class productivity if meat was to become a significant part of their diets. Imagine how putting meat on the plates of children in workhouses would transform their lives, exclaimed some commentators. It would reduce, if not eradicate, scrofulous diseases at the very least.[17] As a promoter of an improved method of slaughtering animals maintained in 1839, the 'more animalised the diet', the healthier the human child.[18]

Indeed, promoters of animal flesh often adopted the rhetoric of efficiency, insisting that meat was a food product ready to be 'swallowed down and assimilated' with the greatest gain in the shortest period of time.[19] Meat was actually 'pre-digested plantfood'. Newspaper editor Arthur Brisbane expressed it most bluntly, arguing that eating meat was 'as necessary as the breathing of air or the drinking of water'. City-living made it indispensable. The 'lives of men are crowded', Brisbane pointed out, and

> their systems cannot readily transform meat into the energies with which they do their work. The digestive power that would be used in grinding vegetables into blood and brain would take too much away from useful effort. We must eat meat – we must eat the cow that eats the grass, leaving her to digest the grass, since we have not the time or the vitality to do it.[20]

According to such commentators, cows were little more than living machines, invented to carry out the labour of predigesting plants for the benefit of fatigued human constitutions.

Hierarchies of Ingestion

However, eating animals was not primarily about people's nutritional needs. It constructed hierarchies of humans. In '"Eating Well", or the Calculation of the Subject', Derrida claimed that the carno-phallogocentrism economy was based on the positive value given to eating animals. He observed that, in Western societies, the virile person 'accepts sacrifice and eats flesh . . . The *chef* [that is, the head of State] must be an eater of flesh'. Both literally and symbolically, the person who eats animal flesh is recognized as fully human, and generally masculine. As a consequence, the status of women, vegetarians and homosexuals can be diminished.[21]

In popular discourse, though, the positive relationship between consuming animal flesh and human status is much less clear-cut. Sometimes it was claimed that fully human people were those who ate vast amounts of flesh; at other times, that they required very little. Some 'lesser humans' were voracious carnivores; others preferred herbs. How can we reconcile these contradictory meanings given to eating animals and being human?

In part, the confusion about whether meat-eating confers high or low status is due to the failure to distinguish between two very different questions. The first asks whether eating vast quantities of animal flesh was the *result of* certain pre-existing traits that made a person more or less human, while the second asks whether eating meat *causes* those traits to develop. For instance, lesser humans were sometimes said to require large quantities of meat because of their lowly developmental stage. At the same time, the excessive consumption of animal flesh was what made these 'savages' less than fully human in the first place. As one food reformer asked in the mid-1930s: how could you explain why certain 'races, and the wild animals with whom they share their taste for animal-flesh food' had a low standard of intelligence and were 'lazy and lethargic when well fed, but capable of tremendous activity' when hungry? He believed the answer lay in the fact that 'large meat consumption' requires considerable activity but, after feasting, animal flesh 'favours the growth of certain bacteria in the intestine, causing poisoning of the blood-stream and consequent mental and physical lethargy'.[22] Enthusiastic eaters of animals risked being associated with lesser forms of humanity.

In direct contradiction to this argument, so-called inferior 'races', as well as women and children, were often assumed to require *less* meat. Based on assumptions that meat was 'brain food', it made sense that the inferior reasoning powers of lesser humans meant that they did not need as much sustenance as others. In the words of a late-nineteenth-century physician, 'savages' subsisted quite well without eating large quantities of meat because they were 'little removed from the common animal stock' from which meat was derived. Therefore, they could 'subsist on forms of life which would be poisonous to us', that is, to 'highly civilized brain-workers'.[23] Of course, if humanity was defined according to the possession of rationality, then those 'savages' who did not require brain food were not simply lesser humans but set outside the human.

When these commentators explored the diets of people they considered to be exemplary humans, both arguments were once again put forward. Many evolutionary-inspired accounts, for instance, pointed to carnivorous appetites as one of the main explanations for the superiority of some people over others. Numerous commentators repeated the sentiment of one lecturer in 1861, when he declared that 'We find in the history of man that those races who have partaken of animal food are the most vigorous, the most moral, and the most intellectual races of mankind.'[24]

The converse was also true, though: a low-protein diet could retard civilization. In 1913 botanists and nutritionists in the highly respected journal *Science* even speculated that 'races' practising a low-protein diet displayed 'physical inferiority' and 'lack of energy, aggressiveness or courage' when compared with 'races' brought up on a protein-rich diet. Might the 'low physical development and efficiency of the native races of India as compared with the Eurasian or the European' be a result of a low-protein diet, these authors asked. Or did the prevalence of certain diseases (such as hookworm) explain these alleged differences? Put even more strongly: might the 'evident inferiority of the races inhabiting India, which enables a mere handful of British soldiers to keep them under control' be evidence of the perils of a meat-free diet?[25] As the naturalist W. H. Hudson observed in 1919, vegetarianism might be acceptable for sick people (and, by extension, nations), but the 'wolf with blood on his iron jaws' was necessary for truly virile and imperial people.[26]

This was not simply a bizarre, racist sentiment of the early twentieth century and before. It was expressed equally dogmatically in evolutionary-inspired accounts in the late twentieth and early twenty-first centuries. For these commentators, meat eating was not merely 'part of our evolutionary inheritance',[27] it was what facilitated the transition from ape to human.[28] Such arguments assumed a link between carnivorous virility and the evolution of 'mankind'. Of course, this was a highly ethnocentric image of the 'ascent' of 'man'. It was also patriarchal. Since males did most of the hunting, the argument implied that men were the driving force behind the evolution of human intelligence, while also ignoring the fact that woman's work as 'gatherers' actually provided more calories than meat.

Once again, the argument is not clear-cut. Although numerous commentators emphasized the link between eating animals and the evolution of 'man' or 'civilization', the opposite argument was made just as frequently. In other words, might the consumption of meat by 'civilized' persons be dangerous? Weren't people who consumed animal flesh and blood coarsened by their diet? The influential American dietary reformer Sylvester Graham made this argument in the 1830s when he insisted that 'nothing is more true than that familiarity with blood always hardens man and makes him more wantonly cruel'. Meat-eaters risked both physical and moral disorder. Blood was 'oppressive to the human stomach', Graham contended. Blood-swollen meat 'always produces a general increased excitement in the system, and tends to febrile and putrid diseases'. At the very least, blood should be 'bled' from the animal flesh (as in Jewish or Muslim slaughter practices) before it could be sold as fit for human consumption. Graham placed even more emphasis on the dangerous moral consequences of consuming animal blood. Anyone who 'devours blood', he argued, deadens his or her moral sensibilities and sympathies. The 'selfish and destructive propensities' of meat-eaters were 'increased and rendered more vehement and ferocious'.[29] The effect was widely believed to be greater if the animal had died while in a state of terror, an argument often employed by reformers of the animal industry. As George Bernard Shaw famously declared, 'If I were to eat meat, my evacuations would stink.' According to him, the stench of fear exuded by an animal on approaching her death would contaminate her flesh and, therefore, the body of whoever subsequently consumed her carcass.[30]

Vegetarians and people advocating a low-meat diet routinely assumed that a diet heavy in animal meat excited male virility, martial vigour and moral corruptibility. According to their way of thinking, pacific nations were vegetarian nations. Fantasies of 'the Orient' stimulated many of these discussions. In 'rice-eating Japan', boasted one health reformer of the 1890s, 'the only harsh words heard are those spoken by the Englishman, for geniality prevails even among the children of the street'.[31] For other commentators, proof of the link between vegetarianism and a pacific temperament could be found closer to home. As Elizabeth Gaskell reported, the Brontë siblings

> never were such good children. I used to think them spiritless, they were so different to any children I had ever seen. In part, I set it down to a fancy Mr Brontë had of not letting them have flesh-meat to eat . . . They had nothing but potatoes for their dinner.[32]

Conversely, the 'English roast' led to the 'Englishman's bad temper'.[33] 'Half-oxidised albumen products' were responsible for upsetting 'mind and body, overtaxing the liver, and causing the proverbial "English liver"', claimed the author of 'Do We Eat Too Much Meat?', printed in *Hearth and Home* in 1893. Although the solution could be as simple as administering a teaspoonful of Oppenheimer's Euonynim Cocoa each morning, wasn't it more natural to simply 'partake less freely of meat?', she asked.[34]

Again, such comments were not simply a product of Victorian culture. The role of consuming animal flesh in devising hierarchies of humans can also be seen in the debates about Jewish and Muslim practices of slaughtering animals without prior stunning. For instance, Arnold Spenser Leese (an ardent British fascist and founder of the Imperial Fascist League) launched a major campaign against Shechita,* claiming it was proof of Jewish danger and degradation. In 1940 Leese promised that 'one of the first acts of a Fascist government in Britain' would be to abolish the legal exemption that Jews and Muslims had been granted in relation to methods of slaughtering animals for food.[35] Leese died in 1956, but as late as 1992 *Vegetarian Living* was republishing his violent attacks on Shechita in their magazine.[36]

Other racialized accounts were less vicious. As late as the 1960s, the author of *Rejuvenation Through Dietic Sex Control* advised readers to observe the 'mild sexual feeling' of the Irish who subsist on a diet of potatoes and buttermilk. In contrast, he asked readers to look at the French, whose 'highly stimulating' diet of meat, seafoods and wine explained their fixation on all things sexual.[37] This was a highly selective history of the relationship between diet and aggression. It overlooked centuries of martial conflict in Ireland – from the bloody episodes of the mid-seventeenth century, in which nearly one-third of the Irish population were killed or forced into exile, to the early twentieth-century war of independence and civil war. Facts aside, as one periodical bluntly declared, there was 'no denying the fact that the practice [of meat-eating] tends to brutalize the race'.[38]

Contagion

Much of the disgust experienced at the thought of ingesting the organs, muscles and blood of animals was associated with the conviction that animals were so radically inferior to people that ingestion risked

---

* Shechita refers to ritual slaughter in accordance with Jewish dietary laws. Controversially, the animal cannot be stunned prior to having her throat cut.

'animalizing' or 'bestializing' humanity. Vegetarianism could be driven more by a disgust of animal corporeality than any concern for animal welfare or rights.

This process of contagion was often a magical one. Just as the 'Obeah fetish' or rag doll mentioned in 'The Black Demons of Hayti' was believed to have the power to kill any voodoo believer who touched it, so too people who ate meat risked 'catching' the characteristics of the dead animal. A kind of 'sympathetic magic' invisibly transferred the characteristics of one object or person to another.[39] Sometimes these fears were linked to the miasma theory of disease, which was prevalent before the discovery of germs. According to this theory, illness was spread through miasma, or bad smells. Slaughterhouses, for instance, were believed to contaminate neighbouring areas. The poisonous odours of blood, sweat and terror radiated outwards, infecting nearby residents and pedestrians. In the words of Thomas Beames in The Rookeries of London (1852), the 'stench from such a Necropolis, or colony of the dead, is dreadful, – must feed disease, and, when fever breaks out, aid its ravages!' He noted that an epidemic 'raging in Lambeth with unprecedented severity' had been 'aggravated by the miasma generated from the decomposed bones'.[40]

Close proximity to dying and dead animals was even worse. Merely coming into intimate contact with dead animals and their spilt blood – as butchers did – was defiling. In 1791 the author of The Cry of Nature; or, An Appeal to Mercy and to Justice on Behalf of the Persecuted Animals warned that a man who could slaughter an animal was capable of murdering humans. Any 'ruffian' capable of

> behold[ing], unmoved, the supplicating looks of innocence itself, and, reckless of the calf's infantile cries, plunges, pitiless, in her quivering side, the murdering steel; will he turn, I say, with horror from human assassination? . . . From the practice of slaughtering an innocent animal, to the murder of man himself, the steps are neither many nor remote.[41]

Typically, the feminist and temperance activist Clara Balfour worried that the 'cruel man or boy who has had his heart hardened, and his feelings blunted in the slaughterhouse, becomes a most dangerous member of society'.[42] A contributor to the Woman's Herald of September 1892 stated the case more mildly, observing that while she harboured no 'personal animus towards the honest tradesman', in her experience she had never 'encountered a butcher who owned a refined face'.[43] In

"AM NOT **I** A BRUTE AND A BROTHER?"

Figure 1. 'Am Not *I* a Brute and a Brother?', from *Punch*, 1869. The image shows a brutal-looking man in an abattoir, wielding a stick against a passive, miserable bull. The caption neatly twists the anti-slavery slogan, 'Am I Not a Man and a Brother?', as I discussed further in Chapter Thirteen, The image is similar to that used in Bovril advertisements from the late 1890s, which used the slogan 'Alas! My poor Brother!' (see Figure 1 in Chapter Five).

Punch, 1869

other words, physiognomic principles confirmed the belief that butchers were a radically inferior species of humanity.

Such sentiments were widely shared. Indeed, it was common for commentators to explicitly set butchers outside humanity (see Figure 1). At the turn of the century, an author in *New Age* encouraged his readers to visit the slaughterhouses of Chicago (he described them as 'the most wicked things in creation'). The men working there were 'more brutes than the animals they slaughter'.[44] Anna Kingsford was even clearer: such men were set outside the human and the rights that humans enjoyed. She bewailed the fact that these 'unfortunate and brutalised men' stood all day in 'pools of blood', and were thus 'condemned by modern "civilisation"'. But, it was 'impossible not to conclude that such men are deprived of all chance of becoming themselves civilised, and are consequently disinherited of their human rights, and defrauded of their human dignity'.[45] Horace Lester, a member of the Humanitarian League, concurred, claiming that it was 'taken for granted that ordinary human nature shrinks instinctively from shedding the blood of the lower animals', but immediately went on to narrow the definition of 'human'. According to him, 'human nature' belonged 'to the average man in a community removed several steps from mere barbarity'. It was obvious, then, that 'the average European or Asiatic would rather be excused from the task of providing his own beef or mutton' since they had reached that 'degree of education or refinement'. In contrast, 'savages' might not feel repugnance in butchering animals.[46] They had yet to attain a truly 'human nature'.

Of course, butchers refused to allow themselves to be besmirched so categorically. They hit back. In the *Meat Trades' Journal*, one responded to an unnamed 'vegetarian agitator' (I suspect he was referring to Lester, who had used the term 'dregs'):

> People don't treat me as an unclean creature that I know of; and as to talking about the 'deep degradation of the nature of the whole class of men', I can tell him that he does misrepresent me and others, and that I do my duty as well and am quite as honest as this vegetarian agitator . . . We are not even now 'dregs' and never were.[47]

But such protests – published in specialist journals read only by fellow butchers – barely registered in the minds of the middle classes as they sat down to their Sunday roasts.

Ingestion

Given these fears of contagion, how much more dangerous was actually *ingesting* the slaughtered carcasses? Ingestion was one of the strongest forms of contagion because it involved 'taking inside' the human body a once-sentient animal. In this way, it exerted a greater magical influence than second-level ingestion (drinking milk, for instance) or peaceable contact (petting an animal). One significant risk in eating animal flesh, many people warned, was to turn the consumer into that 'lesser' animal. This occurred in two distinct ways: it could magically impart the characteristics of *specific* animals or it could 'animalize' the eater in a general fashion. 'You are what you eat' was read literally.

The view that people who consumed large quantities of meat would gradually metamorphose into the animals they most enjoyed consuming was more common in satire than in serious reportage. *Punch* published a witty account of such a transformation in 1856 when it reported on an unnamed professor who had been a 'hippophagist' (eater of horsemeat) for ten years. To the dismay of his wife and the wonderment of his neighbours, the professor gradually became horse-like. His face, a veterinary surgeon corroborated,

> is growing larger every month. The nose has fallen into a straight line with the forehead – the nostrils have expanded to an inordinate degree, and the mouth has stretched itself to more than three times its former width.

In time, he went on, 'all traces of the human face divine will be completely obliterated', and the 'melancholic patient will be walking about a pitiable object with a pitiable horse's head on its shoulders!'[48] Once again, the physiognomic imaginary appears in literal form.

The prevalence of such satires conceals a curious omission in the magical laws associated with eating: the adage 'you are what you eat' was most persuasive when it involved consuming sentient animals rather than plants. In the same year that *Big Budget* published its gruesome account of carnivorous sacrifice set in Haiti, a very different journal – *Hearth and Home. An Illustrated Weekly Journal for Gentlewomen* – launched its own, rather more mild-mannered, attack on the vegetarian diet. It took the form of a satire in which vegetables were portrayed as equally likely to exert a metamorphosis on their consumers. The article poked fun at an unnamed 'lady at the Vegetarian Congress' for claiming that 'those who eat Pig become Piggified'. 'Well!', exclaimed the respondent, 'it's all a matter of taste'. Not being particularly fond of pork, the author imagined that she was more likely to become 'Sheepified or mayhap [sic] Oxenised', and that was probably a better fate. 'There is something so calmly restful, so placidly dignified about your Sheep, while the Cattle on the hill-side have long been my admiration for their beauty, and strength, and amiable docility', she mused. However, of one thing she was certain: she would 'sooner resemble a Cow than a Cabbage, rather assimilate the habits of the Mutton than those of the Artichoke'.[49] The satire was effective simply because vegetarians were not generally seen as at risk of turning into cabbages; while carnivores routinely risked taking on the traits of the 'scorched corpses' (as one vegetarian put it) they devoured.[50]

More commonly, carnivorous appetites were portrayed as 'animalizing' the eater in less specific ways. Thus, social critic John Oswald insisted in 1791 that

> Animal food overpowers the faculties of the stomach, clogs the functions of the soul, and renders the mind material and gross. In the difficult, the unnatural task of converting into living juice the cadaverous oppression, a great deal of time is consumed, a great deal of danger is incurred.[51]

For Sylvester Graham, writing in the 1830s, excessive meat eating 'impairs the symmetry of the [human] body and the beauty of the person'. Meat-eaters had a poor complexion, 'fetid' breath and a short life expectancy. The 'energy and violence' of men's 'selfish propensities and passions' were enhanced by eating meat, rendering them more like animals. They were 'more dull, stupid, sluggish and sensual'.[52] In short, eating meat increased those so-called 'animalistic propensities' in the consumer.

Henry Salt (that prominent humanitarian) was another proponent of this view. In *The Logic of Vegetarianism* (1899), he pointed out that since the human body was literally 'built' by assimilating food, diet obviously altered a person's character. 'Animal food' contained 'highly wrought organic forces' which could

> liberate within our system powers which we may find it difficult or even impossible to dominate – lethargic monsters, foul harpies, and sad-visaged lemures – which may insist on having their own way, building up an animal body not truly human.[53]

It was a concept of human identity that was profoundly unstable: it only took a few mouthfuls of 'the animal' to annihilate 'the human'.

Given the persistent equation of 'the animal' with genital potency, it is not surprising that, of all transformations that took place after eating animal flesh, sexual ones predominated. Its logic was based on taking metaphors literally. As Salt warned,

> Beefy meals are not infrequently the precursors of beefy morals. Carnalities of one kind are apt to lead to carnalities of another, and fleshly modes of diet to fleshly modes of thought.[54]

Indeed, abstaining from meat could only 'enfeeble nature', in the words of the distinguished eighteenth-century French naturalist Georges-Louis Leclerc, Comte de Buffon. 'At least in our climate', de Buffon insisted, abstention would mean that people would neither 'multiply or exist'.[55] People only had to look at the 'somewhat flaccid, nerveless' vegetarians to recognize the truth, a journalist in *The Times* warned.[56]

Of course, a valid question was: is 'animalistic vitality' desirable? While de Buffon and the journalist at *The Times* implied that carnivore habits conferred power, virility even, that was not the view of most food reformers of the nineteenth and early twentieth centuries. Graham was definitely of the opinion that sexual expressiveness was unhealthy. Leading the debate from the 1830s, he claimed that eating meat and other 'stimulating and heating substances' (less predictably, he included rice in this list) increased 'concupiscent excitability and sensibility of the genital organs'. Graham lamented the fact that parents were teaching their children to enjoy meat, thus 'constantly tortur[ing]' the 'delicate sensibilities of youth'. He accused parents who fed meat to their sons of literally 'heating' their 'young blood'. Thus the boys' 'animal propensities' would develop much more rapidly than their 'rational and moral powers', inducing 'a preternatural excitability of the nerves of organic life'. An 'anarchical depravity' is 'thrown . . . over the whole domain of instinct'.[57] Meat-eating pushed boys dangerously out of the realm of rationality, causing them to regress to lower, instinctive life forms. It was an argument that signalled a hearty disapproval of sexuality, as well as drawing attention to the treacherous influence of animal flesh over its human counterpart.

Sylvester Graham ignored daughters. Consuming the bodies of animals was gendered. While meat-eating was assumed to be a *personal* problem for men, it was a *social* problem for women. While men risked personal deterioration of their own bodies and souls through eating meat, women were the victims of male over-consumption. Inflamed male desire – a consequence of the carnivorous diet – was hazardous for women. As the author of an article in the *Woman's Herald* warned in 1892, 'excessive meat-eating, like wine-drinking, tends to inflame the animal instincts' and 'gives the rein to violent passion, which, like "a full hot horse", is apt to carry destruction in its way'.[58] Although this author was willing to admit that the instincts of female carnivores were also inflamed by their diet, feminists of the late nineteenth century were much more likely to code meat-eating as masculine, and to blame carnivorous men for the sexual abuse of women.

This point has been developed in Carol Adams's controversial manifesto, *The Sexual Politics of Meat. A Feminist–Vegetarian Critical Theory* (1990).[59] In it, she praised her feminist predecessors of the nineteenth century for recognizing the intimate ties between carnivorous appetites and patriarchal institutions. One of Adams's heroines is Anne Kingsford, whose principled feminism led her to vegetarianism. In *The Perfect Way to Diet. A Treatise Advocating a Return to the Natural and Ancient Food of Our Race* (1881), Kingsford lamented that the

> young man of the present day, accustomed from childhood to frequent and copious meals of flesh . . . carries about with him and fosters an increasingly disordered appetite, which not infrequently assumes the character of true disease, destroying all capacity for the duties and the higher pleasures of intellectual and refined life.

Indeed, Kingsford insisted that the carnivorous appetites of men were the 'deepest, truest, and most general causes of prostitution in all great cities'. 'Abolish kreophagy and its companion vice, alcoholism', she predicted, and more would be done 'to abolish prostitution than can be achieved by any other means soever'.[60]

However, Kingsford's opposition to meat was born not only of her laudable desire to eradicate prostitution. Part of it was linked to her love of animals – a love that verged on misanthropy. As Kingsford admitted when explaining why she decided to go to medical school,

> I do not love men and women. I dislike them too much to care to do them any good. They seem to be my natural enemies. It is not for them that I am taking up medicine and science, not to cure their ailments; but for the animals and for knowledge generally. I want to rescue the animals from cruelty and injustice, which are for me the worst, if not the only sins.[61]

She even attempted the 'psychic murder' of a leading vivisectionist.[62]

Kingsford's views were also driven by a rigid sexual Puritanism that sits less easily with contemporary mores. She was dismayed by meat-eating because the 'constant ingestion of highly nitrogenised and exciting meats' irritated the nervous system and influenced 'the genital functions in a powerful degree'. It led to a 'condition of pressing insatiability'.[63] Kingsford's feminist utopia was to be governed by diminished desires, not sated ones.

Confirmation that meat tended to inflame sexual passions seemed to be found in an experiment conducted in 1919 by a group of nutritionists from the Carnegie Institution of Washington. They asked: what effect would a low-protein diet have on the physical and intellectual vitality of young men? Based on a four-month analysis of twenty-four men staying at the International Young Men's Christian Association College in Springfield, Massachusetts, the results were published in a huge tome entitled *Human Vitality and Efficiency Under Prolonged Restricted Diet*.

When these nutritionists compared the sexual vitality of men on the restricted diet with those on an 'ordinary' diet, they found that the men denied meat reported a 'marked diminution or a complete disappearance of the sex desire'. They no longer experienced nocturnal emissions and failed to have erections during the daytime as well. As one of the men complained, in the past he frequently had erections, especially when 'embracing his girl, and every morning on awakening'. Once restricted to a low-protein diet, however, he reported that

> there was no emission I can recall and, I believe, no erection. My roommate at college noticed this and one morning said, 'Say! You have lost your manhood!' When with my fiancée during this period, nothing of a sexual nature would come to my mind. I think that if I had not been engaged, I would have left off visiting the lady or attending to any social functions.

Another man on the reduced-meat diet concurred, claiming that the diet had 'unsexed' him. Indeed, he had attempted sexual intercourse during the first two weeks of the diet but there was 'no keen desire for passion, nor did the occasions produce the normal pleasures associated with them'. He recalled thinking, 'How foolish to indulge in this [sexual intercourse] simply by habit!'[64]

The nutritionists conducting the experiment were cautious about assigning a reason for the men's lowered sex drive. They observed that their experimental subjects were all devoted Christians who might have believed that masturbation and unrestrained sexuality were morally wrong. Since the Young Men's Christian Association had hosted the experiment, the men might also have regarded a lowered sex drive as the desired outcome. Casting a cold scientific eye over the men's genital performance, these nutritionists noted further that since many of the men on the restricted diet

> had to rise at an earlier hour than was their usual habit, the bladder was seldom as full as it might normally be, and since frequently this is associated with erection, this influence must not be neglected in weighing the evidence.

What was much less clear was whether a lower sexual drive was a desirable outcome. The authors of *Human Vitality and Efficiency Under Prolonged Restricted Diet* viewed 'unsexing' negatively. In fact, they maintained that reducing men's sex drive was 'disadvantageous to society'. The conclusion was clear: animal flesh seemed imperative for masculine sexual imaginary and performance.

Food reformers, however, eagerly cited *Human Vitality and Efficiency Under Prolonged Restricted Diet*, believing that it offered much-needed proof that a meat-free diet dampened sexual desires. Unlike the original nutritionists, though, the vegetarians believed that this was a positive outcome: sexual expressiveness was personally and socially destructive, if not positively evil. They read the entire book extremely selectively, as well. After all, the sexual side effects of the diet took up only a few of its seven hundred pages. The rest documented the fact that the men on the low-protein diet felt less alert, were not as proficient at mental work and had difficulty concentrating.[65] None of these side effects interested the vegetarians.

Dr Raymond Bernard was one of many food reformers who cited the experiment in his publications. Writing in the early 1960s, Bernard concluded that this 1919 experiment proved that sex ('among civilised human beings') was not a 'product of natural instinct' but had been artificially stimulated by the consumption of meat, alcohol, coffee and tobacco. Nocturnal emissions, too, he alleged, were not natural physiological phenomena that provided a 'necessary release of semen when not discharged through voluntary sexual acts'. Instead, they were simply the 'vicarious elimination of the end-product of protein metabolism and indicate that the protein intake is excessive'.[66]

For food reformers like Bernard and feminists like Kingsford, it was precisely the aphrodisiac effect of meat-eating that proved the wickedness of a carnivorous diet. Morris Krok, the renowned promoter of a raw fruit diet, also equated meat's aphrodisiac quality with a polluting toxin. 'Substances rich in high protein, fat, and other stimulating properties,' he

lectured, 'not only draw on the reserve vitality of the body by heighten-
ing the sexual impulse but create a loss of valuable nutrients in seminal
loss.' The most damaging of these losses was that of 'vitality . . . for without vitality the wheel cannot turn, and the activities of the body are
retarded'. When an aphrodisiac such as meat was consumed, the diner
would experience a brief period of elation and heightened sexual impulses,
followed by a much longer period of depression while the 'reserve [bio-
logical] force' was 'diverted' from (presumably) more important matters
in order to deal with the 'toxin'. After a prolonged diet of meat,

> the reflexive action is no longer so responsive, and so to maintain the
> same amount of stimulation, a greater dose of aphrodisiac is needed.
> Eventually the tone of the organism becomes so depleted that the
> body is no longer capable of putting up a defensive attempt to ward
> off the insidious nature of the toxin used. During such a lax period, no
> stimulation occurs to uncoil the serpent of desire.[67]

Such views were dependent upon a notion of the male sexed body
that was both profoundly evil (a 'serpent of desire') and easily drained
of its vital force.

So what exactly was it about meat that was dangerous to the masculine spermatic economy? The most common answer was uric acid.
'Some Sexual Disorders in the Male: Impotence and Involuntary
Seminal Emissions' was forthright in its warning about the effects of
uric acid, produced by meat-eating. According to its author, an instruc-
tor in genitourinary surgery at Northwestern University Medical
School, uric acid irritated the mucous lining of the 'prostatic urethra'
and caused 'intestinal putrefaction' and constipation. Because the seminal vesicles (the glands on each side of the male bladder that secrete
seminal fluid and promote the movement of spermatozoa through the
urethra) were situated between the colon and bladder, a 'distended
colon filled with hardened fecal matter' placed undue pressure on
these glands and encouraged emissions. This was both 'unnatural' and
'pathological', causing 'a sensation of weakness and lassitude that is not
imaginary'. The author challenged his readers to

> Show me a lawyer who does not dread a nocturnal emission on a night
> preceding an appeal where his mental and physical forces must be at
> their best; or a pugilist who does not fear such a drain the nightbefore
> [sic] a combat.[68]

Or, as another reformer argued, foods such as meat, milk, butter and 'demineralized' white bread produced uric acid and an excess of mucus in the body – eventually resulting not only in tuberculosis, cancer, ulcers, diabetes, colds and asthma, but also in blindness and 'loss of sexual potency'. In particular, this lecturer claimed, ingested meat was transformed into uric acid crystals inside the body. These crystals 'have a ground glass appearance and, after entering the blood stream, lodge on the retina and tear it down so that blindness is produced'. Similarly, they 'enter the prostate and destroy it by a grinding process'.[69] Male potency was in danger of being ground to dust through dietary infractions.

As all of these commentators imply, the problem of carnivorism was not only the threat of contagion or the risk that men's sexual ardour would be excited. It was also about illness. The author of the 1866 Prize Essay of the Alumni Association of the Medical Department of Columbia College put it succinctly:

> What is more likely to cause disease in us than converting the flesh of animals that we eat into our own bodies, and are we not thus liable to be involved in the same maladies with which they are troubled?[70]

These fears sometimes contained racist or anti-Semitic assumptions. In the late nineteenth century, for instance, Jewish practices of inspecting meat to ensure that it was a 'wholesome and proper article' were thought by some commentators to be sinister. In the words of the president of a society for improving abattoirs in London, 'The Jewish inspectors reject as improper food for their people 35 per cent of oxen, 25 per cent of calves, and 25 per cent of sheep. The whole of this rejected substance finds its way into the Gentile organism.'[71] More frequently, though, anxieties that eating meat was physically dangerous were generalized. In the words of Clara Balfour, writing in 1866,

> What sort of condition must the flesh of these animals be in after they have suffered such tortures? The overdriven ox, his feet and head one mass of bruises and aches; the flayed sheep; the slowly expiring calf – what feverish anguish must have poisoned all the fibres of their bodies before death came! Do not the miseries the victims endured make themselves felt by man? How many sudden ailments, obstinate, mysterious maladies, deadly diseases, comparatively unknown to our ancestors (as diphtheria) are rife among us, and defy the doctor's

skill and all the appliances of modern civilization! Does not the cruelty of man to the brute creation thus become cruelty to man
himself?[72]

But what kind of diseases was she referring to? Until the late twentieth century, the three most common dangers involved in masticating
animals were thought to be tuberculosis, constipation and cancer. The
first cannot be underestimated. The rise of veterinary medicine and
comparative pathology from the late nineteenth century introduced
fears related to animals infected with tuberculosis. In 1882 the German
bacteriologist Robert Koch was able to prove what had long been suspected: that bovine and human tuberculosis were caused by the same
organism. As one butcher admitted in the 1890s, poor families were
being fed meat that was 'possible a shade above carrion, but very
little'.[73] Bovine tuberculosis had become '*the* paradigm zoonosis', as
BSE was to become a century later.[74]

After the lungs, the next organ believed to be most threatened by
animal muscle and blood was the bowels. As James Whorton documented in *Inner Hygiene: Constipation and the Pursuit of Health in Modern
Society* (2000), the late nineteenth century saw a demonization of the
large bowel, dubbed the body's 'cesspool'.[75] The ingestion of animal
products, as well as over-processed foods, led to constipation, which
poisoned body, mind and soul. Decaying fecal matter caused autointoxication, resulting in any number of functional disorders, including
insomnia, indigestion and splitting headaches. If that wasn't bad
enough, autointoxication rendered men impotent and women unmar-
riageable. The prominent English surgeon Sir Arbuthnot Lane advised
men that they were better off marrying a 'drunken woman rather than
a toxic one' because 'a drunken person is occasionally merry, but a
toxic one never!'[76] In Lane's words, the 'poor, wretched, stupid, feeble
woman' suffering from constipation was 'ugly and unattractive'. She
had 'cold, clammy hands' and 'aches and pains in her legs, loins, and
arms'. Only by cleaning up her body's 'cesspool' would she be transformed into a 'bright eyed woman, sweet smelling, active mentally and
physically'.[77]

Even meat-eaters could be internal cleansed. For sufferers of constipation who were willing to go under the knife, Lane offered to
shorten or even entirely remove their colon. It was an option chosen by
a surprising number of people, most of whom were women. There
were less dramatic options, though. Exercise, for instance, was crucial.

Lane pointed out that 'while the civilized woman dances with her legs, the native woman dances with her trunk, every movement performed having as its object the stimulation of the intestines into activity'.[78] In this area (dancing), 'civilized' women might learn something from their less 'civilized' sisters. But harried, autointoxicated people were more likely to turn for help via paraffin oil, All-Bran, or DinaMite.[79] If this did not help, entrepreneurs such as Charles Tyrell invented the J. B. L. Cascade, a high-volume enema bag. The initials, J. B. L. stood for Joy, Beauty and Love.[80]

Constipation, and its associated moral effects, was linked to the third most significant danger (particularly for women)[81] inherent in ingesting animal proteins: cancer. Dr Ernest Tipper of the West African Medicine Service was a firm believer in a direct association between meat-eating and cancerous growths. According to Tipper, cancer was a 'disease of civilisation' and he drew attention to the absence of cancer in West African regions, such as Southern Nigeria, where people subsisted almost entirely on vegetable food.[82] In seeking to convey the danger to a lay audience, he drew his metaphors from the Foreign Office and the body politic. For Tipper, meat was an undesirable immigrant who needed to be expelled. However, due to weakness of the body corporeal, this invader had insinuated itself within its host, making 'mischief' and, ultimately, poisoning and killing it. Developing the metaphor further, Tipper explained that the 'upper part of the Digestive Tract functions as the Foreign Office to our internal economy'. Both were responsible for guarding the system from 'the intrusion of delirious substances'. Bodies that had been weakened in some way were incapable of adequately preparing certain foods – meat, in particular – for 'the ultimate assimilation'. As a consequence, the body's Foreign Office 'refuses to grant that food a passport'. Instead, it relegated the indigestible meat to the lower bowel where it *should* be 'properly ejected'. Unfortunately, the lower bowel of people who had a long history of meat-eating was unable to function properly. The result? 'Habitual constipation'. 'Butcher's meat', therefore, was 'allowed to linger about it in a semi-digested state' and 'after a time gets absorbed into the system under a false passport'. But that was particularly hazardous because meat retained its 'biochemically-active principles' and thus carried into the body corporeal 'all its latent potentiality for malignant mischief; in this case, the growth-accelerating and hyperesthenic properties of the young bullock cell'. In other words, meat was not an 'inert' substance. 'The Physicist tells us that nothing

in Nature is DEAD', Tipper harangued, and 'even in inorganic substances the IONS composing the molecular are in a state of extremely
rapid rhythmic activity'. Because the composition of animal meat was
so close to that of human tissues, it was 'all the more subtly dangerous'.
The molecules of animal meat would 'set our IONS revolving at their
own speed', and, he predicted, they would worm their way into 'some
locally scar-irritated highly vascular adult human tissue, such as the
breast, cervix, uteri, tongue, or the bowel constantly irritated by the
presence of a mass of formed faeces' to devastating, cancer-inducing
effect.[83] Sacrificing the animal proved to be a deadly rite indeed: instead
of placating the gods, it brought down their wrath.

From the 1970s, when vegetarianism became more popular, warnings about the dangers of eating meat increased exponentially. The
consumption of slaughtered animals was said to be raising cholesterol
levels to heart-breaking heights; it was responsible for salmonella and
a host of other bacterial dangers (such as E. coli and vancomycin-
resistant enterococci or VRE). The massive use of antibiotics in animal
husbandry was causing bacterial resistance. The sacrificial animal
seemed determined to wreak havoc on those consuming its flesh.

Most frightening, eating meat could, literally, drive you crazy. The
first human disease recognized as a prion disease (that is, a fatal, degen-
erative disease of the nervous system) was Kuru. It was described by
Carleton Gajdusek and Vincent Zigas after their study of the Fore tribe
of the Eastern Highlands of New Guinea[84] and, it was claimed (with
almost no evidence), had been transmitted through ritual cannibalism.[85]
The other disease spread through cannibalism – albeit cannibalism
by animals – was BSE, or bovine spongiform encephalopathy. In 1993,
when the BSE epidemic peaked, it was revealed that three-quarters of
all American cattle were being fed animal parts. By forcing animals to
become cannibals, people set the scene for their own destruction.[86] In
the words of Brian J. Ford in BSE – The Facts. Mad Cow Disease and the
Risk to Mankind (1996), 'Through greed, expediency, and ignorance of
science we have liberated the ancient cannibals' plague [kuru] in
Western society.'[87] It was a particularly potent scare because of beef's
connection to the British national identity.

In the end, however, the number of people dying from vCJD was relatively small. For most meat-eaters today, the dangers are more prosaic:
eating animals threatens to destroy a person's appearance, increases
their propensity to obesity, and is regarded as a low-status diet compared with fish, exotic fruit and vegetables. This problem is exacerbated

by the ways in which the flavours and textures of dead animals are made seductive to many human palates by the cooking process. For instance, raw chicken contains only 110 calories per 100 grams and is less than 3 per cent fat – but once turned into a McNugget it boasts 314 calories per 100 grams and 54 per cent food energy in fat.[88] Over half of the food energy in Burger King's Whopper, McDonald's Chicken McNuggets, Big Mac, and many kinds of Mexican fast food (especially beef enchiladas and chimichangas) consists of saturated fat. This is in contrast to 5 per cent in wild meat. The American Heart Association recommends that no more than 30 per cent of food energy should comprise fat.[89] Finally, these negative consequences of sacrificing animals do not include the numerous environmental effects, including high emissions of greenhouse gases and soil erosion. The costs to animals are incalculable.

CHAPTER SIXTEEN

Eating People

The anxieties expressed in the last chapter about the meaning of eating dead animals were part of a broader problem: the difficulty of distinguishing between the dismembered flesh of certain animals and that of humans. In William Shaw Rae's 'The Black Demons of Hayti', animal husbandry and cannibalism were presented as identical practices. Stephen and Alan (two 'long-pigs') and Evan (the 'little white goat widout de horns') were being fattened up for slaughter. 'Does the English farmer starve his turkeys before Christmas?', Alan whimpered and, immediately afterwards, the chief cannibal greeted the captives with the words, 'aha, my birds!' No distinction was made between the ingestion of the flesh of pigs, poultry, goats or people. This was a serious dilemma for anyone attempting to produce clear and decisive definitions for concepts such as 'human', 'humanity' and the 'humane'.

Comparative Gastronomy

In the first section of the previous chapter, I presented evidence about the staggering consumption of animal flesh in Anglo-American societies, particularly from the mid-nineteenth century onwards. If consuming the muscle and tissue, blood and bone of animals could nourish entire societies, could the same be said about the nutritional value of consuming *human* flesh? In fact, the notion that human flesh could be physically sustaining was simply assumed in debates about 'survival cannibalism'. In extreme circumstances, and faced with no alternative food source, it was widely accepted that eating other people would prolong the lives of survivors. There are innumerable examples of this practice, often prefaced by the comment that the eating of fellow humans was only undertaken 'after consultation and prayer'.[1] As vegan Amos Bronson Alcott (philosopher and father of Louisa May Alcott, the author of Little Women) told Ralph Waldo Emerson, who was waxing lyrical about the horrors of cannibalism while carving a roast: 'But Mr Emerson, if we are to eat meat at all, why should we not eat the best?'[2]

Prior to the 1970s, however, the nutritional value of anthropophagy (Greek for 'man' and 'to eat') was assumed but only rarely explicitly investigated. One exception was the work of Frederick Gowland Hopkins, eminent biochemist and discoverer of vitamins. In 1909 he informed members of the Royal Institution that the cannibals get 'precisely the quality and proportion of the foodstuff needed by the human body by taking them directly from that organism'.

> [By] consuming his own kind he eats exactly the right stuff. The nearer species are allied . . . the less difference is there between the chemical constituents of the tissues of individuals, and therefore the less work thrown on the processes of digestion and conversion, and therefore ape must be more nourishing to man than is beef or mutton.

Following this logic, the 'most efficient food of man' had to be other 'men'.[3]

Hopkins's forthright statement was unusual, but the reluctance to discuss the nutritional value of cannibalism changed in the 1970s. The key commentators were anthropologists, caught up in impassioned debates about whether cannibalism had even existed, let alone whether it was healthful. Andrew Vayda, for instance, pondered the nutritional value of human-on-human feasting. In traditional societies where 'protein intake' was 'marginal', Vayda speculated, the 'consumption of the flesh of sacrificial animals' would be important. Meat would help sick or injured people reverse the 'negative nitrogen balance' crucial for the 'healing of wounds and the production of antibodies'. If people did not have 'ready access to such animals as cattle or pigs as sacrificial items and sources of high-quality proteins', why wouldn't 'the consumption of human flesh . . . function in the same or similar way'?[4] Vayda's focus was on 'primitive' societies. In modern societies, the question of whether human flesh would even reach the 'necessary and appropriate standards' for ingestion by people faced a different hurdle.

As another anthropologist worried, might not 'the ingestion of pesticides, radioactive minerals, therapeutic (and other) drugs, food additives, and so on' mean that human flesh harvested in industrialized societies would be unhealthy anyway?[5]

The nutritional value of human flesh was an intriguing question but, again, experts wondered whether it was the most *efficient* source of energy. This was what concerned academics at the University of Michigan, who concluded that, even if other foods were available, a group of sixty people would need to slaughter one fifty-kilogram man every week in order for cannibalism to be nutritionally worthwhile.[6] Ironically, this research was carried out at a centre devoted to 'Human Growth and Development'.

Before the 1970s were over, one of the academics from the University of Michigan was showing signs of having been infected by a kind of dietetic mania. Stanley Garn's article, 'The Noneconomic Nature of Eating People' (1979), set out to make the strongest possible case against the economic value of cannibalism. With chilling objectivity, Garn asked readers to consider 'the energy cost of catching and returning a captive for immediate festive consumption'. Assume that the 'search-and-capture team' comprised ten men over four days. That alone would require an 'energy cost' of 160,000 kilocalories, not including the cost of rations given to the captive and the 'caloric cost of training and maintaining a search-and-capture team between forays'. Then, the captive would need to be fattened up – 'for more succulent appearance and improved caloric yield'. If the captive was tranquil for the entire hundred days of 'fattening', this would incur 200,000 kilocalories to maintain his weight and an additional 300,000 to properly fatten him. The additional energy cost of guards and cooks, as well as building and maintaining 'public-viewing fattening pens', should not be forgotten. In the end, then, a fifty-kilogram captive might yield '80,000 kilocalories if butchered immediately, or 120,000 kilocalories (at most) if scientifically fattened'. Even these estimates ignored 'inefficiencies in butchering, shrinkage in cooking, and losses in distribution', and so a cannibalistic community would actually 'incur a caloric debt of substantial proportions'. Briefly put, 'people-capturing and people-eating' was 'necessarily an uneconomic enterprise'. Given that it required a 'large and continually renewable' source of humans and incurred a prohibitively high cost in terms of energy, cannibalism was only practicable if practised 'for ceremonial and gustatory pleasure, but (like truffle-hunting) scarcely for caloric

Figure 1. Pamela Anderson for the PETA campaign, 'All Animals Have the Same Parts'. The article beneath this poster begins with the words 'Voluptuous vegetarian Pamela Anderson is proving that all animals have the same parts'. Browsers are encouraged to 'Click here to get your own copy of Pamela's sexy ad!'
Eamonn McCormack/WireImage

profit'.[7] In Garn's anthropophagic accountancy, those aspects of cannibalism that were ceremonial and orally pleasurable were presented as more convincing reasons for eating other people than the more prosaic arguments typically banded about by 'survival cannibals'. 'Eating Well' required sacrificial rituals, not simply a knife, pot and fire.

Collapsing the difference between human and non-human flesh was not simply a witty (and, it sometimes seems, obsessive) exercise for anthropologists. It was also a popular recruitment strategy for vegetarians. Food reformers throughout the centuries were fond of citing Diogenes' comment that 'we might as well eat the flesh of men, as the flesh of other animals'.[8] In the late twentieth century, People for the Ethical Treatment of Animals (PETA) transformed this statement into dramatic images that equated women's bodies with cuts of animal meat. They even co-opted an image that had originally been created by feminists protesting against the objectification of women in the Miss Universe contest. PETA's advertisement showed a woman with the different cuts of meat clearly delineated on her naked back: chuck, shoulder, rib, loin, rump and round. The caption read: 'All Animals Have the Same Parts' (see Figure 1). PETA's poster was, in fact, complicit in objectifying women as nothing more (or less) than 'my birds!' or passive objects to be consumed by male carnivores. Their poster was not a radical critique of the phallocentrism of society: rather, it exploited the phallocentric gaze in order to draw attention to another form of exploitation, that of non-human female animals.

Setting aside, for the moment, the presumed gender of consumable flesh (women as docile cows, cute piglets and sexy chicks), according to such approaches *all* meat-eating was cannibalism. Human tissue, muscle and bone were simply different 'cuts of meat', a theme that had been exploited in every century. As John Oswald put it in 1791, 'The corpse of a man differs in nothing from the corpse of any other animal.'[10] Proselytizing food reformers reported Damascene conversions arising from being struck by the similarities between gorging on animal and human muscle. Thus, in his 1921 reflections on English culture, the indefatigable reformer Henry S. Salt admitted that he regularly questioned friends about why they ate meat and was astonished by the zeal with which they 'sought to parry my awkward importunities'. Salt observed that their responses were evasive, reminding him of 'the quibbling explanations which travellers have received from cannibals when they inquired too closely into certain dietetic observations'. His conclusion? 'As far as diet was concerned', Salt lamented, 'we differed in degree only from the savages whom we deemed so debased'. In that time-honoured fashion of denigrating other peoples, he titled these reflections *Seventy Years Among Savages* (1921). (See Figure 2).

By the time Salt penned his reflections, he was a veteran campaigner for the vegetarian life. His thoughts can be traced back to *The Logic of Vegetarianism*, published two decades earlier, where he drew an evolutionary parallel between contemporary meat-eaters and their 'savage' ancestors. He quipped that there was 'nothing so pleasant as the reunion of long-separated kinsfolk'. 'The glories of the old English roast', Salt teased, 'may be instructively compared with the glories of the old African roast man'. It was his 'cheerful duty', he claimed, to introduce 'flesh eaters' to their ignored relatives, the 'Cannibal and Blood-sportsman'. Written in 1899, the year that 'The Black Demons of Hayti' appeared, Salt's 'Cannibal and Blood-sportsman' mirrored the characters of Sable Gross and Stephen Dining.

Figure 2. The original caption reads: 'THE TOURIST (late traveller for Blobb's Vegetable Tabloids': "Er – gentlemen, before you proceed further in this matter, allow me once more to impress upon you, not only for yourselves, but for your children also, the great advantage of a vegetarian diet." It was published in *Pearson's Magazine* in 1909.

Pearson's Magazine (September 1909)

Salt insisted that eaters of animal and human flesh were, like butchers and hunters,

> but different branches of one and the same great predatory stock. The cannibal and the sportsman are the wicked uncles of the pious flesh-eater, unrespectable descendants from a common ancestry, who have failed to adapt themselves to modern requirements, and, like belated Royalists in a Commonwealth have continued to play the old privileged games when its date is over-past.[11]

Like Ernest Tipper in the last chapter, who used metaphors drawn from the Foreign Office to explain the effects of meat-eating on the human body, Salt was also drawn to the body politic. He believed that in a commonwealth supposed to respect all sentient life, the carnivore, cannibal, butcher and hunter were throwbacks to earlier times of savagery and despotism. Eaters of animal flesh were like monarchists in a democracy: they should heed the proselytizing of vegetarians and give up their archaic habits, just as missionaries and other bearers of civilization convinced cannibals that their diet was 'something monstrous and abnormal, a dreadful perversion of taste'.[12] 'Civilization' itself could be read through sacrificial practices.

Cannibalism and 'Race'

It was no coincidence that Salt drew on metaphors of statecraft – monarchies and commonwealths – when making comparisons between the ingestion of human and animal corpses. The consumption of flesh was central to a range of politics that drew distinctions between humans. This was the third assumption made by Alan in 'The Black Demons of Hayti' when he asked the enslaved Haitian, 'What sort of refreshment can you offer? What are these joints cooking before the fire; man-flesh?' Eating meat created hierarchies of humans. In the last chapter, I explored hierarchies based upon eating animals while here I turn to hierarchies based on the carnivorous consumption of other people.

As we have just seen, there was, according to Salt, no distinction between kreophagists (eaters of animals) and anthropophagists (eaters of humans): both were cannibals. In 'The Black Demons of Hayti', Mona made a similar point when she proclaimed that 'God's curse lies heavily on the Black Republic' because, she believed, the voodoo religion made the ingestion of humans possible. God, who created 'man' to rule over the 'beasts', would forsake any nation that did not hold humanity above the animal. Practices of carnivorous sacrifice and ingestion defined who was within or without the polity.

For those inclined to chew on the bone, accusations of cannibalism generated excited discussions. Travellers, traders, missionaries, anthropologists and other emissaries of the West accused practically every group outside their own of cannibalism. In 1933 John Houston Craige famously dubbed Haitians 'woolly-headed cannibals'.[13] Indeed, the trope of cannibalism was made into a universal symbol of 'the primitive', originating at the birth of humanity yet capable of being hurled at any number of denigrated societies in the present.

Accusation of cannibalism as a way of differentiating the civilized from the bestial has a long history. 'Cannibal' first appeared in the English

language in 1553, in writings about Christopher Columbus. The word
was derived from the Arawak 'caniva', a corruption of 'cariba' (meaning
'bold'). It was a term the Caribbean Islanders of the Lesser Antilles used
to describe themselves, only becoming a synonym of barbarity when
used by their peace-loving neighbours, the Arawak. Anthropophagy dismembered the human from her or his human 'family'. Instead of eating
being an act of communion with fellow humans – in Derrida's words,
'eating well' meant offering 'infinite hospitality'[14] – cannibalism set the
victim outside that communion. It also set the *consumer* of human flesh
outside the fellowship, causing 'civilized' people to instinctively 'recoil
with loathing from the cannibal – a creature human only in form'.[15]

In the West, accusing conquered or supposedly inferior 'races' of
being cannibals was a way of distinguishing so-called civilized human
societies from the 'rest'; that is, 'wild' semi-human societies.
Infamously, Edward Long in *The History of Jamaica* (1774) claimed that

> Their old custom of gormandizing on human flesh has in it something
> so nauseous, so repugnant to nature and reason, that it would hardly
> admit of belief, if it has not been attested by a multitude of voyagers,
> some of whom affirm to have been eye-witnesses of it and, what is
> stronger, by reports of Negroes themselves.

He asked,

> Why should we doubt that the same ravenous savage, who can feast on
> the roasted quarters of an ape (that *mock-man*) would be not less
> delighted with the sight of a loin or buttock of human flesh, prepared
> in the same manner?

Long's view that they were cannibals was simply reinforced by his
observation that, although they feasted on apes, they believed that the
'ape species' was 'scarcely their inferiors in humanity'.[16]

It is not surprising that these cannibals – creatures closer to those
'mock-men', the apes, than to 'true' humans – had a distinctive physiognomy. Thus, in *Wuthering Heights*, to portray Heathcliff as animalistic,
bestial even, Emily Brontë gave him 'sharp cannibal teeth' and made him
claim that he wished that he had been 'born where laws are less strict, and
tastes less dainty'.[17] Authors who claimed scientific authority were even
more direct. As the author of 'Cannibal of Central Australia', published
in *The Illustrated Annual of Phrenology and Physiognomy* in 1869, exclaimed

What a hideous countenance! and yet in human form! . . . Little can be said of his intelligence. The perceptive faculties seem to be immensely large; but the forehead recedes sharply . . . There is little space between the ear and eye, consequently little room for those faculties which are more largely indicated in the civilized brain. There would be some mechanical skill, and the necessary faculties to enable him to entrap game without the higher order of mechanism. Little can be said of the social nature of this specimen; still less of the moral or religious. He is little more than an animal, and yet has the same number of bones, muscles, faculties, and organs that the best of us have.

He went on to say that there was 'work' for missionaries in reforming such cannibals, if they managed to 'escape the gridiron' themselves.[18]

Accusations of cannibalism legitimated the colonial subjection of other people, like the Haitians (see Figure 3).[19] Unlike tales of cannibalism in

Figure 3. The original caption was 'Obeah'. A former slave, feeding on the leg of a young white child, is interrupted by an upstanding white planter. As in 'The Black Demons of Hayti', 'Obeahism' or voodoo is deemed responsible.
Wood, *Blind Memory*

the early modern period (in which the practice signalled barbaric *prac-tices*), by the nineteenth century, cannibalism signified barbaric *persons*, all of whom were highly racialized as non-white.[20] Phrenologists, comparative anatomists and colonialists (whether in the guise of explorers, conquerors, or missionaries) identified entire 'racial' groups as 'cannibals'. Tales of cannibalism not only functioned as sensationalist parables, titillating 'civilized' palates, but also provided a means of identifying certain groups as scarcely human. This was at the heart of explorer Hesketh Prichard's derogatory assessment of Haitians in *Where Black Rules White. A Journey Across and About Hayti* (1900). He assured his readers that some Haitians were 'undoubted cannibals', a practice linked to their voodoo practices. For this reason, he argued, the answer to the question 'Can the Negro rule himself?' had to be 'no'.[21]

The lurid cannibalism of 'The Black Demons of Hayti' was not at all unusual, therefore. Second only to tales about zombies, cannibalism was at the core of Western images of the first black republic. Typically, Haitian hordes were described as meeting in a forest in the dead of night. There, the 'primitive instinct of the blacks' was 'given full rein' and, under the sway of voodoo incarnations and the hypnotic 'rumble of the tom-toms', Haitians gave themselves to 'demonical dances, mad drinking orgies, and sexual frenzies'. As one such storyteller claimed in the 1930s,

> out of these sexual orgies grew the atavistic impulse towards cannibalism. Definite feasts were instituted at which there was a ritual slaughter of children and even grown men, followed by a meal of roast flesh.[22]

The viciousness of these accounts was practically unbounded. In fact, the authors frequently claimed that the cannibals themselves recognized their own inferiority: they feasted on white Europeans or Americans in order to take on their superior traits. Thus, the young white Evan in 'The Black Demons of Hayti' was highly prized, in contrast to the 'black fellow . . . wery old, an' wery tough' who was being roasted on the fire near the start of that story. It was a theme that recurred in the virulently racist *Black Bagdad* [sic] (1933), a memoir by John Houston Craige, an American captain in the US Marine Corps. Craige had served a three-year term in Haiti, much of it in the mountain village of Hinche, eighty miles from Port au Prince. Craige believed that some Haitians were cannibals. One US Marine, Craige alleged, had crashed his plane in the mountains. Initially the locals regarded the Marine as a god because 'they thought the planes were big birds trained by the *blancs*, and that the whites who rode them were all-powerful *bocours*, a species of god'. But the local *Papallon* convinced them that the Marine was

> not a god . . . He is a fool, like the young *blancs* that straggle from the marine patrols on the trails. He is valuable meat. I am going to eat him. He may not be a wise *blanc* nor a brave one, but his organs have the mystic properties of the organs of *blancs*. If we eat his heart, we will have the white man's courage in battle.[23]

In this memoir, the Haitians were both naïve – believing that the American occupiers were gods – and conscious of their own inferiority. The only way to repel the *blanc* invaders was to consume them, magically transferring qualities that the *noir* lacked.

Consuming the Bodies of Slaves

Cannibalism was an accusation intended to deny certain humans entry into full humanity. In the examples given so far, it was used by economically dominant and militarily superior Westerners to denigrate people they enslaved and exploited.

What these Westerners omitted to mention was that *they* were the ones responsible for consuming the bodies of other peoples. In 'The Black Demons of Hayti' the bodies of the enslaved were literally (as well as symbolically) consumed by their masters. Alan Malcolm, son of the white planter, asked the slave Yam Pete, 'What can I eat *of* you to refresh me?' William Shaw Rae's excited narrative about Haitian cannibalism effectively masked the physical, moral and economic cannibalism of the plantation owners. Sugarcane plantations like the one owned by the Malcolm family were notorious for their brutality. It is noticeable that although fields of 'waving cane' appear at the start of the story, the fact that these fields were the site of slave labour is never alluded to. The only time readers are given any hint of the sadistic power relations operating on the plantations is when the father Malcolm vocally disapproved of the fact that his overseer (the notorious Sable Gross) was beating the young mulatto maid. But his displeasure was based on his view that chastising workers was *his* prerogative as their owner. A mere overseer had no right to usurp the right of the white owner.

Slaves and their advocates recognized that they were in danger of being eaten – again, they meant this literally as well as symbolically. This was implicitly noted in the Somerset v. Steuart legal case of 1772, which I discussed in Chapter Eight, when a lawyer speaking on behalf of the slaveholder explicitly acknowledged the risk of the slave being eaten when he followed his declaration that slaves were simply 'property', with the promise that, nevertheless, 'I won't, I assure them, make a rigorous use of my power; I will neither sell them, eat them, nor part with them'.[24]

Slaves' fears that they might be eaten were expressed in many contexts. For instance, poet William Cowper in 'Sweet Meat has Sour Sauce: or, the Slave-Trader in the Dumps' has a slave-trader fantasizing that his cargo are fish to be grilled and eaten:

> 'Twould do your heart good to see 'em below,
> Lie flat on their backs all the way as we go,
> Like sprats on a gridiron, scores in a row.[25]

Cowper was making his protest from a position of immense power and privilege. Not so former slave Olaudah Equiano. His *The Interesting Narrative of the Life of O. Equiano, or G. Vassa, the African, Written by Himself* (1789) voiced the fear of being served up as fodder after he was forcibly hauled on board a slave ship. He asked the other slaves whether 'we were not to be eaten by those white men with horrible looks, red faces, and long hair?'[26] Two years later, abolitionist Richard Hillier in *A Vindication of the Address to the People of Great-Britain on the Use of West India Produce* also protested against cannibalistic practices on slave ships. Hillier's tract was a response to one distributed by a female *apologist* for slavery. In his response, Hillier conjured up the image of an African forced on to a slave ship. The slave was in despair, not understanding why he was 'torn' from 'his country and his friends' and

> why the wretches who have laden him with chains, are desirous that he should eat; he cannot account for their brutal kindness; he concludes that they mean to fatten him, in order to feast upon him at a convenient season.

As a result, the slave refused to eat. He was 'whipt' and 'the *speculum oris* is resorted to'. A 'broken tooth gives an opportunity for its introduction; his mouth is forced open, rice is crammed down his throat, and he is compelled to live'.[27]

Figure 4. James Gillray, 'Barbarities in the West Indies', c.1791. The inscription beneath the image comes from a speech by Philip Francis. It reads: 'An English Negro Driver, because a young Negro thro sickness was unable to work, threw him into a Copper of Boiling Sugar-juice, & after keeping him steeped over head & ears for above Three Quarters of an hour in the boiling liquid, whipt him with such severity, that it was near Six Months before he recover'd of his Wounds & Scalding.' As the overseer boils dismembered slaves, he says, 'B—t your black Eyes! what you can't work because you're not well? – but I'll give you a warm bath to cure your Ague, & a Curry-combing afterwards to put spunk into you.' On the wall are dismembered arms, ears and other bodily parts. Historian Ronald Paulson claims that the print may actually parody abolitionists' rhetoric, while historian Marcus Wood goes even further, suggesting that Gillray was 'enacting a fantasy of execution and dismemberment upon an anonymous set of black bodies, a fantasy in which the viewer is invited to participate'.

Still other writers made the cannibalistic link in even stronger terms (see Figure 4).[28] In the same year as Hillier was writing, William Fox (founder of the Sunday School Society) confirmed the fears of slaves, explicitly claiming that they were being cannibalistically consumed. Since the sugar trade was dependent on slavery, he argued, everyone who consumed sugar was therefore a cannibal. Every pinch of sugar was 'steeped in the blood of our fellow-creatures'. He shrugged aside

the idea that consumers of sugar were less guilty of the crime of cannibalism than the 'slave-dealer, the slave-holder, and the slave-driver':
these men were 'the agents of the consumer, and may be considered as
employed and hired by him to procure the commodity'. As we saw earlier, like much cannibal discourse, a grisly accountancy was indulged in.
Even leaving aside the unimaginable misery caused to the slave, his or
her family and the community, Fox insisted, 'in every pound of sugar
used (the produce of slaves), we may be considered as consuming two
ounces of human flesh'. He maintained that,

> A family that uses 5lbs. of sugar per week, with the proportion of
> rum, will, by abstaining from the consumption 21 months, prevent
> the slavery or murder of one fellow-creature; eight such families in
> 19½ years, prevent the slavery or murder of 100, and 38,000 would
> totally prevent the Slave Trade to supply our islands.

The 'rights of man' were 'not limited to any nation, or to any colour'.
And it included the right not to be cannibalized.[29]

A Second Address to the People of Great Britain was published the following year, and was even plainer about exactly which bodily
excretions were being consumed when sugar was eaten. The author of
this tract was Andrew Burn, and he was determined to disgust his
readers, especially female ones. For Burn, it was not only the case
that 'the Consumers of Sugar and Rum' were the 'first and moving
cause of those torrents of Blood and Sweat, that annually flow from the
body of the poor African', but they were also cannibals. In his direct
language, he claimed that women who

> use soft sugar, either in Puddings, Pies, Tarts, Tea, or otherwise . . .
> literally, and most certainly, in so doing, eat large quantities of that
> last mentioned fluid [blood], as it flows copiously from the Body of the
> laborious Slave.

Even more distressing, sweet-toothed consumers were not only sip-
ping the blood of slaves, but also the 'warm stream' of sweat, lice, the
'disgusting fluid . . . arising from a disorder called the Yaws' and other
infections. Burn went further, reciting two anecdotes about a 'roasted
Negro' and the 'skeleton of a Child' that had been found at the bottom
of superior-flavoured rum and sugar. He affirmed 'as a certain fact' that
'the Carcase of a Dog, Cat, Sheep, Goat, Man or Woman' would

'greatly tend to meliorate and soften' the taste of rum.[30] As a poem 'for Youthful Readers, on Colonial Slavery' (1832), urged,

> If good people at home, when they sweeten their food,
> Would abstain from the cane-juice that's water'd with blood.[31]

The repugnant consumption of human blood was not simply a prerogative of white slave owners in places like Haiti, but an integral part of capitalist production. Radical critiques of twentieth-century capitalism were incensed by exploitation within the meat industry – an industry that was portrayed as literally 'consuming' desperate labourers. The best illustration of this can be found in Upton Sinclair's best-selling novel *The Jungle* (1905), which was set in the Chicago Union Stockyards. Because Sinclair had already written about chattel slavery, an editor challenged him to 'do the same thing for wage slavery'. What Sinclair found wandering about the stockyards was profoundly shocking: a 'veritable fortress of oppression', slaughtering animals in the most cruel ways and virtually 'eating' the human operatives.

The novel accused industrialists of cannibalism: workers who fell into vats, or whose body parts were caught in the machinery, were rendered into leaf lard or tinned meat products. He also repeated the accusation that anti-slavery activists had made from the eighteenth century onwards: the entire process was also symbolically cannibalistic.

As a result of the furore over Sinclair's book, the 1906 Pure Food and Drug Act was passed through Congress. Although Sinclair had set out to transform the lives of the grossly exploited workers, the result was nothing more than controls over the adulteration and labelling of food and drugs. Sinclair's dream that the newly formed working men's unions would enable the exploited workers to 'look out for themselves' more effectively never eventuated. Americans were reassured that the animals they ate were hygienically killed, but the labouring men were disposable; they could be consumed, and at virtually no cost. As Sinclair complained, 'I aimed at the public's heart, and by accident I hit it in the stomach.'[32] It was a point that has been cinematically exploited ever since, as in *White Zombie* (a film about a sugar-cane plantation in Haiti) and, most notoriously, in *Night of the Living Dead* (1968), and its many imitations (see Figure 5).

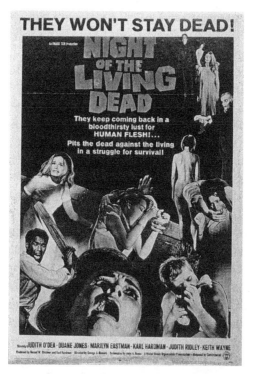

Figure 5. Film poster for *Night of the Living Dead*, 1968. The film, directed by George A. Romero, featured zombies, cannibalism and graphic violence within a Pennsylvania community. Duane Jones, who later became executive director of the Black Theater Alliance, played its hero, Ben.
Getty Images

Bringing the Cannibal Home

White Zombie and *Night of the Living Dead* were unusual in that the cannibals were white- as well as brown-skinned. Outside of the slavery debates of the late eighteenth century and in extreme examples of survival, there has been great resistance to any suggestion that cannibalism existed amongst Europeans. In an 1866 talk to the Anthropological Society of London, Richard Stephen Charnock admitted that it was 'unpalatable to Europeans' to be reminded that 'the inhabitants of Europe were at one time quite as savage as those who have practised, or who still practise this crime'. Absolutely unpalatable! exclaimed respondents to his talk. After all, Charnock's many critics asserted, human flesh simply did not 'agree with' civilized stomachs and 'even' Fiji-islanders generally felt ill after eating it.[33] The only occasion on which cannibalism could be admitted was in the context of disasters of unprecedented magnitude: in such circumstances, it was even possible (reluctantly, and with much debate and soul-searching) to admit Sir John Franklin, Britain's greatest Arctic explorer and national hero, into the company of cannibals.

Of course, the rejection of cannibalism within Europe was dependent upon a highly specific definition of 'people-eating'. Take the Roman Catholic Eucharist, in which believers hope to become more Christ-like by devouring His body and blood. When believers kneel for the Sacrifice of the Mass, the bread and wine becomes 'His body and blood'. For believers, there is nothing metaphorical about it. The ingestion of the host (from the Latin *hostia*, meaning victim) is, theologically speaking, literal. Yet no kinship with other cannibalistic practices (even symbolic ones, as in Obeahism) is confessed.

The definition excludes many secular rituals as well. In Britain and America, in the past as well as today, it is not uncommon for mothers who have recently given birth to eat the placenta – but who would dare call this most maternal ingestion 'cannibalism'? Keen placentophagists are reminded that the placenta 'should not be more than three days old'. Recipes for roast placenta, placenta cocktail and placenta lasagne are easy to find. Experienced cooks blandly inform potential digesters that a placenta generally weighs about one-sixth of the baby's weight, so if it was too much to consume immediately, it can be dehydrated and stored in gel caps. Mothers are advised to add a spoonful to their cereal or drink when required. This incestuous feasting is credited with the magical properties of warding off post-partum depression and bringing happiness to new mothers. As one mother quipped, 'It is the only piece of meat you can eat that you don't have to kill to do so.'[34] (See Figure 6.)

The problem of definitions is even more serious if we turn our gaze to medicine. Blood transfusions, growth hormones (Creutzfeldt-Jakob Disease was transmitted, in part, by a growth hormone made from human pituitaries) and organ transplants all involve the taking other human tissues and flesh inside one's own body: crucially, perhaps, they do not involve mastication. In the future the definition of human-on-human cannibalism might be further complicated by animal–human chimeras. Currently, by injecting human stem cells into sheep, chimeras whose livers are 80 per cent human can be created.[35] As a science correspondent for *Reason* magazine asked, 'would eating a liver composed chiefly of human liver cells grown in a sheep be cannibalism?' His answer? 'Yes; don't do it. Save them for transplants.'[36]

Figure 6. A placenta on a chopping board. This photograph is from a web-site providing recipes for cooking and eating placentas. Browsers are told that 'Each placenta weighs approximately ⅙ the baby's weight. Cut the meat away from the membranes with a sharp knife. Discard the membranes.' The directions for placenta lasagne tell cooks to 'Use your favorite lasagne recipe and substitute this mixture for one layer of cheese'.
http://www.twilightheadquarters.com/placenta.html

Even if we stick to conventional definitions of cannibalism, however, the practice can be found close to home. In the nineteenth and twentieth centuries, British and American reports of cannibalism (excluding 'survival cannibals' and the exceptionally rare cannibalistic psychopath, both of which have generated a vast literature)[37] took two forms: individual pranks and cruelty associated with the exploitation of the bodies of the poor. In the first instance, reports of cannibalism were linked to hazing practices, usually within medical schools. In a fairly typical example, a physician in the 1860s confessed that a 'horrid practical joke' had been played on a medical student: his fellow students had 'cut a piece [of flesh] from a body in the dissecting-room, and had it fried and served up to him as beef-steak, which he ate, and thought very good'.[38] In the same decade, *The Times* and the *Lancet* reported that a lab assistant at St Thomas' Hospital (London) carried out the 'abominable action' of cooking and eating a small piece of human flesh 'out of bravado'. *The Times* was relieved to be able to report that the 'disgusting act' had been carried out by a lower-class assistant, rather than the medical students who were 'gentlemen both by birth and education'.[39] Class could be as potent an explanation as 'race'.

From the nineteenth century, however, another form of cannibalism began to 'speak its name': that is, people-eating arose in the context of the political economy of pauperism. In nineteenth-century Britain, paupers could occasionally be heard protesting that their bodies were – literally – being consumed. One such panic occurred in 1829 when a pauper newly admitted to the workhouse of St Paul's, Shadwell (in the Tower Hamlets area of London) complained that the food they were being served contained human as well as animal remains. Why might the other inmates have good reason to think that this was plausible? Shortly before this accusation, Parliament had been debating the Anatomy Bill (passed in 1832), which proposed that the bodies of paupers who had died inside workhouses and whose bodies had not been claimed by their family could be sent to medical schools for dissection. If the wealthy were prepared to dismember paupers' bodies in the study of anatomy, why not suppose they would be willing to use these bodies in other humiliating ways? The *Morning Chronicle* reported that 'many of the paupers' at St Paul's 'became so frightened' by gossip that they were being fed human remains that 'they refused to partake of their food'. The pauper who sparked the panic – described by a magistrate as 'one of the most turbulent paupers in existence' – was eventually sentenced to twenty-one days in a house of correction for making unfounded allegations. Nevertheless, the master of the workhouse was anxious to prove that he was not serving up 'Nattomy Soup', so he brought a bowl of the workhouse broth and its recipe to court.[40]

This was not the only time that paupers feared that they were being made to eat each other. Ten years later an anxious inspector of workhouses in Kent reported that rumours were spreading that 'the children of the workhouses were killed to make pies with, while the old, when died, were employed to manure the guardian's fields, in order to save the expense of coffins'.[41] There was even a ballad circulating in the mid-nineteenth century: 'The Workhouse Boy' featured a young pauper who went missing after the master of the workhouse promised that 'You'll all get fat on your Christmas cheer!' After searching for him, the other paupers found his remains in the soup pot:

> A dollop of bones lay a grizzling there,
> In the leg of the breeches the poor boy did wear!
> To gain his fill the boy did stoop,
> And, dreadful to tell, he was boil'd in the soup!
> And ve all of us say, and ve say it sincere,
> That he was push'd in there by an overseer.
> Oh the Poor Vorkhouse [sic] Boy, etc.[42]

Around the same time as this ballad was being sung, a highly publicized instance of alleged cannibalism took place in Hampshire. At the Andover workhouse male paupers had been put to work crushing bones for use as fertilizer. In 1845 a local farmer and member of the Board of Guardians discovered that the paupers were so hungry that they were fighting over the bones in order to eat them. To great consternation, it was revealed that some of the bones came from the local cemetery. Paupers, it was claimed, had been sucking on the bones of dead people.

The gruesome story caused uproar, forcing the government to institute a parliamentary inquiry into what had happened. The scandal was a godsend for people protesting against the stringent new Poor Law, which was based on the principle of 'less eligibility' (the idea that life within the workhouse should be 'less eligible', or less preferable, than the lowest life outside). The master of the Andover workhouse – ex-Sergeant Major Colin M'Dougal, a veteran of Waterloo – was accused of introducing increasingly harsh measures to prevent the workhouse from becoming overcrowded by the growing numbers of unemployed men and women. The callous acceptance of the situation by the master, the matron, and many members of the board of guardians shocked reporters. *Punch* penned 'The Andover War-Song', a satirical attack on the guardians' attitude. The last stanza went:

> We wunt be beat! We wunt be beat!
> On we will goe, and wunt retreat.
> No; by our Chairman we will stand,
> 'Gin all the rason in the land.
> We've got no ears for paupers' groans,
> What zignifies their gnawun' bones?
> What matters what be Workus meat!
> We wunt be beat! We wunt be beat![43]

Newspapers and journals throughout the country broadcast the message that the misery of the Andover paupers – and their comrades in poverty – should be reflected upon by every true Englishman and woman. The *English Gentleman* exhorted 'the minister, while he picks his teeth' to 'think of his fellow-man picking a human bone' and 'the goodly citizen, while undergoing repletion' to 'dispense with the marrow-bone and toast' and sigh, in the fullness of his stomach, over the thoughts of 'perverted appetites'. Everyone 'capable of reflection, and desirous to benefit mankind' should 'shudder' when they realized what had been going on in their own nation.[44] This was not simply a matter of retaining the dignity of Englishmen. It was also a question of the rights of all men and women created in God's image to be accorded compassion. People were 'not placed by his Maker upon any one spot throughout this broad land to be starved'. Every person was

> entitled to food – it is his inherent right, as much as the air he breathes – but he is bound to earn it honestly. If we cannot employ him – if we cannot accept his labour – or if he is incapable of work – still he is one of us, and must not be shut up to gnaw the bones of dead men. Policy and Christianity teach us otherwise.[45]

Policy and Christianity endorsed honest labour, not anthropophagy.

The crisis was also linked to anxieties about what distinguished humans from animals. In attempting to explain how men could come to 'resemble beasts', readers were encouraged to imagine what it felt like to be starving. The hunger of these paupers was not the hunger of 'gentlemen who hunt, and ladies who take proper exercise', nor was it that of 'the poor sickly maiden who labours all day for a sixpence'. Their hunger was much more than 'the sinking of a stomach': these paupers had been reduced to an animalistic level, the 'famished state of the wolf'.[46]

To add insult to the story, while the pauper-men were 'savagely fighting' over flesh and bones, master M'Dougal was 'pilfering from these poor wretches', getting drunk and 'otherwise disgracing himself and humanity' by sexually abusing the female inmates.[47] M'Dougal, too, had 'animal propensities', earning him the nickname 'Dougal Creature'.[48] As the *Satirist; or, the Censor of the Times* informed readers,

> M'Dougal has certainly been a devil among the female paupers. It was not merely now and then an occasional indiscretion, but he seems never to have been able to let them alone. He is obviously endowed with a most ungovernable and indiscriminative liking for the sex, and, numerous as the female paupers were, he had 'stomach for them all'. He evinced his gallantry nearly to all alike.

M'Dougal was dubbed 'the sultan of his pauper seraglio' and a 'Scotch Turk'. The workhouse was 'a sort of Mahometan paradise, and the feminine paupers the houris with which it was thickly peopled'.[49] In other words, everyone involved in this workhouse had been degraded. The master set the scene and corrupted everyone around him. While the men were 'bestialised' by the nature of their work and inadvertent cannibalism, the women were rendered less than fully human by the female equivalent: an abuse of their sexuality.

The periodical press united in condemnation and horror that such scenes should take place in this respectable Hampshire town, or indeed any English town (see Figure 7). Three features of the scandal earned the most comment: the disparity between rich and poor, the animalization of paupers and the contrast between an allegedly civilized Britain and 'true cannibal savages'.

How could there be such a disparity between rich and poor Britons, asked people throughout the country. The *Penny Satirist* published a poem written by Joe Miller, entitled 'Food for the Poor: Song of the Andover Union', which juxtaposed rich and poor eating habits. In some homes, Miller wrote, 'men had feasted far and wide' on animal flesh, and then these

> fat and torpid things
> Were sleeping like the drones,
> The meat was eaten all away!

Figure 7. From *Punch* (25 March 1914). The cartoon is not only a play on English cannibalism, but also on the parochialism of English culture. Kendal is slightly to the south-west of Appleby in Cumbria. The original caption reads: *Doctor (to old Appleby dame whose son has been eaten by cannibals in the South Sea Islands)*: 'I am so very sorry to hear the bad news about your son. Can you tell me where it happened?'
Dame: 'Nay, a don't rightly knaa. It was soomwhar below Kendal.'
Punch

Meanwhile,

> The paupers grouped around THEIR feasts –
> Every – every one!
> The shreds and patches of putrid flesh
> Clung to their whitening thrones,
> And the marrow ouzed with a sickening breath
> Up from the tainted bones.
>
> The paupers sat like a ghastly crew
> After a staving wreck,
> And they saw the black flesh quiver and reek
> And the bones wear a plague-like speck.
> But as famine shrilled forth its deadly shriek,
> They leaped to its echoing tones;
> And they scratch'd for the carrion brought for the flesh,
> And howl'd for the marrowy bones![50]

It was a story that delighted satirists (see Figure 8).

In both of these examples, as well as in the many other commentaries on the scandal, the shock was as much about the animalization of paupers as it was about the chewing on human bones. These paupers had been relegated, unwittingly, to 'nearly the last state of human

THE ANDOVER BASTILE.

Figure 8. 'The Andover Bastile', in *Penny Satirist*, 1845. On the left is an image of 'The Poor Picking the Bones to Live', depicting bestial-faced paupers fighting over bones to eat. The caption states that they had been 'ground down by hunger to a condition as low as that of the very dogs'. On the right is a sketch of 'The Commission of Inquiry Discussing the Subject over a Good Dinner', in which seven well-fed men tuck in to roast beef and liquor.
Penny Satirist (6 September 1845)

degradation', lamented the *Satirist*. They 'have been treated like brutes, and their hankering after decaying bones and refuse meat, have accorded with the brutal regime to which they have been subjected'.[51] The inmates of the Andover Union Workhouse went so far as to remind the Poor Law commissioners that farm animals in the UK were being better fed than they were. All over the county, they petitioned, 'certain animal called swine are greatly over-fed, and thereby rendered much fatter than any pork ought rightly to be'.[52]

Furthermore, how could this have happened in a 'civilised' country? The *English Gentleman* insisted that 'we did not think it possible that human beings could be found among us quarrelling for a loathsome bone, indifferent as to whether it belonged to man or beast!'[53] It harangued readers to remember that 'we are in a Christian land and not among Savages – that we are in *England*, whose people pay millions for the maintenance of the poor'.[54] Cannibalism in Andover had exposed a fundamental corruption at the heart of political life in England: 'What shall be said of the system – or laws – or party – or persons – who shall have driven them to so terrible an extremity?'[55] Such depravity could be imagined in less civilized parts of the world. 'The New Zealand Savages', the *Satirist* pointed out, 'have been proven to eat their enemies, and occasionally, perhaps, their friends, with a keen appetite'. But even they would never think of 'devouring carcases while in a putrid state'. Indeed, while the Englishman might 'deplore' the 'eccentric taste' of indigenous New Zealanders for eating a member of a 'hostile tribe' or even for being tempted by a 'stray missionary' (if sufficiently 'plump'), 'we must still rejoice that famine has nothing to do with its display'.[56] *John Bull* even imagined an 'intelligent foreigner' saying, on hearing of the case, 'Monsieur Jean Bull is certainly a most incomprehensible animal.'[57]

While deeply shocking to people of the time and leading to major reforms of the workhouse system (which was, after all, the reason journalists and politicians propagated such myths), this panic over cannibalistic workhouse practices was short-lived. A century later, however, a very different panic arose over eating people. This time, the focus was on the exploitation of middle-class girls and women rather than working-class men. In the 1980s and 1990s allegations of cannibalistic practices became linked to satanic rituals. Therapists such as Colin A. Ross, author of *Satanic Ritual Abuse: Principles of Treatment* (1995), professed to have met 'dozens of people who claim to have participated in ritual cannibalism, drinking of human blood, and human and animal sacrifice, and who believe themselves to be demon-possessed'. Because cannibalism is seen as belonging to a 'primitive phase of cultural development', Ross went on, such practices 'pose a major challenge to our usual beliefs about human history and the cultural evolution of our race'.[58]

His concerns were widely shared. Although only about two per cent of adults in North America claimed to have experienced possession by the devil,[59] stories of satanic abuse often included cannibalistic vignettes. The story of 'Gina', published in Daniel Ryder's *Breaking the Circle of Satanic Ritual Abuse. Recognizing and Recovering from the Hidden Trauma* (1992), was fairly typical of the genre (see Figure 9, a 'patient's' sketch from his book).[60] Gina's mother was a Sunday-school teacher and mission leader in the local Baptist church in Oklahoma, but Gina's main memories were of being immersed in a satanic cult. Her life story was one of rape from the age of six. The perpetrators included both her parents as well as dozens, maybe hundreds, of other cult members. Once again, the flesh of animals and persons were intertwined. Gina

Figure 9. The original caption read, 'A woman killed this infant in a ritual and then as part of the ceremony walked among the participants with the child placed on the sword, blood dripping down. The child was later dismembered and eaten by all. The infant was brought to the cult meeting by inducing premature labor in one of the women.' From Daniel Ryder, *Breaking the Circle of Satanic Ritual Abuse.*

Ryder, *Breaking the Circle of Satanic Ritual Abuse*

recalled that they were fed large quantities of raw and barely cooked meat. 'We ate hamburger meat, eggs, and occasionally steak, which we bought from a store. The rest of the meat was raised at the section house – goat meat, chicken meat, horse meat, and cat meat', she remembered, explaining that 'Satanists believe that eating animal or human flesh gives them more power and domination. Drinking blood is believed to do the same thing.' At the ceremonies, black-robed men and women would chant 'in another tongue . . . Just as some Christians "speak in tongues" to get closer to God, they spoke in a satanic language to get closer to Satan.' In grotesque terms, she described how she was forcibly impregnated and made to give birth to an infant every year; these babies were then sacrificed and eaten.[61]

Such lurid accounts were standard fare, and closely resemble older stories about the potency of ingesting human body parts. Given that Haiti was the paradigm 'cannibal country', it should come as no surprise that it sometimes made an appearance in these stories.[62] More commonly, however, the sacrificed person was not a racial 'other'. Indeed, the power of the ritual could be particularly strong precisely because the victim was an intimate companion. As one 'expert' observed, the phallus or fingers of satanic cult members were sometimes eaten, 'an act very effective in restoring potency'.[63] Like the older narratives explored earlier in this chapter, infants and children were favoured victims. As the author of *Cults that Kill* (1988) explained,

> When you sacrifice someone, for the instant just before they die, they supposedly emit their life energy. That power, Satanists believe, can be harnessed for their use. They believe babies are best because babies are pure . . . When you sacrifice a baby, you get greater power than if you sacrifice an adult.[64]

How can these stories be explained? Some investigators embraced a highly reductive version of psychoanalysis. Thus Lloyd deMause, director of the Institute for Psychohistory and editor of a special issue on the cult abuse of children in the *Journal of Psychohistory* in 1994, claimed that cannibalistic acts were attempts by 'deeply regressed individuals' to 'avoid castration and engulfment fears and reassure themselves of their potency and separateness'. DeMause's psychohistorical explanation was that these cult members were re-enacting 'fetal trama' [sic]. 'It may seem arbitrary and excessive', he admitted, 'to claim that cultic ritual involves regression all the way back to birth', but

I think this is the only way to make sense out of the specific elements of cult rituals. Cults relive each traumatic moment of birth in their rituals. They put children in cases, boxes and coffins as symbolic wombs. They hang them upside down, the position of fetuses . . . They drink victim's blood as fetuses 'drink' placental blood . . . When did we all ever 'drink' blood? Only in the womb.[65]

In contrast to the cannibalistic scares arising out of exploitative practices within workhouses, anthropophagy in the late twentieth century was internalized – literally, its origin could be traced to the mother's womb. It was only in the 1990s, with the feminist attack on 'recovered memory', that people-eating was politicized and, to coin a rather ugly word, de-literalized. For second-wave feminists, feasting on the bodies of girls and women was symbolic. Patriarchy was the real ogre.

Conclusion to Part 5: What Does it Mean to Eat Flesh?

In this Part, 'Eating: Carnivorous Consumption', I have explored how people have been ranked as human, lesser human, and pure animal according to their response to the consumption of a variety of flesh. Entire groups could be labelled 'barbaric' by accusing them of cannibalism, but what was depicted as cannibalistic in white European societies was highly selective. When it did include the literal mastication of another person's flesh, the causes were primarily economic (paupers in the nineteenth century) or satanic (infants and young girls in the late twentieth century).

The meaning of animal flesh also turns out to be a sensitive marker of status because the animal becomes human inside the stomach, intestines, pancreas, liver, bone and blood. As the president of a society dedicated to improving abattoirs expressed it in the 1890s, 'the animal substance which to-day may be beef, mutton, or pork, may to-morrow be human substance, part and parcel of man, bone of his bone and flesh of his flesh'.[1] The 'executions of ingestion, incorporation, or introjection of the corpse' (as Derrida put it)[2] constituted the human and set her outside the animal, who could be killed. For Derrida, this 'non-criminal putting to death' of animals exposed the limitations of Levinas's philosophy. For Levinas, the responsibility not to kill ('Thou shalt not kill') was partial: it only referred to 'thy neighbour'. As Derrida pointed out,

The 'Thou shalt not kill' — with all its consequences, which are limitless — has never been understood within the Judeo-Christian tradition, nor apparently by Levinas, as a 'Thou shalt not put to death the living in general'.

As I discussed in the last Part, Levinas remained a humanist, even if not a traditional one. Sacrifice was still present in his work: Levinas did not 'sacrifice sacrifice' because it was 'not forbidden to make an attempt on life in general, but only on the life of man, of other kin'. In contrast, Derrida wanted to 'link the question of the "who" to the question of "sacrifice"'. Autonomy and authority could only be achieved within a carno-phallogocentric economy that privileged the human (not legitimately edible) over the animal; the man (carnivorous supreme) over the woman.[3] Such hierarchies decided who could be eaten – sometimes literally; other times, symbolically.

The underlying tensions, however, have appeared time and again. Even though considerable cultural energy went into abstracting the living animal from the marinated chop, the repressed knowledge of animal life – of sentience – constantly breaks through. Many animals resembled humans; they possessed recognizable traits that might be passed on if taken inside the human body. Fears of miscegenation (especially for those humans anxious to cast the 'human' in a wholly superior moral universe to the 'animal') could make these acts of consumption discomforting. Becoming a living being depends upon absorbing elements from inside, outside, around. Eating is intimate. It exposes the fluidity of the human subject. It is a Möbius strip turned into a river of blood in the shape of a figure-of-eight. Like it or not, there is violence there.

Xenografts and Metamorphosis

CHAPTER SEVENTEEN

Stephanie and Goobers

This is the story of Stephanie and Goobers, who were born seven months apart. Stephanie was born on 14 October 1984. Along with twelve thousand other premature children in America that year, she suffered from hypoplastic left-heart syndrome: that is, the left-hand side of her heart was underdeveloped. Two weeks after Stephanie's birth the healthy Goobers was killed on her behalf. Goobers's walnut-sized heart was excised and sewn into Stephanie's chest. For three weeks, Stephanie's simian heart-beat kept her alive. Then she too died.

Who were these two infants, whose bodies were successfully fused for a few weeks? Goobers had been raised in California's Loma Linda Medical Center, run by the Seventh Day Adventist Church. She was one of a small research colony of baboons kept in the basement of that hospital. I was unable to find out anything else about her.

In contrast, Stephanie's short life has a long biography. Her mother was twenty-three-year-old Teresa Fae. Stephanie's unmarried parents had separated shortly before her birth, and her mother was dependent on Aid to Families with Dependent Children. Told of her daughter's heart condition, Teresa had taken Stephanie home to die. When Teresa received a telephone call from a paediatric cardiac surgeon at the Loma Linda Medical Center, suggesting that a revolutionary new operation might save her daughter's life, Teresa would not have hesitated.

The surgeon's name was Leonard L. Bailey. He claimed to be governed by 'medical altruism' as much as by scientific ambition, and justified his experiments by arguing that the fact that the possibility of transplantation 'even exists today is a tribute to the humanness of mankind'.[1] He had

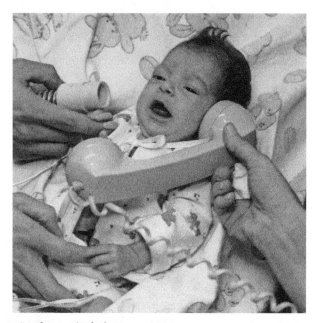

Figure 1. Stephanie ('Baby') Fae in 1984.
Press Association

spent the previous seven years performing around 160 cross-species organ transplants on sheep and goats. Although none of these animals had survived for more than six months, Bailey was convinced that Baby Fae (as Stephanie came to be known in the media) could be saved by replacing her heart with one taken from a baboon. Surgeons were experiencing increasing success in carrying out human-to-human organ transplantations, so animal-to-human transplantations (xenotransplanation, after the Greek 'xenos', meaning 'stranger') were a logical step. Bailey was optimistic. The US government had recently approved a new immunosuppressive drug called cyclosporine, and he believed that because the immune system of an infant was immature it was less likely to reject the organ. As Bailey put it, 'A newborn is a gracious host.'[2]

Initially, the operation seemed to have worked (for Stephanie, that is; Goobers's death had been inevitable from the start). Four days after surgery, a poignant video was released to the media, which showed her yawning and stretching (see Figure 1). After eleven days, *The Times* reported that five-pound Baby Fae was 'sucking strongly, crying lustily and as cute as a button'.[3] This did not last long, however. Stephanie's kidneys and heart failed as a result of the drugs and progressive graft necrosis, and she died.

Millions of people followed the story. Had Bailey created a human–animal chimera? When Stephanie died, the public was aghast. Her death renewed discussions about human–animal relations. The surgeon who had removed Goobers's healthy heart and used it as a 'spare part' one was accused of not acting in the best interests of either Goobers or Stephanie. In the context of his human patient, why hadn't he attempted to find a human donor? Shouldn't Stephanie have been referred to Dr William Norwood at the Children's Hospital in Boston, who had since 1979 been repairing the underdeveloped hearts of infants, with considerable success? Some critics even questioned Bailey's scientific competence, especially after it was reported that, when questioned about why he had chosen to transplant the heart of a baboon, given its evolutionary distance from humans, Bailey had replied, 'Er, I find that difficult to answer. You see, I don't believe in evolution.'[4]

The bitterest accusations, however, came from the pro-animal lobby. Had Goobers been treated appropriately? Animal rights campaigners belonging to PETA (People for the Ethical Treatment of Animals) dubbed xenografting a form of 'ghoulish tinkering', arguing that it 'boils down to having killed a perfectly healthy baboon in order to prolong a child's suffering'.[5] Philosopher Tom Regan admitted that it was easy to grieve the death of Stephanie. After all, she

> was *somebody*. A distinct individual with an unknown but partly imaginable future. If we allowed ourselves, we could share her first taste of ice cream, feel the butterflies in her stomach before the third-grade play, endure her [dental] braces.

In contrast, Regan complained, the other victim seemed to be beyond empathetic responses. That 'lifeless corpse, the still beating heart wrenched from the uncomprehending body' was a '*something*', an 'it'. Goobers had 'a life whose quality and duration mattered to him [sic], independently of his utility to us', he insisted. Just as Baby Fae did not exist simply as a resource to save the life of a sick Goobers, Regan continued, so Goobers 'did not exist as her resource either'. The surgeons who 'seized his heart' had 'grievously violated Goobers [sic] right to be treated with respect'.[6]

Regan certainly had a point, but Baby Fae was also little more than an experimental resource in a dramatic surgical drama. In the words of critics of the attempted xenograft, the physicians had acted as though Stephanie was nothing more than 'a pathetic sacrificial victim whose dying was exploited and prolonged on the altar of scientific progress'.[7] Baby Fae faltered even in the empathy stakes. Goobers generated more sympathy than did Stephanie, who was stigmatized as the dying daughter of an unmarried mother who had dropped out of high school, 'passed bad checks', smoked heavily and was dependent on welfare handouts.[8] After the deaths of Goobers and Stephanie, thirteen thousand people accused the Loma Linda Medical Center of acting cruelly towards Goobers while only seventy-five made a similar complaint about cruelty towards Stephanie.[9] *Time* even referred to the child as a '5-lb. *object*'.[10] She was an 'it' too.

Critics of the procedure claimed that the surgeons treated Stephanie as a means to an end rather than an end in herself. This is a reference to the Kantian 'categorical imperative' that has been mentioned elsewhere in this book, and is a charge levelled at most of the pioneers of xenotransplantations. Was it any coincidence, asked critics, that the early recipients of animal organs were overwhelmingly poor and disenfranchised? In the words of one of these patients, Jefferson Davis (a forty-three-year-old African-American dying of glomerulonephritis), 'You told me that's one chance out of a thousand. I said I didn't have no choice . . . You told me it gonna be animal kidneys. Well, I ain't had no choice.'[11] At the New Orleans Charity Hospital on 5 November 1963, surgeon Keith Reemtsma replaced Davis's kidney with one harvested from a chimpanzee. The chimpanzee died immediately, and Davis followed suit on 6 January 1964. Later that month, James D. Hardy performed the first heart transplant to use a chimpanzee heart. It was inserted into Boyd Rush, a poverty-stricken sixty-eight-year-old deaf-mute. Rush was in a coma when the time for the operation arrived, so his stepsister had signed the consent form. She was not told that the heart belonged to a chimpanzee. As opponents to vivisection constantly argued, a lack of consideration for animals would inevitably seep into attitudes towards 'lesser humans' such as the physically or mentally handicapped, the poor and women. Stephanie Fae, Jefferson Davis, Boyd Rush, Goobers and a host of unnamed primates were disadvantaged animals to be experimented upon without qualm.[12]

These people and events complicate further our understanding of being human, being animal and becoming animal/human. What does it mean for Stephanie Fae, her mother and the millions who followed her progress in the media to have a baboon's heart beating in her tiny all-too-human chest? Was she part-human part-animal, a chimera? The following two chapters investigate this question by describing how the secretions and organs of animals have been utilized within the human body. The first chapter tackles nineteenth- and early twentieth-century attempts to exploit animal bodies in the name of rejuvenating the human frame. Here, I refer to medical experiments with animal secretions and sexual organs. Then I turn to procedures involving the xenotransplantation of whole organs from animals to humans (although, as we shall see, there were some attempts to transplant *from* humans to animals). Was Bailey correct when he attacked the bioethical furore that exploded in the aftermath of Stephanie Fae's death as 'too quick, too ill-informed, too self-assured'? He admitted that 'some of it hurt my feelings', claiming that he had

> often compared the ethical rhetoric of those days to the phenomenon of 'pack journalism', and have considered it 'semi-ethics' – close, but not quite the real thing. What was missing was *wisdom* and a sense of perspective.[13]

Ethicists will have a lot to say in response to scientific belittlement. I conclude by discussing the implications of twenty-first-century therapies involving stem cells harvested from other species.

In what follows, then, the creation of chimeras – that is, organisms that have been said to possess partly human and partly animal bodies – both incites anxieties about 'species integrity' and reminds us that such integrity has always been an illusion of Western science and philosophy. The Möbius strip of *zoe* evades attempts to assert an inflexible, 'natural' boundary between discrete creatures. As we will be seeing, what is 'natural' can change with remarkable speed, as a result of scientific technologies, ideological imperatives and the power of creative visions. Attempts by people within their historical time and geographical place, as well as a host of other contexts (including gendered ones), to create others and themselves in the image of some kind of imagined ideal – human or animal – are a story of ingenuity, to be applauded as well as feared.

CHAPTER EIGHTEEN

Rejuvenation

Bodies are made up of fluids, fat, tissue, muscle and bone, all encased in skin and decorated in practical ways with hair, fur or feathers. All bodily components eventually disintegrate. In mammals such as humans, apes and dogs, bones grow brittle and snap; muscle tone relaxes; fat stores melt away or (more unfortunately) accumulate; sex hormones cease production, causing penises to droop and vaginas to dry up; hair grows dull and may fall out. Those of us who have observed, or are beginning to observe, the process in ourselves may be forgiven for occasionally thinking: not a pretty sight.

But what if scientists discovered a way to reverse, or at least delay, the inevitable? What if bodily parts and secretions could be shared around a bit more, passing from virile bodies, like Goobers's, to impaired ones, like Stephanie Fae's? Or from younger to older creatures? Scientists in the affluent West have enthusiastically grasped this challenge, identifying non-human animals as possessing the 'some-*thing*' that 'some*one*' (human) desired. How could an 'it' be truly 'sacrificed' because 'its' are not 'ends in themselves'? They are nothing more than 'means to an end'. Humans have been charged with raising themselves 'above all other beings in the world that are not men', as Kant famously expressed it.[1] Surely part of 'being human' means being engaged in a relentless process of self-perfection.

The 1984 experiment involving Goobers and Stephanie Fae was, therefore, part of a wider philosophical and scientific momentum towards the exploitation of animal bodies in the interest of human ones. In fact, attempts to regenerate the human through inserting animals under our flesh (and not just in the form of dead meat) have a very long history. The first documented heterologous graft was performed in 1668, when the Dutch surgeon Job van Meekeren used a bone from a dog's skull to repair that of a soldier.[2] It took another three hundred years before such processes began to be understood scientifically. From the 1880s, scientific interest in xenotransplants reached new heights. Initially, though, the excitement was directed toward the possibility of regenerating elderly bodies rather than infantile ones such as Stephanie Fae's.

In the nineteenth and early twentieth centuries, scientists increasingly turned their attention to the last period of a person's lifespan and, more specifically, to attempts to reverse the process of ageing. Grey hair was no longer 'a glorious crown; it is found in the way of righteousness',[3] as the Bible would have it. Old age was no longer that stage in life when men and women should welcome the opportunity to relinquish the incessant search for the pleasures of this world in expectation of greater glories in the next. Rather, ageing persons demanded the right to gratification in the here and now.

On the contrary, ageing was increasingly seen as a chronic disease. 'No living organism can ultimately escape Death', the author of a book entitled *Rejuvenation* admitted in 1923, but with the help of science 'we can at least push back his kingdom'. Science could uncover 'a charm to wean us from the vulgar habit of growing old'.[4] The author of *Outwitting Middle Age* (1926) concurred, explaining that human life no longer needs to be 'darkened by the grim shadow of Age'.[5] By exploiting the organs and internal secretions of animals, men and women could do more than merely 'outwit middle age': they could significantly defer the appearance of the grim reaper.

As we will see, these scientific experiments contrasted strongly with those performed by late twentieth-century surgeons such as Leonard L. Bailey, who operated on Goobers and Stephanie Fae. For one thing, they were relatively uninterested in infants. They also differed from twenty-first-century scientists, whose most significant interventions into the physiology of life typically focused on the very earliest stage of development – on molecular, cellular and embryonic life (issues which will be explored in the next chapter).

Rejuvenation and Xenografts

What were the techniques used by late nineteenth-century scientists to perfect the human? How did they exploit the bodies of animals? And how did their interventions seek to affect the future status of the human?

The quest to discover the 'elixir of life', which would transform the human lifespan and aid in the perfection of the human body, took a dramatic turn in 1889. In June of that year, the renowned French-American-Mauritian neurologist and physiologist Charles Édouard Brown-Séquard excitedly informed the distinguished members of the Société de Biologie that the testicular extracts of dogs and guinea pigs had remarkable anti-ageing properties. Brown-Séquard was no quack. After a distinguished career in Paris, Virginia, New York and London (where he served as inspiration to Robert Louis Stevenson for *Dr Jekyll and Mr Hyde*), he was appointed in 1878 to replace the renowned physiologist Claude Bernard in the Collège de France.

By 1889, however, Brown-Séquard was seventy-two years old and feared that his physical and intellectual powers were waning. Using himself as his experimental subject, he concluded that injecting extracts from animals' testicles were rejuvenating. As he put it in an article in the *Lancet* in 1889, injecting ground-up guinea pig and dog testes improved 'all the functions dependent on action of the nervous systems': they gave energy, muscular strength, stamina and mental agility.[6] Brown-Séquard claimed that he felt thirty years younger. Even better, as the *British Medical Journal* frankly reported, 'defæcation and micturition were also discharged with greater ease'. Brown-Séquard also boasted that the extract meant that he had been able to *rendre visite* to his young third wife. Within four years of his announcement, Brown-Séquard claimed to have collected evidence of 1600 uses of his 'orchitic liquid', of which between 85 and 90 per cent were deemed successful.[7] He eagerly marketed the testicular extracts as 'sequarine – the medicine of the future'.

Although the scientific community were initially aghast, fretting that Brown-Séquard had brought medical science into disrepute by such a blatant harvesting of animals' sexual organs, his findings reverberated around the world. In fact, his ideas were in line with much popular Victorian thought. Anglo-American historians have often described the nineteenth century as the century of the 'spermatic economy', in which semen was believed to possess extraordinarily invigorating properties. As historian Chandak Sengoopta explained in *The Most Secret Quintessence of Life: Sex, Glands, and Hormones, 1850–1950* (2006), in the nineteenth century

any inordinate loss of semen, whether through masturbation or excessive venery, was supposed to cause immense damage to health and
morals. Since the loss of semen was harmful, the absorption of semen
was likely to be of some benefit.[8]

In 1905, the British physiologist Ernest Starling formally renamed
Brown-Séquard's 'internal secretions' 'hormones', after the Greek
word *hormōn* ('exciting or arousing'). Although embarrassing to
modern scientists, this was the birth of the science of endocrinology.

Brown-Séquard's 'organotherapy' (sometimes known as 'opother-
apy', or the treatment of illness and disease with extracts made from
animal glands) involved crushing the glands of guinea pigs, dogs or bulls
and injecting the liquid under the skin or into the rectum. In the 1920s,
however, Serge Voronoff, a Russian-French physician, proposed a much
more radical use of animals' sexual organs. Like Brown-Séquard,
Voronoff was persuaded that the 'internal secretions' of testicles were
responsible for much more than merely enabling the 'sexual function'.
Indeed, they were a stimulant to the 'organism as a whole'. Voronoff
encouraged physiologists to scrutinize the bodies of male eunuchs who
could not be classed as 'truly men'. In a visit to Cairo in 1898,
Voronoff was 'immensely struck' by the appearance of these eunuchs.
They were

> long in the leg, with small craniums and smooth, hairless faces. In the
> majority of instances they are obese, with pendulous cheeks, developed
> breasts, and enlarged pelves. They look, in fact, like old women, and
> the resemblance is enhanced by their characteristic high-pitched voices.
> The muscles are flabby, the walk and movements lethargic, the gums
> and sclerotics [white of the eye] pallid. They present, in short, all the
> signs so characteristic of the anæmic, feeble and flabby organism.

Further evidence for their lack of manly characteristics included their
'slow' intelligence and lack of 'courage and enterprise'. He concluded
that the 'internal secretions of the testicle' must be important in the
development of the truly human: the testicle 'stimulates the intelligence, maintains courage, and prolongs life'. Men who were 'vigorous
and energetic, with lively imagination, a capacity for work, and the
power of resisting fatigue' have been blessed with 'highly active testicles'.[9] In effect, as Voronoff candidly lectured, 'decrepit old men are,
in reality, eunuchs', emasculated by the 'cruel law of nature'.[10] It is

thus important to observe that, for Voronoff and his colleagues, the 'human' they sought to rejuvenate and make into a perfect specimen was almost without exception male. Eunuchs were scarcely human because they were like women. Most importantly, they lacked 'highly active testicles'.

What could be done? Voronoff argued that Brown-Séquard's testicular extracts were a 'weak' and 'palliative' way to deal with men whose endocrine secretions were inadequate. As Voronoff put it in *The Study of Old Age and My Method of Rejuvenation* (1926),

> The inert substances of glands which have been crushed, dried or macerated in glycerine, contains very few active principles. What is more, in order to imitate the processes of nature, this substance would not have to be taken in massive doses once or twice in the twenty-four hours, but in minute quantities constantly repeated during the day and for the remainder of life.[11]

Surely, he insisted, there was a more direct and effective way to revive true human vigour within the bodies of old and decrepit men.

Like Brown-Séquard, Voronoff believed that mutilating and destroying the bodies of animals would solve human inadequacies. He spent years experimenting, grafting the testicles of young he-goats and rams into old, 'miserable' ones. According to Voronoff, the elderly animals metamorphosed from incontinent, senile, 'thin, melancholic, and timid' creatures to animals that were 'young in gait, bellicose and aggressive . . . Full of vitality and energy'.

Heartened, Voronoff decided to extend his experiments to people. Despite his enthusiastic attempts to persuade healthy men to donate one of their testicles to aid older men ('Nature is generous, she is even prodigal' in giving men two testicles when they only required one, he urged), his male colleagues and acquaintances could not be convinced. Worse: he discovered that it was 'forbidden by law' to harvest testicles from men who had been executed or had been victims of fatal accidents. Voronoff lamented that he could do little more than hope for the day when 'special hospitals, equipped with special facilities' would exist, at which 'candidates for glandular grafting will remain, in readiness to receive the required organs from the fatally injured cases who will be hurried thither'.[12]

Until that utopian day, Voronoff turned his scientific mind to the 'daring' possibilities posed by anthropoid apes (see Figure 1). These

Figure 1. A sketch of Serge Voronoff and an unnamed assistant performing a rejuvenating operation at the College of France. The image is entitled 'L'Homme qui rend la Jeunesse' or 'The man who restores youth', and was published on the cover of *Le Petit Journal* on 22 October 1922.

Doctor Serge Voronov (1866–1951) The Man who Restores Youth, from 'Le Petit Journal', 22nd October 1922 (colour litho), French School (20th century)/Private Collection/Archives Charmet/The Bridgeman Art Library

near-relatives of humans could be captured in India and Africa, transported to Europe and their live sex organs grafted into the scrotums of ageing and impotent men. Unlike Leonard Bailey, who harvested Goobers's heart and gave it to Stephanie Fae, Voronoff believed in evolution and therefore recognized that, in evolutionary terms, the anthropoid ape immediately preceded the emergence of the human. Humans were simply 'the final link in a long evolutionary chain'. As Voronoff explained,

> Among other well-known facts, it is extremely difficult to distinguish the three-months' foetus of the ape from the human foetus . . . So close is the early resemblance, that if I had had to make a graft on a three months' foetus, I should probably have taken my graft from man or ape indifferently, for I should not have been able to distinguish between them, and I should not have considered that I had made a heterograft.[13]

Voronoff admitted that the species boundary was impossible to determine in early fetal life. However, he was convinced that evolutionary
development at a later stage varied by 'race'. In his book *Rejuvenation
by Grafting* (1925), he included a note stating that there was 'nothing
surprising in the fact that grafted organs or tissues of the chimpanzee
behave as would corresponding structures taken from a man, such as a
negro or native Australian of certain races'.[14] In the long chain of evolution, 'negroes' and indigenous Australians were only marginally
positioned above chimpanzees. Voronoff's potential patients – white,
wealthy male Europeans – were to benefit from the harvesting of the
organs of these lower life forms.

What was his actual procedure? (See Figure 2.) Surgically, xenografting was a straightforward procedure for two surgeons. A chimpanzee
rendered unconscious with chloroform and a man who had been
drugged with a local anaesthetic such as novocaine would be laid on
adjacent operating tables. Surgeon A would open the chimpanzee's

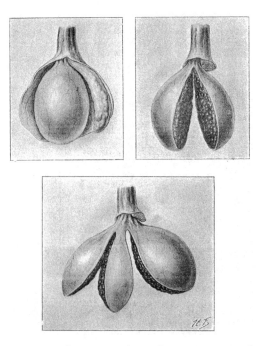

Figure 2. A simian testicle cut into three slices prior to implantation in a
human scrotum. From 'Opération sur le Singe Donneur', in Serge
Voronoff and George Alexandrescu, *La Greffe Testiculaire du Singe à l'Homme*.
Voronoff and Alexandrescu, *La Greffe Testiculaire du Singe a l'Homme*

scrotum, while Surgeon B would prepare the human scrotum by opening it and pulling back the membrane as far as possible. The internal surfaces of this 'pocket' would be 'scarified by short cutting movements of the scalpel', thus promoting new blood connections between the tissues and the graft. Surgeon A would then remove the simian's testicle (being careful not to cut its vascular connections since the graft needed nutrition until the moment of transplantation), scarify it, then cut it into four slices. 'As the testicle of the chimpanzee is small', Voronoff explained, each slice would probably be only two centimetres in length, half a centimetre in width, and a few millimetres in depth. In contrast, if the testicles of yellow baboons were used, thinner slices would be necessary and one testicle would be enough for two men. Surgeon B then needed to detach the slice and stitch it inside the 'pockets' of the man's scrotum. Two grafts were placed inside each scrotum. The incisions in both man and animals were then sutured closed.[15]

Although nearly all discussion concerned men, a female equivalent of this operation was performed, albeit extremely rarely. After all, it was sometimes necessary to 'stimulate the vitality of a worn-out [female] organism' as well. Intra-abdominal grafting of the ovaries of female chimpanzees into women was considered too risky. Fanciful critics might wonder if there was a small chance that the woman would give birth to a chimpanzee, or a monkey/human chimera. Practical risks were more plausible. Making an incision through a woman's abdominal wall was a 'bold exercise', Voronoff admitted (especially, he added, because most women seeking rejuvenation were 'old and usually fat'). As a consequence, he experimented with alternative implantation sites. In the end, he decided that the best location for grafting chimpanzee ovaries was inside the *labia majora*. Voronoff would make an incision

> on the upper part of these folds and after vigorous irritation of that region, the grafts are planted at the level of the terminal fibres of the round ligaments. This scarification has the purpose of producing, just in man, a marked hyperæmia and an abundant new vascularisation susceptible if ensuring the survival of the grafts.[16]

It was an extreme form of cosmetic surgery, scarifying a woman's genitals in order to rejuvenate her face and torso.

Voronoff claimed that his results were as spectacular for humans as they had been for his 'melancholic' goats and rams. He boasted that in the vast majority of operations the men were rejuvenated (I could find no data for the number of women he operated on, nor about the effect of the operation on them). Between June 1920 and October 1923 Voronoff performed fifty-two testicular grafting operations. In all cases except one, the glands had been harvested from apes. In *Rejuvenation by Grafting*, Voronoff reported on the success of forty-three of these animal-to-man grafts, and claimed that the others were too recent to be conclusive. While nobody died as a result of the operation, he admitted that between 5 and 12 per cent of these post-operative patients suffered from neurasthenia, myopathy (a muscular disease), infantilization of the genitalia ('the chimpanzee . . . being too young'), and inflammation of the testicles. In contrast, between 36 and 88 per cent of patients experienced 'absolute . . . physical and mental restoration', while in 26 to 55 per cent of cases 'the physical and mental rehabilitation was accompanied by complete restoration of sexual activity'[17] (see Figure 3). In addition, Voronoff asserted that the gland operation was successful in 'curing' homosexuality in 57 per cent of patients seeking remedy for their sexual preference (but the total number of patients is not given).[18] Although Voronoff was careful to insist that testicular grafts should not be done simply for their aphrodisiac effects, he admitted that the transplantation often excited a man's sexual energies. It could also extend life, but only

> if, after the graft, men were to conduct themselves with the same sagacity as do the beasts, whose physiological expenditure is in proportion to their true needs and who do not kill themselves by various excesses.

In other words, humans had to imitate the animal world, by avoiding the excesses of human civilization and only eating, drinking, sleeping and engaging in sexual intercourse according to their basic needs. As a warning, he presented the case of a seventy-seven-year-old man who, as a result of the graft, turned from a 'senile old man' into 'a man in full and striking possession of all his faculties'. Unfortunately, because he was overly exuberant about the result, the patient threw himself into a hedonistic lifestyle and died in an alcoholic fugue.[19]

As most of Voronoff's comments imply, the main indicator of 'success' was a revival of the patient's essential humanity, which was characterized by masculinity. This was one reason why he was always much more ambivalent about operating on women. Implanting

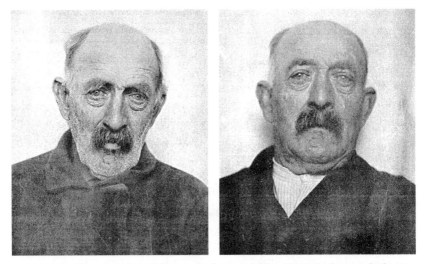

Figure 3. Photographs of George Behr, aged 73 and 74, before and after Voronoff's operation. He had lived 'a long life of hard work and want', but three months after the operation he took a job with a chemist, 'washing bottles, keeping the garden, and looking after the fowls'. From Serge Voronoff and George Alexandrescu, *La Greffe Testiculaire du Singe à l'Homme*.

Voronoff and Alexandrescu, *La Greffe Testiculaire du Singe a l'Homme*

chimpanzee ovaries in women was ideologically problematic. Observers fretted that such a procedure might represent a reversion to 'primitive' practices. After all, there was a long tradition of 'foreign peasant women' ingesting pregnant sows' uteruses and ovaries (collected from abattoirs) to cure them of barrenness.[20] Even worse, might rejuvenated women become sexually voracious? That was decidedly making women more animalistic, a characteristic to which the female 'species' was already regrettably prone.

In contrast, male vitality and prowess was held in very high esteem in the West. In his case studies, Voronoff strongly emphasized the fact that his patients' 'capacity for work' had been greatly enhanced. In addition to the 'awakening of . . . genital powers', patients claimed that they could 'work all day now' and felt 'like a young oak'.[21] The recovery of masculinity was explicit, as in Voronoff's discussion of one of the earliest grafts he carried out on a human. In 1913 he grafted a chimpanzee's thyroid gland into a boy named Jean who was suffering from *myxœdœmatour*, or cretinism.[22] Shortly after the operation, the child (who had been 'so backward as to be almost reduced to the animal level') was on the road to complete recovery. For Voronoff, however, the proof of the effectiveness of the graft lay in the fact that

> four years later, when eighteen years of age, young Jean, whom I had known in 1913 as a poor little imbecile, having but a rudimentary brain and the body of a child of eight, was found suitable for military service and accomplished his duty in the trenches most gallantly.[23]

'The greatest deeds of life', Voronoff insisted, were 'performed during the activity of the sexual gland'.[24] These deeds obviously included the most manly act of all: military combat.

Brown-Séquard and Voronoff, as well as their numerous imitators, shared a scientific and moral vision of the world. They were optimistic that, through manipulating the bodies of animals, 'the human' could be transformed. People would live better and longer lives. They would be more content. Men would be more masculine. Women? Well, that was less clear. They would be more youthful-looking (good), but perhaps it would also bring out women's innate animal-like sensuousness (bad). Nevertheless, the 'eyes of distressed humanity', as one anonymous author put it in the *Scientific Monthly* in 1922, 'turned eagerly' towards the new gland cures for 'health and happiness'. The author noted that only a few years previously psychoanalysis had been 'all the rage' but endocrinology now reigned supreme. Indeed, he exclaimed, 'those who formerly were rushing to have complexes extracted are now anxious to have glands implanted. Away with psychology! 'Rah for physiology.' He did admit that 'as fads there is not much to choose between them' but 'popular expectations always run far ahead of the march of sober science'. Both psychoanalysis and gland theory had 'a certain foundation of fact', but

> the scientific basis of the glandular idea is much more solid and substantial. An emotional complex is after all a figment of the imagination, but when you get out a chemical compound, extracted, purified and identified, you have hold of something tangible and when you put it back into the patient you can regulate the dose and record the reaction.[25]

Gland treatments were precise and straightforward: there was no need to struggle with mutable complexes or riotous instincts. With the help of animal secretions and organs, the human body was extraordinarily malleable. A phial of extracts or a minor operation could literally change what it meant to be human.

Critics

For Voronoff, all of human progress was 'due to the triumph of Man over Nature'. In this way,

> Man [sic] demonstrates his superiority over the rest of creation, and it is thanks to this superiority that he has arrived at his present state of evolution. But for the constant struggle against Nature, we should be still in the predicament of the cave man.

In case his readers had not quite grasped his point, he added: 'To subdue Nature is to ensure the progress of Humanity.'[26]

Scientists and experimenters like Voronoff shared a vision of 'the human' that was strenuously rejected by many people, both then and now. For one thing, the new technologies were developed through experimenting on live animals. From the 1880s onwards self-styled 'animal guardians' routinely referred to Brown-Séquard as the 'most eminent experimenter in vivisection now living – one who ... has probably inflicted more animal suffering than any other man in his time'.[27] The *Herald* even published a letter from a repentant former vivisector who attacked Brown-Séquard's 'pottering, happy-go-lucky "vivisections"'. The correspondent admitted that

> we may indeed have learned something but at what a cost! ... the curious illustrations and ingeniously varied superfluity of verifications hit upon by [Brown-Séquard] were produced through the wholesale sacrifice and torture of thousands of sentient beings with feelings as acute as our own.[28]

Readers of the *Anti-Vivisection Journal* were aghast at unverified claims that it took the adrenal glands of twenty thousand oxen to produce one pound of adrenalin.[29] Voronoff was also proclaimed guilty of torturing animals. Not only did his animals not consent to having their sexual organs removed but, in order to have sufficient supplies of testicles, Voronoff had to transport thousands of monkeys from India or Africa. Sometimes, anti-vivisectionists reported, he crammed as many as twenty monkeys into a crate 5½ feet long, 2½ feet wide and 18 inches high.[30] Purveyors of the 'elixir of life' were overlooking the 'price of pain and death to the helpless dumb creatures'.[31] For critics, the species boundary was emotionally, as well as scientifically, porous: anyone capable of torturing animals would have few scruples being cruel to humans.

These commentators were also repelled by any notion that science could be redemptive. Writing in 1893, the humanitarian and mystic Edward Maitland warned about the 'serious danger' represented by 'certain scientific classes' who set themselves above fundamental natural laws. According to him, dictatorial scientists would 'trample under foot every principle, sentiment and interest that stands in their way', imposing a way of life that was 'utterly incompatible, not only with religion and morality but with humanity itself'.[32] Thirty-four years after Maitland's warnings, anxieties about the 'tyranny of science' were echoed by the novelist Sir Philip Gibbs in an article on rejuvenation. 'We have already to make up our minds whether we are going to allow these scientists to tinker about with the human body and experiment with the human mind', he informed readers. Was it

> good for men and women to let the scientists experiment like this with their bodies and brains? Will it not lead to great dangers, and be an outrage against some divine law in nature which will lead us to a new form of hell here or hereafter? Will it not put our very souls into the hands of the scientists, who in the future may be evil men – as some are now – who may be the paid servants of some frightful Scientific State which has control over the bodies of men and women, or may be the actual dictators of that State?

He foresaw 'dangers ahead by which humanity may fall under a tyranny of science and lose its soul in trying to alter the natural laws of evolution, and the Design which some of us perceive'.[33]

As these examples make clear, there was a strong moral undertone to these arguments. 'Nature' was sacred, propelled to ultimate perfection by the laws of a great deity: evolution could even be seen as one of His mechanisms. 'Nature' should not be tampered with. The transplantation of animal organs into humans was an unnatural act, turning men into 'human vampires', protested the *Animals' Guardian* in 1897.[34]

Worse, scientists who experimented on living flesh – whether animal or human – were debasing nature even further by systematically commercializing life forces. Bodies were corrupted 'simply for the sake of commercial profit'.[35] In the words of Ouida (the pen name of the novelist Marie Louise de la Ramée), writing in 1893, organotherapists were treating animals' bodies as mere 'vessels' filled with organs and blood for 'the human invalid'.[36] As the president of the Animal Defence and Anti-Vivisection Society sneered in 1929, 'Is your magneto – your human magneto – working well? If it is not, Dr Voronoff may within a short time be able to sell you a substitute from his stock of "spares"'. Lind-af-Hageby continued, pointing out that Voronoff and his ilk regarded the human body as nothing more than a 'machine'; its organs were the 'motor', and its glands were the 'magneto'. In the near future, she warned,

> if a man or woman needs a new part of any sort, in a year or two he or she will be able to go to [Voronoff's] chimpanzee farm at Mentone [on the French Riviera] and pick out a likely-looking chimpanzee, and a surgeon will cut the 'spare' out of the animal and sew it into the human being.[37]

Men and women who undertook rejuvenation treatments were, literally, selling their souls and debasing their bodies in exchange for eternal – or at least extended – life. Frightening images of a modern re-enaction of the Faustian myth were invoked. In the words of the editor of the *Anti-Vivisection and Humanitarian Review* in 1929, 'The compact of Faust with Satan for the restoration of youth fades before the blatancy of modern attempts at cheating Nature. (Nature is sure to exact payment.)'[38]

'Nature' was being cheated at every level: individual, societal and species. Critics of rejuvenation were disgusted by reports that elderly men who should be thinking of their grandchildren and the hereafter were being transformed into 'gross sensualists'. In 1889, one unnamed physician distributed six thousand copies of a pamphlet attacking Brown-Séquard's methods. 'I consider the idea of injecting the seminal fluid of dogs and rabbits into human beings a disgusting one', he began, adding that

> when the treatment also involves the practice of masturbation, I think it is time for the medical profession in England to repudiate it. One may be a vivisector without also encouraging a loathsome vice … Vivisection may be an open question, but self-abuse is not.[39]

It is not clear whether he was claiming that it was wrong for animals to be masturbated in order to excrete their semen or whether he believed that Brown-Séquard's patients masturbated after their rejuvenating treatment. I suspect he was referring to the latter. After all, Voronoff's patients testified to a 'return of sexual vigour' that was 'abnormal both in degree and character'. It was 'morbid eroticism'.[40] As Dr Maurice Beddow Bayly, an ardent opponent of both vivisection and vaccines, complained in *The Gland Grafting Operation of Dr Voronoff* (1928), two of the photographs reproduced in Voronoff's book showed signs of 'gross deterioration': the 'before' photograph showed a 'senile but mild and harmless old man' while the 'after' photograph showed 'a coarse and bloated sensualist'.[41] Bayly protested that Voronoff's operation induced the 'abnormal and morbid accentuation of the sexual function'.[42] The 'restitution of the sex-powers to the profligate and the roué' could only result in an 'increase in prostitution, venereal disease and illegitimacy'. Unless the men's wives were also 'rejuvenated', the outcome would be dire.[43] The idea of breeding monkeys in huge farms simply for the purpose of harvesting their sex organs and having them 'transplanted into old men and women who, through numerous transgressions of the laws of life, have reached a premature decay' was merely a way of 'vamperizing on the lives of others'. It enabled profligate people to avoid 'reaping' what they had 'sown'.[44]

Feminists sarcastically questioned why they were expected to 'give admiring attention' to rejuvenated septuagenarians who experienced 'a kind of eroticism' and 'exaltation' of 'function' (as one coyly put it).[45] Indeed, exclaimed Ouida, Brown-Séquard's remedy was 'nothing more or less than this, the permanent or momentary stimulation of lost vigour, through forces borrowed from animal life'. Rather than being met with any 'shout of joy or ecstatic admiration', this 'infernal process' should be 'hissed and damned as an unspeakable filth and shame!' Hundreds of animals had been 'sacrificed' simply for the 'noble end of enabling worn-out man to stimulate the desires and passions of youth!'[46]

At the centre of these concerns about the corruption of humanity was the assumption that there was something innately unclean about animals. It is no coincidence that, at the time organotherapists and early endocrinologists were being criticized, a very similar disputation was taking place concerning the new science of inoculation. In 1898, for example, the *Freethinker* protested against 'the dirty practice of

Figure 4. James Gillray, *The Cow Pock – or – The Wonderful Effects of the New Inoculation*, 1802. The sketch satirizes fears that arose about inoculation, after it was introduced by Edward Jenner in 1796. For many people of the time, inoculation with material from an animal was poisoning people, who had been made in God's image. It shows people being vaccinated with cow pox, and developing bovine features. Cows are emerging from their mouths, ears, limbs and buttocks. Satanic horns have sprouted from one man's head.

The Cow Pock or the Wonderful Effects of the New Inoculation, published by H. Humphrey, 1809 (coloured engraving), Gillray, James (1757–1815)/Private Collection/The Bridgeman Art Library

inoculating human beings with the filthy matter from diseased cows'.[47] The author of *Vaccination, or, Blood Poisoning with Animal Diseases* (1899) made the point even more strongly, telling readers that he had

> seen children after vaccination develop the most violent maniacal tempers, not previously existent. I have seen a child of two to three years assume a most fiendish expression and kick and strike its mother.[48]

He viewed 'ingrafting [sic] of human beings with animal diseases and animal taints' as an action that would inevitably '*animalise* man'.[49] Intimate contact with animal secretions and organs was inherently polluting. It could actually turn people into the animal from which the virus had been taken (see Figure 4). As Dr Benjamin Moseley warned,

> Can any person say what may be the consequences of introducing a
> bestial humour [meaning, fluid] into the human frame, after a long
> lapse of years? . . . Who knows, also, that the human character may
> undergo strange mutations from quadruple sympathy.[50]

He also worried that 'owing to vaccination the british [sic] ladies might
wander in the field to receive the embraces of the bull'.[51]

Rejuvenating technologies did more than simply disrupt individual
lifecycles and human purity; they disturbed the stability of society as a
whole. Would older generations become, in effect, 'younger' than
their children, protégés, or spouses? By killing off a significant part of
an entire generation of young men, the First World War had already
seriously upset the orderly progression of generations. Might governments compel people to use the new scientific means of rejuvenation to
engineer new life? In 1928, one anti-vivisectionist quoted Voronoff as
saying that it was 'not beyond the bounds of the possible that in a time
of great national emergency a government may make the operation
compulsory'. This critic dryly predicted a time when 'men who fought
in the later war may still take part in another war in say, 1980, and
mothers may be stimulated to bear children at sixty and over, so as to
augment the man-power of the nation'.[52]

Finally, might xenografts transfer animal traits into the human stock?
As the author of an article entitled 'Monkeying with Man' (1928) put
it, Voronoff's operation risked endangering the 'purity of our race'.
Long-standing anxieties about miscegenation came to the fore. Might
there be 'transference to the re-activated human of less desirable attributes which civilized man is accustomed to boast that he has mastered
or outlived'? It was plausible, the author went on, to assume that the
'human germ-plasm includes a number of suppressed genes, carried
over from the germ-plasm of ancestors common to us and our arboreal
cousins'. Consequently, there was a possibility 'of endocrine secretions
manufactured by simian glands stirring into activity these dormant
elements'.[53]

Transplanting animal organs into humans deliberately blurred the
boundary between people and animals, thus threatening notions about
the integrity of the human species itself. As the *Anti-Vivisection Journal*
anxiously observed in 1926, Voronoff had bragged that he had managed
to transplant a human ovum into a female chimpanzee and fertilize it
with human sperm. This was both 'debased and debasing' and was 'evidence, if such were needed, of where vivisection leads those who

practice it'.[54] Inserting animal parts into human persons was polluting. In the words of one critic of organotherapy, there was something 'essentially revolting' about harvesting organs from animals at the moment of death and inserting them into people. Echoing the concerns expressed about meat-eating, the impurity of 'slaughterhouse offal' was stressed: many of the animals were already diseased and, even if healthy, the extreme fear they must have been experiencing at the moment of death must have flooded their bodies with unnatural properties.[55] 'Natural' evolutionary processes would be soiled by such interventions.

Bayly was most anxious about this aspect of organ transplantation. 'A race of beings will be created', he thundered, in which apes 'will have been permanently grafted in to the human stock'. He accused Voronoff of claiming that if he was allowed to operate on the 'children of Genius', he could create a 'super-race of men of genius'. According to Bayly, Voronoff would

> give every promising boy a third testicle, an ape's. God having been so careless as only to have provided him with two. Sexual precocity, moral depravity, and probably a predisposition to Cancer and other malignant tissues of a fast-growing character, are three evils which there are good arguments for believing would accrue from such an outrageous interference with the body that we have been taught is the temple of God.

Voronoff was inciting the 'basest instincts in mankind'.[56]

It might perhaps be expected that the greatest dangers of all involved the penetration of women's bodies with animal organs and fluids, and vice versa. At some stage, Bayly feared, women who wanted to defeat 'the ravages of time' might find themselves pregnant with a 'monkey offspring'. A surgeon would inevitably 'succumb to the temptation' to implant a female chimpanzee with a human embryo, resulting in a creature that was 'neither animal nor human, but a creature apart'.[57] And what would happen if a monkey gave birth to a human? Who would be the legal guardian; would the birth be registered in the normal way; who would be named as the parents? Even more crucially, Bayly asked, 'Would the Church baptise it, and would it be considered, in the Christian sense, to possess a soul?'[58] In a lighter tone, another physician asked if there wasn't a risk that offspring from a rejuvenated woman would 'exhibit an awkward proclivity for nut-cracking and tree-climbing'?[59]

He was joking (about nut-cracking, not souls), but the question had a serious side: was it possible for 'Simian characters' to be 'transmitted either to the new host of the graft or to his or her progeny'? Voronoff denied it: for him, organotherapy was similar to eating meat or drinking the 'extracts of dead animal glands'. Bayly was not convinced that it was helpful to compare the 'action of an extract of a dead gland and the natural secretion of a living one'. Wasn't the analogy beside the point anyway, since it was 'recognised by every physiologist that diet affects temperament both in animals and man'? Dr Ernest H. Tipper's research among 'among primitive tribes in Africa' proved, according to Bayly, that the 'perversion of the natural diet of the early races of mankind so as to include the flesh of animals which exceeded man in muscular power, vital cell-activity and rate of growth' has resulted in a 'predispositiion [sic] in the cells of the human body to assume the same degree of vital activity, to swing to the same rhythm, and hence to the wide and growing incidence of Cancer and other malignant growths among civilised communities'.[60] Bayly argued that the 'barrier of the intestinal mucous membrane' still acted as some 'safeguard' but was not sufficient since it was often 'damaged or weakened by constipation'. These were similar to anxieties about eating animal flesh, but Bayly warned that the risk was even greater when live animal organs were incorporated into the human body:

> Replace one gland with that of another species and if, as is the case with the anthropoid ape, its vital rhythm sufficiently approximates to that of the human species, so that it finds its humeral environment similar to that to which it has been accustomed, it will grow in its new host, and moreover the superior vitality of the ape's tissues will enable them to establish themselves amid surroundings in which a homograft, although more nearly synchronised in vital rhythm, would be absorbed.

The cells of this ape gland would, therefore, multiply in its host; in time, its 'essential rhythm' would be transferred to the host's body.

There was one further question that obsessed Bayly. If the characteristics of the grafted animal could alter the physiological composition of the rejuvenated man or woman, might it also be transferred to the next generation (the scientifically discredited view of biologist Jean-Baptiste Lamarck, that traits an organism acquires during its lifetime can be passed on to its offspring)? Bayly argued that there was evidence that 'acquired characteristics' could be transmitted. Indeed, he went further, citing the German anatomist Max Westenhöfer's view that 'the anthropoid ape is descended from man and not man from the ape'. Bayly noted that 'the foetal Chimpanzee passes through a stage at the third month when it is indistinguishable from a woman-borne child'. It only became 'ape-like' as pregnancy advanced. The ape's teeth, corpuscles and 'serological agglutination reactions' were also similar to man's. It was

> precisely this close approximation which suggests the possibility that when the grafting of ape's glands has been practised for some time and in successive generations, ultimately the crossing of ape and man in the normal way of mating may become an accomplished fact, and that nature may thereby be cheated in her attempt to preserve the human stock from such a possible contamination.

He called upon people to accept that 'in some remote age' man 'became gradually changed until by the transmission and accentuation of such modifications, the race of anthropoid apes was produced'. If that could happen in the distance past, Bayly warned, it could occur again: Voronoff's operations, he concluded, 'constitute a MENACE TO THE HUMAN RACE'.[61]

Fortunately, fears of men like Bayly and the 'animal guardians' were not realized – in part because neither the testicular extracts of Brown-Séquard nor the organ transplants of Voronoff actually worked. Despite their popularity, the experiments were deeply flawed and sceptics argued that any improvements were the result of the placebo effect. 'Imagination was a powerful factor in producing the beneficial result', observed one critic as early as 1894: the passionate organotherapist was 'only deceiving himself and others'.[62] Furthermore, there were exaggerated reports of incredible cures: 'the paralysed immediately walk, the lame throw aside canes and crutches, the deaf hear, and the blind see', scorned the *Lancet*.[63] The popularity of techniques of rejuvenation attracted cranks, who treated animal serums as a 'soda-fountain affair, to be dished out at every street corner'.[64] One of the most notorious of these was John R. Brinkley, who advertised his goat-gland implants on the radio from his home in rural Kansas. He claimed to hold three MD degrees when, in reality, his qualifications were the result of bribery and other chicaneries. He chose to implant goat sexual glands, as opposed to chimpanzee ones, because (in the words of David

Hamilton), 'to the simple people of the mid-west, the goat was a symbol of sexual prowess and stamina'. When his first patient subsequently gave birth to a son, the boy was named 'Billy'.[65] As one surgeon lamented, 'Fakirs and charlatans were quick to smell the unlimited gold' that organotherapy 'put within reach of their grasping fingers'.[66]

Nevertheless, although they were often mocked and their surgical claims were demolished, their theories about the role played by glands gradually earned scientific respectability. Brown-Séquard's work with sex extracts harvested from animals was superseded in the 1930s when laboratory biochemists discovered how to make sex hormones in synthetic form. As Chandak Sengoopta has argued in *The Most Secret Quintessence of Life* (2006), scientists in the late nineteenth century developed a dramatic new way of understanding the body. In earlier decades, medical understandings of the workings of the body had been dominated by the nervous system, particularly the spinal cord, ganglia and nervous fibres. This 'solidistic conception' of the body was questioned by experimentalists like Brown-Séquard and Voronoff, who drew attention to what they called 'internal secretions'. Glands pumped powerful chemicals into the bloodstream, literally affecting every aspect of an individual's biological make-up. These secretions were dubbed 'hormones' in 1905 by the British physiologist Ernest Starling.[67] Although Brown-Séquard and Voronoff's experiments are embarrassing to modern scientists, their ideas eventually led to the science of endocrinology.

The debates also expose the fragility of the notion of species integrity, and the extent to which both the proponents of organotherapy and its critics sought to patrol different – albeit equally artificial – boundaries between the animal and the human. As we shall see next, both groups' attempts were to suffer severe tests in the decades that followed.

CHAPTER NINETEEN

Transplantation and Species Boundaries

Human bodies could clearly be altered by coming into close contact, or even merged, with the fluids and glands of animals.
Recipients seemed to be infused with so-called animalistic qualities,
including sexual rapaciousness and energy. Its proponents argued that
this made them more, rather than less, human. As in the case of cosmetic surgery, the procedure simply ensured that the 'authentic inner
self' could shine though its deteriorated façade. Even critics might
agree, but they retorted that this authentic self might be a 'natural'
male beastliness. Whether humanizing or bestializing, organotherapy
promised people that they would attain success in the great trilogy of
human culture: employment, politics and marriage.

From the start, however, the vision of men like Brown-Séquard and
Voronoff was much greater than merely injecting testicular extracts
and stitching animals' sex glands into male scrotums and (very rarely)
female labia. They always believed that the scientific paradigm would
eventually proffer immeasurably more radical ways to exploit animals for the benefit of humanity. In particular, they looked forward to
the day when entire organs would be spliced to the bodies of their
patients, who would then flourish with a bit of 'the animal' working
inside.

Even in their time, this was a possibility. In fact, as Voronoff was
aware, surgeons at the beginning of the nineteenth century had
identified kidneys, not sex organs, as the 'best bet' for successful
inter-species transplants. In 1905, the French surgeon Dr M.
Princeteau had successfully grafted a rabbit's kidney into a young

patient suffering kidney failure. His patient survived two weeks. The following year, a pig's kidney was grafted onto the blood vessels of a woman's arm and, in 1909, the kidney of the first non-human primate (a macaque) was grafted onto a woman's thigh. In both cases, the patients died within hours. There were even transplants from humans to animals. In 1908, I. Unger took the kidneys of a human who had died at birth and grafted them into a baboon. The baboon survived for eighteen hours before dying of 'acute tubular necrosis'.[1]

In the next three decades, surgeons made other attempts, including transplanting organs taken from pigs, goats, lambs and primates, but none of the patients survived for any length of time. The procedure was revived in the late 1950s, when scientific understanding about immunosuppression had improved and so chances of survival rose. Notably, Dr Keith Reemtsma, a surgeon at Tulane University in New Orleans, grafted chimpanzee kidneys into patients: all the chimpanzees died, of course, but one patient survived for nine months. Again, some of these transplantations involved human organs being moved into animal bodies. In 1964, for instance, the *Annals of Surgery* reported transplantation operations carried out at the UCLA hospital from human cadavers to dogs, monkeys and chimpanzees. As the surgeon tersely reported, however, 'All of these have been rejected, usually with an accelerated pattern.'[2]

Other prominent scientists such as Christiaan Barnard and Thomas Starzl carried on their research in the 1960s. They were greatly aided by a new definition of death that was based on the cessation of brain function as opposed to heartbeat, thus enabling them to experiment using the organs of human cadavers. In 1984, as we saw in Chapter Seventeen, paediatric cardiac surgeon Leonard Bailey of the Loma Linda Medical Center grafted Goobers's heart into the young Stephanie Fae.

After Leonard Bailey's audacious experiment, the transplantation of major animal organs into humans became a reality. The procedures – that is, the transplantation of both human and animal organs – were spurred on by what promoters of transplant technologies call the 'grim' disparity between the supply of donor organs and the demand for them.[3] As we shall see at the end of this chapter, though, new knowledges about stem cells might provide an even more radical way to redress human ills by 'harvesting' ever-more intricate elements of human and animal bodies.

Critics of Whole-Organ Xenotransplants

What is remarkable about the late twentieth- and early twenty-first-century debates about the ethics of whole-organ transplantation from animals to humans is how little changed in three-quarters of a century. Six main anxieties have been dominant. To a large degree, the first five were shared by the earlier critics of xenografts: they include alarm about the commodification of the human body, the 'unnaturalness' of the procedures, the polluting aspects of mingling animal bodies with those of humans, the fracturing of individual bodily integrity and the undermining of human identity as a discrete species. The final troubling fear, though, is new: might infectious agents jump species?

First, as in the early decades of organotherapy and rejuvenation-orientated xenografts, the ethics of commodifying the body has been prominent in the debates. With the help of immunosuppressant drugs, the body is universalized, with 'parts' made exchangeable even between species. Internal organs are simply 'replaceable parts' or property. In the words of 'Organ Wars', an article published in the *Medical Anthropology Quarterly* in 1995, 'transplantation surgeries contribute to conceptions of the body as a collection of replaceable parts and of the self as distinct from all but its neural locus'.[4] Blood, ova, sperm and genetic material can regularly be exchanged. Procuring, preparing and replacing the bodily 'parts' is extremely expensive, and the marketplace is always in flux. Transplanted tissues and organs, then, are simply another way in which bodily boundaries can be breached in the medical marketplace.

In this sense, xenotransplantation has been seen as the ultimate in biopolitics, or the political control of populations at the biological and species level. In the affluent West, governments have become increasingly concerned with the regulation of bodily parts by the biotechnological industry, trans-national corporations and national health regulatory groups such as the National Institutes of Health (NIH) and US Food and Drug Administration (FDA).

Late twentieth-century anxieties about biopolitics, and what it might mean for the uniqueness of individual identity when bodily parts can be exchanged for money, is similar but not identical to those anxieties expressed earlier in the century. In the earlier period, commodification was much more likely to be conceived of in terms of the ways that middle- and upper-class men were exploiting animals. Chimpanzees, apes, goats, rams, oxen, rabbits and dogs were mutilated and killed in

vast numbers in order to rejuvenate humans. In contrast, in the contemporary world only a relatively small number of people (primarily
highly vocal activists for animal rights) worry about individual animal
donors. More typically, the disadvantaged bodies that are portrayed as
being exploited are not the animal donors but human recipients of the
experimental procedures – the vulnerable people mentioned in
Chapter Seventeen, such as Stephanie Fae, Jefferson Davis and Boyd
Rush. The proliferation of discussions about the dangers of biopolitics
remains wedded to a humanist tradition, with very little emphasis on
how biopolitics affects animal wellbeing. With the exception of
Goobers (one of the very few experimental animals whose name is
known outside the laboratory setting), the animals are nothing more
than an undifferentiated set of consumable 'its', manipulated by a marketplace that is run by corporations. Their body parts seem to emerge
from nowhere specific.

The commodification of the body is problematic in another way, too:
it introduces a false sense of 'choice'. People are assumed to be able to
'choose' to have bodily parts improved (as in plastic surgery) or
exchanged (transplantation). Not only does this elide the problem of
animal consent, it also means that those people who 'fail' to 'choose'
correctly, or who lack the resources to do so, are further stigmatized.

Second, critics of xenotransplantation regularly castigate it as 'unnatural'. Thus, a textbook for nurses on medical ethics, published in the
mid-1940s, decreed that the

> unnatural character of the operation rests in the fact that the trans-
> planted organ is said to continue to function in a non-human manner,
> effecting notable physical and psychical changes in the subject.

As such, it was 'manifestly immoral'.[5] More recently, one patient
protested, he did not want a 'monster inside me' because 'these are not
natural things'.[6] Admittedly, the unnaturalness of the procedure did not
bother most proponents and recipients. All of human culture is 'unnatural'. After all, as one patient argued, leather

> goes through quite a refined process, so you couldn't really say it is
> natural for us to make leather shoes. In the same way that the process
> that the pigs organs would go through to get into us isn't natural, but
> we've now got that technology. It's developed, that's happened, so
> why not use it?

He argued that everything in the world, including animal life, was available to be exploited by humans. Appealing to the mantra of 'choice', he argued that it was

> a personal preference where you draw the line as to the extent that you utilize that resource. If you only want to use it for food and clothing, rather than for preserving lives, then that seems a little illogical.[7]

Animals are, therefore, infinitely exploitable: if humans develop a preference to eat them, skin them for leather or excise their hearts, livers and kidneys for xenotransplantation, then so be it. The conversion of living animals into steak, shoes and substitute organs is as 'natural' as any other act of human culture.

Others were more squeamish. Those critics who wanted to insist that xenotransplantation was 'unnatural' could often be heard making a third argument: the mingling of animal and human organs is inherently polluting for the human. As one critic tersely summarized it: 'We have been made superior to animals and it would be degrading to be made part pig, part human.'[8]

In the last chapter, as well as in that on eating animal corpses (Chapter Fifteen), the polluting nature of blood-engorged muscles and organs was discussed. When this is compounded with fears of hybridity (drawing on anxieties related to 'racial' differences and miscegenation) the contaminating status of the procedure is heightened. As anthropologist Mary Douglas explained in her classic *Purity and Danger*, disgust is elicited from things being 'out of place'.[9] This was certainly the case with early attempts to graft the skin of pigeons, roosters, dogs and frogs onto burn victims. As the author of an article entitled 'Dermepenthesis' (a neologism for skin grafting) complained in the *Medical Record* in 1888, using the skin of frogs was 'so repulsive to most people, and especially to women and children, that after two trials I gave it up'.[10]

Disgust was amplified when the 'matter out of place' was whole organs originally belonging to humans, monkeys, pigs or dogs – and that ranking-order was clear. Thus, in the late 1990s, when one hundred patients who had human-organ transplants were asked about their attitude to xenotransplantation, 96 per cent said that transplanted human organs were acceptable. In contrast, the acceptability of monkey and pig organs ranged between 42 and 44 per cent, while the organs of dogs were acceptable to only around one-third of patients.[11] As one person admitted when questioned about his attitude toward xeno-transplantation:

> Well the idea of putting anybody else's . . . you know the idea of an operation and taking out a major organ makes me feel queasy. It's not a nice thing. And then putting in something . . . I mean, pigs. Dirty, horrible farmyard animals, is how they're classically seen. And then putting something like that inside you. It's not a nice idea but . . . it's worth it, I reckon! [Laughs].[12]

As the patient implicitly recognized, the suffering body is never truly whole or organically bounded: it is often consumed by pain that can seem boundless; it is prey to phantom limbs (that is, it feels pain in limbs even after they have been amputated); it is routinely fed pills and potions that are inherently poisonous. Nevertheless, the prospect of animal organs operating independent of the individual's will inside the human body remains profoundly disquieting.

Fourth, arguments about commodification and pollution both assume that individuals possess some kind of innate bodily integrity that will be threatened once animals and human organs can be easily and routinely exchanged. According to the *Proposed Canadian Standard for Xenotransplantation* (1999), xenografts challenge

> the basic integrity and intrinsic value of the human person and human species . . . As xenotransplantation involves cells, tissues or organs from another species, it questions the very 'nature' of what makes us human . . . Our homology, coevolution and interdependence with other species may be biologically evident but that does not necessarily make it ethically acceptable to foster the development of these techniques.[13]

Each individual human is no longer considered unique, indivisible; she is a jigsaw-like entity consisting of interchangeable parts. The dualistic separation of the self from the body allows for the fragmentation and marketing of those parts. Given the status in the West of the (imagined) concept of individual integrity, this is widely viewed as dehumanizing.

At the very least, might the dismemberment of human parts within one's own self incite psychological tensions, especially if those parts had been harvested from animals? As a professor of Christian ethics at

Georgetown University's Kennedy Institute of Ethics put it after the
death of Baby Fae,

> Special concerns would arise when the transplanted organ is the
> heart. True, the heart is only a pump. But that is an abstract, anatom-
> ical statement. More important, do people think of it in that way
> only? Ask the poets, the novelists, the mystics, the lovers . . . anyone.
> Concretely, if the patient survives, how would she be viewed by other
> people, and eventually and most importantly, by herself? Would she
> be so medically signalized [sic], at least early on, that a social brack-
> eting would stamp her early years? What effects would this have?[14]

In attempting to answer these questions, the sciences of philosophy
and psychology have come to the fore. On the one hand, the crucial
question has been seen by some as quantitative: what *amount* of tissue
from another species will be regarded as necessary to redefine the
individual? Is it one thing to walk around with a pig's kidney filtering
your blood, but quite another to depend on that pig's kidneys, heart,
lungs and pancreas? It raises questions about the biological trajectory
of identity as well as about an individual's species integrity. As one
patient said, 'The last thing I want in this short life of mine is to
have a monster inside me and perhaps become one . . . These are
not natural things.'[15] On the other hand, equally uncertain questions
of psychology have been posited. As a report produced by
Compassion in World Farming and the British Union for the Abolition
of Vivisection observed in 1998, patients might accept a transplant
of an animal organ 'on the understanding that its "animal presence" is
strictly confined to one organ, in one place'. They warned that recipients might not realize that 'this animal presence cannot be prevented
from spreading to every other organ and tissue', a fact that would
'fundamentally challenge some people's concept of themselves as a
human being and their notions of selfhood, as well as affecting how
others see them'.[16] The psychological effects of having a significant
quantity of 'animal presence' inside one's body had repercussions for
human identity.

The fifth anxiety is linked to all those above. Human fantasies of possessing a bounded identity were threatened by the idea that xenografts
could make humans into something more animal-like and vice versa.
Might xenotransplantation result in a 'scientifically-created, living
embodiment of the once-mythical concept of the chimera',[17] that is,

the fabled fire-spouting monster with a goat's body, a lion's head and a serpent's tail?

A century before whole-organ transplants became a practical possibility, H. G. Wells eerily imagined such a happening. In *The Island of Doctor Moreau* (1896) he described 'creatures' who, despite the 'rough humanity' of their 'bodily form', were actually hybrids:

> Each of these creatures had woven into it, into its movements, into the expression of its countenance, into its whole presence, some now irresistible suggestion of a hog, a swinish taint, the unmistakable mark of the beast.[18]

Such nightmarish creatures would seriously fracture human identity. If simply eating dead animal flesh could provoke insidious processes of animalization, how much more dangerous was assimilating fully functioning animal organs? One-quarter of transplant patients in the late 1990s believed that their appearance, personality, dietary preferences and sexual habits would change after a xenograft.[19] One-fifth of this sample believed that animals possessed souls, a worrying notion for those who had faith in the existence of an afterlife.[20]

Although greatly exaggerated, these fears are not pure whimsy. Transplant surgeon Thomas Starzl and his collaborators found evidence of what they called 'metabolic baboonization' after the transplantation of baboon livers into human patients. The white blood cells of baboons did actually spread throughout the bodies of transplant recipients. Hearts, kidneys and lymph nodes were all affected:

> The fall of the patient's serum acid postoperatively to the nearly undetected level that is normal for the baboon was a particularly dramatic demonstration of the creation by the hepatic xenograft of its own chemical environment . . . The result was that the graft as well as the recipient became genetic composites . . . If xenotransplantation is to be successful, it seems evident that the persistence of the double cell population is both inevitable and obligatory.

Starzl and his associates mused about whether 'incomplete or even full chimerism' would 'change the image of the baboon organs enough to make them viewed as allografts by humans'.[21]

Such results, representing a benign shift in molecular structures, enabled scaremongering critics of the procedure to go on the attack.

Not surprisingly, the biotechnological industry responded vigorously. In the words of the CEO of the United Therapeutics Corporation,

> All life is fundamentally chimeric. The intermixing of all life arises from the evolutionary processes by which every species, genus, family, order, class, phylum and kingdom branches from, and hence partially incorporates, another. Anti-chimeric sentiment is fundamentally a position that opposes any *additional* admixture of species beyond that which has 'naturally' evolved. Depending on the advocate, chimerism might be wrong for animals but acceptable in plants, wrong in primates but acceptable in domesticated beasts, or perhaps just wrong if the human species is involved.[22]

They could also have pointed out that, although the scale of transformation in modern xenotransplantation is extraordinary when compared with earlier xenografts, the admixture of animal and human organs has a distinguished history. Just to take a few examples: human bones and tendons have long been replaced with cow bones and tendons; surgical sutures are made from sheep intestines; polio vaccines are developed from monkey kidney cells; porcine fetal ventral mesencephalon cells are implanted to treat Parkinson's disease; encapsulated porcine pancreatic cells are used to treat diabetes mellitus. None of these procedures have caused much consternation. In fact, nearly a decade before the first full heart transplant, pig heart valves had already been substituted for the human equivalent without controversy. It seems that many people feel that *whole* animal organs – whole pigs' hearts as opposed to just their valves – are a different issue altogether.

Concerns about the so-called animalization of humans are only one side of the problem. There is also anxiety about humanizing animals in an attempt to make their organs more easily assimilated into human biology. This debate was sparked by the creation of the first transgenic pig in 1992. The scientist responsible was David White, an immunologist at Cambridge University. White's pig carried the genetic code for human regulator proteins. Since then, techniques of modifying the genetic makeup of pigs in order to 'humanize' their organs have made great strides. As *The Times* reported in 2008, 'The humanisation process of the organs is expected to be achieved by breeding genes directly into the pigs, probably by injecting them directly into the parent boar's testicles.'[23] Harvesting the organs of transgenic animals would greatly reduce the likelihood that the patient's immune system would reject them. By transferring human genetic material into pigs, the animal would carry the 'protective human "armour" of "complement regulating proteins" – the proteins that naturally coat the human cells and inhibit the activation of the toxic complement protein that causes rejection'.[24]

'How can you criticize the use of pig tissue for therapeutic procedures that save lives,' David White asked, 'while at the same time accepting the existence of a ham sandwich?'[25] The procedure was 'nothing different from what is already occurring in nature', argued another scientist, adding that 'nature' was in fact 'more dangerous' because the genetic mutations were not controlled as they would be in a laboratory setting.[26] It was simply not the case that 'humans will start to look like pigs, or pigs will begin to behave like humans', John Wallwork, head of the transplant unit at Papworth Hospital in Cambridgeshire, calmly attempted to persuade people.[27]

Finally, while the five main concerns I have looked at were shared (to a greater or lesser extent) by the early critics of xenografts, a much more dangerous fear emerged in the late twentieth century. In my view, this is the only one with any justification. The threat can be expressed simply: what is the risk that xenotransplantation will spread xenozoonoses, or infectious agents that are capable of jumping species? Ebola and HIV are the most obvious examples of the transmission of deadly diseases from primates to humans. Was it possible that porcine retroviruses, for example, could be transmitted to the human population? Does this create a unique epidemiological risk?

Although no one knows how great the risk is, there is no doubt that it is a risk. The legitimacy of this fear means that recipients will be required to be monitored all their lives to guard against the emergence and spread of new diseases. As the author of an article on xenotransplantation, writing in the *Lancet* in 1998, observed, patients would be required to adhere to

> a schedule of frequent, long-term, or life-long medical surveillance; the granting of permission to public-health agencies to examine private hospital records; the granting of consent to a complete necropsy at time of death; the responsibility to educate close contacts about the risks and control of infections; and detailed information about the trying, sometimes traumatic psychological effects of immunosuppressive drugs.[28]

Perhaps it would be necessary to forcibly quarantine patients who did not obey the rules. After all, xenotransplantation differs from other experimental treatments in that the risk is to the entire society, and not simply to the individual patient. Furthermore, mutations and gene swapping are particular problems for transplant patients because their immune systems had been suppressed, making them even less able to restrict the proliferation of viruses. Xenotransplantation kills animals: unwittingly, those animals could take revenge.

Twenty-First-Century Chimeras

In the nineteenth and early twentieth centuries, fears of half-man, half-beast creatures were stimulated by fairly basic organotherapies (the ingestion of animal secretions) and primitive xenografts. From the mid-twentieth century, the transplantation of entire organs incited concerns about the 'animalization' of humans. At what point would the identity of the 'animal' override that of the human? Might some animals become human-like? How should we respond to any of these permeations?

Such questions have become even more relevant in the twenty-first century, with the invention of radical biotechnological techniques involving stem cells. The turning point came when human embryonic stem cells were discovered to be pluripotent. In other words, these cells have the capacity to divide into almost all types of tissue. Their extreme plasticity means that there is potentially no further need for whole-organ transplants.

Stem-cell technologies profoundly influence definitions of humanity. It was obvious that Voronoff's 'rejuvenated' men remained human despite having the testes of monkeys sewn into their bodies. Similarly, the transplantation of a whole heart from a baboon into Baby Fae never threatened her humanity. Recipients of xenografts today may fret or joke about the 'beast within', but nobody is seriously questioning the fact that they retain their human identity.

In the twenty-first century, though, chimeras are part-animal and part-human at a cellular level. In early 2004, scientists at the Mayo Clinic injected human stem cells into forty-day-old fetal pigs. They effectively produced chimeras, organisms with both human and animal cells throughout their bodies. Such organisms are different from both hybrids (mules, for instance, who are the result of sexual reproduction between a male donkey and a female horse) and clones (including Dolly the Sheep, who was produced with identical genetic material).

They are even distinct from organisms created by recombinant DNA technology, which inserts isolated genes from one organism in another. Rather, chimeras are created by injecting stem cells from one species into the embryo of another. As a result, chimeras possess two or more different populations of cells, derived from different organisms. In the future, it is easy to imagine that chimeras will be created in whom most of the nervous tissue is human or have a majority of human cells, including brain cells. Humanness becomes a question of a continuum, from chimeras with a few human cells to those with primarily human cells.

Chimeras have been created for a range of reasons. In many cases it has been seen as a logical extension of other practices in which the animal is sacrificed for the good of the human. For instance, chimeras could be used to test pharmaceutical drugs or study human development in situations where people or human embryos are considered inappropriate. Thus, human–mice chimeras have provided valuable models for human diseases such as Aids and hepatitis. Particularly if attempting to understand viruses that do not infect mice cells – the HIV virus is one example – these humanized mice were invaluable in tracking infection and understanding how the virus replicates.[29] Most importantly, much scientific research into chimeras focuses upon the usefulness of these animal hybrids in growing organs that could be transplanted into the bodies of desperately ill humans. Because chimeras contain human cells, they are more likely to be transplanted successfully. Indeed, chimera sheep whose livers are 80 per cent human have already been created.[30]

A serious problem arises, however: when is a chimera 'human'? There is no answer.

Should we be surprised? If, as I argue throughout this book, there is not and has never been any agreed definition of either 'human' or 'animal', then why should it be different for human/animal chimeras? As I said in the Introduction, we can never know on which side the ants treading that Möbius strip are walking. What we can do, though, is see where competing voices in the debate about human/animal boundaries choose to tie a knot in that Möbius strip in order to declare '*here!* and not *there!* is the place where the human starts and the animal ceases'. As we shall observe – again – it is a process infused with human vanity.

Some scientists adopt a formulaic approach. They impose a threshold, insisting, for instance, that any organism whose cells are genetically more than 50 per cent human can be designated 'human'. As we have seen, others draw inspiration from the 'personhood debates', which have tended to valorize cognitive factors. Thus chimeras who lack traits such as intelligence would be placed in a similar category as embryos, the newly born, those who are severely intellectually impaired and the legally dead. Still others recommend a 'sliding scale' approach, with different levels of humanness being governed by an assessment of higher-level human cognitive traits and the possession of crucial human biological tissue.[31] In most definitions, attention is paid to developmental stages. After all, as one expert sensibly warned, 'it may not be clear how sentient or intelligent a human–animal chimera will be until it has been produced and raised'.[32] Any judgement of humanness must be made according to the 'average, mature member of a species'.[33] As will be obvious from the various approaches, all are either biologically essentialist or speciesist. They define humanity according to an ur-human, or the degree to which the chimera conforms to a particular vision of humanity.[34]

It is thus hardly surprising that, like the other scientific technologies discussed in this and the last chapter, the production of chimeras at the cellular level has incited intense anxiety. Again, many familiar arguments have been rehearsed. Chimeras are 'monsters', 'immoral inventions'.[35] Their creation would be 'injurious to the well-being, good policy, or good morals of society'.[36] Religious objections have been particularly vociferous. Writing for the Catholic pro-life website LifeIssues, Tara Seyfer based her objections on her belief that humans were made in the image of God and set above other animals. She reminded her readers of the 'dignity of being human'. After all,

> Jesus Christ did not come as an animal, but specifically as a human being, in a human body. This bespeaks the dignity which God accords human beings and their bodies and how specially He views the human race. It thus seems to lead toward the blasphemous to purposefully combine the genetic or bodily material of a human being and an animal in a way that changes either of their identities. To mix the imago Dei with non-imago Dei seems a violation, and evokes a certain repugnance. Perhaps this repugnance is a sign of wisdom.

The Old Testament has 'strong proscriptions against sexual relations with animals', she noted, adding that the 'injunctions were so strong that death was the punishment for transgression'. Perhaps, she speculated, the anti-bestiality regulations serve to keep the human (i.e., the *imago Dei*) separate from the nonhuman (the non-*imago Dei*) with regards to pro-creation and potential genetic crossing. One could venture that God not only abhors the unspeakable act of sexual relations between ani-mals and humans, but also the combining of their genetic constitutions at a certain level.[37]

Reading Seyfer's article, I cannot help but fear that she would be sim-ilarly judgemental in condemning homosexual and lesbian sexual relations. Perhaps we should remind ourselves that, until 1967, homo-sexual men in Britain were legally prosecuted under legislation banning bestiality.[38]

But are chimeras 'unnatural'? Many people believe that transferring human cells into non-humans in ways that would change their function is contrary to 'nature'. In this view, they are adhering to Aristotelian principles that insist that every living being has a *telos*, or an appro-priate end or goal. The use of stem cells to create mixed beings would violate a being's natural teleology. The problem with this argument is that it is unclear what an organism's 'natural' state actually is. It makes it impossible to argue when intervention into nature should be allowed, and when not. Is *in vitro* fertilization legitimate, but not growing organs? Is a blood transfusion or the implantation of a pig's heart valve justifiable, but not the transplantation of a whole pig's heart?

Worries about the potential dangers of 'crossing species bound-aries' are also raised, although scientists have been doing it for centuries, such as when they breed animals. Part of the problem lies in actually defining 'species'. As I discussed in the Introduction, in the eighteenth and nineteenth centuries the designation of different species was based primarily on outward appearance. Carl Linnæus, the father of biological taxonomy, divided animals into six classes – Mammalia, Aves, Amphibia, Pisces, Insecta and Vermes.[39] When he set out to dis-tinguish humans from the rest of mammals he invented the term *Homo sapiens* – 'man of wisdom'. The gendered implication of this taxonomy is discussed in the Introduction.

Although Linnæus's taxonomy remains crucial to the way we group different types of animals, the designation of 'species' today is more liable to be based upon genetic similarities. But this is also not without its problems. As some critics observed in the *Kennedy Institute of Ethics Journal* in 2005,

Setting genetic species boundaries around humans and chimpanzees, for instance, seems straightforward until it becomes necessary to select a relevant threshold of genetic similarities. What threshold would produce the most accurate phylogeny between these organisms? If one were to restrict the relevant genetic grouping to a subset of the eukaryotic genome, one might not only distinguish between humans and chimpanzees, but also establish separate species categories among humans.[40]

Defining who is genetically 'human' is not self-evident.

These debates about 'species boundaries' and the dangers of 'crossing' them continue to divide scientists. There is a wider community of critics, however, who point to the potential ethical risks involved in creating chimeras. Genetic engineering could result in the creation of chimeras who are 'decerebrate' (and therefore unable to feel pain) and who could then be used to produce cost-effective organs for transplantation into the bodies of 'full humans'. They might also be exploited in experiments to study the course of diseases. Supporters of chimeras went to the other extreme, warning that too generous a definition of 'human' might ensure that many chimeras would be classed as 'persons', thus delivering 'a deathblow to a valuable field of medical research'.[41]

Chimeras could even be exploited as the 'new slaves' of the twenty-first century. Not everyone believes this is a bad thing. In the words of Joseph Fletcher, author of *The Ethics of Genetic Control. Ending Reproductive Roulette* (1988), chimeras

> might legitimately be fashioned to do dangerous or demeaning jobs. As it is now, low grade work is shoved off on moronic and retarded individuals, the victims of uncontrolled reproduction. Should we not 'program' such workers thoughtfully instead of accidentally, by means of hybridization?[42]

The idea that 'low grade work is shoved off on moronic and retarded individuals' displays a shocking degree of malice towards many working-class men and women, as does the eugenic subtext.

Mark Dowie, a critic of 'new slavery', satirized such commentators. Because chimeras are not human, he sneered, liberal-minded people might be excused from 'worrying their silly little heads about inalienable human rights and the resulting law and conditions that demand safe working conditions'.[43] As Dowie correctly recognized, proponents of chimeric slavery were espousing a philosophy with potentially disastrous consequences not only for chimeras but also for every human and non-human animal. At the very least, its dangers will be obvious to anyone who has thought about racial discrimination, class oppression or the history of slavery. Making a distinction between 'pure' and 'impure' humans introduces a language with dangerous historical precedents. As early as 1982, the President's Commission for the Study of Ethical Problems in Medicine and Biomedicine and Behavioral Research fretted,

> Could genetic engineering be used to develop a group of virtual slaves – partly human, partly lower animal – to do people's bidding? Paradoxically, the very characteristics that would make such creatures more valuable than any existing animals (that is, their heightened cognitive powers and sensibilities), would also make the moral propriety of their subservient role more problematic. Dispassionate appraisal of the long history of gratuitous destruction and suffering that humanity has visited upon the other inhabitants of the earth indicates that such concerns should not be dismissed as fanciful.[44]

There was another side to these fears: if new biotechnologies could be used to create chimeras designed to carry out menial labour, similar technologies could be used to enhance the traits of other members of *Homo sapiens*. In other words, the deliberate downgrading of certain organisms could be mirrored by the upgrading of others. As one author speculated, brain implants could create 'extremely efficient and powerful interfaces between brains and external computers'. Consider, he continued,

> a possible future in which a few or even a majority, but not all, adults are able, through some combination of advanced technologies, to process information with the speed of today's Google, but with far greater incisiveness, focus, discretion, judgment, and practical wisdom. The remainder of the adult population, the unenhanced, would realistically be in no position to compete for the corresponding number of appealing jobs, or for genuine political and economic influence.[45]

The horrors of science fiction do not seem so fantastic.

Conclusion to Part 6
'Have We Created a Chimera?'

Scientists claim to be able to transform what is meant by the human. In this chapter and the previous one, we saw how intoxicating potions (such as Brown-Séquard's animal essences), reproductive tricks (Voronoff's rejuvenating hormones) and surgical wizardry (xenotransplantation and the creation of transgenic beings) could engender human–animal hybrids as fantastical as the classical chimera.[1] What is conveniently set aside is the fact that all life is fundamentally chimeric. As we have seen, though, choices about what are acceptable forms of difference are highly contingent, often changing with startling rapidity in response to technological and scientific innovation, the power of competing groups within society (Catholics, feminists and animal rights activists, for instance) and even more banal factors such as the 'passing of time', which can lead to familiarization. Most dramatically, research into stem cells has demonstrated the extraordinary plasticity of early embryonic material, which has the capacity to divide into almost all tissue types. The development of an embryo, in other words, can no longer be regarded as inevitably leading to a human person. As feminists Catherine Waldby and Susan Squier point out, stem-cell scientists have shown us 'the *perfect contingency* of any relationship between embryo and person, [and] the non-teleological nature of the embryo's developmental pathways'.[2]

For animals like Goobers, it is hard to see that any of the techniques explored can be beneficial, at least in the forms that they are currently being discussed. Organotherapy and early xenografting involved the extreme exploitation of animals. In the first sentence of a book written when he was in his seventies, Serge Voronoff wrote movingly about his 'deep debt of gratitude to animals', especially monkeys, 'who have been my best collaborators'. Ironically, given that he made a career out of vivisecting animals, he went on to say that these animals 'have a sensibility closely approaching our own'. He wanted to 'repay my debt by proving that animals are deserving not only of our protection, but that they should be treated as being endowed with intelligence and feelings'. Remarkably, he concluded the paragraph with the claim that, 'in certain circumstances', animals even 'give proof of a mental refinement and an abnegation which may even carry them to the extreme limit of willingly laying down their lives'.[3] Voronoff was an old man when he wrote those words. Perhaps he was trying to make amends for a life devoted to sacrificing his beloved animals in the interests of science. More likely, he sincerely believed it.

For other surgeons and scientists, the pain that was necessarily inflicted on animals had to be weighed against the benefits to humans. Take A. M. Phelps's article 'Transplantation of Tissue from Lower Animals to Man', which was published in the *Medical Record* in 1891. In this paper, he responds to anti-vivisectionists who protested against grafting the leg of a dog onto a young boy at the Charity Hospital on Blackwell's Island in New York (the dog had her vocal cords 'carefully severed . . . to prevent any disturbance' of the patient, had her leg amputated 'near the paw' and was immobilized in plaster of Paris to enable the graft to 'take'). 'Those who understand the motive which activates the surgeon', he explained,

> can comprehend how, with all sympathy for the brute, his sacrifice of limb may be demanded for the good of his master, man. They, too, can appreciate the reluctance of the surgeon to inflict wanton suffering, whether upon man or brute, and can understand how such an operation only seemed commendable when a more than commensurate benefit was promised. To those whose eyes are blind to human suffering, and whose sympathies are all for the brute, I have nothing to say.[4]

Late twentieth- and twenty-first-century technologies of xenotransplantation also only cause harm, usually lethal, to animals. In contrast to discussions about the human donation of organs to other humans, the 'gift metaphor' cannot be employed when referring to animal donors. Languages of consent or altruism have no role. As one transplant patient admitted, there was a difference between the 'gift of love' made by a donor who had died accidentally and the 'sacrifice' of an animal donor specifically chosen for him.[5] With only very rare exceptions, it is always assumed that one set of animals (non-human ones) will be sacrificed for another set (human). It is not plausible to imagine a time in the near future that living humans might become donors for animals. I doubt it will happen in the distant future either. Although xenotransplantation could enable people and other animals to become cyborgs, rather than Donna Haraway's dream of feminist empowerment and 'fruitful couplings',[6] it is more likely to lead to further mastery over animals.

Even the new biotechnological possibilities involved in the creation of chimeras do not look likely to lead to anything that could elevate the status of animals. Chimeric animals are created simply as objects to be used; their organs, tissues and blood 'harvested'. In the end, transgenic animals are killed, albeit in kinder ways than animals who have been bred for our dinner tables. As David White bragged, his transgenic pigs 'will live lives of luxury. And they will die better – quietly, under anaesthetic, not stunned by an electric charge, then get their throats cut in some abattoir.'[7]

For human lives, though, xenotransplantation offers hopes as great as those of allo-transplants (human-to-human). Intervening at earlier and earlier stages of development – particularly at the level of stem cells – holds the greatest hope for human wellbeing. Eliminating the risks of the spread of xenozoonoses remains a challenge for scientists throughout the world, and is best solved by employing the patients' own stem cells.

The exploitation of non-human animals in the struggle to improve the human species has been a central quest in Western society. To achieve perfect health and to prolong human life, the animal is, literally, placed under our skin, not as dead corpses but as living organisms. In the modern period, the creation of human–animal hybrids is central to a vast array of scientific procedures. It is at the financial hub of countless multinational corporations. It is not surprising that medical technologies involving the ingestion of animal fluids or the grafting of animal organs possess such cultural resonance: they have the potential to transform identity, corporeality and the understanding of what constitutes the human and human culture. Such techniques transgress dichotomies such as human/animal, self/non-self and life/death. Organ transplantation, for instance, presents a vision of the 'real self' that is divorced from the 'bodily self'; embodiment becomes divorced from identity.[8] The body is fragmented and the 'self' is seen to reside elsewhere. Incorporating animal organs and exploiting transgenic technologies enable humans to become cyborgean; we are more obviously 'animalized' humans. By controlling and regulating this 'animalistic' being, politics seeks to retain the privileged status of (selected) humans.

CHAPTER TWENTY

Concluding Words: Negative Zoélogy

Telling stories about what makes us human can be fun, vicious, mischievous, reassuring, disheartening and fulfilling. Some of the most remarkable stories in this book have been told by people whose identities are shrouded in anonymity. Their pseudonyms are revealing. It matters that the Earnest Englishwoman chose to envelop her anonymity in a particular gender, nationality and personality. It matters that Ellis Bell is a man's name. It matters that Heathcliff and Red Peter are denied full names, that Haitians are given diminutive ones (Sable Gross and Yam Pete, for example) and that some of the women in this book are known solely by their husbands' surnames ('Mrs —'). It is significant that many creatures are only identified according to some superficial characteristic. By designating complex personalities 'animals', 'slaves', 'Haitians', 'Orientals', 'pygmies', 'baboons', 'dogs' and 'cats' we radically diminish their worlds. Naming makes a difference.

My favourite stories, though, have been told by people who have donned the skin, fur or feathers of non-human animals. What would an animal say if she could speak? Perhaps she would agree with the wise vulture in 'Essay on the Language of Animals' (1819), who told her offspring that the human propensity for mass killing in war was simply the way a benevolent 'Nature' provided food for vultures. Humans have

only the *appearance* of animal life, being really vegetables, with the power of motion; and that as the boughs of an oak are dashed together by the storm, that swine may fatten upon the falling acorns, so men are, by some unaccountable power, driven one against another [in war] until they lose their motion that vultures may be fed.[1]

Throughout this book, we have heard people declaim the glories of being human; the wise old vulture reminds us not only of the violence of human culture, but also that the autonomous, self-willed 'human' at the heart of humanist thinking is a fantasy, a chimera.

Of all the speaking animals in this book, I am particularly fond of Red Peter and Bob the spotted terrier. Both these persons (and, yes, for all my scepticism about the revolutionary potentialities of rights discourse, I do think that the ape and the dog can be designated as persons in law) struggled with the ascription of human/animal. Both recognized the violence such naming did to them and to others: Red Peter couldn't bear to look into the eyes of his companion – the captive, half-trained female chimpanzee – and Bob empathized with Caribbean slaves. Humanity's obsessive attempts to demarcate the territory of the human from that of the animal – to tie a knot in that Möbius strip in order to declare '*here!* is the fully-human. *There!* are the others, the animals, the women, the economically and politically disenfranchised, the subaltern' – is both the greatest driving force of history and also the inspiration for systematic violence.

The question, then, becomes: what is to be done? In the introduction, I argued that we need to acknowledge the unknowability of all beings, including human ones. It is this celebration of the 'unsubstitutable singularity' of people and animals that permeates this book. But, readers might legitimately ask, what does this actually mean?

I am a historian, and so this book is populated by literate people telling stories about how they made their worlds; they often speculate eloquently on the worlds of others. However, they do both of these things within incommensurable limits. I am particularly interested in two very different types of limits. One has been the central focus of this book: that is, the limits set by specific historical and topological contexts. This is the territory historians have been trained to excavate. Each person is born into a world forged by others. We resist, create and recreate – but always from a starting point that is never of our own choosing. Many of us rail against the injustices of pre-existing hierarchies created by species, sex, skin colour, wealth, religion, sexual preference and a host of other characteristics.

For those of us at the 'wrong end' of these predetermined hierarchies, it is frustrating to realize that not everyone is willing to acknowledge the way in which our worlds are radically diminished. The lives of animals are obviously exceptionally vulnerable to violence, even though they attempt to make the best of things. For those designated lesser humans, the task is equally daunting, even if they have the advantage of being able to articulate their own objections. Unfortunately, it is the nature of hierarchical ladders that those on the bottom rungs often find it easiest to attack others in the immediate vicinity. Thus, they often find themselves struggling against other groups who are also protesting inequality and prejudice. In pessimistic moments, we might wonder (along with many of the activists discussed in Chapter Six) whether there is a limited economy of sympathy. Non-Western feminists, for instance, end up devoting considerable energy battling the assumptions of some Western feminists who believe that their particular (Western) war against patriarchy is a global struggle based on universal values. In an increasingly globalized world, characterized by rapid changes induced by mass media, technology, migration and global capitalism, the key question becomes: how do we decide which values are universal (that is, able to transcend cultural peculiarities) and which are local (and, by implication, peripheral). The question is crucial because globalization is primarily an issue of power – of the ability of one group (European feminists, for instance) to define its own local values or characteristics as 'global' while designating another group's values or characteristics (those of Haitian feminists, for instance) as 'local'. The group with most clout decides. It makes little difference that liberal, feminist humanism as defined in the West, with its emphasis on individual dignity and personhood, cannot stand the weight of systemic inequality and violence experienced by many women elsewhere in the world.

Like the Earnest Englishwoman, those of us who find ourselves relegated to the lower rungs of various hierarchies can be formidably disruptive. Our strategies are legion. The Earnest Englishwoman, for instance, fantasized about becoming animal. Rather than forging an alliance with her oppressors (men as the only fully human creatures and therefore the only ones capable of 'giving' women the vote), she defiantly proclaimed solidarity with her fellow sufferers (animals). In doing so, however, she left the pecking order intact. She reconciled herself (admittedly, in satire) to the fact that women *are* animals, with all the subordination that such a position entails. Philosopher Giorgio Agamben can be accused of a similar failure of nerve. He rails against the 'anthropological machine' that raises 'man' higher than 'animal', but he fails to deplore the 'andrological machine' or the assumption of male superiority over women.[2] As I have suggested throughout this book, these two oppressive political practices are inherently intertwined. In my view, Derrida's more radical vision is better placed than other philosophies to challenge – to 'deconstruct' – the full range of hierarchies and subjections. It is also my view that the image of the Möbius strip provides a way of challenging tyrannical dichotomies such as biology/culture, animal/human, colonizer/ed, and fe/male.

There is, however, a second and more abstract constraint that we encounter in every attempt to understand radically different worlds. This problem resides not in the specificities of individual creatures, with all their needs, desires, alliances and conflicts (the passion of historians), but with the broader incommensurability of zoe, or 'life itself' (more typically, the obsession of philosophers). In the twenty-first century, we have become obsessed with defining, categorizing and identifying zoe. Life itself has become the central focus of every form of institutionalized knowledge, from biology to politics and from philosophy to history. However, the genome project and emerging technologies for creating life forms notwithstanding, zoe remains beyond description, categorization, prediction. The vast and exciting knowledges we are acquiring simply make our questions proliferate. In the end, all we know for certain is that we don't.

There is another way of expressing this problem: we are faced with the fundamental unknowability of zoe. But how can zoe be 'unknowable' if we 'know' it is not-known? How to get out of this quandary?

I find it helpful to think in terms of what might be called a 'negative zoélogy'.* The term is a neologism, taking its inspiration from 'negative theology', albeit with God resolutely excised. In other words, theologians and philosophers have faced the problem of incommensurability before: in their struggles to talk about God. Famously, in the late fifth and early sixth centuries, Pseudo-Dionysius (or Dionysius the Areopagite) asked, How can human beings talk about God, a transcendent being beyond all human knowledge, language and mystical intuition? The only solution, he concluded, is to exchange all positive descriptions (God is great, omnipotent, good, omnipresent and so forth) for apophantic or negative ones. As Pseudo-Dionysius said of the Divine, 'words cannot contain him, and no name can lay hold of him.

---

* Pronounced 'zow-EE-low-gee'.

He is not one of the things that are and he cannot be known in any of them.'[3] God cannot be spoken of in terms of 'similarity or dissimilarity'; God is both 'beyond assertion and [beyond] denial'.[4] Speaking about God requires some form of affirmation, which must then be denied, only to then deny the denial, and so on.

Shorn of its mysticism, this is, I believe, a useful concept when thinking about the radical making of worlds here on earth. As with the Möbius strip, negative zoélogy enables us to move beyond comparisons based on similarities and dissimilarities. It injects instability and indeterminacy into our discussions, and serves as a (much needed) reminder that we are not masters of the universe and that all our knowledges are contingent. In our century, I find its negativity generative: it incites imagination. The Möbius strip is a reminder of the fluidity of *zoe*, which is always in motion, affirming and negating, subverting identity and claims of sameness. Negative zoélogy merges with this twisting strip, insisting that violence is done by assertions of ontological solidities: unity or disunity, sameness or difference. Bluntly, it undermines assumptions of superiority/inferiority, inevitably popping up when making comparisons with other worlds ('different *compared with what/whom?*').[5]

Admittedly, the relationship between negative theology and negative zoélogy is simply allegorical. At the most basic level, there is nothing otherworldly or redemptive in negative zoélogy, unlike negative theology. It insists on a radical alterity that is not liberating in itself, but only within the milieu of specific political and historical struggles. As we saw in Part Four, Emmanuel Levinas was a keen proponent of absolute alterity, or what he referred to as Otherness. He once wrote that the 'epiphany of the Other . . . comes to us not only out of the context but also without mediation'.[6] To my mind, this abstraction does violence to flesh-and-blood creatures engaged in struggles within situations that they have not chosen. Rather, encounters with other sentient beings occur in temporal and topographical contexts, albeit profoundly complex ones.

This is what makes historians sympathetic to negative zoélogy. History as a discipline has an inbuilt tendency to apophantic or negative utterances: historians are taught to be sceptical about all universals, all assumptions that the world as we know it has always existed. Every history student is taught that the world is *not* as we know it; that whatever we think is stable and certain is *not*; that there is *not* an unambiguous 'us'; and – paradoxically – that the joy of history is in affirming the relevance of what is *not* like 'us' for the present. In this sense, the discipline of history itself is infused with practices conducive to negative zoélogy. Geoffrey Harpham made a similar point, albeit about the humanities more generally, positing that the humanities produce

> not certain but *un*certain knowledge, knowledge that solicits its own revision in an endless process of refutation, contestation, and modification. Humanists aspire to speak the truth, but none would wish to have the very last word, for such a triumphant conclusion would bring an end not just to the conversation but to the discipline itself.[7]

The historian's mantra is: we must always acknowledge the material, ideological and historical contexts that has brought any *particular* version of Möbius's spiralling strip into being. Negative zoélogy goes further, reminding historians of the dangers involved in attempting to pinch the strip in any one place in order to appropriate other worlds. The title of one of the most eminent historical journals tells it all: *Past and Present*; incommensurable worlds, in dialogue.

This emphasis on the historical contexts of all acts of world-making, including ones that focus upon *zoe* itself, returns us to the productive forces and material practices of social interaction. Put another way, it foregrounds those power relations that have interested us throughout this book. Otherness should never become an absolute good. As we have observed, difference is readily co-opted in the name of greed: zoological gardens cater for voyeuristic urges, chimeras are exploited in the name of fashionable art and some humanitarians have made fortunes ministering to the hungry. Worse, allegations of difference routinely justify violence, such as eating animals, denigrating women, maligning Muslims, enslaving Haitians and massacring Jews, to name just a few.

Perhaps the political work of radical alterity that is integral to negative zoélogy can be illustrated by thinking of it in terms of translation. How can we ever know what strangers (human or non-human) are truly saying? It is not that animals or humans are imperceptible; their speech is simply incomprehensible. As William James joked in 1943, in an article entitled 'On a Certain Blindness in Human Beings', referring to the starkly different pleasure worlds of dogs and humans,

> Take our dogs and ourselves . . . how insensible, each of us, to all that makes life significant for the other! – we to the raptures of bones

under hedges, or smells of trees and lamp-posts, they to the delights of literature and art.[8]

More seriously, Martin Heidegger explained,

> When we say that the lizard is lying on the rock, we ought to cross out the word 'rock' in order to indicate that whatever the lizard is lying on is certainly given *in some way* for the lizard, and yet is not known to the lizard as rock.

The lizard has 'its *own relation* to the rock, the sun, and to a host of other things'.[9] The lizard possesses a world as well as a way of communicating that world; it is just unknowable to us.

This is the insight that we get from studying the dance-language of bees (see Chapter Three). The dance is a complex symbolic system that scientists have learned to decode. Human translations of the bees' language are, in the words of Eileen Crist in 'Can an Insect Speak?' (2004), a '*realistic* vehicle for clarifying the meaning and function of the dance'. However, Crist goes on to observe, although humans can translate the bees' dance 'starkly and concisely', we paradoxically cannot actually 'convey literal meaning'. By translating (bees') dance into (human) speech, we reveal the dance's

> simultaneous proximity to and distance from our linguistic form of life: by revealing its sense through translation, its indefiniteness of sense in the medium of human language is simultaneously exposed. Any performative renders the baseline of the dance as doing something – pointing to a state of affairs in the world and eliciting action. Yet the dance cannot be rendered isomorphically to human language, so its meaning remains irredeemably unsettled: opaqueness lingers in the wake of its conversion into words. This feeling of imprecision, however, is less about the intrinsic nature of the dance, and far more about out partiality to the belief that meaning is only crystal clear in *words*.[10]

As Derrida put it, it is 'not that the animal has a lesser relationship, a more limited access to entities', but she has 'an *other* relationship'.[11] Or, as Maurice Merleau-Ponty reminded his readers in *Signs* (1964), 'We have the feeling that our language expresses totally. But it is not because it expresses totally that it is ours; it is ours because we believe it expresses totally.'[12]

In the philosophy of language, this is incommensurability or a situation in which, despite good intentions, it is impossible to translate between radically different cultures and languages. In translating the words of strangers, even the most basic linguistic structures are inevitably distorted by the language of the (more dominant) translator. Let me illustrate this point by turning to Theodor Georg Heinrich Strehlow's influential text, *Aranda Phonetics and Grammar* (1944). In his painstaking research on the grammar of the Arrente of Australia he discovered that they had no grammatical distinctions for gender:

> The Aranda nouns know no distinctions of gender: masculine, feminine and neuter, are all meaningless terms to the Central Australian tribesman [sic]. Not even the common animals of the chase are differentiated according to sex.

We should not be fooled by this seemingly neutral archaeology of Arrente grammar. Given Strehlow's consistent use of the masculine gender, we might paraphrase the Earnest Englishwoman's question and ask: 'Are women Aranda?' Strehlow's own text exposes his moral viewpoint when he notes that the Arrente '*refuse* to acknowledge in its grammar the prima distinctions of gender'.[13] Strehlow considered gender (as understood within European languages and, in Strehlow's case, prioritizing the masculine over the feminine or neutral) to be fundamental to 'human articulateness'. In the words of anthropologist Elizabeth Povinelli, gender 'becomes a moral insistence on what "primal distinctions" humans must acknowledge to be human as such'. The power relations involved in this articulation of alterity are evident when we ask, why did Aranda grammar eventually gain gender rather than English losing it?[14]

Negative zoélogy, radical alterity and the Möbius strip, then, insist on resisting all attempts of appropriation, whether of Aranda, women, animals or the subaltern. I may be wrong, but I imagine that the Earnest Englishwoman would have liked thinking with representations of the Möbius strip, in particular, even though her satire remained welded to hierarchical models. The strip is consistent with her critique of the great Chain of Being. It is also in harmony with her implicit criticism of humanism, with its patently false insistence on the autonomous, wilful human subject who acts independently in the world.

The Earnest Englishwoman's question – 'are women animals?' – and its inverse – 'are animals women?' – cannot be categorically answered, then. Of course, collapsing differences between humans and animals, despite all peculiarities of group and personality, have been a popular pursuit in Western culture. Some of the ways this has been done have been explored in these *Reflections*. Thus misogyny, racial sciences and the creation of the *Homo sacer* (or the creature reduced to bare life) have appealed to notions of degraded animals to denigrate humans. Others have humanized animals. Vegetarians deny that there is any significant difference between human and animal flesh; physiognomists look into the eyes of animals and see the reflections of their children; primatologists and animal rights advocates equate the societies of particular animals with humans, sometimes even raising the animal above certain people. The effect, in my mind, is a radical flattening out of the contours of our world.

In contrast, negative zoélogy, radical alterity and the dizzy circling of the Möbius strip provide us with more optimistic ways of thinking *with* different worlds. They provide a way of playing with difference, while avoiding the tendency to invent other creatures (human or animal) in our own image or to use them simply as pawns in our own ideological or material battles. They are tools, if you like, that offer a subversive critique of identity politics, based on a play of difference ('them') versus sameness ('us'). They deny the hierarchies that work against justice while, at the same time, paying homage to a *desire* for authenticity, certainty and community. Most importantly, they refuse to deify other beings, while still reminding us of the beauty of motion, of affirmation and denial and further affirmation. By situating fellow creatures within specific temporal and geographical spaces, we keep them resolutely in the real world, with all its suffering, joy, identifications and struggles. Located within history and politics, negative zoélogy, radical alterity and Möbius's strip encourage us to affirm knowledge while simultaneously gesturing towards the fact that there is more – much more – always to come. They point to a politics that is as committed to uniqueness of all life forms as much as to the creative, exhilarating desire and struggle for community and communion, authenticity and certainty.

Notes

CHAPTER ONE: INTRODUCTION: 'ARE WOMEN ANIMALS?'

1 'An Earnest Englishwoman', 'Letter to the Editor. Are Women Animals?', 11.
2 Pope, *An Essay on Man*, 39.
3 Ibid., 43–4.
4 Rawick (ed.), *The American Slave*, vol. 7, 117.
5 Agamben, *The Open*, 26.
6 Derrida, '"Eating Well"', in Cadava, Connor and Nancy (eds), *Who Comes After the Subject?*, 114.
7 Stockdale, *A Remonstrance Against Inhumanity to Animals*, 17.
8 Grant Allen, from an unnamed 'American magazine', in Women's Franchise League, *Report of Proceedings at the Inaugural Meeting*, 7.
9 Morris, *The Naked Ape*, 9 and 79.
10 MacKinnon, *Are Women Human?*, 1–3.
11 Linnæus, *Systema naturæ per regna tria naturæ*.
12 For a brilliant analysis, see Schiebinger, 'Why Mammals are Called Mammals'.
13 Aristotle, 'Politica', in *The Works of Aristotle* (ed. Ross), vol. x, 1253a.
14 Evelyn, *The History of Religion*, 260–1.
15 Descartes, *Discourse on Method and Other Writings*, 73–6.
16 Kant, *Anthropology from a Pragmatic Point of View*, 226.
17 Freud, 'Civilization and its Discontents' in *The Standard Edition of the Complete Works of Sigmund Freud*, vol. xxi, 99.
18 Lloyd, *Humanitarianism and Freedom*, 14.
19 Derrida, 'Violence Against Animals' in Derrida and Roudinesco (eds), *For What Tomorrow . . . A Dialogue*, 66.
20 Lavater, *On Physiognomy*, 3–4.
21 Darwin, 'The Descent of Man, and Selection in Relation to Sex', in *The Portable Darwin*, 330.
22 Diamond, *The Third Chimpanzee*, 23.
23 For example, see the editors' preface to Cavalieri and Singer (eds), *The Great Ape Project*, 2.
24 Derrida, '"Eating Well"', op. cit., 114.
25 Derrida, 'The Animal that Therefore I Am (More to Follow)', 400.
26 Derrida, 'On Reading Heidegger', 183.
27 Wollstonecraft, *A Vindication of the Rights of Woman* (ed. Lynch), 56.
28 Fontaine, *The Complete Fables of Jean de La Fontaine*, 47–8. I have edited the last line of his translation. I am also grateful for a slightly different inflection in the translation in Fontaine, *Selected Fables*, 23–4.
29 Derrida, 'The Animal that Therefore I Am (More to Follow)', 374 and 378–9.

CHAPTER TWO: RED PETER

1 Kafka, 'A Report to an Academy', in *The Transformation and Other Stories*, 187–95.
2 Ames, *Carl Hagenbeck's Empire of Entertainment*, 27.
3 Hagenbeck, *Beasts and Men*, 58.
4 Darwin, *The Origin of Species*, 130–1.
5 Ibid., 135.
6 For instance, see Lorenz, 'Transatlantic Perspectives on Men, Women, and Other Primates'; Robertson, *Kafka*; Rubinstein, 'Franz Kafka: A Hunger Artist'.
7 Hagenbeck, *Beasts and Men*, 20.
8 Ames, *Carl Hagenbeck's Empire of Entertainment*, 89.
9 Derrida, 'The Animal that Therefore I Am (More to Follow)', 400.
10 Hagenbeck, *Beasts and Men*, 282.
11 See Chapter Ten for many examples.
12 For some examples, see Traill, 'Observations on the Anatomy of the Orang Outang', 5; 'Our Simian Cousins', 751; Boulenger, *Apes and Monkeys*, 29; 'Monkeyana', 651–2.
13 Felce, *Apes*, 85.
14 Ibid., 88.
15 Ibid., 35–8.
16 For an incisive discussion, see Schiebinger, 'The Gendered Ape', in Benjamin (ed.), *A Question of Identity*, 119–51.

CHAPTER THREE: TALKING ANIMALS

1 'The Origin of Species. A New Song', 616–17.
2 'Monkeyana', 651.
3 For a concise but excellent summary, see Crist, 'Can an Insect Speak?'
4 Aristotle, 'Politica', in *The Basic Works of Aristotle* (ed. McKean), 1253a.
5 Aristotle, *Aristotle's Historia Animalium*, 73–83.
6 Johns, 'The Language of Dumb Animals', 671.
7 Mill, *On Liberty and Other Essays*, 65 and 77.
8 Scott, 'The Genesis of Speech', xxvii.
9 Noble and Davidson, 'The Evolutionary Emergence of Modern Human Behaviour', 224.
10 Agamben, *The Open*, 26–7.
11 Descartes, *Discourse on Method and Other Writings*, 73–6. Emphasis added.
12 Pepys, *The Diary of Samuel Pepys*, 90.
13 La Mettrie, *Man a Machine*, 103.
14 Traill, 'Observations on the Anatomy of the Orang Outang', 42–3.
15 Primatt, *A Dissertation on the Duty of Mercy and Sin of Cruelty to Brute Animals*, 136–9.
16 Goulburn, *The Idle Word*, 4.
17 Ibid., 11–12.
18 Ibid., 12.
19 'Language of the Lower Animals', 414.
20 Farrar, *An Essay on the Origin of Language*, 53.
21 Ross, *On Aphasia*, 121–2.
22 Maxwell, 'Speech', 828.
23 Darwin, *The Descent of Man, and Selection in Relation to Sex*, ii, 390–1.
24 Darwin, 'The Descent of Man, and Selection in Relation to Sex', in *The Portable Darwin*, 330.
25 'Sigma', 'My Cousin the Gorilla', 135–40.
26 Scott, 'The Genesis of Speech', liii.

27 Yerkes, *Almost Human*, 25–6 and 51.

28 Bateman, *Darwinism Tested by Language*, 86.

29 Ibid., 108 and 111.

30 Ibid., 154.

31 Ibid., 181, 188 and 224. Also see Bateman, *On Aphasia*, 154–65.

32 Edward Meyrick Goulburn (Dean of Norwich), in the preface to Bateman, *Darwinism*, xvii–xviii.

33 Müller, 'On the Classification of Mankind by Language or by Blood', 429.

34 Müller, 'Forgotten Bibles', in *The Essential Max Müller on Language, Mythology, and Religion*, 259–60. Also see Müller, *Lectures on the Science of Language Delivered at the Royal Institution of Great Britain in April, May, and June, 1861*, 360–70; Phillips, 'A Record of Monkey Talk', 1050; Romanes, 'Intellect in Brutes', 122–5; Romanes, *Mental Evolution in Animals*. For historical analyses, see Jeffords, 'The Knowledge of Words', 66–83; Burrow, 'The Use of Philology in Victorian England', in Robson (ed.), *Ideas and Institutions of Victorian Britain*, 180–204; Costall, 'How Lloyd Morgan's Canon Backfired', 113–22.

35 Morgan, 'The Limits of Animal Intelligence', 44.

36 Morgan, 'Animal Intelligence', 524.

37 Garner, 'The Simian Tongue II', 430. For a superb, detailed analysis of Garner's work, see Radick, *The Simian Tongue*.

38 Garner, 'The Simian Tongue II', 48.

39 Garner, *Apes and Monkeys*, 12.

40 Garner, 'The Simian Tongue [I]', 314.

41 Garner, 'The Simian Tongue II', 428.

42 Garner, *Apes and Monkeys*, 12 and 20.

43 Garner, 'The Simian Tongue II', 428.

44 *Apes and Monkeys*, 66 and 71.

45 Ibid., 108–14.

46 Ibid., 35.

47 Ibid., 8–10.

48 Darwin, *Charles Darwin's Marginalia*, vol. 1, 164.

49 Garner, *Apes and Monkeys*, 95.

50 Garner, 'What I Expect to Do in Africa', 715.

51 Richard L. Garner, cited in Phillips, 'A Record of Monkey Talk', 1050.

52 Lloyd Morgan, quoted in 'Mr Garner and his Apes', 444.

53 'A Few Questions for Professor Garner', 480; 'Thinks Well of Gorillas', 1; *Truth* (27 December 1894), 1513–14, and (12 November 1896), 1232–3.

54 'Mr Garner and his Apes', 444.

55 For an excellent discussion, see Radick, 'Primate Language and the Playback Experiment, in 1890 and 1980', 461–93.

56 Ker, 'In a Haytian Village', 139.

57 'Aphasia', *Lancet*, 386.

58 Purser, *Current Theories on Aphasia*, 3.

59 Bateman, *On Aphasia*, 18.

60 For critics, see Freud, *On Aphasia*, 103–4. For a more detailed analysis, see Greenberg, *Freud and His Aphasia Book*, 3.

61 'Aphasia', *Lancet*. Also see Bateman, *On Aphasia*, 533.

62 Mygind, *Deaf-Mutism*, 22. He also makes the interesting observation that more boys are deaf-mutes than girls, perhaps due to the higher mortality rates of deaf-mute girls, the 'greater development of the male organs of hearing', and their 'predisposition to pathological changes' (p. 27).

63 Evelyn, *The History of Religion*, 260.

64 Ibid., 260–1.

65 Love, *Deaf Mutism*, 262.

66 'The Lost Senses. Vol. I, Deafness: Vol. ii. Blindness by John Kitto', 334.

67 'The Dumb Alphabet', 156.

68 Charlotte Elizabeth, *The Happy Mute*, 9–10.

69 Gallaudet, 'A Sermon on the Duty and Advantages of Affording Instruction to the Deaf and Dumb', in Barnard, *Tribute to Gallaudet*, 186.

70 Seiss, *The Children of Silence*, 123.

71 'The Dumb and Deaf', in *Encyclopædia Americana*, cited in Seiss, *The Children of Silence*, 124.

72 Rev. Colin Stone, quoted in Seiss, *The Children of Silence*, 127.

73 Kant, *Anthropology from a Pragmatic Point of View*, 47 and 86. Also see James, 'Thoughts before Language'.

74 'Record of Events', 560.

75 C. Burnett, 'Animals', 45.

76 Scott, *The Deaf and Dumb*, 1.

77 Love, *Deaf Mutism*, 10 and 256.

78 'Our Medical Corner', 348.

79 Unnamed teacher in a Pennsylvanian institution, cited in Seiss, *The Children of Silence*, 115.

80 Archbishop Whately in *Lessons on Reasoning*, quoted in Hubbard, 'Deaf-Mutism', 578.

81 Max Müller, quoted in Hubbard, 'Deaf-Mutism', op. cit., 578.

82 Laurie, 'A Marvellous Conquest', 332–4.

83 'L. N. S.', 'A Plea for the Speechless', 111.

84 Mann, *The Deaf and Dumb*, 77–8.

85 Goulburn, *The Idle Word*, 17. He is slightly confusing because he uses the word 'speech' when he really means language, which is why I have 'translated' his 'speech' into 'language'.

86 Dr Gallaudet, cited in Hubbard, 'Deaf-Mutism', op. cit., 578. Emphasis added.

87 For a few examples, see Burch, *Signs of Resistance*, 35–9; Baynton, *Forbidden Signs*; Jackson and Lee (eds), *Deaf Lives*; Lang, *Silence of the Spheres*; Parks, 'Treatment of Signed Languages in Deaf History Textbooks', 72–93; Van Cleve (ed.), *Deaf History Unveiled*.

88 Yellon, *Surdus in Search of his Hearing*, 80.

89 Blackburn, 'Our Deaf and Dumb', 592.

90 Myklebust, *The Psychology of Deafness*, 241–2.

91 Stokoe, *Language in Hand*, 7. Also see Stokoe, *Sign Language Structure*.

92 See Klima and Bellugi, *The Signs of Language*.

93 Kellogg and Kellogg, *The Ape and the Child*, 3–4; W. N. Kellogg, 'More About the "Wolf Children" of India'; W. N. Kellogg, 'A Further Note on the "Wolf Children" of India'. He was responding to Squires, '"Wolf Children" of India'.

94 Kellogg and Kellogg, *The Ape and the Child*, 5–6. In the 1990s, a similar comment was made in Tomasello, Savage-Rumbaugh and Kruger, 'Imitative Learning of Actions on Objects by Children, Chimpanzees, and Enculturated Chimpanzees', 1703.

95 Kellogg and Kellogg, *The Ape and the Child*, 11.

96 Ibid., frontispiece.

97 Ibid., 307.

98 Ibid., 315–19.

99 Ibid., 281 and 292.
100 C. Hayes, *The Ape in Our House*, 11.
101 Ibid., 64.
102 Hayes and Hayes, 'The Intellectual Development of a Home-Raised Chimpanzee', 108.
103 Ibid.
104 For example, see Gardner, Gardner and VanCantfort (eds), *Teaching Sign Language to Chimpanzees*; Griffin, *Animal Minds*; Miles, 'ME CHANTEK', in Parker, Mitchell and Boccia (eds), *Self-Awareness in Animals and Humans*, 254–72; Savage-Rumbaugh, Shanker and Taylor, *Apes, Language, and the Human Mind*.
105 Robert M. Yerkes cited in 'Apes to Talk with Fingers?', 197.
106 Yerkes, *Almost Human*, 180.
107 Cited in Hill, 'Apes and Language', 91.
108 Gardner and Gardner, 'Ethological Roots of Language', in Gardner, Gardner, Chiarelli, and Plooij (eds), *The Ethnological Roots of Culture*, 205.
109 There are dissenters. For example, see Pinker, *The Language Instinct*.
110 Terrace, *Nim*, 30.
111 Ibid., 28.
112 For a discussion, see Radick, *The Simian Tongue*, 320–64.
113 Terrace, *Nim*, 30.
114 Ibid., 202.
115 Savage-Rumbaugh, Shanker and Taylor, *Apes, Language, and the Human Mind*, 194–5.
116 Segerdahl, Fields and Savage-Rumbaugh, *Kanzi's Primal Language*, 7.

CONCLUSION TO PART 1

1 Walker, 'Current Studies of Animal Communication as Paradigms for the Biology of Language', in Walker (ed.), *Explorations in the Biology of Language*, 204.
2 Weedon, *Feminist Practice and Poststructuralist Theory*, 31.
3 Crist, 'Can an Insect Speak?', 13. I am grateful to Crist's article for drawing my attention to the bees' dance language.
4 Lindaver, *Communication Among Social Bees*, 38–9.
5 Crist, 'Can an Insect Speak?', 20.
6 Ibid., 25.
7 Kafka, 'A Report to An Academy', in *The Transformation and Other Stories*, 195.
8 Derrida, 'The Animal That Therefore I Am', in Calarco and Atterton (eds), *Animal Philosophy*, 126.
9 Kafka, 'A Report to An Academy', op. cit., 187.

CHAPTER FOUR: AN EARNEST ENGLISHWOMAN

1 Singer, *Rethinking Life and Death*, 182.
2 Bentham, *An Introduction to the Principles of Morals and Legislation*, ccix.
3 'An Earnest Englishwoman', 'Letter to the Editor. Are Women Animals?'

CHAPTER FIVE: SENTIENCE AND WELFARE

1 Smith, *The Theory of Moral Sentiments*, 11–12.
2 Thomas Jefferson to Thomas Law (13 June 1814), cited in *The Writings of Thomas Jefferson*, xiv, 141.
3 Bentham, *An Introduction to the Principles of Morals and Legislation*, ccix.
4 Young, *An Essay on Humanity to Animals*, 8. In the same year (1798), John Lawrence also used the term 'rights of beasts' and in Germany in 1788 Wilhelm Dieter wrote that 'animals can have rights' just as children do.

5 Descartes, *Discourse on Method and Other Writings*, 73–6.

6 Dean, *An Essay on the Future Life of Brutes*, vol. 2, 49–50 and 104–5.

7 Primatt, *A Dissertation on the Duty of Mercy and Sin of Cruelty to Brute Animals*, 13–14. Also see p. 7.

8 Dr David H. Cochran, speaking to the Vivisection Hearing before the Senate Committee on the District of Columbia, cited in Lederer, 'The Controversy over Animal Experimentation in America, 1880–1914', in Rupke (ed.), *Vivisection in Historical Perspective*, 244.

9 For instance, see 'Knackers, Pork-Sausages, and Virtue', 2; 'Do Horses Ever Cry?', 142.

10 Originally published in *Hull Times*, but reproduced in *Bristol Mercury* (25 August 1838); *Preston Chronicle* (1 September 1838); *Morning Post* (1 September 1838); *Blackburn Standard* (5 September 1838); Drummond, *The Rights of Animals, and Man's Obligation to Treat Them With Humanity*, 91–2. For other accounts of animal suicides, see various editions of *Animals' Guardian*: November 1908 (138 and 142), May 1910 (111), June 1910 (134), March 1911 (47–8). Also see Oldfield, 'The Scientific View', in Salt (ed.), *The New Charter*, 69; Rhodes, *The Nine Circles or the Torture of the Innocent*, 131–3; 'Monkeyana', 651; Drummond, *The Rights of Animals*, 91–2.

11 'Shell Shock in Cows', 187–8.

12 For a discussion, see my *Fear*; *An Intimate History of Killing*; *Dismembering the Male*; 'The Malingerers' Craft', in Davison, Jalland and Prest (eds), *Body and Mind*, 91–115; 'Shell-Shock, Psychiatry, and the Irish Soldier During the First World War', in Gregory and Paseta (eds), *Ireland and the Great War*, 155–70; 'Psychology at War, 1914–1945', in Bunn, Lovie and Richards (eds), *Psychology in Britain*, 133–49; 'Effeminacy, Ethnicity, and the End of Trauma', 57–69.

13 'Animal Sufferers from Shell Shock', 9. Also see Carver and Dinsey, 'Some Biological Effects Due to High Explosives', 36–51.

14 Primatt, *A Dissertation on the Duty of Mercy and Sin of Cruelty to Brute Animals*, 34–46.

15 'M.C.', 'Letter to the Editor. The Non-Human Races and Continued Existence', 14.

16 'F. G. N.', 'Letter to the Editor. Is There a Future Life for Animals?', 132. Also see Vanasseur, 'A Friend of Mine', 29.

17 'M. C.', 'Letter to the Editor. The Non-Human Races and Continued Existence'. The writer is a woman.

18 Summary of a lecture given by Evan Morris, in 'Destiny of the Lower Animals', 88.

19 For an analysis of the broader debate, see Keith Thomas's brilliant *Man and the Natural World*, 43.

20 'The Feminine Soul', 3.

21 Fowler, 'Is There a Future State for Animals?', 43.

22 'The Immortality of Animals', 27.

23 Summary of a lecture given by Evan Morris, in 'Destiny of the Lower Animals'.

24 Grahame, *Vivisection*, 6.

25 Warbasse, *The Conquest of Disease Through Animal Experimentation*, 16–17.

26 For a discussion, see Pernick, *A Calculus of Suffering*.

27 For debates about whether fetuses feel pain, see Warbasse, *The Conquest of Disease Through Animal Experimentation*, 18; Fitzgerald, *Foetal Pain*; Glover and Fisk, 'Do Fetuses Feel Pain?'; Giannakoulopoulos, Sepulveda, Kourtis, Glover and Fisk, 'Fetal Plasma Cortisol and Beta-Endorphin Response to Intrauterine Needling'; RCOG, *Fetal Awareness*; David James, 'Recent Advances: Fetal Medicine'.

28 Love, *Deaf Mutism*, 10; he is arguing against this common perception.

29 For examples, see Lewis, 'Animal Models of Pain'; Timberlake, 'The Attribution of Suffering', in Baird and Rosenbaum (eds), *Animal Experimentation*, 71–6; Harrison, 'Animal Pain', in Baird and Rosenbaum (eds), *Animal Experimentation*, 128–39.

30 Rickaby, *Moral Philosophy or Ethics and Natural Law*, 248 and 250, and Rickaby, *Moral Philosophy*, 248–9.

31 Warbasse, *The Conquest of Disease Through Animal Experimentation*, 18–20.

32 Carlille, 'Are Animals Happy?', 268.

33 Girdlestone, *Vivisection*, 15, 17 and 22.

34 Robinson, *The Religion of Nature*, 6 and 116.

35 Salt, *Consolations of a Faddist*, 10.

36 Robinson, *The Religion of Nature*, 126–31 and 202. For other arguments about animal insensitivity, see 'Remarks on the Comparative Pleasures and Sufferings of Animals', 351.

37 For a spirited refutation of Harrison's arguments, see House, 'Harrison on Animal Pain', 376–9.

38 Harrison, 'Do Animals Feel Pain?', 25–40. Also see Grandin and Johnson, *Animals in Translation*, 179–240.

39 Bennett, 'Animal Models and Their Clinical Implications', in Merskey, Loeser and Dubner (eds), *The Paths of Pain 1975–2005*, 245–6.

40 Kant, *The Metaphysics of Morals*, 238. Also see Primatt, *A Dissertation on the Duty of Mercy and Sin of Cruelty to Brute Animals*, 286–9, and Salzmann, *Elements of Morality*, vol. 2, 7.

41 Hoare, *Memoirs of Granville Sharp*, vol. 2, 291–2.

42 Rickaby, *Moral Philosophy*, 249.

43 This can been seen in any of the publications of the Society for the Protection of Animals from Vivisection, but see 'A Member of Parliament', *Vivisection and the United Kingdom*, 4; 'Human Grafting as an Aid to Longevity', 58; Ricketts, 'Blessed are the Merciful', in *Appeals for Mercy*, 3; Oakley, *A Plea For Dumb Animals*, 8; Oxenham, *Moral and Religious Estimate of Vivisection*, 17.

44 Shaw, *The Doctor's Dilemma*, lxiii. Also see Beirne, 'On the Sexual Assault of Animals', in Creager and Jordan (eds), *The Animal–Human Boundary*, 123, which links serial killers and animal abusers.

45 Jenyns, *Disquisitions on Several Subjects*, 1–2, 8–11 and 17–18.

46 Ballantyne, *The Child's Ark*, 65 and 67. Also see *The Alphabet of Animals*; *The Children's Picture-Book of the Sagacity of Animals*; Bolton, *Chickens Teach Children*.

47 Jackson, *Our Dumb Neighbours*, 182.

48 Ibid. Emphasis added.

49 Charlotte Elizabeth, *The Happy Mute*, no page.

50 Shaw, *The Doctor's Dilemma*, lix–lx.

51 Brayfytte, 'Experimental Physiology', 39.

52 *The Vivisector*. Also see Barlow-Kennett, *Address to the Working Classes*, 1.

53 'Mercy's Voice', *Vivisection*, 4.

54 Salt, 'The Rights of Animals', 219–20. See also Bigelow, *A Great Surgeon on Vivisection*, 2.

55 For histories, see Lederer, *Subjected to Science*.

56 'F. P. C.', *Cancer Experiments on Human Beings*, 1–2.

57 'M. D.', *The Scientist at the Bedside*, 2–3.

58 Anna Kingsford, cited in Lansbury, 'Gynaecology, Pornography and the Antivivisection Movement', 417.

59 'M. D.', *The Scientist at the Bedside*, 2–3.

60 Hutton, 'The Anti-Vivisectionist Agitation', 511.
61 Frey, 'Vivisection, Morals and Medicine', 94–7.

CHAPTER SIX: HUMANITARIANISM AND THE LIMITS OF SYMPATHY

1   Lubinski, 'Screw the Whales, Save Me!', 401.
2   Angell, *Protection of Animals*, 8
3   'The Woman About Town', 423.
4   Foster, 'Vivisection', 140.
5   Girdlestone, *Vivisection*, 9 and 14.
6   Oakley, *Vivisection*, 54–5.
7   Singer, *Animal Liberation. Towards an End to Man's Inhumanity to Animals*, ix.
8   Regan, *The Case for Animal Rights*, xii.
9   'The Birmingham Association', 23.
10 For instance, see Reece, *The Public Health Act and the Contagious Diseases Acts*, 5.
11 Playfair, *Motion for the Repeal of the Contagious Diseases Acts*, 4 and 11–13.
12 'Personal Examination of Prisoners Contrary to English Law', 61.
13 Hopkins, *The Ride of Death*, 5–6.
14 Taylor, *The Contagious Diseases Act*, part 1, 4–5.
15 Hume-Rothery, *A Letter Addressed to The Right Hon. W. E. Gladstone, MP, and the Other Members of Her Majesty's Government*, 5 and 10.
16 'Discipulus', 'Letter to the Editor. The "Pall Mall Gazette" and the Dog Bill'.
17 'Vanessa', 'Vivisection is Demoralizing to Vivisectors and Spectators. Part III'.
18 Butler, *Speech Delivered by Mrs Josephine Butler at the Fourth Annual Meeting of the Vigilance Association for the Defence of Personal Rights*, 8. Emphasis added.
19 Hillier, *A Vindication of the Address to the People of Great-Britain on the Use of West India Produce*, 18. Hillier disagrees with this sentiment.
20 'A Gentleman of the Partie', *A Journal of Eight Days*, 70.
21 Burney, *The Wanderer*, vol. 3, 241. Also see Dinwiddy, 'The Early Nineteenth-Century Campaign Against Flogging in the Army', 308–31, for the debate about flogging.
22 *National Society for the Prevention of Cruelty to Children, Scottish Branch report for the Year 1901. Moray, Nairn and Banffshire*, 9–10.
23 Turner, *Reckoning with the Beast*, 37.
24 Mann, *Tom Mann's Memoirs*, 38. For an even more strongly worded attack by social-ists on animal rights movements, see 'B&B', *Animal Liberation*, 5–24.
25 Winsten, *Salt and His Circle*, 64–5.
26 Salt, 'The Rights of Animals', 217.
27 Girdlestone, *Vivisection*, 53 and 55.
28 'H', 'On the Notion of the Souls of Beasts', 569.
29 Hartmann, *Anthropoid Apes*, 293.
30 'Vanessa', 'Vivisection is Demoralizing to Vivisectors and Spectators'.
31 'J. E. H.', *Is it Natural?*, 3–4.
32 De Cyon, 'The Anti-Vivisectionist Agitation', 509.
33 Ibid., 506–10.
34 'Hysterical Old Maids', 248–50. In a latter issue, readers were informed that the woman who had attacked Brown-Séquard with her parasol as he was vivisecting a monkey without anaesthetic was not an 'old maid' but the wife of a 'literary gentle-man'. She was Marie Huot, wife of Anatole-Théodore-Marie Huot, editor of the leftist Parisian magazine *L'Encyclopédie Contemporaine Illustrée*.
35 C. F. Hodge, cited in Kaylor, 'Feelings, Thought, and Conduct of Children Toward Animal Pets', 206.

36 Ibid., 236–7.
37 Sully, *Studies of Childhood*, 234–5 and 247.
38 Freud, *Totem and Taboo*, 127.
39 Shaw, *When I was a Child*, 51–2.
40 Manning and Waugh, 'The Child of the English Savage', 696 and 691.
41 Waugh, 'Notes' (April 1890), 43.
42 For some examples, see 'The Factory Question', 7; 'Outrages on Women', 849; Wesley, 'Letter to the Editor. A Day's March', 11; Howell, 'Letter to the Editor. Young Children in Mines', 12; Waugh, 'Letter to the Editor. Unwanted and Illtreated Children. A New Law and a New Departure for Them', 3.
43 'A Word for Children', *Home Journal* (20 June 1866).
44 'Cruelty to Animals: Also to Women and Children'.
45 'A Lady Who Is Deeply Interested'.
46 Ibid.
47 Shelman and Lazoritz, *The Mary Ellen Wilson Child Abuse Case*, 13.
48 Initially, it was called the London Society for the Protection of Children.
49 Manning and Waugh, 'The Child of the English Savage', 688–99.
50 Waugh, 'Notes' (May 1889), 83–4.
51 Ricketts, 'The Whole Creation Groaneth', in *Appeal for Mercy*, 17.
52 They changed their name to the National Society for the Prevention of Cruelty to Children in 1889. The NSPCC was granted its Royal Charter in 1895, when Queen Victoria became patron. It did not change its title to 'Royal Society for the Prevention of Cruelty to Children' or similar, as the name NSPCC was already well established, and to avoid confusion with the RSPCA, which had already existed for more than fifty years.
53 Waugh, 'Notes' (October 1897), 130.
54 Warren, 'Dogs of London', 104–5.
55 Cited in Young-Bruehl, *Hannah Arendt*, 513.
56 For an excellent discussion, see Boddice, *A History of Attitudes and Behaviours Towards Animals in Eighteenth and Nineteenth Century Britain*.
57 Bentham, *The Works of Jeremy Bentham*, part xix, 17.
58 Bentham, *An Introduction to the Principles of Morals and Legislation*, ccviii.
59 Bentham, 'Letter to the Editor', cited in Bentham, *The Works of Jeremy Bentham*, part xix, 549–50.
60 Bentham, 'Anarchical Fallacies', in *The Works of Jeremy Bentham*, vol. 2, 496–501, 505, 508, and 521.
61 RSPCA, *Trustees' Report and Accounts. 2008*, 6–7.
62 Beck, 'Population Aspects of Animal Mortality', op. cit., 45, and Wiswall, 'Animal Euthanasia and Duties Owed to Animals', 801–3.
63 Beck, 'Population Aspects of Animal Mortality', op. cit., 45 and 47.
64 Bryant, 'Animals Unmodified', 150.
65 Morin and Deane, 'Americans Split on How to Interrogate'. Also see http://www.pollingreport.com/terror5.htm, accessed 25 February 2010.
66 http://www.pollingreport.com/terror5.htm, a poll of November 2008, accessed 25 February 2010.
67 Ibid.
68 For example, see Finley, *The Torture and Prisoner Abuse Debate* (Westport, CT: Greenwood Press, 2008); Lomax, 'The *Real* American Gulag'; Conroy, *Unspeakable Acts, Ordinary People*; Dayan, 'Legal Slaves and Civil Bodies', 3–39.
69 For an interesting discussion, see Ashcroft, Griffiths and Triffin (eds), *The Empire Writes Back*, 122–4 and 168.

70 Morgan, *A Sermon. Animal and Man*, 4.

71 Singer, 'Animal Liberation'.

72 Burke, *A Philosophical Enquiry into the Origin of our Ideas of the Sublime and Beautiful*, 73–4

73 Carroll, 'Some Popular Fallacies About Vivisection', 851.

74 Edgeworth, 'The Grateful Negro', in *The Juvenile Tale-Book*, 23–4.

75 Ritchie, *Natural Rights*, 107–8.

76 Singer, 'Severe Impairment and the Beginning of Life'. For a critique, see Oppenheimer, 'Who lives? Who dies?'

77 Tooley, 'Abortion and Infanticide', in Singer (ed.), *Applied Ethics*, 57 and 84.

78 Derrida, 'Force of Law'.

79 Malchow, 'Frankenstein's Monster and Images of Race in Nineteenth Century Britain', 119.

80 It is important to recognize that many scientists continued to refuse to acknowledge animal sentience, as was seen in the pro-vivisectionists debates.

CHAPTER SEVEN: MR HEATHCLIFF

1 E. Brontë, *Wuthering Heights*, 136.

2 Ibid.

3 For the text, see http://www.hrcr.org/docs/frenchdec.html.

4 Letter from Rev. Henry Martyn to William Wilberforce (14 February 1804), in P. Brontë, *The Letters of the Reverend Patrick Brontë*, 317.

5 Letter from Patrick Brontë to the editors of the *Leeds Mercury* (8 March 1834), in ibid., 96.

6 Green, *Patrick Brontë*, 188.

7 E. Brontë, *Wuthering Heights*, 112. Not all scholars agree that Heathcliff was a slave. Another strong argument has him labelled as one of the Irish orphans who populated British cities in the 1840s as a consequence of the Famine: see Michie, 'From Simianized Irish to Oriental Despots', 125–40, and Terry Eagleton, *Heathcliff and the Great Hunger*.

8 E. Brontë, *Wuthering Heights*, 37.

9 Ibid.

10 Morgan, 'Liverpool's Dominance in the British Slave Trade, 1740–1807', in Richardson, Schwarz and Tibbles (eds), *Liverpool and Transatlantic Slavery*, 15. Other important cities include Bristol and London.

11 Muir, *Bygone Liverpool* (Liverpool: Henry Young and Sons, 1913), 59. This was also said of Bristol and other slave cities.

12 E. Brontë, *Wuthering Heights*, 36 and 330.

13 Ibid., 54–5.

14 Ibid., 37 and 50.

15 Ibid., 46.

16 Ibid., 37.

17 Ibid., 39.

18 Ibid., 163.

19 Ibid., 169.

20 Ibid., 178, 103 and 107.

21 Ibid., 151. Also see 174 and 181.

22 Letter from Charlotte Bronte to W. S. Williams (14 August 1848), in Hafley, 'The Villain in Wuthering Heights', 201.

23 E. Brontë, *Wuthering Heights*, 270.

24 Ibid., 112.

25 Ibid., 3.
26 C. Brontë, *Jane Eyre*, 114.
27 Douzinas, *The End of Human Rights*, 372–3.
28 Schmitt, *Political Theology*, 5.
29 Agamben, *State of Exception*, 1–11.

CHAPTER EIGHT: HUMAN RIGHTS

1 For the text, see http://www.ushistory.org/declaration/document/index.htm.
2 For the text, see http://www.hrcr.org/docs/frenchdec.html.
3 Douglass, *The Frederick Douglass Papers*, series 1, vol. 5, 528–9. Speech in Chicago 2 January 1893.
4 For a history, see Douzinas, *The End of Human Rights*.
5 See http://www.un.org/en/documents/charter/.
6 S   e   e
http://www.ohchr.org/EN/UDHR/Documents/UDHR_Translations/eng.pdf.
7 For a helpful summary of these and others, see http://www.caslon.com.au/humanrightsprofile6.htm, accessed 5 April 2010.
8 Tom Campbell, *Rights: A Critical Introduction* (London: Routledge, 2006), 3.
9 de Gouges, 'Declaration of the Rights of Woman'.
10 In the postamble of de Gouges's 'Declaration', op. cit.
11 For a discussion, see Kadish, 'The Black Terror', 673, and Beckstrand, *Deviant Women of the French Revolution and the Rise of Feminism*, 97–121.
12 Quoted by many historians, but see Scott, 'French Feminists and the Rights of "Man"', 16–17.
13 Wollstonecraft, *A Vindication of the Rights of Woman* (ed. Lynch), 7, 9–10, 55 and 203.
14 Vorzimmer, 'The Darwin Reading Notebooks (1838–1860)', 140.
15 Anonymous review published in *Critical Review*, 7.4 (1792), 389–93, and cited in Wollstonecraft, *A Vindication of the Rights of Woman* (ed. Lynch), 273.
16 Wardle (ed.), *Godwin and Mary*, 119.
17 Godwin, *Memories of the Author of 'A Vindication of the Rights of Woman'*, 188.
18 For a discussion, see Richards, 'The Body of Her Work, the Work of Her Body', 565–92.
19 Polwhele, 'The Unsex'd Females', in *Poems*, 36–44.
20 Graves, 'Maternal Despotism', in Lonsdale (ed.), *The New Oxford Book of Eighteenth-Century Verse*, 791–2.
21 'Launcelot Light' and 'Lætitia Lookabout', *A Sketch of the Rights of Boys and Girls*, 14 and 63.
22 Nietzsche, *Beyond Good and Evil*, 103–5.
23 C. Brontë, *Jane Eyre*, 114.
24 E. Brontë, *Wuthering Heights*, 174.
25 Ibid., 150.
26 Grant Allen, from an unnamed 'American magazine', in Women's Franchise League, *Report of Proceedings at the Inaugural Meeting*, 7.
27 She was responding to Grant Allen in ibid.
28 Miss Arabella Shore in *Opinions of Women on Women's Suffrage*, 27. For a sample of similar comments from a range of different feminist perspectives, see Harrison, *'Homo Sum'*, 4–6; Mellone, *The Position and Claims of Woman*, 9–10; Zangwill, *One and One are Two*, 3.
29 Women's Social and Political Union, 'Woman This, and Woman That'.

30 Billington-Greig, *Towards Woman's Liberty*, 1, 3 and 84.

31 Haslam, *The Rightful Claims of Women*, 3.

32 For a discussion, see Bergoffen, 'February 22, 2001', 117, and Campbell, 'Legal Memories', 149–78. Cynically, it may be noted that male-on-male rape was also a prominent part of these conflicts.

33 Women writers who linked the subjection of women and slaves included Aphra Behn, Mary Chudleigh, Sarah Fyge Egerton, Anne Finch, Katherine Philips and Elizabeth Rowe.

34 Wollstonecraft, *A Vindication of the Rights of Woman: With Strictures on Political and Moral Subjects*, 330.

35 I am grateful to Richard Dellamore for making this connection: see his 'Earnshaw's Neighbor/Catherine's Friend', 546–7.

36 Fox, *An Address to the People of Great Britain on the Propriety of Abstaining from West India Sugar and Rum*, 1.

37 Walvin, *Black Presence*, 110.

38 Hargrave, *An Argument in the Case of James Sommersett*, 16 and 78.

39 Washburn, *Extinction of Villenage and Slavery in England*, 20.

40 Cowper, *The Task*, 33.

41 Letter from Benjamin Franklin to abolitionist Anthony Benezet (22 August 1772), in *The Writings of Benjamin Franklin*, vol. v, 431–2.

42 R. Paley, 'Imperial Politics and English Law', 663.

43 Canning, cited in Dew, 'Abolition of Negro Slavery', in Faust (ed.), *The Ideology of Slavery*, 60.

44 Haywood, *A Manual of the Laws of North-Carolina*, vol. 1, 141.

45 Dayan, 'Legal Terrors', 49.

46 Rawick (ed.), *The American Slave*, vol. ix, 114 and 117.

47 Douglass, *The Frederick Douglass Papers*, series 1, vol. 2, 254.

48 Cresswell's Executor v. Walker (1861).

49 US v. Amy, 24 F. Cas. 792 (C.C.D. Va. 1857) (no. 14,445), 795–810.

50 Nott, 'Two Lectures on the Natural History of the Caucasian and Negro Races', in Faust (ed.), *The Ideology of Slavery*, 237 and 236. My emphasis.

51 Harper, 'Memoir on Slavery' (first pub. 1852), in Faust (ed.), *The Ideology of Slavery*, 88–9.

52 Train, *Train's Speeches in England, on Slavery and Emancipation*, 19.

53 Paterson, 'Toussaint L'Overture', 326.

54 Ritchie, *Natural Rights*, 104.

55 'Caught!', in Barry, 'Slavery in the South To-day', reproduced in Daniel, *The Shadow of Slavery*, 116. I am grateful to Daniel's book for the text and context of the article.

56 Jones, *The Dispossessed*, 107.

57 J. D. Lucas to John E. Wilkie (11 April 1907), file 50-162-6, Department of Justice, US National Archives RG 60, cited in Daniel, *The Shadow of Slavery*, 22. The image comes from Richard Barry, 'Slavery in the South To-day', op. cit., 485.

58 According to Kara, *Sex Trafficking*, ix.

59 Foreword by Richard Holbrooke in Skinner, *A Crime So Monstrous*, xi. For estimates on slavery in the twenty-first century, see Hendricks, 'Modern Slavery and the Production of Consumer Goods in a Global Economy', 431–51.

60 Gorden, 'Haitian Forced Labor and the Dominican Republic', 206–49.

61 Skinner, *A Crime So Monstrous*, 12.

62 Kara, *Sex Trafficking*, x.

63 Bales, *Disposable People*, 5.

64 Campbell, *Rights*, 3.

65 Ignatieff, *The Lesser Evil*, vii and 141.

66 Elshtain, 'Reflection on the Problem of "Dirty Hands"', in Levinson (ed.), *Torture*.

67 Dershowitz, *Why Terrorism Works*, 135, 144, 156, and 182. My emphasis.

68 Wantchekon and Healy, 'The "Game" of Torture', 596–609.

69 McCloskey, *Meta-Ethics and Normative Ethics*, 180–1.

70 Bagaric and Clarke, 'Not Enough Official Torture in the World?', 608–9 and 615. Also see their 'Tortured Responses (A reply to Our Critics)', 703–37.

71 Agamben, *State of Exception*, 3–4.

72 http://www.mirror.co.uk/news/allnews/content_objectid=14042696 _method=full_siteid=50143_headline=-MY-HELL-IN-CAMP-X-RAY- name_page.html.

73 Cited in Honigsberg, *Our Nation Unhinged*, 89.

74 Smith, 'Inside Guantanamo'.

75 Justice Ginsburg, Oral Arguments, Rasul v. Bush, 542 U.S. 466 (2004), (Nos. 03-334, 03-343), 51, http://www.supremecourtus.gvt/oral_arguments/ argument_transcripts/03-334.pdf, accessed 3 April 2007.

76 Jamison, 'The Sins of the Father', 88–151.

77 Weil, 'Human Personality', in *Simone Weil: An Anthology*, 60, and cited in Diamond, 'Injustice and Animals', in Elliott (ed.), *Slow Cures and Bad Philosophers*, 121.

78 Campbell, *Rights*, xv.

79 Douzinas, *The End of Human Rights*, 99.

80 Marx, *Grundrisse*, in *Selected Writings*, 346.

81 Anatole France quoted in Douzinas, 'Left or Rights', 627.

82 Brown, *States of Injury*, 99.

83 Arendt, *The Origins of Totalitarianism*, 279–80.

84 Ibid., 299–300.

85 Agamben, *Homo Sacer*, 126.

86 Lennox, 'Refugees, Racism, and Repatriations', 687.

87 Payen, 'Lavalas', 767–8. My emphasis.

88 Brown, *States of Injury*, 98.

89 Bhabha, 'On Minorities'.

90 Simone Weil, quoted in Diamond, 'Injustice and Animals', 128.

CHAPTER NINE: ANIMAL RIGHTS AND 'SPECIESISM'

1 Primatt, *A Dissertation on the Duty of Mercy and Sin of Cruelty to Brute Animals*, 11–12.

2 Stockdale, *A Remonstrance Against Inhumanity to Animals*, 1–3. Also see Raff, *A System of Natural History*, 106.

3 *The Dog of Knowledge*, 70–2.

4 Fitz-Gerald, *Barbarous Cruelty to Living Animals Made Legal in Great Britain*, 48.

5 Oakley, *Vivisection*, 40–1 and 44.

6 'Women Legislators'.

7 Wise, *Though the Heavens May Fall*, 225.

8 Wise, *An American Trilogy*, 226–7.

9 Best and Nocella, 'Introduction: Behind the Mask: Uncovering the Animal Liberation Front', in their (eds) *Terrorists or Freedom Fighters?*, 12.

10 Spiegel, *The Dreaded Comparison*, 14, 24–5, 37, and 43.

11 According to Disraeli, *Vaurien*, vol. 2, 165–82. Taylor was also 'Sipsop the Pythagorean' in Blake, *An Island in the Moon*, 7.

12 *Public Characters of 1798–1799*, 132–3.

13 Taylor, *Vindication of the Rights of Brutes*, iii–iv, vi, 10, 13, 15, 18–19, 76, 81–3, and 89–90.

14 Sellars, *The Rise and Rise of Human Rights*.

15 Regan, *The Case for Animal Rights*, 327 and 329. My emphases.

16 Ibid., 329 and 207–10.

17 'A Declaration on Great Apes', in Cavalieri and Singer (eds), *The Great Ape Project*, 4–6.

18 Wise, *Rattling the Cage* and *Unlocking the Cage*.

19 Wise, *Unlocking the Cage*, 35–8.

20 For example, see Tooley, 'Abortion and Infanticide', in Singer (ed.), *Applied Ethics*, 57 and 84, and Peter Singer, 'Severe Impairment and the Beginning of Life'. For a critique, see Oppenheimer, 'Who lives? Who dies?'

21 Bryant, 'Sacrificing the Sacrifice of Animals', 282.

22 Chris Ronald Tame speaking at the Libertarian Alliance conference on environmentalism. 26 September 1992, cited in The ITMA Team, 'Shechita Barbaric? Oy Vay!', 10.

23 Marquardt, with Levine and La Rochelle, *Animalscam*, 6–7, 17–19, and 125.

24 'Laicus', *The Right to Torture*, 3.

25 Salt, *The Humanities of Diet*, 11.

26 Bryant, 'Sacrificing the Sacrifice of Animals', 283.

27 Redden, 'A Few Words about the Deaf and Dumb', 177.

28 Max Müller, cited in Jenkins, 'The Scientific Testimony of "Facts and Opinions"', 185.

29 Grace and Marks, 'The Great Ape Project and Disability Rights', 818–22.

30 For instance, see Frey, 'Vivisection, Morals and Medicine', 94–7.

31 Cupp, 'A Dubious Grail', 16.

32 Ibid., 18.

33 Ibid., 43–5.

34 'A Declaration on Great Apes', in Cavalieri and Singer (eds), *The Great Ape Project*, 5.

35 E. Brontë, *Wuthering Heights*, 17.

36 Ritchie, *Natural Rights*, 109.

37 Bryant, 'Sacrificing the Sacrifice of Animals', 266.

38 Wise, 'Animal Rights, One Step at a Time', in Sunstein and Nussbaum (eds), *Animal Rights*, 33.

39 Bryant, 'Sacrificing the Sacrifice of Animals', 253.

40 Haraway, *The Haraway Reader*, 141.

41 Braidotti, *Transpositions*, 107.

42 Douzinas, *The End of Human Rights*.

43 Derrida, 'Violence Against Animals', in Derrida and Roudinesco (eds), *For What Tomorrow . . . A Dialogue*, 64–5.

44 Ibid., 68.

45 MacIver, 'Ethics and the Beetle', 65–6.

46 See Heidegger in Sheehan, 'Heidegger and the Nazis', 41–3.

47 Singer, *Enemies*, 145 and 357.

48 For some examples, see Blum, *The Monkey Wars*, 6; Coe, *Dead Meat*, 72–3; Gold, *Animal Rights*, 37; Mason, *An Unnatural Order*, 48, 118–19 and 218–19; Rollin, *Animal Rights and Human Morality*, 216; Ryder, 'Speciesism', in Baird and Rosenbaum (eds), *Animal Experimentation*; Sapontzis, *Morals, Reasons, and Animals*, 86; Schleifer, 'Images of Death and Life', in Singer (ed.), *In Defence of*

Animals, 63; Singer, *Animal Liberation* (1990), 83–5; Wynne-Tyson, *The Extended Circle*, 29.

49 Panaman, 'How to Do Animal Rights – and Win the War on Animals'.

50 Lane, 'Imagine', 45. For another camp analogy, see Lee, 'Unjustifiable Explosions', 40.

51 Churchill, 'Foreword: Illuminating the Philosophy and Methods of Animal Liberation', in Best and Nocella (eds), *Terrorists or Freedom Fighters?*, 3. For another example of making comparisons to the Holocaust, see Sax, *Animals in the Third Reich*, 18–19.

52 For her CV, see http://www.upc-online.org/karenbio.htm, accessed 5 April 2010.

53 Davis, *The Holocaust and the Henmaid's Tale*, xi.

54 Ibid., 108.

55 Ibid., 111. Davis is quoting from Patterson, *Eternal Treblinka*, 167.

56 Davis, *The Holocaust and the Henmaid's Tale*, 112. Also see Chris McIntosh (who pleaded guilty to arson at McDonald's restaurant in Seattle), quoted in Liddick, *Eco-Terrorism*, 89–90, and Sax, *Animals in the Third Reich*.

57 For example, see Jehl, 'Officials Told to Avoid Calling Rwanda Killings "Genocide"'; Winter, 'Journey into Genocide'; MacDonald, 'Daring to Compare', 383–403; Sztybel, 'Can the Treatment of Animals Be Compared to the Holocaust?', 97–132.

58 Friedberg, 'Dare to Compare', 365–7.

59 Bettelheim, 'The Holocaust – One Generation After', in Gottlieb (ed.), *Thinking the Unthinkable*, 379.

60 For example, see 'Jewish "Kapparot" Ritual Killing of Animals'.

61 Douzinas, 'The End(s) of Human Rights', 13 and 21.

62 'Cruelty to Animals' (7 April 1826), 89.

63 'Cruelty to Animals' (1 June 1841), 135.

64 Tonna, *Kindness to Animals*, no page.

65 Ricketts, 'The Whole Creation Groaneth', in *Appeals for Mercy*, 16–17.

66 'A Vivisector's Nightmare', 131.

67 Hodgins, *Aims and Objects of the Toronto Humane Society*, 31–2.

68 'Animal Rights Terror Tactics'.

69 'Staying on Target and Going the Distance'.

70 Bolz, Dundonis and Schulz, *The Counterterrorism Handbook*, 158.

71 For estimates, see ibid. 158; Doward, 'Kill Scientists, Says Animal Rights Chief' and 'Animal Rights Terror Tactics'.

72 For a particularly crude example, see Mundi Club, *A Pictorial History of the Royal Animal Terrorists*.

73 Lee, 'Unjustifiable Explosions', 39.

74 John Lewis, cited in Schorn, 'Burning Rage'. This can also be found at http://www.animalliberationfront.com/Philosophy/JerryVlasak.htm, accessed 12 March 2011.

75 Best, 'Who's Afraid of Jerry Vlasak?'. Also see McDonald, 'Monkey Madness at UCLA'.

76 Hepburn, 'What Price Violence', 42.

77 Fenland Fox, 'Not the IRA Way', no page.

78 Ryder, 'Sentientism', no page. My emphasis.

79 Cited in Spicer, 'Not a Game of Cricket', 38.

80 'Neil from Shrewsbury', 'Speaking Out', 45.

81 'Neil', 'A Retort', no page. This presumably is the same man as 'Neil from Shrewsbury'.

82 http://student.maxwell.syr.edu/ajnocell/, accessed 28 January 2010.
83 Best and Nocella, 'Introduction', in their (eds) *Terrorists or Freedom Fighters?*, 23. Also see McClain, 'ALF. A Secret Interview with a Compassionate Commando', 12.
84 Maxwell Schnurer, 'At the Gates of Hell: The ALF and the Legacy of Holocaust Resistance', in Best and Nocella (eds), *Terrorists or Freedom Fighters?*, 113–14.
85 See *Uniting and Strengthening America by Providing Appropriate Tools Required to Intercept and Obstruct Terrorism (USA PATRIOT Act) Act of 2001*, 107th Congress, 1st Session (2001) and Senate Committee on Environment and Public Works, *Oversight on Ecoterrorism Specifically Examining the Earth Liberation Front (ELF) and the Animal Liberation Front (ALF)*, 109th Congress, 1st Session (2005). They were labelled terrorist in counterterrorism handbooks as well: see Bolz, Dundonis and Schulz, *The Counterterrorism Handbook*.

CONCLUSION TO PART 3

1 Humphrey, *The Politics of Atrocity and Reconciliation*, 1.
2 E. Brontë, *Wuthering Heights*, 11, 129, 224 and 274.
3 Douzinas, *The End of Human Rights*, 187–8.
4 Gourevitch, *We Wish To Inform You That Tomorrow We Will be Killed With Our Families*, 6–9.

CHAPTER TEN: BOBBY THE DOG

1 Levinas, *Totality and Infinity*, 39.
2 Kant, *The Metaphysics of Morals*, 255.
3 Levinas, 'The Name of a Dog', in *Difficult Freedom*, 152–3.
4 Steeves, 'Lost Dog', in Pollock and Rainwater (eds), *Figuring Animals*, 24.
5 Interview of Emmanuel Levinas after his article 'The Name of a Dog; or, Natural Rights', in Calarca and Atterton (eds), *Animal Philosophy*, 49.
6 For a discussion, see Davy, 'An Other Face of Ethics and Levinas', 43.
7 'H', 'On the Notion of the Souls of Beasts', 569.
8 See Ellis, *Man and Woman*, 51. Also see Hartmann, *Anthropoid Apes*, 291.
9 'Our Simian Cousins', 751.
10 Bell, *The Hand*, 16.
11 Rochet, 'Analytical Account of the Chief Characters Tending to Separate Man from Animals', 168–70. Also see Wolff, 'The Form and Dermatoglyphs of the Hands and Feet of Certain Anthropoid Apes', 347, and Heidegger, cited in Derrida, '*Geschlecht* II: Heidegger's Hand' in Sallis (ed.), *Deconstruction and Philosophy*, 169.
12 Graham, *Lectures on the Science of Human Life*, vol. 2, 16.

CHAPTER ELEVEN: PHYSIOGNOMIC ARTS

1 Aristotle, 'Physiognomonics', in *The Complete Works of Aristotle* (ed. Barnes), vol. 1, 1237. My emphasis.
2 Ibid.
3 Graham, 'Lavater's Physiognomy in England', 562.
4 Lavater, *Essays on Physiognomy*, vol. 3, part 2, 391.
5 Scoutetten, *Eléments de Philosophie Phrénologique*, 57.
6 It is not clear who actually wrote the poem.
7 Lavater, *Essays on Physiognomy*, 389–90.
8 Ibid., 296.
9 Lavater and Sue, *Lavater's Looking Glass*, 175.

10 Steeves, 'Lost Dog', in Pollock and Rainwater (eds), *Figuring Animals*, 24.

11 Bell, *The Anatomy and Philosophy of the Expression*, 25–30 and 54.

12 Ibid., 30.

13 Ibid., 88—92.

14 Ibid., 89 and 121.

15 Ibid., 121.

16 Ibid., 92.

17 W. Paley, *Natural Theology*, 7 and 12.

18 Bell, *The Anatomy and Philosophy of the Expression*, 264.

19 Ibid., 32.

20 Ibid., 165.

21 Ibid., 140–1.

22 Ibid., 145.

23 Ibid., 83.

24 Ibid., 101–3.

25 Redfield, *Comparative Physiognomy*, 330.

26 'Knackers, Pork-Sausages, and Virtue', 2.

27 Searing, 'My Story', cited in Esmail, 'The Power of Deaf Poetry', 357.

28 Bateman, *On Aphasia*, 215.

29 Love, *The Deaf Child*, 38.

30 *The American Annals of the Deaf and Dumb* (October 1854), cited in Seiss, *The Children of Silence*, 118.

31 Lavater, 'Memoir of the Life of J. K. Lavater', in *On Physiognomy*, vol. 1, xcv. Report of a conversation between Lavater and Emperor Joseph.

32 'Letter to the Editor. Defence of the Female Claim to Mental Equality', 115. The sex of the writer is ambiguous: at times in the letter, s/he uses pronouns that may imply that the author was of either sex. However, the predominance of female pronouns supports my assumption that the author is a woman.

33 Thackeray quoted in Honour, *The Image of the Black in Western Art*, vol. 4, 204.

34 Jenyns, *Disquisitions on Several Subjects*, 8–9.

35 Thompson, 'Facial Expression and its Psychology', 72.

36 Ker, 'In a Haytian Village', 139.

37 Redfield, *Comparative Physiognomy*, 253–4. Also see Smith, *Vagabondiana*, 30, and Napier, 'Resemblance Between Man and Animals', clxx.

38 Redfield, *Comparative Physiognomy*, 117–18, 167, 171 and 328.

39 Ibid., 334.

40 'E. R.', 'Familiar Lectures on Physiognomy', 313.

41 Lavater, *On Physiognomy*, vol. 1, 132–33.

42 Ibid., 90.

43 Ibid., 166. Also see *How to Read the Face*, 3; Redfield, *Comparative Physiognomy*, 15; Thompson, 'Facial Expression and its Psychology', 71.

44 Lavater, *Essays on Physiognomy*, vol. 1, 135.

45 *Encyclopedia Britannica* (1853–60), cited in Graham, 'Lavater's Physiognomy in England', 561–2.

46 E. Brontë, *Wuthering Heights*, 50.

47 Ibid., 7.

48 Pennell, *Mary Wollstonecraft*, 108.

49 Wollstonecraft, *Letters Written During a Short Residence in Sweden, Norway, and Denmark*, 36 and 171.

50 Juengel, 'Godwin, Lavater, and the Pleasures of Surface', 74.

51 Shelley, *Frankenstein*, 276.

52 Ibid., 344.

53 Reported in 'Lavater', 183.

54 Darwin, *The Autobiography of Charles Darwin and Selected Letters*, 27.

55 Bray, 'The Physiology of the Brain', 277.

56 Thompson, 'The Descent of Facial Expression', 128.

57 'On Physiognomy', 115.

58 Thompson, 'Facial Expression and its Psychology', 68 and 71. Also see Thompson, 'The Descent of Facial Expression', 128.

59 'Physiognomy', 137–8.

60 For a discussion, see Gilman, *A Cultural History of Madness and Art in the Western World*.

61 Morison, *The Physiognomy of Mental Disease*, 1.

62 Shaw, *The Physiognomy of Mental Disease and Degeneracy*, 3.

63 'Physiognomy', 137 and 141. Also see Woolnoth, *The Study of the Human Face*, 5–7.

64 Beale, 'A Letter to the Editor', 375.

65 Levinas, *Entre Nous*, 10.

66 Lavater, 'Memoir of the Life of J. K. Lavater', in *On Physiognomy*, vol. 1, xcv. Report of a conversation between Lavater and Emperor Joseph.

67 Ibid.

68 Lavater, *On Physiognomy*, vol. 1, 152–4. Also see p. xcv.

69 'E. R.', 'Familiar Letters on Physiognomy', 98.

70 Lavater, *On Physiognomy*, vol. 1, 24.

71 Ibid., 3–4.

72 Thompson, 'Facial Expression and its Psychology', 70.

CHAPTER TWELVE: DARWINIAN REVOLUTIONS

1 Darwin, *The Life and Letters of Charles Darwin*, vol. 2, 171.

2 Barrett, Gautrey, Herbert, Kohn and Smith, *Charles Darwin's Notebooks, 1836–1844*, 542.

3 Darwin, *The Expression of the Emotions in Man and Animals*, 20.

4 Watson, 'Commentary', in Watson (ed.), *Darwin*, 1063.

5 Darwin, *The Expression of the Emotions in Man and Animals*, 20.

6 Ibid., 45.

7 Ibid., 45 and 57.

8 Ibid., 65–7.

9 Ibid., 74.

10 Ibid., 86–8.

11 Barrett et al., *Charles Darwin's Notebooks*, 541–2.

12 Some commentators seem to imply that there was a link. For instance, see Rachels, *Created from Animals*; Sholtmeijer, *Animal Victims in Modern Fiction*; Midgley, 'Practical Solutions', in Paterson and Palmer (eds), *The Status of Animals*, 18; Singer, *Animal Liberation. A New Ethics for our Treatment of Animals*.

13 Preece, 'Darwinism, Christianity, and the Great Vivisection Debate', 399–419.

14 Darwin, *The Descent of Man*, part 1 and 2, 119–20.

15 Barrett et al., *Charles Darwin's Notebooks*, 264.

16 Watson, 'Commentary', in Watson (ed.), *Darwin*, 1062.

17 Suckling, *Anti-Darwin*, 168–9.

18 Baynes, '*The Expression of the Emotions in Man and Animals* by Charles Darwin', 512.

19 Ibid., 492–528.

20 Letter to Alexander Bain (9 October 1873), in Darwin, *The Life and Letters of Charles Darwin*, 173.

21 'Our Simian Cousins', 751.

22 Suckling, *Anti-Darwin*, 1.

23 'The Emotions'.

24 Thompson, 'Facial Expression and its Psychology', 72.

25 Huber, *Evolution of Facial Musculature and Facial Expression*, 101.

26 Ibid., 99–101, 152–60.

CHAPTER THIRTEEN: SURGICAL SCIENCES

1 Lavater, *On Physiognomy*, vol. 1, 154.

2 Yousif, 'Introduction', 203.

3 For example, see Nahai, *The Art of Aesthetic Surgery*.

4 BAAPs website: www.baaps.org.uk.

5 Aitkenhead, 'Most British Women Now Expect to have Cosmetic Surgery in their Lifetime'.

6 The statistic is for 2004: Rondilla and Spickard, *Is Lighter Better?*, 106.

7 For example, see Brons, *Facial Harmony*; Hueston, 'Duchenne Today', in Duchenne de Boulogne, *The Mechanism of Human Facial Expression*, 257–69; Hueston and Cuthbertson, 'Duchenne de Boulogne and Facial Expression', 411–20; Farkas, Hreczko, Kolar and Munro, 'Vertical and Horizontal Proportions of the Face in Young Adult North American Caucasians', 328–37.

8 Gonzalez-Ulloa, 'Aesthetic Plastic Surgery', 3.

9 Ekman, *Telling Lies*.

10 Gonzalez-Ulloa, 'Aesthetic Plastic Surgery'.

11 For some examples, see Asthana, 'Half of British Women Consider Plastic Surgery'; Brown, 'Sometimes Nips and Tucks Can be Career Moves', 3–6; Bull and Rumsey, *The Social Psychology of Facial Appearance*; Dion, 'Young Children's Stereotyping of Facial Attractiveness', 183–8; Niechajev and Haraldsson, 'Ethnic Profile of Patients Undergoing Aesthetic Rhinoplasty in Stockholm', 139–45; Kalick, 'Aesthetic Surgery', 128–33; Shaw, 'Folklore Surrounding Facial Deformity and the Origins of Facial Prejudice', 237–46; Solis, 'Plastic Surgery Wooing People Hoping to Move Up Career Ladder', 1.

12 Gonzalez-Ulloa, 'Aesthetic Plastic Surgery'.

13 Roe, 'The Deformity Termed "Pug Nose" and Its Correction by a Simple Operation'.

14 Sarwer and Magee, 'Physical Appearance and Society', in Sarwer, Pruzinsky, Cash, Goldwyn, Persing and Whitaker, *Psychological Aspects of Reconstructive and Cosmetic Plastic Surgery*, 24–5. Also see Jones, 'An Evolutionary Perspective on Physical Attractiveness', 97–109.

15 Sarwer and Magee, 'Physical Appearance and Society', op. cit. 24.

16 Aronsohn, *Your Looks*, 49.

17 For further discussion, see Gilman, *Making the Body Beautiful*, especially 85–118; Gilman, *The Jew's Body*, 169–93.

18 Porter, 'Analysis of the African American Female Nose', 623.

19 For another analysis, see Kaw, 'Medicalization of Racial Features', 81.

20 Niechajev and Haraldsson, 'Ethnic Profile of Patients Undergoing Aesthetic Rhinoplasty in Stockholm', 144.

21 Haiken, *Venus Envy*, 202.

22 McCurdy and Lam, *Cosmetic Surgery of the Asian Face*, 5.

23 Millard, 'The Oriental Eyelid and its Surgical Revision', cited in Kaw, 'Medicalization of Racial Features'.

24 Aronsohn and Epstein, *The Miracle of Cosmetic Plastic Surgery*, 135–6.

25 Rondilla and Spickard, *Is Lighter Better?*, 106.
26 Yousif, 'Introduction', 203.
27 For example, see Borman, Ozgür and Gürsu, 'Evaluation of Soft-Tissue Morphology of the Face in 1,050 Young Adults', 280–8; Farkas, Forrest and Litsas, 'Revision of Neoclassical Facial Canons in Young Afro-Americans', 179–84; Farkas, Hreczko, Kolar and Munro, 'Vertical and Horizontal Proportions of the Face in Young Adult North American Caucasians', 328–37; Le, Farkas, Ngim, Levin and Forrest, 'Proportionality in Asian and North American Caucasian Faces Using Neoclassical Facial Canons as Criteria', 64–9; Porter, 'The Average African American Male Face: An Anthropometric Analysis', 78–81; Porter and Olson, 'Anthropometric Facial Analysis of the African American Woman', 191–7.
28 Butler, *Breeding, Training, Management, Diseases, &c. of Dogs*, 59–60.
29 Bermúdez, 'Experimental Model of Facial Transplant', 1374; Siemionow, Ozmen and Demis, 'Prospects for Facial Allograft Transplantation in Humans', 1421–8.
30 'The Pendleton Panther', 'Plastic Surgery for Animals'.
31 Pavletic, *Atlas of Small Animal Reconstructive Surgery*, 413. Emphasis added.
32 Drury (ed.), *British Dogs*, 274 and 282–3. Also see Barton, *Dogs*, 176–7.
33 Hutt, *Genetics for Dog Breeders*, 182–3.
34 Harrison, *The Breeding of Show Fox Terriers*, 17.
35 Shaw, *The Illustrated Book of the Dog* (London: Cassell and Co., 1890), 155.
36 Gwynne-Jones, *Talking About Dogs*, 137.

CONCLUSION TO PART 4

1 Aronsohn and Epstein, *The Miracle of Cosmetic Plastic Surgery*, 334–5.
2 With greater or lesser success, radical environmentalists since Levinas have attempted to broaden the ethical scope of face-to-face encounters, some not only insisting that animals have faces but also attempting to move Levinas 'beyond the inter-human' by claiming that plants and stones have 'faces' as well. For an interesting example, see Davy, 'An Other Face of Ethics in Levinas', 39–65.
3 *The Dog of Knowledge*, 70–2.
4 Kant, *The Metaphysics of Morals*, 255.
5 Seabrook, *The Magic Island*, 101.
6 Cited in http://www.nndb.com/people/695/000113356/.

CHAPTER FOURTEEN: 'THE BLACK DEMONS OF HAYTI'

1 I am indebted to Marcus Wood in *Blind Memory* for drawing this image to my attention, and for his analysis.
2 Rae, 'The Black Demons of Hayti', 274–7.
3 Derrida, '"Eating Well"', in Cadava, Connor and Nancy (eds), *Who Comes After the Subject?*, 112.

CHAPTER FIFTEEN: EATING ANIMALS

1 Jenyns, *Disquisitions on Several Subjects*, 16–18.
2 'Cruelty to Animals' (7 April 1826), 89.
3 http://wiki.answers.com, accessed 20 December 2009.
4 All these statistics are from The Animal Studies Group, 'Introduction', in their (eds), *Killing Animals*, 1.
5 http://www.vegsoc.org/nvw/2002/presspac2.html, accessed 7 October 2009.
6 Wolfson and Sullivan, 'Foxes in the Hen House', in Sunstein and Nussbaum (eds), *Animal Rights*, 206.
7 Smil, 'Eating Meat', 628, and http://www.vegsoc.org/nvw/2002/presspac2.html,

accessed 7 October 2009, and Lacobbo and Lacobbo, *Vegetarians and Vegans in America Today*, 6.

8   Schmitt, 'Meat's Meat', 185.

9   Dodge, *The Plains of the Great West and Their Inhabitants*, 211.

10 Murray, *Factors Affecting the Prices of Livestock*, 2.

11 Waddington, '"Unfit for Human Consumption"', 636, and Capie and Perren, 'The British Market for Meat 1850–1914', 504.

12 All these statistics are indebted to Smil, 'Eating Meat', 610–13.

13 Hickman, 'Excessive meat-eating "kills 45,000 each year"'.

14 All these statistics are indebted to Smil, 'Eating Meat', 610–13.

15 Ibid., 609.

16 Ibid.

17 Carson, *A New Method of Slaughtering Animals for Human Feed*, 30–1.

18 Ibid.

19 Arthur Brisbane, cited (disapprovingly) in Carqué, *An Appeal to Common Sense*, 3.

20 Ibid., 2.

21 Derrida, '"Eating Well"', in Cadava, Connor and Nancy (eds), *Who Comes After the Subject?*, 114.

22 Belfrage, 'Diet and Race', in Lane (ed.), *The New Health Guide*, 18–19.

23 George Beard, cited in Adams, *The Sexual Politics of Meat*, 31.

24 Lankester, *On Food*, 173.

25 Wherry, 'Does a Low-Protein Diet Produce Racial Inferiority?', 908–9 and Mitchell, 'Does a Low-Protein Diet Produce Racial Inferiority?', 156–8.

26 Hudson, *The Book of a Naturalist*, 296–7.

27 Smil, 'Eating Meat', 599.

28 For a more sophisticated account than most, see Stanford, *The Hunting Apes*.

29 Graham, *Lectures in the Science of Human Life*, vol. 2, 375–6. Also see Carson, *A New Method of Slaughtering Animals for Human Feed*, 30–1, which also warned against the consumption of non-bled meat.

30 George Bernard Shaw, cited in Jones, 'Food Choice, Symbolism, and Identity', 140.

31 Mrs Ernest Jones, writing in *Hospital*, quoted in 'Do We Eat Too Much Meat?', 595.

32 Gaskell, *The Life of Charlotte Brontë*, vol. 1, 41. There were also occasional complaints that vegetarians were irritable: 'Vegetarianism', 4.

33 Mrs Ernest Jones, op. cit.

34 'Do We Eat Too Much Meat?' I have assumed that the author is a woman.

35 Leese, *The Legalized Cruelty of Scechita*, 5. Also see Leese, *Out of Step*; Leese, *My Irrelevant Defence*. The RSPCA and other groups also protested against Shechita: see Slotki, *History of the Manchester Shechita Board, 1892–1952*, 41–5, for some examples.

36 Leese, 'Barbaric', 48. Note that Leese's letter was published on the *Vegetarian Living* letters page, as though he had just sent it to them.

37 Bernard, *Rejuvenation Through Dietic Sex Control*, 6.

38 *Judy* (23 May 1900), 243.

39 For a fascinating analysis, see Fraser, *The Golden Bough*.

40 Beames, *The Rookeries of London*, 209.

41 Oswald, *The Cry of Nature*, 24.

42 Balfour, *Cruelty and Cowardice*, 6 and 13. Also see Gangee, *The Cattle Plague and Diseased Meat in Their Relation with the Public Health*, 15–16, and Salt, *The Logic of Vegetarianism*, 61 and 63.

43 'Vegetarianism', 4.

44	MacDonald, 'Problems of the Great Republic', 115.
45	Kingsford, *The Perfect Way in Diet*, 61–2.
46	Lester, *Behind the Scenes in Slaughter-Houses*, 3–4. See pp. 5–6 for use of term 'dregs'.
47	'The Attack on London Slaughterhouses', 618.
48	'The Effects of Eating Horse-Meat', 27.
49	'Passing Events', 784.
50	Ibid.
51	Oswald, *The Cry of Nature*, 21.
52	Graham, *Lectures in the Science of Human Life*, vol. 2, 368–9.
53	Salt, *The Logic of Vegetarianism*, 76 and 79–81.
54	Ibid.
55	Buffon, cited (disapprovingly and with slightly different wordings) in Graham, *Lectures in the Science of Human Life*, vol. 2, 44, and Graham, *The Physiology of Feeding*, 137.
56	'Those Estimable People, the Vegetarians', 9.
57	Graham, *A Lecture to Young Men on Chastity*, 40 and 52–3.
58	'Vegetarianism', 4.
59	Adams, *The Sexual Politics of Meat*.
60	It was an argument also made in Holliday, *The Violent Sex*, 40.
61	Maitland, *Anna Kingsford*, 48.
62	*Vegetarian Review* (February 1896), 73, cited in Twigg, 'The Vegetarian Movement in England, 1847–1981', chapter 6.
63	Kingsford, *The Perfect Way in Diet*, 58–9.
64	Benedict, Miles, Roth and Smith, *Human Vitality and Efficiency Under Prolonged Restricted Diet*, 639–40.
65	Ibid., 640.
66	Bernard, *Rejuvenation Through Dietic Sex Control*, 18–19.
67	Morris Krok, in his preface to ibid., no page.
68	Mowry, 'Some Sexual Disorders in the Male', cited in ibid., 19–20.
69	Rymer and Rymer, 'Psychological Medicine as Practiced by the Quack', 697–8. They were attacking such 'quacks'.
70	Percy, *What Effect Has the Meat or Milk from Diseased Animals Upon the Public Health?*, 47.
71	Richardson, 'Public Slaughter-Houses', 637.
72	Balfour, *Cruelty and Cowardice*, 12–13.
73	Behrend, *Cattle Tuberculosis and Tuberculous Meat*, 8.
74	The best accounts are by Keir Waddington: '"Unfit for Human Consumption"', 636, and *The Bovine Scourge*, 3.
75	Sir Arbuthnot Lane, cited in Whorton, *Inner Hygiene*, 69.
76	Cited in ibid.
77	Cited in ibid.
78	Lane, *The Prevention of the Diseases Peculiar to Civilization*, 56.
79	Whorton, 'Civilization and the Colon', 426.
80	Tomes, 'The History of Shit', 403.
81	For example, see Keith, *Fads of an Old Physic*, 82.
82	Tipper, *The Cradle of the World and Cancer*, 9–10 and 20–1.
83	Ibid. Scaremongering about the dangers of eating meat continued into the early twenty-first century. For a couple of examples of this vast popular literature, see Cox, *Why You Don't Need Meat*, and Waldman and Lamb, *Dying for a Hamburger*. For a fascinating history of a meat-poisoning, see Smith and Diack, *Food Poisoning, Policy, and Politics*.
84	For an insightful analysis, see Anderson, *The Collectors of Lost Souls*.
85	Johnson, 'Maxime Schwartz', 528.

86 Schlosser, *Fast Food Nation*, 272. It was also transmissible by inoculation of infected tissue.
87 Ford, *BSE – The Facts*, 199.
88 Smil, 'Eating Meat', 627.
89 Ibid., 626.

CHAPTER SIXTEEN: EATING PEOPLE

1 Bancroft, *History of Oregon*, 469–75. Also see Schmitt, 'Meat's Meat', 197–8.
2 Shepard, *Pedlar's Progress*, 441.
3 As reported in Salt, *The Humanities of Diet*, 14.
4 Vayda, 'On the Nutritional Value of Cannibalism', 1462–3.
5 Posinsky, 'Cannibalism', 269.
6 Garn and Block, 'The Limited Nutritional Value of Cannibalism', 106.
7 Garn, 'The Noneconomic Nature of Eating People', 902–3. For an almost identical argument, but in relation to cannibalism by other primates, see Hiraiwa-Hasegowa, 'Cannibalism Among Non-Human Primates', in Elgar and Crespi (eds), *Cannibalism*, 333–4, and Elgar and Crespi, 'Ecology and Evolution of Cannibalism', in their (eds) *Cannibalism*, 1–12.
8 Smith, *Fruits and Farinacea*, 60.
9 PETA's 'All Animals Have the Same Parts' can be found at https://secure.peta.org/site/Advocacy?cmd=display&page=UserAction&id=3205, accessed 15 October 2010.
10 Oswald, *The Cry of Nature*, 25.
11 Salt, *The Logic of Vegetarianism*, 99 and 101.
12 Ibid., 99 and 101.
13 Craige, *Black Bagdad*, 1–2.
14 Derrida, '"Eating Well"', in Cadava, Connor and Nancy (eds), *Who Comes After the Subject?*, 115.
15 Ricketts, 'The Whole Creation Groaneth', in *Appeals for Mercy*, 17.
16 Long, *The History of Jamaica*, vol. 2, 381–2.
17 E. Brontë, *Wuthering Heights*, 178 and 270.
18 Wells, 'Cannibal of Central Australia', 47. Also see Train, *Train's Speeches in England, on Slavery and Emancipation*, 22.
19 Anonymous wood-carving from *Illustrated Police News* (c.1860), in Wood, *Blind Memory*, 191.
20 Wheeler, *The Complexion of Race,* and Lestringant, *Cannibals.*
21 Prichard, *Where Black Rules White*, 79, 81, and 281–4.
22 Loederer, *Voodoo Fire in Haiti*, 31.
23 Craige, *Black Bagdad*, 105.
24 Walvin, *Black Presence*, 110.
25 Cowper, 'Sweet Meat has Sour Sauce'.
26 Equiano, *The Interesting Narrative of the Life of O. Equiano*, 85.
27 Hillier, *A Vindication of the Address to the People of Great-Britain on the Use of West India Produce*, 17–18.
28 Paulson, *Representations of Revolution (1789–1820)*, 204–5, and Wood, *Blind Memory*, 155.
29 Fox, *An Address to the People of Great Britain on the Propriety of Abstaining from West India Sugar and Rum*, 1–6.
30 Burn, *A Second Address to the People of Great Britain*, 6–12. Also see Cooper, *Considerations on the Slave Trade* and Allen, *The Duty of Abstaining from the Use of West India Produce.*

31 'T. P.', 'Rhymes for Youthful Readers, on Colonial Slavery', 151.

32 Sinclair, *The Autobiography of Upton Sinclair*, 108–10, 122 and 126.

33 Charnock, 'Cannibalism in Europe', xxiii and xxix.

34 For an example from past century, see Guttmacher, *Life in the Making*, 21. For a few examples from today, see http://www.mothers35plus.co.uk/plac_rec2.htm, http://www.twilightheadquarters.com/placenta.html, http://www.moon-dragon.org/parenting/placentadisposalrituals.html http://www.ourfirstmarriage.com/index.php/2009/07/23/placenta-recipies/, and http://www.birenandkris.com/serendipity/index.php?/archives/14-Whats-for-dinner-tonight-Roast-Placenta....html, accessed 7 May 2008.

35 Bennett, 'Chimera and the Continuum of Humanity', 353.

36 Bailey, 'What is Too Human?'

37 There is a large literature on 'survival cannibalism' and cannibalistic psychopaths. For a few examples, see Askenasy, *Cannibalism*; Constantine, *A History of Cannibalism from Ancient Cultures to Survival Stories and Modern Psychopaths*; Cunningham, *The Place Where the World Ends*; Hanson, *The Custom of the Sea*; Read, *Alive*.

38 Dr Caplin quoted in Charnock, 'Cannibalism in Europe', xxx.

39 'Cannibalism', 10.

40 May 1829, cited in the *Morning Chronicle*, cited by Ruth Richardson's wonderful book *Death, Dissection, and the Destitute*, 221.

41 E. C. Tufnell, 10 January 1839, National Archives MH 32/70.

42 Ashton, *Modern Street Ballads*, 352.

43 'The Andover War-Song', 143.

44 'The Sunderland Election', 264.

45 Ibid.

46 'The Andover Union Inquiry', 364.

47 Ibid.

48 'The "Dougal Creature"', 314.

49 'Working of the Workhouse System', 291.

50 Miller, 'Food for the Poor', 1.

51 'The Andover Horrors', 308.

52 'A Reasonable Request', 101.

53 'The Sunderland Election', 264.

54 Ibid.

55 Ibid.

56 'The Andover Horrors', 308.

57 'We Hardly Know How to Approach the Andover Inquiry', 580.

58 Ross, *Satanic Ritual Abuse*, 14. Also see Emon, *Occult Criminal Investigation*, quoted in Hicks, 'The Police Model of Satanism Crime', in Richardson, Best and G. Bromley (eds), *The Satanism Crime*, 178. Both the 'babysitter' story and the 'Cross of Nero' were also told in Ryder, *Breaking the Circle of Satanic Ritual Abuse*, 22.

59 Ross and Joshi, 'Paranormal Experiences in the General Population', 357–61.

60 Ryder, *Breaking the Circle of Satanic Ritual Abuse*, 251.

61 Ibid., 218–31.

62 For an example, see Noblitt and Perskin, *Cult and Ritual Abuse*, 60.

63 deMause, 'Why Cults Terrorize and Kill Children', 511.

64 Kahanes, *Cults that Kill*, 140.

65 deMause, 'Why Cults Terrorize and Kill Children', 513.

CONCLUSION TO PART 5

1 Richardson, 'Public Slaughter-Houses', 635.
2 Derrida, '"Eating Well"', in Cadava, Connor and Nancy (eds), *Who Comes After the Subject?*, 112.
3 Ibid., 112–14.

CHAPTER SEVENTEEN: STEPHANIE AND GOOBERS

1 Bailey, 'Organ Transplantation: A Paradigm of Medical Progress', 25.
2 Wallis, 'Baby Fae Stuns the World'.
3 'Lusty Baby', 6.
4 Gould, 'The Heart of Terminology', 31.
5 Unnamed protester, quoted in Munson, *Raising the Dead*, 159.
6 Regan, 'The Other Victim', 9–10.
7 Annas, 'Law and the Life Sciences', 15.
8 Wallis, 'Baby Fae Stuns the World'.
9 http://www.geocities.com/organdonate/ashorthistoryofhumanandxeno-transplanting. html, accessed 23 May 2009.
10 Wallis, 'Baby Fae Stuns the World'. My emphasis.
11 Cited in Annas, 'Law and the Life Sciences', 15.
12 For eighteenth-century concerns about transplantation (albeit allo-grafting) and commodification, see Blackwell, '"Extraneous Bodies"', 21–68.
13 Bailey, 'Organ Transplantation', 27.

CHAPTER EIGHTEEN: REJUVENATION

1 Kant, *The Metaphysics of Morals*, 255.
2 Haeseker, 'Van Meekeren and his Account of the Transplant of Bone from a Dog into the Skull of a Soldier', 173–4.
3 Proverbs, 16:31.
4 Corners, *Rejuvenation*, v.
5 Ramus, *Outwitting Middle Age*, 3.
6 Brown-Séquard, 'The Effects Produced on Man by Subcutaneous Injections of a Liquid Obtained from the Testicles of Animals', 105–7.
7 Brown-Séquard, 'On a New Therapeutic Method Consisting in the Use of Organic Liquids Extracted from Glands and Other Organs', 1212.
8 Sengoopta, *The Most Secret Quintessence of Life*, 37.
9 Voronoff, *Rejuvenation by Grafting*, 13–17.
10 Voronoff, 'The Conquest of Old Age', in Forbath (ed.), *Sidelights from the Surgery*, 18.
11 Voronoff, *The Study of Old Age and My Method of Rejuvenation*, 30.
12 Voronoff, *Rejuvenation by Grafting*, 31–2.
13 Ibid., 34. Note that he uses the word 'heterograft' whereas today we would use 'xenograft'.
14 Appendix by Dr Baudet in ibid., 135.
15 Voronoff, *The Study of Old Age and My Method of Rejuvenation*, 133–55. See this for images of the operation.
16 Ibid., 127–8.
17 Voronoff, *Rejuvenation by Grafting*, 11.
18 Voronoff and Alexandrescu, *Testicular Grafting From Ape to Man*, 114–19.
19 Voronoff, *Rejuvenation by Grafting*, 33, 37 and 45–50.
20 'C. B. F.', 'The 1933 Year Book of Neurology and Psychiatry', 719, and Guttmacher, *Life in the Making*, 211.

21 Voronoff, *The Study of Old Age and My Method of Rejuvenation*, 97–124.
22 In French, *myxœdœmatour* is a form of congenital idiocy or cretinism. However, he could have been referring to myxoedema, an acquired thyroid failure. I am indebted to Professor Tom Treasure for this reference.
23 Voronoff, *The Study of Old Age and My Method of Rejuvenation*, 73.
24 Voronoff, 'The Conquest of Old Age', op. cit., 18.
25 'The Progress of Science', 189 and 191.
26 Voronoff, 'The Conquest of Old Age', op. cit., 20.
27 Leffingwell, *The Vivisection Question*, 5.
28 Letter from James Adams, *Herald* (13 April 1875), cited in Grahame, *Vivisection*, 38.
29 Allinson, 'Organotherapy', 16.
30 'The "Rejuvenation" Treatment', 16.
31 Ouida, *The New Priesthood*, 388.
32 Maitland, 'An Appeal to Hearts and Heads' in Carpenter and Maitland, *Vivisection*, 19 and 22.
33 Gibbs, 'We May all Stay Young'.
34 'Human Grafting as an Aid to Longevity', 58
35 Bayly, *Voronoff*, 4.
36 Ouida, *The New Priesthood*, 388.
37 Lind-af-Hageby, *'Ecrasez l'Infâme!'*, 25.
38 Ibid., 58.
39 'Letter to the Editor. Dr Brown-Séquard's Experiments', 347.
40 Bayly, *The Gland Grafting Operation of Dr Voronoff*, 4.
41 Ibid.
42 Bayly, *Dr Sergius Voronoff and Rejuvenation by Means of Grafting Monkey-Glands*, 5.
43 Ibid.
44 Bayly, *Voronoff*, 5.
45 Lind-af-Hageby, *'Ecrasez l'Infâme!'*, 58.
46 Ouida, *The New Priesthood*, 388.
47 *Freethinker* (7 August 1898), 504.
48 Heath, *Vaccination*, 20–1.
49 Ibid., 31. Emphasis in the original.
50 Moseley, *Treatise on the Lues Bovilla*, 214.
51 Cited in Thornton, *Vaccinae Vindicia*, 4–5.
52 Bayly, *Dr Sergius Voronoff and Rejuvenation by Means of Grafting Monkey-Glands*, 11.
53 'Quaero', 'Monkeying with Man', 722.
54 'Debased and Debasing', 1.
55 Allinson, 'Glands Again', 4.
56 Bayly, *The Gland Grafting Operation of Dr Voronoff*, 9–10.
57 Bayly, *Voronoff*, 5 and 8.
58 Ibid., 8.
59 Haire, *Rejuvenation*, 6.
60 He is referring to Tipper, *The Cradle of the World and Cancer*, 16.
61 Bayly, *The Gland Grafting Operation of Dr Voronoff*, 6–9, and 11–15.
62 'Brown-Séquard's Rejuvenating Fluid', 118. Also see 'C. B. F.', 'The 1933 Year Book of Neurology and Psychiatry', 720.
63 'Dr Brown-Séquard's Elixir of Life', 57–8.
64 Thorek, *A Surgeon's World*, 169–70.
65 For the full story, see Hamilton, *The Monkey Gland Affair*, 36–8.
66 Thorek, *A Surgeon's World*, 169–70.
67 Sengoopta, *The Most Secret Quintessence of Life*.

CHAPTER NINETEEN: TRANSPLANTATION AND SPECIES BOUNDARIES

1 Reported in Dubernard, Bonneau and Latour, *Heterografts in Primates*, 39.
2 Goodwin, 'Discussion', 409. For other examples, see Stone and Kennedy, 'Survival of Heterologous Mammalian Transplants', 645–51.
3 Siegel, 'Re-Engineering the Laws of Organ Transplantation', 917.
4 Joralemon, 'Organ Wars', 335.
5 McFadden, *Medical Ethics for Nurses*, 218.
6 Papagaroufali, 'Xenotransplantation and Transgenesis', in Descola and Pálsson (eds), *Nature and Society*, 249.
7 Michael and Brown, 'The Meat of the Matter', 390.
8 Nuffield Council on Bioethics, *Animal-to-Human Transplants*, 105.
9 Douglas, *Purity and Danger*.
10 Quoting G. F. Cadogan-Masterman, in 'Dermepenthesis', 638–9.
11 Coffman, Sher, Hoffman, Rojter, Folk, Cramer, Vierling, Villamel, Podesta, Demetriou and Makowka, 'Survey Results of Transplant Patients' Attitudes on Xenografting', 379.
12 Michael and Brown, 'The Meat of the Matter', 388.
13 Health Canada, *Proposed Canadian Standard for Xenotransplantation*, cited in Mortensen, 'In the Shadow of Doctor Moreau', 57.
14 McCormick, 'Was There Any Real Hope for Baby Fae?', 12.
15 Papagaroufali, 'Xenotransplantation and Transgenesis', op. cit., 249.
16 Langley and D'Silva, *Animal Organs in Humans*, 41–2.
17 Ibid.
18 Wells, *The Island of Doctor Moreau*, 99.
19 Coffman et al., 'Survey Results of Transplant Patients' Attitudes on Xenografting', 379.
20 Ibid.
21 Starzl, Valdiva, Marase, Demitris, Fontes, Rao, Manez, Marino, Todo, Thomson and Fung, 'The Biological Basis of and Strategies for Clinical Xenotransplantation', 218–19 and 232.
22 Rothblatt, *Your Life or Mine*, 89.
23 Smith, 'Pig Organs "Available" to NHS Patients in a Decade', 13.
24 Woods, 'Have a Heart', 1.
25 David White in the *Sunday Times* (5 July 1992).
26 Unnamed scientist quoted in Hanson, 'The Seductive Sirens of Medical Progress', 5.
27 Cited in James, 'Operation Hope', 30.
28 Vanderpool, 'Critical Ethical Issues in Clinical Trials with Xenotransplants', 1348.
29 Loike and Tendler, 'Reconstituting a Human Brain in Animals', 348.
30 Bennett, 'Chimera and the Continuum of Humanity', 353.
31 For the best discussion, see ibid., 350.
32 Ibid., 381.
33 Rivard, 'Toward a General Theory of Constitutional Personhood', 1433.
34 For a discussion, see Cassuto, 'Bred Meat', 84.
35 Hon. Bruce Lehman, US Commissioner of Patents, cited in Dowie, 'Gods and Monsters'.
36 Ibid.
37 Seyfer, 'The Ethics of Chimeras and Hybrids'.
38 For a discussion, see Brady, *Masculinity and Male Homosexuality in Britain 1861–1918*, 97.

39 Linnæus, *Systema naturæ per regna tria naturæ*.
40 Karpowicz, Cohen and van der Kooy, 'Developing Human–Non-Human Chimeras in Human Stem Cell Research', 117.
41 Bennett, 'Chimera and the Continuum of Humanity', 365.
42 Fletcher, *The Ethics of Genetic Control*, 172–3.
43 Dowie, 'Gods and Monsters'. Dowie is, of course, a critic of 'new slavery'.
44 President's Commission for the Study of Ethical Problems in Medicine and Biomedical and Behavioral Research, *Splicing Life*, 58.
45 Wright, 'Personhood 2.0', 1053.

CONCLUSION TO PART 9

1 The Chimera was the fabled fire-spouting monster which possessed a goat's body, a lion's head and a serpent's tail, who terrorized the Lycians of Asia Minor before being slain by the young Bellerophon.
2 Waldby and Squier, 'Ontogeny, Ontology, and Phylogeny', 33. Emphasis in original.
3 Voronoff, *Love and Thought in Animals and Men*, 3–4.
4 Phelps, 'Transplantation of Tissue from Lower Animals to Man', 225.
5 Coffman et al., 'Survey Results of Transplant Patients' Attitudes on Xenografting', 381.
6 Haraway, *The Haraway Reader*, see especially 39.
7 David White, cited in James, 'Operation Hope', 30. Also see Rollin, *Science and Ethics*, 209.
8 See Sharp, 'Organ Transplantation as a Transformative Experience', 357–89.

CHAPTER TWENTY: CONCLUDING WORDS: NEGATIVE ZOÉLOGY

1 'Essay on the Language of Animals', 262–3.
2 This point was also made by Kelly Oliver in her brilliant *Animal Lessons*. Unfortunately for me, I only discovered her book after mine was completed. She is interested in many of the same philosophers.
3 Pseudo-Dionysius, 'The Divine Names', in *Pseudo-Dionysius. The Complete Works*, 109.
4 Pseudo-Dionysius, 'Mystical Theology', in ibid., 141.
5 An interesting example of this problem has been given by Donna Haraway in *The Haraway Reader*, 58–9.
6 Levinas, 'Meaning and Sense', in *Emmanuel Levinas: Basic Philosophical Writings*, 53.
7 Harpham, 'Beneath and Beyond the "Crisis in the Humanities"', 30. He is propagating humanist thought, but his argument works equally well for those writing within an anti-humanistic tradition.
8 James, 'On a Certain Blindness in Human Beings', in *Essays on Faith and Morals*, 260.
9 Heidegger, *The Fundamental Concepts of Metaphysics*, 198.
10 Crist, 'Can an Insect Speak?', 21–2.
11 Derrida, *Of Spirit*, 49.
12 Merleau-Ponty, *Signs*, 89–90. He was drawing on the work of linguist Ferdinand de Saussure. I am grateful to Crist, 'Can an Insect Speak?' for drawing my attention to this work.
13 Strehlow, *Aranda Phonetics and Grammar*, 59.
14 Povinelli, 'Radical Worlds', 328–34.

Bibliography

'A Declaration on Great Apes', in Paolo Cavalieri and Peter Singer (eds), *The Great Ape Project. Equality Beyond Humanity* (London: Fourth Estate, 1993)

'A Member of Parliament', *Vivisection and the United Kingdom. An Appeal to Working Men* (London: Society for the Protection of Animals from Vivisection, 1893)

Adams, Carol, *The Sexual Politics of Meat. A Feminist–Vegetarian Critical Theory* (Cambridge: Polity, 1990)

Adams, James, 'Letter', *Herald* (13 April 1875)

Agamben, Giorgio, *Homo Sacer: Sovereign Power and Bare Life*, trans. Daniel Heler-Roazen (Stanford: Stanford University Press, 1998)

——, *The Open: Man and Animal*, trans. Kevin Attell (Stanford: Stanford University Press, 2004)

——, *State of Exception*, trans. Kevin Attell (Chicago: University of Chicago Press, 2005)

Aitkenhead, Decca, 'Most British Women Now Expect to have Cosmetic Surgery in their Lifetime', *Guardian* (14 September 2005)

Allen, William, *The Duty of Abstaining from the Use of West India Produce. A Speech Delivered at the Coach Makers' Hall, Jan. 12, 1792* (London: T. W. Hawkins, 1792)

Allinson, Bertrand P., 'Glands Again', *Anti-Vivisection Journal* (January 1926)

——, 'Organotherapy', *Anti-Vivisection Journal* (February 1921)

'Am Not *I* a Brute and a Brother?', *Punch* (25 September 1869)

Ames, Eric, *Carl Hagenbeck's Empire of Entertainment* (Seattle: University of Washington Press, 2008)

Amunts, Katrin and Karl Zilles, 'A Multimodal Analysis of Structure and Function in Broca's Region', in Yosef Grodzinsky and Katrin Amunts (eds), *Broca's Region* (Cambridge: Cambridge University Press, 2006)

'An Earnest Englishwoman', 'Letter to the Editor. Are Women Animals?', *The Times* (16 April 1872)

Anderson, Warwick, *The Collectors of Lost Souls. Turning Kuru Scientists into Whitemen* (Baltimore: Johns Hopkins University Press, 2008)

'The Andover Bastile', *Penny Satirist* (6 September 1845)

'The Andover Horrors', *Satirist; or, The Censor of the Times* (28 September 1845)

'The Andover Union Inquiry', *English Gentleman* (27 September 1845)

'The Andover War-Song', *Punch* (27 September 1845)

Angell, George T., *Protection of Animals* (New York: American Social Sciences Association, 1874)

'Animal Rights Terror Tactics', http://news.bbc.co.uk/2/hi/uk_news/902751.stm (30 August 2000), accessed 1 January 2010

The Animal Studies Group, *Killing Animals* (Urbana: University of Illinois Press, 2006)

'Animal Sufferers from Shell Shock', *The Times* (28 December 1917)

Annas, Geary J., 'Law and the Life Sciences: Baby Fae: The "Anything Goes" School of Human Experimentation', *Hastings Center Report*, 15.1 (February 1985)

Anonymous, *The Alphabet of Animals. Intended to Impress Children with Affection for the Brute Creation* (London: Society for Promoting Religious Knowledge Among the Poor, 1863)

Anonymous [Thomas S. Baynes], 'The Expression of the Emotions in Man and Animals by Charles Darwin', *Edinburgh Review*, cxxxvii (April 1872)

'Apes to Talk with Fingers?', *Science News-Letter*, 11.311 (26 March 1927)

'Aphasia', *Lancet*, 92.2351 (19 September 1868)

Arendt, Hannah, *The Origins of Totalitarianism* (1951; New York: Harcourt Brace Jovanovich, 1973)

Aristotle, 'Physiognomonics', in *The Complete Works of Aristotle*, ed. Jonathan Barnes (Princeton: Princeton University Press, 1984)

——, 'Politica', trans. Benjamin Jowett, in *The Basic Works of Aristotle*, ed. Richard McKean (New York: Modern Library, 2001)

——, 'Politica', trans. Benjamin Jowett, in *The Works of Aristotle*, ed. W. D. Ross, vol. x (Oxford: Clarendon Press, 1921)

——, *Aristotle's Historia Animalium*, vol. 2, trans. A. L. Peck (London: William Heinemann, 1860)

Aronsohn, Richard B. and Richard A. Epstein, *The Miracle of Cosmetic Plastic Surgery* (Los Angeles: Sherbourne Press, 1970)

Aronsohn, Richard B., *Your Looks. Younger and Better Through Cosmetic Surgery* (Pacific Palisades: Nurseco, 1981)

Ashcroft, Bill, Gareth Griffiths and Helen Triffin (eds), *The Empire Writes Back: Theory and Practice in Post-Colonial Literatures* (1989; London: Routledge, 2002)

Ashton, John, *Modern Street Ballads* (London: Chatto and Windus, 1888)

Askenasy, Hans, *Cannibalism: From Sacrifice to Survival* (Amherst, NY: Prometheus, 1994)

Asthana, Anushka, 'Half of British Women Consider Plastic Surgery', *Guardian* (25 September 2005)

'The Attack on London Slaughterhouses', *Meat Trades' Journal*, 297 (4 January 1894)

'B&B', *Animal Liberation. A Case of Moral Indignation?* (Brighton: Unemployed Centre, 1987)

Bagaric, Mirko and Julie Clarke, 'Not Enough Official Torture in the World? The Circumstances in which Torture is Morally Justifiable', *University of San Francisco Law Review*, 39 (2004–2005)

——, 'Tortured Responses (A Reply to Our Critics): Physically Persuading

Suspects is Morally Preferable to Allowing the Innocent to be Murdered', *University of San Francisco Law Review*, 40 (2005–2006)

Bailey, Cathryn, 'We Are What We Eat: Feminist Vegetarianism and the Reproduction of Racial Identity', *Hypatia*, 22.2 (spring 2007)

Bailey, Leonard L., 'Organ Transplantation: A Paradigm of Medical Progress', *Hastings Center Report*, 20.1 (January–February 1990)

Bailey, Ronald, 'What is Too Human? The Ethics of Human/Animal Chimeras', http://www.reason.com/archives/2004/11/24/what-is-too-human, accessed 1 January 2010

Baird, Robert M. and Stuart E. Rosenbaum (eds), *Animal Experimentation. The Moral Issues* (New York: Prometheus, 1991)

Bales, Kevin, *Disposable People. New Slavery in the Global Economy* (1999; Berkeley: University of California Press, 2004)

Balfour, Clara Lucas, *Cruelty and Cowardice: A Word to Butchers and Their Boys* (London: S. W. Partridge, 1866)

Ballantyne, Randall H., *The Child's Ark. Being Short Descriptions of Some of the Animals Mentioned in Scripture; with Simple Remarks Adapted for Children*, 2nd edn (London: John Johnstone, 1848)

Bancroft, Hubert Howe, *History of Oregon* (San Francisco: McGraw-Hill, 1888)

Barlow-Kennett, Richard, *Address to the Working Classes* (London: Victoria Street Society for the Protection of Animals from Vivisection, n.d.)

Barrett, Paul H., Peter J. Gautrey, Sandra Herbert, David Kohn and Sydney Smith, *Charles Darwin's Notebooks, 1836–1844* (Cambridge: Cambridge University Press, 1987)

Barry, Richard, 'Slavery in the South To-day', *Cosmopolitan Magazine*, 42 (March 1907)

Barton, Frank Townend, *Dogs. Their Selection, Breeding and Keeping* (London: Jarrold and Sons, n.d.)

Bateman, Frederic, *Darwinism Tested by Language* (London: Rivington, 1877)

——, *On Aphasia, or Loss of Speech, and the Localisation of the Faculty of Articulate Language*, 2nd edn (London: J. & A. Churchill, 1890)

Bateson, Gregory and Margaret Mead, *Balinese Character: A Photographic Analysis* (New York: New York Academy of Sciences, 1942)

Bayly, M. Beddow, *Dr Sergius Voronoff and Rejuvenation by Means of Grafting Monkey-Glands* (London: Animal Defence and Anti-Vivisection Society, 1928)

——, *The Gland Grafting Operation of Dr Voronoff* (London: privately, 1928)

——, *Voronoff* (London: Animal Defence and Anti-Vivisection Society, 1928)

Baynes, Thomas S., '*The Expression of the Emotions in Man and Animals* by Charles Darwin', *Edinburgh Review*, 137 (1873)

Baynton, Douglas C., *Forbidden Signs: American Culture and the Campaign Against Sign Language* (Chicago: University of Chicago Press, 1996)

Beale, Henry B., 'A Letter to the Editor', *Girl's Own Paper* (11 March 1893)

Beames, Thomas, *The Rookeries of London: Past, Present and Prospective* (London: Thomas Bosworth, 1852)

Beck, Alan M., 'Population Aspects of Animal Mortality', in William J. Kay,

Herbert A. Nieburg, Austin H. Kutscher, Ross M. Grey and Carole E. Fudin (eds), *Pet Loss and Human Bereavement* (Ames: Iowa State University, 1984)

Beckstrand, Lisa, *Deviant Women of the French Revolution and the Rise of Feminism* (Madison: Fairleigh Dickinson University Press, 2009)

Behrend, Henry, *Cattle Tuberculosis and Tuberculous Meat* (London: F. Calder-Turner, 1893)

Beirne, Piers, 'On the Sexual Assault of Animals: A Sociological View', in Angela N. H. Creager and William Chester Jordan (eds), *The Animal–Human Boundary: Historical Perspectives* (Rochester, NY: University of Rochester Press, 1999)

Belfrage, S. Henning, 'Diet and Race', in Sir William Arbuthnot Lane (ed.), *The New Health Guide* (London: Geoffrey Bles, 1935)

Bell, Charles, *The Anatomy and Philosophy of the Expression as Connected with the Fine Arts*, 5th edn (1806; London: Henry G. Bohn, 1865)

——, *The Hand. Its Mechanism and Vital Endowments as Evincing Design* (London: William Pickering, 1833)

Benedict, Francis G., Walter R. Miles, Paul Roth and H. Monmouth Smith, *Human Vitality and Efficiency Under Prolonged Restricted Diet* (Washington DC: Carnegie Institute of Washington, 1919)

Bennett, D. Scott, 'Chimera and the Continuum of Humanity: Erasing the Line of Constitutional Personhood', *Emory Law Journal*, 55 (2006)

Bennett, Gary J., 'Animal Models and Their Clinical Implications', in Harold Merskey, John D. Loeser and Ronald Dubner (eds), *The Paths of Pain 1975–2005* (Seattle: IASP Press, 2005)

Bentham, Jeremy, *An Introduction to the Principles of Morals and Legislation. Printed in the Year 1780 and Now First Published* (London: T. Payne and Son, 1789)

——, *The Works of Jeremy Bentham, Now First Collected; Under the Superintendence of his Executor, John Bowring. Part XIX. Containing Memoirs of Bentham by John Bowring; Including Autobiographical Conversations and Correspondence* (Edinburgh: William Tait, 1842)

——, *The Works of Jeremy Bentham, Published Under the Superintendence of His Executor, John Bowring* (Edinburgh: William Tait, 1843)

Bergoffen, Debra, 'February 22, 2001: Toward a Politics of the Vulnerable Body', *Hypatia*, 18.1 (winter 2003), 117

Bermúdez, Luis Eduardo, 'Experimental Model of Facial Transplant', *Plastic and Reconstructive Surgery*, 110.5 (October 2002)

Bernard, Raymond, *Rejuvenation Through Dietic Sex Control* (Durban: Essence of Health Publishing Company, 1962)

Best, Steven, 'Who's Afraid of Jerry Vlasak?', Animal Liberation Press Office (undated)

Best, Steven and Anthony J. Nocella (eds), *Terrorists or Freedom Fighters? Reflections on the Liberation of Animals* (New York: Lantern Books, 2004)

Bettelheim, Bruno, 'The Holocaust – One Generation After', in Roger S. Gottlieb (ed.), *Thinking the Unthinkable* (New York: Paulist, 1990)

Bhabha, Homi K., 'On Minorities: Cultural Rights', *Radical Philosophy*, 100

(March–April 2000), http://www.radicalphilosophy.com/default.asp?channel _id=2187&editorial_id=10064, accessed 5 April 2010

Bigelow, Henry J., *A Great Surgeon on Vivisection* (London: National Anti-Vivisection Society, n.d.)

Billington-Greig, Teresa, *Towards Woman's Liberty*, new edn (London: Women's Freedom League, 1913)

Bird, Mark Baker, *The Black Man; or, Haytian Independence. Deduced from Historical Notes and Dedicated to the Government and People of Hayti* (New York: privately, 1869)

Birdwhistell, Ray L., *Kinesics and Context. Essays on Body Motion Communication* (Philadelphia: University of Pennsylvania Press, 1970)

'The Birmingham Association', *Shield* (21 March 1870)

Blackburn Standard (5 September 1838)

Blackwell, Mark, '"Extraneous Bodies": The Contagion of Live-Tooth Transplantation in Late-Eighteenth-Century England', *Eighteenth-Century Life*, 28.1 (winter 2004)

Blake, William, *An Island in the Moon*, facsimile edn introduced, transcribed and annotated by Michael Phillips (Cambridge: Cambridge University Press, 1987)

Blanchard, Dallas A. and Terry J. Prewitt, *Religious Violence and Abortion: The Gideon Project* (Gainesville: University Press of Florida, 1993)

Blum, Deborah, *The Monkey Wars* (New York: Oxford University Press, 1994)

Boddice, Rob, *A History of Attitudes and Behaviours Towards Animals in Eighteenth and Nineteenth Century Britain. Anthropocentrism and the Emergence of Animals* (Lewiston: Edwin Mellen Press, 2008)

Bolton, Rev. J., *Chickens Teach Children. A New Year's Address to Sunday Scholars* (London: Church of England Sunday School Institute, c.1850s)

Bolz, Frank, Kenneth J. Dundonis and David P. Schulz, *The Counterterrorism Handbook. Tactics, Procedures, and Techniques*, 3rd edn (Boca Raton: Taylor and Francis, 2005)

Borman, H., F. Ozgür and G. Gürsu, 'Evaluation of Soft-Tissue Morphology of the Face in 1,050 Young Adults', *Annals of Plastic Surgery*, 42.3 (March 1999)

Boulenger, E. G., *Apes and Monkeys* (London: George G. Harrap, 1936)

Bourke, Joanna, *Dismembering the Male: Men's Bodies, Britain and the Great War* (London: Reaktion Press, 1996)

——, 'Effeminacy, Ethnicity, and the End of Trauma: The Sufferings of "Shell Shocked" Men in Great Britain and Ireland, 1914–39', *Journal of Contemporary History*, 35.1 (January 2000)

——, *An Intimate History of Killing: Face-to-Face Killing in Twentieth Century Warfare* (London: Granta and Basic, 1999)

——, *Fear: A Cultural History* (London: Virago, 2005)

——, *Rape: A History from 1860 to the Present* (London: Virago, 2007)

——, 'The Malingerers' Craft: Mind Over Body in Twentieth Century Britain and America', in Graeme Davison, Pat Jalland and Wilfrid Prest (eds), *Body and Mind. Historical Essays in Honour of F. B. Smith* (Melbourne: Melbourne University Press, 2009)

——, 'Psychology at War, 1914–1945', in G. C. Bunn, A. D. Lovie and G. D. Richards (eds), *Psychology in Britain. Historical Essays and Personal Reflections* (London: British Psychological Society, 2001)

——, 'Shell-Shock, Psychiatry, and the Irish Soldier During the First World War', in Adrian Gregory and Senia Paseta (eds), *Ireland and the Great War. 'A War To Unite Us All?'* (Manchester: Manchester University Press, 2002)

Brady, Sean, *Masculinity and Male Homosexuality in Britain 1861–1918* (Basingstoke: Palgrave, 2009)

Braidotti, Rosi, *Transpositions. On Nomadic Ethics* (Cambridge: Polity, 2006)

Bray, Charles, 'The Physiology of the Brain', *Anthropological Review*, vii (1869)

Brayfytte, 'Experimental Physiology', *Animals Guardian*, ii.3 (December 1891)

Bristol Mercury (25 August 1838)

British Association of Aesthetic Plastic Surgeons website: www.baaps.org.uk.

Brons, Rijnko, *Facial Harmony. Standards for Orthognathic Surgery and Orthodontics* (London: Quintessence, 1998)

Brontë, Charlotte, *Jane Eyre. A Novel* (New York: Carleton, 1864)

Brontë, Emily, *Wuthering Heights*, ed. Pauline Nestor (1847; London: Penguin Classics, 2008)

Brontë, Patrick, *The Letters of the Reverend Patrick Brontë*, ed. Dudley Green (Stroud: Nonsuch, 2005)

Brown, Eryn, 'Sometimes Nips and Tucks Can be Career Moves', *New York Times* (12 February 2006)

Brown, Simon, *Secrets of Face Reading. Understanding Your Health and Relationships* (London: Godsfield, 2008)

Brown, Wendy, *States of Injury. Power and Freedom in Late Modernity* (Princeton: Princeton University Press, 1995)

Brown-Séquard, C. E., 'Note on the Effects Produced on Man by Subcutaneous Injections of a Liquid Obtained from the Testicles of Animals', *Lancet*, 134.3438 (July 1889)

——, 'On a New Therapeutic Method Consisting in the Use of Organic Liquids Extracted from Glands and Other Organs', *British Medical Journal* (10 June 1893)

'Brown-Séquard's Rejuvenating Fluid', *Animals' Guardian*, iv.8 (May 1894)

Bruner, J. S. and R. Tagius, 'The Perception of People', in G. Lindzey (ed.), *Handbook of Social Psychology*, vol. 2 (Reading, MA: Addison Wesley, 1954)

Bryant, Taimie, 'Animals Unmodified: Defining Animals/Defining Human Obligations to Animals', *University of Chicago Legal Forum* (2006)

——, 'Sacrificing the Sacrifice of Animals: Legal Personhood for Animals, the Status of Animals as Property, and the Presumed Primacy of Humans', *Rutgers Law Journal*, 39 (2007–8)

Bull, Ray and Nichola Rumsey, *The Social Psychology of Facial Appearance* (New York: Springer-Verlag, 1988)

Burch, Susan, *Signs of Resistance. American Deaf Cultural History, 1900 to World War I* (New York: New York University Press, 2002)

Burke, Edmund, *A Philosophical Enquiry into the Origin of our Ideas of the Sublime and Beautiful*, first pub. 1757 (Menston: Scolar Press, 1970)

Burn, Andrew, *A Second Address to the People of Great Britain: Containing a New, and Most Powerful Argument to Abstain from the Use of West India Sugar. By An Eye Witness to the Facts Related*, 2nd edn (London: M. Gurney, 1792)

Burnett, C., 'Animals', *Saturday Magazine*, 24.744 (3 February 1844)

Burney, Fanny, *The Wanderer; or, Female Difficulties*, vol. 3, 2nd edn (London: Longman, Hurst, Rees, Orme and Brown, 1814)

Burrow, J. W., 'The Use of Philology in Victorian England', in Robert Robson (ed.), *Ideas and Institutions of Victorian Britain* (London: G. Bell and Sons, 1967)

Butler, Francis, *Breeding, Training, Management, Diseases, &c. of Dogs* (New York: privately, 1857)

Butler, Josephine, *Speech Delivered by Mrs. Josephine Butler at the Fourth Annual Meeting of the Vigilance Association for the Defence of Personal Rights, Held at Bristol, October 15th, 1874* (Bristol: Vigilance Association for the Defence of Personal Rights, 1874)

Calarco, Matthew and Peter Atterton (eds), *Animal Philosophy: Essential Readings in Continental Philosophy* (London: Continuum, 2006)

Cameron, Nigel M. de S. and David S. Short, *On Being Human. 'Speciesism' and the Image of God* (London: Christian Medical Fellowship, 1991)

Campbell, Kirsten, 'Legal Memories: Sexual Assault Memory and International Humanitarian Law', *Signs*, 28.1 (autumn 2002)

Campbell, Tom, *Rights: A Critical Introduction* (London: Routledge, 2006)

'Can Dogs Commit Suicide?', *Animals' Guardian* (November 1908)

'Cannibalism', *The Times* (20 September 1867)

Capie, Forrest and Richard Perren, 'The British Market for Meat 1850–1914', *Agricultural History*, 54.4 (October 1980)

Carlille, Briggs, 'Are Animals Happy?', *Nineteenth Century: A Monthly Review*, 20.114 (August 1886)

Carqué, Otto, *An Appeal to Common Sense: The Folly of Meat-Eating* (London: L. N. Fowler, 1904)

Carroll, Lewis, 'Some Popular Fallacies about Vivisection', *Fortnightly Review*, 23 (June 1875)

Carson, James, *A New Method of Slaughtering Animals for Human Feed*, 2nd edn (London: Whittaker and Co., 1839)

Cartwright, Samuel A., 'Report on the Diseases and Physical Peculiarities of the Negro Race', *New Orleans Medical and Surgical Journal*, 7 (1851)

Carver, Alfred and A. Dinsey, 'Some Biological Effects Due to High Explosives', *Proceedings of the Royal Society of Medicine. Section of Neurology*, 12.2 (1918–19)

'A Case for the Society for the Prevention of Cruelty to Animals', *Moonshine* (19 September 1896)

Caslon Analytics Human Rights, http://www.caslon.com.au/humanrightsprofile6.htm, accessed 8 September 2010

Cassuto, David N., 'Bred Meat: The Cultural Foundations of the Factory Farm', *Law and Contemporary Problems*, 70 (2007)

Cavalieri, P. and Peter Singer (eds), *The Great Ape Project. Equality Beyond Humanity* (London: Fourth Estate, 1993)

'C. B. F.', 'The 1933 Year Book of Neurology and Psychiatry', *American Journal of Psychiatry*, 91 (1934)

Charnock, Richard Stephen, 'Cannibalism in Europe', *Journal of the Anthropological Society of London*, 4 (1866)

Chevalier-Skolnikoff, Suzanne, 'Facial Expression of Emotion in Nonhuman Primates', in Paul Ekman (ed.), *Darwinism and Facial Expression. A Century of Research in Review* (Cambridge, MA: Malor Books, 2006)

The Children's Picture-Book of the Sagacity of Animals (London: Sampson Low, Son and Co., 1862)

Chomsky, Noam, *Language and the Mind*, 3rd edn (Cambridge: Cambridge University Press, 2006)

Church, F. S., [illustration], *Harper's Weekly* (1891)

Churchill, Ward, 'Foreword: Illuminating the Philosophy and Methods of Animal Liberation', in Steven Best and Anthony J. Nocella (eds), *Terrorists or Freedom Fighters? Reflections on the Liberation of Animals* (New York: Lantern Books, 2004)

Coe, Sue, *Dead Meat* (New York: Four Walls Eight Windows, 1993)

Conroy, J., *Unspeakable Acts, Ordinary People: The Dynamics of Torture* (New York: Alfred A. Knopf, 2000)

Constantine, Nathan, *A History of Cannibalism from Ancient Cultures to Survival Stories and Modern Psychopaths* (London: Arcturus, 2006)

Cooper, Thomas, *Considerations on the Slave Trade; and the Consumption of West Indian Produce* (London: Darton and Harvey, 1791)

Corners, George F., *Rejuvenation. How Steinach Makes People Young* (New York: Thomas Seltzer, 1923)

Costall, A., 'How Lloyd Morgan's Canon Backfired', *Journal of the History of the Biological Sciences*, 29 (1993)

Cowper, William, 'Sweet Meat has Sour Sauce: or, the Slave-Trader in the Dumps', written early 1788, http://cfmb.icaap.org/content/33.3/BV33.3art7.pdf, accessed 5 April 2010

——, *The Task* (London: John Sharpe, 1825)

Cox, Peter, *Why You Don't Need Meat* (Rochester, VT: Tharsons Publishing Group, 1986)

Craige, John Houston, *Black Bagdad* (New York: Minton, Balch and Co., 1933)

Crist, Eileen, 'Can an Insect Speak? The Case of the Honeybee Dance Language', *Social Studies of Science*, 34.1 (February 2004)

Crollius, Oswaldus, *Bazilica Chymica and Praxis Chymiatricae or Royal and Practical Chymistry*, trans. John Hartman (London: Hartman, 1609)

'Cruelty to Animals', *Children's Friend* (7 April 1826)

'Cruelty to Animals', *Children's Friend* (1 June 1841)

'Cruelty to Animals: Also to Women and Children', *New York Ledger* (3 August 1867)

Cummings, Frederick, 'Charles Bell and the Anatomy of Expressions', *Art Bulletin*, 46.2 (June 1964)

Cunningham, Richard, *The Place Where the World Ends: A Modern Story of Cannibalism and Human Courage* (New York: Sheed and Ward, 1973)

Cupp, Richard L., 'A Dubious Grail: Seeking Tort Law Expansion and Limited Personhood as Stepping Stones Towards Abolishing Animals' Property Status', *SMU Law Review*, 60 (2007)

'Cutting His Old Associates', *Harper's Weekly*, 17 January 1863

Daniel, Pete, *The Shadow of Slavery: Peonage in the South 1901–1969* (Urbana: University of Illinois Press, 1972)

Darwin, Charles, *The Autobiography of Charles Darwin and Selected Letters*, ed. Francis Darwin, first pub. 1892 (New York: Dover, 1958)

——, *Charles Darwin's Marginalia*, vol. 1, ed. Mario A. Di Gregorio with the assistance of N. W. Gill (New York: Garland, 1990)

——, *The Descent of Man, and Selection in Relation to Sex*, ii (1871; Princeton: Princeton University Press, 1981)

——, 'The Descent of Man, and Selection in Relation to Sex' (first pub. 1871), in Duncan M. Porter and Peter W. Graham (eds), *The Portable Darwin* (New York: Penguin, 1993),

——, *The Descent of Man. Part 1 and 2* (1871; Charlestown: BiblioBazaar, 2008)

——, *The Expression of the Emotions in Man and Animals* (New York: D. Appleton and Co., 1899)

——, *The Expression of the Emotions in Man and Animals*, ed. Paul Ekman, 3rd edn (New York: Oxford University Press, 1998)

——, *The Life and Letters of Charles Darwin Including an Autobiographical Chapter*, vol. 2, ed. Francis Darwin (London: John Murray, 1887)

——, *The Origin of Species by Means of Natural Selection* (1859; London: Penguin, 1985)

David, Tom, *Sacred Work. Planned Parenthood and its Clergy Alliances* (New Brunswick: Rutgers University Press, 2005)

Davis, Karen, *The Holocaust and the Henmaid's Tale. A Case for Comparing Atrocities* (New York: Lantern Books, 2005)

——, 'United Poultry Concerns', http://www.upc-online.org/karenbio.htm, accessed 8 September 2010

Davy, Barbara Jane, 'An Other Face of Ethics in Levinas', *Ethics and Environment*, 12.1 (2007)

Dayan, Colin (a.k.a. Joan Dayan), 'Legal Terrors', *Representations*, 92 (autumn 2005)

Dayan, Joan, 'Legal Slaves and Civil Bodies', *Nepantla: Views from South*, 2.1 (2001)

De Beauvoir, Simone, *The Second Sex*, trans. Constance Borde and Sheila Malovany-Chevallier (1949; New York: Alfred A. Knopf, 2010)

De Cyon, E., 'The Anti-Vivisectionist Agitation', *Contemporary Review*, 43 (January–June 1883)

de Gouges, Olympe, 'Declaration of the Rights of Woman'(1791), http://www.library.csi.cuny.edu/dept/americanstudies/lavender/decwom2.html.

Deal, C., *The Greenpeace Guide to Anti-Environmental Organizations* (Berkeley: Odonian Press, 1993)

Dean, Richard, *An Essay on the Future Life of Brutes*, vol. 2 (London: G. Kearsley, 1768)

'Debased and Debasing', *Anti-Vivisection Journal* (October 1926)

'The Declaration of Independence', http://www.ushistory.org/declaration/document/ index.htm, accessed 8 September 2010

Dee, Jonathan, *Simply Face Reading* (New York: Sterling Publishing Co., 2005)

'Defence of the Female Claim to Mental Equality', *Lady's Monthly Museum* (1 February 1801)

Dellamore, Richard, 'Earnshaw's Neighbor/Catherine's Friend: Ethical Contingencies in *Wuthering Heights*', *ELH*, 74.3 (2007)

deMause, Lloyd, 'Why Cults Terrorize and Kill Children', *Journal of Psychohistory*, 21.4 (spring 1994)

'Dermepenthesis', *Medical Record*, 33 (9 June 1888)

Derrida, Jacques, 'And Say the Animal Responded', trans. David Wills, in Cary Wolfe (ed.), *Zoontologies* (Minneapolis: University of Minnesota Press, 2003)

———, 'The Animal That Therefore I Am', trans. David Wills, in Matthew Calarco and Peter Atterton (eds), *Animal Philosophy: Essential Readings in Continental Philosophy* (London: Continuum, 2006)

———, 'The Animal that Therefore I Am (More to Follow)', *Critical Inquiry* (winter 2002)

———, '"Eating Well", or the Calculation of the Subject: An Interview with Jacques Derrida', in Eduardo Cadava, Peter Connor and Jean-Luc Nancy (eds), *Who Comes After the Subject?* (New York: Routledge, 1991)

———, 'Force of Law: The "Mystical Foundation of Society"', trans. Mary Quaintance (October 1989), http://pdflibrary.files.wordpress.com/2008/01/derrida_force-of-law.pdf

———, '*Geschlecht* II: Heidegger's Hand', in John Sallis (ed.), *Deconstruction and Philosophy. The Texts of Jacques Derrida* (Chicago: University of Chicago Press, 1987)

———, *Of Spirit. Heidegger and the Question*, trans. Geoffrey Bennington and Rachel Bowlby (Chicago: University of Chicago Press, 1989)

———, 'On Reading Heidegger: An Outline of Remarks to the Essex Colloquium', *Research in Phenomenology*, 17 (1987)

———, 'Violence Against Animals', trans. Jeff Fort, in Jacques Derrida and Elisabeth Roudinesco (eds), *For What Tomorrow . . . A Dialogue* (Stanford: Stanford University Press, 2004)

Dershowitz, Alan M., *Why Terrorism Works. Understanding the Threat, Responding to the Challenge* (New Haven: Yale University Press, 2002)

Descartes, René, *Discourse on Method and Other Writings*, ed. F. E. Sutcliffe (Harmondsworth: Penguin, 1968)

'Destiny of the Lower Animals', *Animals' Guardian* (March 1894)

Dew, Thomas Roderick, 'Abolition of Negro Slavery', in Drew Gilpin Faust (ed.), *The Ideology of Slavery; Proslavery Thought in the Antebellum South, 1830–1860* (Baton Rouge: Louisiana State University Press, 1981)

Diamond, Cora, 'Injustice and Animals', in Carl Elliott (ed.), *Slow Cures and Bad Philosophers: Essays on Wittgenstein, Medicine, and Bioethics* (Durham, NC: Duke University Press, 2001)

Diamond, Jared, *The Third Chimpanzee* (New York: Harper Collins, 1992)

Dimitrius, Jo-Ellan and Mark Mazzarella, *Reading People. Secret Tips That Reveal the Truth Behind Body Language* (London: Vermilion, 1998)

Dinwiddy, J. R., 'The Early Nineteenth-Century Campaign Against Flogging in the Army', *English Historical Review*, 97.383 (April 1982)

Dion, Karen K., 'Young Children's Stereotyping of Facial Attractiveness', *Developmental Psychology*, 9 (1973)

'Discipulus', 'The "Pall Mall Gazette" and the Dog Bill', *Shield*, 24 June 1871

Disraeli, Isaac, *Vaurien: or, Sketches of the Times: Exhibiting Views of the Philosophies, Religions, Politics, Literature, and Manners of the Age*, 2 vols (London: T. Cadell, 1797)

'Do Animals Commit Suicide?', *Animals' Guardian* (May 1910)

'Do Animals Commit Suicide?', *Animals' Guardian* (June 1910)

'Do Animals Commit Suicide?', *Animals' Guardian* (March 1911)

'Do Horses Ever Cry?', *Animals' Guardian*, November 1908

'Do We Eat Too Much Meat?', *Hearth and Home. An Illustrated Weekly Journal for Gentlewomen* (14 September 1893)

Dodge, Richard Irving, *The Plains of the Great West and Their Inhabitants. Being a Description of the Pains, Game, Indians, &c. of the Great North American Desert* (New York: G. P. Putnam's Sons, 1872)

The Dog of Knowledge; or, Memoirs of Bob, the Spotted Terrier; Supposed to be Written by Himself (London: J. Harris, 1801)

'The "Dougal Creature"', *Satirist; or, the Censor of the Times* (5 October 1845)

Douglas, Mary, *Purity and Danger. An Analysis of Concepts of Pollution and Taboo* (London: Routledge and Kegan Paul, 1966)

Douglass, Frederick, *The Frederick Douglass Papers* (Princeton: Princeton University Press, 1992)

Douzinas, Costas, *The End of Human Rights* (Oxford: Hart Publishing, 2000)

——, 'The End(s) of Human Rights', *Melbourne University Law Review*, 26 (2002)

——, 'Left or Rights', *Journal of Law and Society*, 34.4 (2007)

Doward, Jamie, 'Kill Scientists, Says Animal Rights Chief', *Observer* (24 July 2004), http://www.guardian.co.uk/society/2004/jul/25/health.animalrights, accessed 26 January 2010

Dowie, Mark, 'Gods and Monsters', Mother Jones (January–February 2004), http://online.sfsu.edu/~rone/GEessays/chimerapatent.htm, accessed 5 December 2009.

'Dr Brown-Séquard's Elixir of Life', *Lancet*, 135.3462 (4 January 1890)

'Dr Brown-Séquard's Experiments', *British Medical Journal* (10 August 1889)

Drummond, William H., *The Rights of Animals, and Man's Obligation to Treat Them with Humanity* (London: John Mardon, 1838)

Drury, W. D. (ed.), *British Dogs: Describing the History, Characteristics, Points, Club Standards and General Management of the Various Breeds of Dogs Established in Great Britain* (London: L. Upcott Gill, 1897)

Dubernard, J. M., M. Bonneau and M. Latour, *Heterografts in Primates* (Villeurbanne: Fondation Merieux, 1974)

'The Dumb Alphabet', *Young Folks* (30 August 1879)

Dunlap, Knight, 'Are Emotions Teleological Constructs?', *American Journal of Psychology*, xliv (1932)

Eagleton, Terry, *Heathcliff and the Great Hunger. Studies in Irish Culture* (London: Verso, 1995)

Edgeworth, Maria, 'The Grateful Negro' (first pub. 1804), in *The Juvenile Tale-Book, or Collection of Interesting Tales and Novels for Youth* (Paris: Truchy, 1837)

'The Effects of Eating Horse-Meat', *Punch* (19 January 1856)

Ekman, Paul, *Telling Lies: Clues to Deceit in the Marketplace, Politics, and Marriage* (1985; New York: W. W. Norton and Co., 2001)

Elgar, Mark A. and Bernard J. Crespi, *Cannibalism. Ecology and Evolution Among Diverse Taxa* (Oxford: Oxford University Press, 1992)

Elliott, Carl (ed.), *Slow Cures and Bad Philosophers: Essays on Wittgenstein, Medicine, and Bioethics* (Durham, NC: Duke University Press, 2001)

Ellis, Havelock, *Man and Woman: A Study of Human Secondary Sexual Characters* (London: Walter Scott, 1894)

Elshtain, Jean Bethke, 'Reflection on the Problem of "Dirty Hands"', in Sanford Levinson, *Torture. A Collection* (Oxford: Oxford University Press, 2006)

Emon, Randall, *Occult Criminal Investigation* (Baldwin Park Police Department (California) Training Bulletin 86(2), 1986)

'The Emotions', *Fun* (16 November 1872)

Equiano, Olaudah, *The Interesting Narrative of the Life of O. Equiano, or G. Vassa, the African, Written by Himself* (London: n.p., 1789)

'E. R.', 'Familiar Lectures on Physiognomy', *La Belle Assemblée; or, Bell's Court and Fashionable Magazine* (1 August 1807)

Esmail, Jennifer, 'The Power of Deaf Poetry: The Exhibition of Literacy and the Nineteenth-Century Sign Language Debates', *Sign Language Studies*, 8.4 (summer 2008)

'Essay on the Language of Animals', *La Belle Assemblée; or Bell's Court and Fashionable Magazine* (June 1819)

Evelyn, John, *The History of Religion: A Rational Account of the True Religion* (London: Henry Coulburn, 1850)

'Evolutionary Electioneering (A Darwinian Drama – Part III)', *Fun* (25 November 1885)

'The Factory Question', *The Times* (10 May 1843)

Farkas, Leslie G., C. R. Forrest and L. Litsas, 'Revision of Neoclassical Facial Canons in Young Afro-Americans', *Aesthetic Plastic Surgery*, 24.3 (May–June 2000)

Farkas, Leslie G., Tania A. Hreczko, John C. Kolar and Ian R. M. B. Munro, 'Vertical and Horizontal Proportions of the Face in Young Adult North American Caucasians: Revision of Neoclassical Norms', *Plastic and Reconstructive Surgery*, 75.3 (March 1985)

Farrar, Frederic William, *An Essay on the Origin of Language: Based on Modern Researchers and Especially on the Works of M. Renan* (London: J. Mura, 1860)

Faust, Drew Gilpin (ed.), *The Ideology of Slavery. Proslavery Thought in the Antebellum South, 1830–1860* (Baton Rouge: Louisiana State University Press, 1981)

Felce, Winifred, *Apes. An Account of Personal Experiences in a Zoological Garden* (London: Chapman and Hall, 1948)

'The Feminine Soul', *Englishwoman's Review and Drawing Room Journal* (21 March 1857)

'Fenland Fox', 'Not the IRA Way', *Arkangel for Animal Liberation*, 1990 or 1991

'A Few Questions for Professor Garner', *Truth*, 35 (1894)

'F. G. N.', 'Is There a Future Life for Animals?', *Animals' Guardian* (November 1917)

Finley, Laura L., *The Torture and Prisoner Abuse Debate* (Westport, CT: Greenwood Press, 2008)

Fitz-Gerald, John Purcell, *Barbarous Cruelty to Living Animals Made Legal in Great Britain; or, The New Act of Parliament Called the 'Cruelty to Animals Amendment Act', Exposed. An Appeal to British Humanity* (London: William Hunt and Co., 1877)

Fitzgerald, M., *Foetal Pain: An Update of Current Scientific Knowledge* (London: Department of Health, 1995)

Fletcher, Joseph, *The Ethics of Genetic Control. Ending Reproductive Roulette* (New York: Prometheus, 1988)

Fontaine, Jean de La, *The Complete Fables of Jean de La Fontaine*, ed. Norman R. Shapiro (Urbana: University of Illinois Press, 2007)

——, *Selected Fables*, ed. Joslyn T. Pine (Toronto: Dover, 2000)

Ford, Brian J., *BSE – The Facts. Mad Cow Disease and the Risk to Mankind* (London: Corgi, 1996)

Foster, Michael, 'Vivisection', *Scientific Monthly*, 71.3 (September 1950)

Fowler, William Weekes, 'Is There a Future State for Animals', *Animals' Guardian* (March 1909)

Fox, William, *An Address to the People of Great Britain on the Propriety of Abstaining from West India Sugar and Rum*, 6th edn (London: privately, 1791)

'F. P. C.', *Cancer Experiments on Human Beings* (London: Victoria Street Society for the Protection of Animals from Vivisection, c.1880s)

Franks, Mary Anne, 'Guantanamo Forever: United States Sovereignty and the Unending State of Exception', *Harvard Law and Policy Review*, 1 (2007)

Fraser, James George, *The Golden Bough: A Study in Magic and Religion*, first pub. 1890 (Oxford: Oxford University Press, 2009)

The Freethinker (7 August 1898)

Freud, Sigmund, 'Civilization and its Discontents', in *The Standard Edition of the Complete Works of Sigmund Freud*, vol. xxi, trans. James Strachey in collaboration with Anna Freud (London: Hogarth Press, 1995)

——, *On Aphasia. A Critical Study* (1891; London: Imago, 1953)

——, *Totem and Taboo. Some Points of Agreement Between the Mental Lives of Savages and Neurotics*, trans. James Strachey (1913; London: Routledge and Kegan Paul, 1950)

Frey, R. G., 'Vivisection, Morals and Medicine', *Journal of Medical Ethics*, 9 (1983)

Friedberg, Lilian, 'Dare to Compare. Americanizing the Holocaust', *American Indian Quarterly*, 24.3 (summer 2000)

Gallaudet, Rev. Thomas H., 'A Sermon on the Duty and Advantages of Affording Instruction to the Deaf and Dumb', in Henry Barnard, *Tribute to Gallaudet. A Discourse in Commemoration of the Life, Character and Services, of the Rev. Thomas H. Gallaudet, LLD, Delivered Before the Citizens of Hartford, Jan. 7th, 1852* (Hartford: Brackett and Hutchinson, 1852)

Gangee, Joseph Sampson, *The Cattle Plague and Diseased Meat in Their Relation with the Public Health, and with the Interests of Agriculture* (London: T. Richards, 1857)

Gardner, R. Allen and Beatrix T. Gardner, 'Ethological Roots of Language', in R. Allen Gardner, Beatrix T. Gardner, Brunetto Chiarelli and Frans X. Plooij (eds), *The Ethnological Roots of Culture* (Dordrecht: Kluwer Academic Press, 1994)

Gardner, R. Allen, Beatrix T. Gardner and Thomas E. VanCantfort (eds), *Teaching Sign Language to Chimpanzees* (Albany: State University of New York Press, 1989)

Garn, Stanley M., 'The Noneconomic Nature of Eating People', *American Anthropologist*, 81.4 (December 1979)

Garn, Stanley M. and Walter D. Block, 'The Limited Nutritional Value of Cannibalism', *American Anthropologist*, 72.1 (February 1970)

'Mr Garner and his Apes', *Speaker* (24 October 1896)

Garner, Richard L., 'The Simian Tongue [I]', *New Review*, 4 (1891)

——, 'The Simian Tongue II', *New Review*, 5.30 (November 1891)

——, 'What I Expect to Do in Africa', *North American Review*, 154.427 (June 1892)

——, *Apes and Monkeys. Their Life and Language* (Boston: Ginn and Co., 1900)

Gaskell, Elizabeth, *The Life of Charlotte Brontë*, vol. 1 (New York: D. Appleton and Co., 1857)

'A Gentleman of the Partie', *A Journal of Eight Days. Journey from Portsmouth to Kingston upon Thames; Through Southampton, Wiltshire, &c. with Miscellaneous Thoughts, Moral and Religious* (London: H. Woodfall, 1761)

Giannakoulopoulos, X., W. Sepulveda, P. Kourtis, V. Glover and N. M. Fisk, 'Fetal Plasma Cortisol and Beta-Endorphin Response to Intrauterine Needling', *Lancet*, 344.8915 (July 1994)

Gibbs, Sir Philip, 'We May all Stay Young', *Nash's Magazine* (October 1927)

Gilman, Sander L., *A Cultural History of Madness and Art in the Western World* (New York: Wiley, 1982)

——, *The Jew's Body* (New York: Routledge, 1991)

——, *Making the Body Beautiful. A Cultural History of Aesthetic Surgery* (Princeton: Princeton University Press, 1999)

Girdlestone, Edward Deacon, *Vivisection: In Its Scientific, Religious, and Moral Aspects* (London: Simpkin, Marshall and Co., 1884)

Glas, Norbert, *Reading the Face. Understanding a Person's Character Through Physiognomy. A Spiritual–Scientific Study* (Forest Row: Temple Lodge, 2008)

Glover, Vivette and Nicholas Fisk, 'Do Fetuses Feel Pain?', *British Medical Journal*, 313 (1996)

Godwin, William, *Memories of the Author of 'A Vindication of the Rights of Woman'*, 2nd edn (London: J. Johnson, 1798)

Gold, Mark, *Animal Rights: Extending the Circle of Compassion* (Oxford: Jon Carpenter, 1995)

Gonzalez-Ulloa, Mario, 'Aesthetic Plastic Surgery: Who are its Practitioners? What Should They Be?', *Annals of Plastic Surgery*, 2.1 (January 1979)

Goodwin, William E., 'Discussion', *Annals of Surgery*, 160.3 (1964)

Gorden, Michelle E., 'Haitian Forced Labor and the Dominican Republic', *Comparative Labor Journal*, 15 (1993–1994)

Goulburn, Edward Meyrick, in the preface to Frederic Bateman, *Darwinism Tested by Language* (London: Rivington, 1877)

——, *The Idle Word: Short Religious Essays Upon the Gift of Speech, and its Employment in Conversation* (London: Rivingtons, 1855)

Gould, Stephen Jay, 'The Heart of Terminology. What Has an Abstruse Debate Over Evolutionary Logic Got to Do With Baby Fae?', *Natural History*, 97.2 (February 1988)

Gourevitch, Philip, *We Wish to Inform You That Tomorrow We Will be Killed with Our Families. Stories from Rwanda* (New York: Picador, 1998)

Grace, Ora Ellen and Jonathan Marks, 'The Great Ape Project and Disability Rights: Ominous Undercurrent of Eugenics in Action', *American Anthropologist*, 102.4 (December 2000)

Graham, John, 'Lavater's Physiognomy in England', *Journal of the History of Ideas*, 22 (1961)

Graham, Sylvester, *A Lecture to Young Men on Chastity. Intended Also for the Serious Consideration of Parents and Guardians* (Boston: Light and Stearns, 1837)

——, *Lectures in the Science of Human Life*, vol. 2 (Boston: Marsh, Capen, Lyon and Webb, 1839)

——, *The Physiology of Feeding* (London: Ideal Publishing Union, 1897)

Grahame, James, *Vivisection: A Reprinted Correspondence Regarding Vivisection* (Glasgow: James Maclehose, 1876)

Grandin, Temple and Catherine Johnson, *Animals in Translation: Using the Mysteries of Autism to Decode Animal Behaviour* (London: Bloomsbury, 2005)

Graves, Richard, 'Maternal Despotism; or, The Rights of Infants' (written 1792, first pub. 1801), in Roger Lonsdale (ed.), *The New Oxford Book of Eighteenth-Century Verse* (Oxford: Oxford University Press, 1987)

Green, Dudley, *Patrick Brontë: Father of Genius* (Stroud: Nonsuch, 2008)

Greenberg, Valerie D., *Freud and His Aphasia Book. Language and the Sciences of Psychoanalysis* (Ithaca: Cornell University Press, 1997)

Griffin, Donald R., *Animal Minds* (Chicago: University of Chicago Press, 1992)

Guttmacher, Alan Frank, *Life in the Making* (London: Jarrolds, 1934)

Gwynne-Jones, Olwen, *Talking About Dogs and their Care and Breeding* (London: Faber and Faber, 1958)

'H', 'On the Notion of the Souls of Beasts', *La Belle Assemblée; or, Bell's Court and Fashionable Magazine* (1 December 1806)

Haeseker, Barend, 'Van Meekeren and his Account of the Transplant of Bone from a Dog into the Skull of a Soldier', *Plastic and Reconstructive Surgery*, 88 (1991)

Hafley, James, 'The Villain in *Wuthering Heights*', *Nineteenth-Century Fiction*, 13.3 (December 1958)

Hagenbeck, Carl, *Beasts and Men. Being Carl Hagenbeck's Experiences for Half a Century among Wild Animals* (New York: Longmans, Green, and Co., 1909)

Haidt, Jonathan and Dacher Keltner, 'Culture and Facial Expression: Open-Ended Methods Find More Expressions and a Gradient of Recognition', *Cognition and Emotion*, 13.3 (1999)

Haiken, Elizabeth, *Venus Envy: A History of Cosmetic Surgery* (Baltimore: Johns Hopkins University Press, 1997)

Haire, Norman, *Rejuvenation. The Work of Steinach, Voronoff, and Others* (London: George Allen and Unwin Ltd., 1924)

Hamilton, David, *The Monkey Gland Affair* (London: Chatto and Windus, 1986)

Hanson, Mark J., 'The Seductive Sirens of Medical Progress. The Case of Xenotransplantation', *Hastings Center Report* (September–October, 1995)

Hanson, Neil, *The Custom of the Sea* (London: Doubleday, 1999)

Haraway, Donna, *The Haraway Reader* (New York: Routledge, 2004)

——, *When Species Meet* (Minnesota: University of Minnesota Press, 2008)

Hargrave, Francis, *An Argument in the Case of James Sommersett, a Negro, Lately Determined by the Court of King's Bench Wherein it is Attempted to Demonstrate the Present Unlawfulness of Domestic Slavery in England, To Which is Appended a State of the Case* (London: privately, 1772)

Harper, William, 'Memoir on Slavery', first pub. 1852, in Drew Gilpin Faust (ed.), *The Ideology of Slavery. Proslavery Thought in the Antebellum South, 1830–1860* (Baton Rouge: Louisiana State University Press, 1981)

Harpham, Geoffrey Galt, 'Beneath and Beyond the "Crisis in the Humanities"', *New Literary History*, 36.1 (winter 2005)

Harrison, Jane, *'Homo Sum'. Being a Letter to an Anti-Suffragists from an Anthropologist*, 2nd edn (London: National Union of Women's Suffrage Societies, 1913)

Harrison, Peter, 'Animal Pain', in Robert M. Baird and Stuart E. Rosenbaum (eds), *Animal Experimentation. The Moral Issues* (New York: Prometheus, 1991)

——, 'Do Animals Feel Pain?', *Philosophy*, 66.255 (January 1991)

Harrison, T. H., *The Breeding of Show Fox Terriers with a Gallery of the Celebrities in the Fox Terrier World* (London: Stock-Keeper Co., 1897)

Hartman, Rhonda Gay, 'The Face of Dignity: Principled Oversight of Biomedical Innovation', *Santa Clara Law Review*, 47 (2007)

Hartmann, Robert, *Anthropoid Apes* (London: Kegan Paul, Trench and Co., 1885)

Haslam, Thomas J., *The Rightful Claims of Women. An Address* (Dublin: Ormond Printing Co., 1906)

Hayes, Cathy, *The Ape in Our House* (London: Victor Gollancz, 1952)

Hayes, Keith J. and Catherine Hayes, 'The Intellectual Development of a Home-Raised Chimpanzee', *Proceedings of the American Philosophical Society*, 95.2 (April 1951)

Haywood, John, *A Manual of the Laws of North-Carolina, Arranged Under Distinct Heads in Alphabetical Order*, vol. 1 (Raleigh, NC: privately, 1808)

Health Canada, *Proposed Canadian Standard for Xenotransplantation* (Draft no. 14) by André La Prairie (Ottawa: Therapeutic Products Programme, July 1999),

http://www.hc-sc.ca/hpb-dgps/therapeut/zfiles/english/bgtd/xeno
_std_e.html

Heath, Edward Alfred, *Vaccination, or, Blood Poisoning With Animal Diseases* (London: Heath and Co., 1899)

Heidegger, Martin, *The Fundamental Concepts of Metaphysics: World, Finitude, Solitude*, trans. William McNeil and Nicholas Walker (1983; Bloomington: Indiana University Press, 1995)

Hendricks, Mary Ross, 'Modern Slavery and the Production of Consumer Goods in a Global Economy', *Thomas M. Cooley Law Review*, 20.3 (2003)

Hepburn, Jim, 'What Price Violence', *Arkangel for Animal Liberation*, 5 (spring 1991)

Hess, Elizabeth, *Nim Chimpsky. The Chimp Who Would Be Human* (New York: Bantam, 2009)

Hickman, Martin, 'Excessive meat-eating "kills 45,000 each year"', *Independent*, 19 October 2010, http://www.independent.co.uk/life-style/health-and-families/health-news/excessive-meateating-kills-45000-each-year-2110289.html, accessed 19 October 2010

Hicks, Robert D., 'The Police Model of Satanism Crime', in James T. Richardson, Joel Best and David G. Bromley (eds), *The Satanism Crime* (New York: Aldine de Gruyter, 1991)

Hill, Jane H., 'Apes and Language', *Annual Review of Anthropology*, 7 (1978)

Hillier, Richard, *A Vindication of the Address to the People of Great-Britain on the Use of West India Produce. With Some Observations and Facts Relative to the Situation of Slaves. In Answer to a Female Apologist for Slavery*, 2nd edn (London: privately, 1791)

Hiraiwa-Hasegowa, Marika, 'Cannibalism Among Non-Human Primates', in Mark A. Elgar and Bernard J. Crespi (eds), *Cannibalism. Ecology and Evolution Among Diverse Taxa* (Oxford: Oxford University Press, 1992)

Hoare, Prince, *Memoirs of Granville Sharp, Esq. Comprised from his Own Manuscripts, and Other Authentic Documents in the Possession of His Family and of the African Institute*, vol. 2, 2nd edn (London: Ellerton and Henderson, 1828)

Hodge, Clifton, *Nature Study and Life* (Boston: Ginn and Co., 1902)

Hodgins, J. George, *Aims and Objects of the Toronto Humane Society* (Toronto: William Briggs, 1888)

Holliday, Laurel, *The Violent Sex: Male Psychobiology and the Evolution of Consciousness* (Guerneville: Bluestocking Press, 1978)

'L'Homme qui rend la Jeunesse', *Le Petit Journal* (22 October 1922)

Honigsberg, Peter Jan, *Our Nation Unhinged. The Human Consequences of the War on Terror* (Berkeley: University of California Press, 2009)

Honour, Hugh, *The Image of the Black in Western Art. IV. From the American Revolution to World War I* (Cambridge, MA: Harvard University Press, 1989)

Hopkins, J. Ellice ['J. E. H.'], *Is it Natural?* (London: Hatchards, 1885)

——, *The Ride of Death* (London: Hatchards, 1883)

House, Ian, 'Harrison on Animal Pain', *Philosophy*, 66.257 (July 1991)

How to Read the Face: or Physiognomy Explained According to the Philosophy of Lavater (London: C. Goodman, 1860)

Howell, George, 'Letter to the Editor. Young Children in Mines', *The Times*, 15 April 1872

Hubbard, H. W., 'Deaf-Mutism', *Leisure Hour* (July 1894)

Huber, Ernst, *Evolution of Facial Musculature and Facial Expression* (Baltimore: Johns Hopkins University Press, 1931)

Hudson, W. H., *The Book of a Naturalist* (London: Hodder and Stoughton, 1919)

Hueston, John T. and R. Andrew Cuthbertson, 'Duchenne de Boulogne and Facial Expression', *Annals of Plastic Surgery*, 1.4 (July 1978)

Hueston, John T., 'Duchenne Today: Facial Expression and Facial Surgery', in G. B. Duchenne de Boulogne, *The Mechanism of Human Facial Expression*, ed. and trans. R. Andrew Cuthbertson (Cambridge: Cambridge University Press, 1990)

'Human Grafting as an Aid to Longevity', *Animals' Guardian*, vii.4 (January 1897)

'Human Rights and Constitutional Documents', http://www.hrcr.org/docs/frenchdec.html, accessed 8 September 2010

Hume-Rothery, Mary Catherine, *A Letter Addressed to The Right Hon. W. E. Gladstone, MP, and the Other Members of Her Majesty's Government, and of Both Houses of Parliament Touching the Contagious Diseases Acts of 1866 and 1869, and Their Proposed Extension to the Civil Population of this Country* (Manchester: Abel Heywood and Son, 1870)

Humphrey, Michael, *The Politics of Atrocity and Reconciliation. From Terror to Trauma* (London: Routledge, 2002)

Hunt, W. A., 'Recent Developments in the Field of Emotion', *Psychological Bulletin*, 38 (1941)

Hutt, Frederick B., *Genetics for Dog Breeders* (San Francisco: W. H. Freeman and Co., 1979)

Hutton, Richard Holt, 'The Anti-Vivisectionist Agitation', *Contemporary Review*, 43 (January–June 1883)

'Hysterical Old Maids', *Englishwoman's Review* (15 June 1883)

Ignatieff, Michael, *The Lesser Evil: Political Ethics in an Age of Terror* (Princeton: Princeton University Press, 2004)

'The Immortality of Animals. Have Animals Souls. Yes: But Some Men Have None?', *Animals' Guardian* (February 1909)

The ITMA Team, 'Shechita Barbaric? Oy Vay! Have You Seen the *Spanish* Method of Cattle Slaughter? A Sideways Look at the Lunatic Fringe Opposition to Kosher Meat from the "Jew-Wise" to the "Animal Rights" Lobby' (London: InfoText Manuscripts, c.1992)

Izard, Carroll E., 'Cross-Cultural Perspectives on Emotion and Emotion Communication', in Harry C. Triandis and John W. Berry (eds), *Handbook of Cross-Cultural Psychology. Basic Processes. Volume 3* (Boston: Allyn and Bacon, 1980)

——, *The Face of Emotion* (New York: Appleton Century-Croft, 1971)

Jackson, Peter W. and Raymond Lee (eds), *Deaf Lives: Deaf People in History* (Feltham: British Deaf Society, 2001)

Jackson, Thomas, *Our Dumb Neighbours; or, Conversations of a Father with his Children on Domestic and Other Animals* (London: S. W. Partridge and Co., 1864)

James, Brian, 'Operation Hope', *Radio Times* (20–26 March 1993)

James, David, 'Recent Advances: Fetal Medicine', *British Medical Journal*, 316.7144 (23 May 1998)

James, William, 'On a Certain Blindness in Human Beings', in *Essays on Faith and Morals* (New York: Longmans, Green, and Co., 1943)

——, 'Thoughts before Language: A Deaf Mute's Recollections', *American Annals of the Deaf and Dumb*, 38.2 (April 1893)

Jamison, Melissa, 'The Sins of the Father: Punishing Children in the War on Terror', *University of La Verne Law Review*, 29 (2008)

Jefferson, Thomas, *The Writings of Thomas Jefferson*, ed. Andrew Lipscomb and Albert Bergh (Washington DC: Thomas Jefferson Memorial Association of the United States, 1903)

Jeffords, Susan, 'The Knowledge of Words: The Evolution of Language and Biology in Nineteenth Century Thought', *Centennial Review*, xxxi.1 (winter 1987)

Jehl, Douglas, 'Officials Told to Avoid Calling Rwanda Killings "Genocide"', *New York Times* (10 June 1994), http://www.nytimes.com/1994/06/10/world/officials-told-to-avoid-calling-rwanda-killings-genocide.html?scp=1&sq=Douglas%20Jehl,%20%E2%80%9COfficials%20Told%20to%20Avoid%20Calling%20Rwanda%20&st=cse

Jenkins, William G., 'The Scientific Testimony of "Facts and Opinions"', *American Annals of the Deaf and Dumb*, 35.3 (1890)

Jenyns, Soame, *Disquisitions on Several Subjects* (Dublin: R. Moncrieffe, T. Walker, P. Byrne and C. Lewis, 1782)

'Jewish "Kapparot" Ritual Killing of Animals', website of the Institute for Historical Research, http://www.ihr.org/rounduparchive/2009_12.shtml, 2009, accessed 5 April 2010.

Johns, Rev. B. G., 'The Language of Dumb Animals. God's Hand in the Book of Nature', *Quiver*, 29.361 (January 1894)

Johnson, Richard J., 'Maxime Schwartz. How the Cow Turned Mad', *Bulletin for the History of Medicine*, 78 (2004)

Jones, Doug, 'An Evolutionary Perspective on Physical Attractiveness', *Evolutionary Anthropology*, 5.3 (1996)

Jones, Jacqueline, *The Dispossessed. America's Underclass from the Civil War to the Present* (New York: Basic Books, 1992)

Jones, Michael Owen, 'Food Choice, Symbolism, and Identity: Bread-and-Butter Issues for Folkloristics and Nutrition Studies', *Journal of American Folklore*, 120.476 (spring 2007)

Joralemon, Donald, 'Organ Wars. The Battle for Body Parts', *Medical Anthropology Quarterly*, 9.3 (September 1995)

Judy: The London Serio-Comic Journal (23 May 1900)

Juengel, Scott, 'Countenancing History: Mary Wollstonecraft, Samuel Stanhope Smith and Enlightenment Racial Science', *ELH*, 68 (2001)

——, 'Godwin, Lavater and the Pleasures of Surface', *Studies in Romanticism*, 35.1 (spring 1996)

Kadish, Doris Y., 'The Black Terror: Women's Responses to Slave Revolts in Haiti', *French Review*, 68.4 (March 1995)

Kafka, Franz, 'A Report to an Academy', in *The Transformation and Other Stories*, ed. and trans. Malcolm Pasley (Harmondsworth: Penguin Classics, 1992)

Kahanes, Larry, *Cults that Kill: Probing the Underworld of Occult Crime* (New York: Warner Books, 1988)

Kalick, S. Michael, 'Aesthetic Surgery: How it Affects the Way Patients are Perceived by Others', *Annals of Plastic Surgery*, 2.1 (January 1979)

Kant, Immanuel, *Anthropology from a Pragmatic Point of View*, trans. and ed. Robert B. Lauden (1978; Cambridge: Cambridge University Press, 2006)

——, *The Metaphysics of Morals*, trans. Mary Gregor (1797; Cambridge: Cambridge University Press, 1991)

Kara, Siddharth, *Sex Trafficking: Inside the Business of Modern Slavery* (New York: Columbia University Press, 2009)

Karpowicz, Phillip, Cynthia B. Cohen and Derek van der Kooy, 'Developing Human–Non-Human Chimeras in Human Stem Cell Research: Ethical Issues and Boundaries', *Kennedy Institute of Ethics Journal*, 15.2 (2005)

Kaw, Eugenia, 'Medicalization of Racial Features: Asian American Women and Cosmetic Surgery', *Medical Anthropological Quarterly*, 7.1 (1993)

Kaylor, M. A., 'Feelings, Thought and Conduct of Children toward Animal Pets', *Pedagogic Seminary*, 16 (1909)

Keith, George S., *Fads of an Old Physic* (London: Adam and Charles Black, 1897)

Kellogg, W. N., 'A Further Note on the "Wolf Children" of India', *American Journal of Psychology*, 46.1 (January 1934)

——, 'More About the "Wolf Children" of India', *American Journal of Psychology*, 43.3 (July 1931)

Kellogg, W. N. and L. A. Kellogg, *The Ape and the Child. A Study of Environmental Influence upon Early Behavior* (New York: Whittlesey House, 1933)

Ker, David, 'In a Haytian Village', *Good Things. The English Boy's and Girl's Magazine* (1876)

Kingsford, Anna, *The Perfect Way in Diet. A Treatise Advocating a Return to the Natural and Ancient Food of Our Race* (London: Kegan Paul, Trench and Co., 1881)

Klima, Edward S. and Ursula Bellugi, *The Signs of Language* (Cambridge, MA: Harvard University Press, 1979)

Klineberg, O., 'Emotional Expression in Chinese Literature', *Journal of Abnormal and Social Psychology*, 33 (1938)

'Knackers, Pork-Sausages, and Virtue', *Penny Satirist* (9 March 1839)

Kruse, Corwin R., 'Gender, Views of Nature, and Support for Animal Rights', *Society and Animals*, 7.3 (1999)

La Mettrie, Julien Offray de, *Man a Machine* (1748; Chicago: Open Court, 1912)

Lacobbo, Karen and Micahel Lacobbo, *Vegetarians and Vegans in America Today* (Westport, CT: Praeger, 2006)

'A Lady Who Is Deeply Interested', *New York Times* (27 January 1872)

'Laicus', *The Right to Torture* (Naas: Leinster-Leader Office, 1905)

Landis, C., 'Studies of Emotional Reactions: II. General Behavior and Facial Expression', *Journal of Social Psychology*, 4 (1924)

Lane, David, 'Imagine', *Arkangel for Animal Liberation*, 3 (1990)

Lane, Sir W. Arbuthnot, *The Prevention of the Diseases Peculiar to Civilization* (London: Faber and Faber, 1929)

Lang, Harry G., *Silence of the Spheres: The Deaf Experience in the History of Science* (Westport, CT: Bergin and Garvey, 1994)

Langley, Gill and Joyce D'Silva, *Animal Organs in Humans: Uncalculated Risks and Unanswered Questions. A Report Produced Jointly by British Union for the Abolition of Vivisection and Compassion in World Farming* (London: British Union for the Abolition of Vivisection and Compassion in World Farming, 1998)

'Language of the Lower Animals', *Bow Bells Weekly*, 26 (29 June 1888)

Lankester, Edwin, *On Food. Being Lectures Delivered at the South Kensington Museum* (London: Robert Hardwicke, 1861)

Lansbury, Carol, 'Gynaecology, Pornography, and the Antivivisection Movement', *Victorian Studies*, 28.3 (spring 1985)

'Launcelot Light' and 'Lætitia Lookabout', *A Sketch of the Rights of Boys and Girls* (London: J. Bew, 1792)

Laurie, A., 'A Marvellous Conquest: A Story of the Bayouda', *Boy's Own Paper* (6 July 1889)

'Lavater', *The Tourist; or, Sketch Book of the Times* (28 January 1833)

Lavater, Johann Kaspar, *Essays on Physiognomy Designed to Promote Knowledge and the Love of Mankind*, ed. Thomas Holloway, trans. Henry Hunter, vol. 1 (London: John Murray, 1789)

——, *Essays on Physiognomy; for the Promotion of the Knowledge and Love of Mankind*, trans. Thomas Holcroft, 2nd edn (London: H. B. Symonds and J. Walker, 1804)

Lavater, Johann Kaspar and Jean Joseph Sue, *Lavater's Looking Glass; or, Essays on the Face of Animated Nature, from Man to Plants* (London: Millar Ritchie, 1800)

Le, T. T., L. G. Farkas, R. C. Ngim, L. S. Levin and C. R. Forrest, 'Proportionality in Asian and North American Caucasian Faces Using Neoclassical Facial Canons as Criteria', *Aesthetic Plastic Surgery*, 26.1 (January–February 2002)

Lebrun, Yvan, *Mutism* (London: Whurr, 1990)

Lederer, Susan E., 'The Controversy over Animal Experimentation in America, 1880–1914', in Nicolaas A. Rupke (ed.), *Vivisection in Historical Perspective* (London: Routledge, 1987)

——, *Subjected to Science: Human Experimentation in America Before the Second World War* (Baltimore: Johns Hopkins University Press, 1995)

Lee, Ronnie, 'Unjustifiable Explosions', *Arkangel for Animal Liberation*, 3 (1990)

Leese, Arnold, 'Barbaric', *Vegetarian Living* (July/August 1992)

——, *The Legalized Cruelty of Shechita: The Jewish Method of Cattle-Slaughter* (Guildford: privately, 1940)

——, *My Irrelevant Defence: Meditations Inside Gaol and Out on Jewish Ritual Murder* (London: IFL Party Publishing, 1938)

——, *Out of Step: Events in the Two Lives of an Anti-Jewish Camel-Doctor* (Guildford: privately, n.d.)

Leffingwell, Albert, *The Vivisection Question* (New Haven: Tuttle, Morehouse and Taylor, 1901)

Lennox, Malissia, 'Refugees, Racism, and Repatriations: A Critique of the United States' Haitian Immigration Policy', *Stanford Law Review*, 45.3 (February 1993)

Lester, Horace Francis, *Behind the Scenes in Slaughter-Houses* (London: William Reeves, 1892)

Lestringant, Frank, *Cannibals: The Discovery and Representation of the Cannibal from Columbus to Jules Verne*, trans. Rosemary Morris (Cambridge: Polity, 1997)

Levinas, Emmanuel, *Entre Nous: On Thinking-of-the-Other*, trans. Michael B. Smith and Barbara Harshav (London: Athlone, 1998)

——, 'Meaning and Sense' (first pub. 1964), in *Emmanuel Levinas: Basic Philosophical Writings*, ed. Adriaan T. Peperzak, Simon Critchley and Robert Bernarconi (Bloomington: Indiana University Press, 1996)

——, 'The Name of a Dog; or, Natural Rights', in *Difficult Freedom: Essays in Judaism*, trans. Seán Hand (London: Athlone, 1990)

——, *Totality and Infinity: An Essay on Exteriority*, trans. A. Lingis (1961; Pittsburgh: Duquesne University Press, 2003)

Levy, Robert I., 'The Emotions in Comparative Perspective', in Klaus Scherer and Paul Ekman (eds), *Approaches to Emotion* (Hillsdale, NJ: Lawrence Erlbaum Associates, 1984)

Lewis, Ricki, 'Animal Models of Pain', http://www.the-scientist.com/2005/03/28/S10/1, accessed 20 December 2009

Liddick, Donald R., *Eco-Terrorism. Radical Environmental and Animal Liberation Movements* (Westport, CT: Praeger, 2006)

Lind-af-Hageby, Louise, *'Ecrasez l'Infâme!' An Exposure of the Mind, Methods, Pretences, and Failure of the Modern Inquisition* (London: Animal Defence and Anti-Vivisection Society, 1929)

Lindaver, Martin, *Communication among Social Bees* (1961; Cambridge, MA: Harvard University Press, 1971)

Linnæus, Carl, *Systema naturæ per regna tria naturæ*, 10th edn (Stockholm, 1758)

Lloyd, Bertram, *Humanitarianism and Freedom* (Manchester: Humane Education Society, 1933)

'L. N. S.', 'A Plea for the Speechless', *British Mother's Journal* (no date, according to online resource 'British Periodicals')

Loederer, Richard A., *Voodoo Fire in Haiti*, trans. Richard I. Vesey (Plymouth: Beacon Library, 1937)

Loike John D. and Moshe Tendler, 'Reconstituting a Human Brain in Animals: A Jewish Perspective on Human Sanctity', *Kennedy Institute of Ethics Journal*, 18.4 (2008)

Lomax, Adrian, 'The *Real* American Gulag: Common, Lethal, Unreported', *Counterpunch* (16 June 2005), http://www.counterpunch.org/lomax06162005.html, accessed 25 February 2010

Long, Edward, *The History of Jamaica. Or, General Survey of the Antient and Modern*

State of that Island: With Reflections on its Situation, Settlements, Inhabitants, Climate, Products, Commerce, Laws, and Government, vol. 2 (London: T. Lowndes, 1774)

Lorenz, Dagmar C. G. 'Transatlantic Perspectives on Men, Women, and Other Primates: The Ape Motif in Kafka, Canetti, and Cooper's and Jackson's *King Kong*', *Women in German Yearbook*, 23 (2007)

'The Lost Senses. Vol. I, Deafness: Vol. ii. Blindness by John Kitto', *North British Review*, 6.12 (February 1847)

Love, James Kerr, *The Deaf Child. A Manual for Teachers and School Doctors* (Bristol: John Wright and Sons, 1911)

——, *Deaf Mutism. A Clinical and Pathological Study* (Glasgow: Maclehose, 1896)

Lubinski, Joseph, 'Screw the Whales, Save Me! The Endangered Species Act, Animal Protection, and Civil Rights', *Journal of Law in Society*, 4 (2002–3)

'Lusty Baby', *The Times* (7 November 1984)

MacDonald, David B., 'Daring to Compare: the Debate About a Maori "Holocaust" in New Zealand', *Journal of Genocide Research*, 5.3 (2003)

MacDonald, J. R., 'Problems of the Great Republic', *New Age. A Journal for Thinkers and Workers* (25 November 1897)

MacIver, A. M., 'Ethics and the Beetle', *Analysis*, 8.5 (April 1948)

MacKinnon, Catharine A., *Are Women Human? And Other International Dialogues* (Cambridge, MA: Harvard University Press, 2006)

——, 'Of Mice and Men. A Fragment on Animal Rights', in Josephine Donovan and Carol J. Adams (eds), *The Feminist Care Tradition in Animal Ethics. A Reader* (New York: Columbia University Press, 2007)

Maitland, Edward, 'An Appeal to Hearts and Heads', in Edward Carpenter and Edward Maitland, *Vivisection* (London: William Reeves, 1893)

——, *Anna Kingsford. Her Life Letters Diary and Work* (London: George Redway, 1896)

Malchow, Howard L., 'Frankenstein's Monster and Images of Race in Nineteenth Century Britain', *Past and Present*, 139 (May 1993)

Mann, Edwin John, *The Deaf and Dumb; Or, a Collection of Articles Relating to the Condition of Deaf Mutes; Their Education and the Principal Asylums Devoted to their Instruction* (Boston: D. K. Hitchcock, 1836)

Mann, Tom, *Tom Mann's Memoirs*, intro. Ken Coates (1923; Nottingham: Spokesman, 2008)

Manning, Henry Edward and Benjamin Waugh, 'The Child of the English Savage', *Contemporary Review* (May 1886)

Marquardt, Kathleen with Herbert M. Levine and Mark LaRochelle, *Animalscam. The Beastly Abuse of Human Rights* (Washington DC: Regnery, 1993)

Marx, Karl, Grundrisse (written 1857–8), in *Selected Writings*, ed. David McLennan (Oxford: Oxford University Press, 1977)

Mason, Jim, *An Unnatural Order: Uncovering the Roots of Our Dominion of Nature and Each Other* (New York: Simon and Schuster, 1993)

Maxwell, Herbert, 'Speech', *Blackwood's Edinburgh Magazine*, 151.920 (June 1892)

'M. C.', 'The Non-Human Races and Continued Existence', *Animals' Guardian* (January 1916)

McClain, Carla, 'ALF. A Secret Interview with a Compassionate Commando', *No Compromise* (March–April 1996)

McCloskey, Henry John, *Meta-Ethics and Normative Ethics* (The Hague: Martinus Nijhoff, 1969)

McCormick, Richard A., 'Was There Any Real Hope for Baby Fae?', *Hastings Center Report*, 15.1 (February 1985)

McCurdy Jr., John A. and Samuel M. Lam, *Cosmetic Surgery of the Asian Face* (New York: Thieme Medical Publishers, 1990)

McDonald, Patrick Range, 'Monkey Madness at UCLA', *LA Weekly* (9 August 2007), http://www.laweekly.com/2007-08-09/news/monkey-madness-at-ucla/1, accessed 25 January 2010

'M. D.', *The Scientist at the Bedside* (London: Victoria Street Society for the Protection of Animals, c. 1882)

Mellone, Sydney Herbert, *The Position and Claims of Woman. A Historical Survey (With Reference to Present Conditions)* (London: Woman's Press, c.1910)

'Mercy's Voice', *Vivisection* (Toronto: Copp, Clark and Coy, 1876)

Merrill, A. P., 'An Essay on Some of the Distinctive Peculiarities of the Negro Race', *Memphis Medical Recorder*, 4 (1855)

Michael, Mike and Nik Brown, 'The Meat of the Matter: Grasping and Judging Xenotransplantation', *Public Understanding of Science*, 13 (2004)

Michie, Elsie, 'From Simianized Irish to Oriental Despots: Heathcliff, Rochester and Racial Differences', *Novel. A Forum on Fiction*, 25.2 (winter 1992)

Midgley, Mary, 'Practical Solutions', in David Paterson and Mary Palmer (eds), *The Status of Animals: Ethics, Education and Welfare* (Wallingford: CAB International, 1989)

Miles, H. L. W., 'ME CHANTEK: The Development of Self-Awareness in a Signing Orangutan', in Sue Taylor Parker, Robert W. Mitchell and Maria L. Boccia (eds), *Self-Awareness in Animals and Humans: Developmental Perspectives* (Cambridge: Cambridge University Press, 1994)

Mill, John Stuart, *On Liberty and Other Essays*, ed. John Gray (1859; Oxford: World Classics, 1991)

Millard, Ralph, 'The Oriental Eyelid and its Surgical Revision', *American Journal of Ophthalmology*, 57 (1964)

Miller, Joe, 'Food for the Poor. Song of the Andover Union', *Penny Satirist* (13 September 1845)

Mintz, Steven, '[Review] Pets in America: A History by Catherine C. Grier', *Journal of Social History* (spring 2007)

Mitchell, H. H., 'Does a Low-Protein Diet Produce Racial Inferiority?', *Science*, new series, 38.970 (1 August 1913)

'Monkeyan'a', *Punch* (18 May 1861)

'Monkeyana', *Chambers's Journal of Popular Literature, Science and Arts*, 13 (10 October 1896)

'Moon Dragon Birthing Services', http://www.moondragon.org/parenting/placentadisposalrituals.html, accessed 8 September 2010

Morgan, C. Lloyd, 'Animal Intelligence', *Nature*, 26 (28 September 1882)

——, 'The Limits of Animal Intelligence', *International Congress of Experimental*

Psychology, Second Session. London, 1892 (London: Williams and Norgate, 1892)

Morgan, Rev. Hamilton, *A Sermon. Animal and Man* (Detroit: Emmanuel Church, 1895)

Morgan, Kenneth, 'Liverpool's Dominance in the British Slave Trade, 1740–1807', in David Richardson, Suzanne Schwarz and Anthony Tibbles (eds), *Liverpool and Transatlantic Slavery* (Liverpool: Liverpool University Press, 2007)

Morin, Richard and Claudia Deane, 'Americans Split on How to Interrogate: Majority Polled Oppose Using Torture', *Washington Post* (28 May 2004), http://www.encyclopedia.com/doc/1P2-182838.html, accessed 25 February 2010

Morison, Sir Alexander, *The Physiognomy of Mental Disease* (London: privately, 1840)

Morning Post (1 September 1838)

Morris, Desmond, *The Naked Ape. A Zoologist's Study of the Human Animal* (London: Jonathan Cape, 1967)

Mortensen, Melanie J., 'In the Shadow of Doctor Moreau: A Contextual Reading of the Proposed Canadian Standard for Xenotransplantation', *University of Ottawa Law and Technological Journal*, 2 (2005)

Moseley, Benjamin, *Treatise on the Lues Bovilla; or Cow Pox*, 2nd edn (London: privately, 1805)

'Mothers 35 Plus', http://www.mothers35plus.co.uk/plac_rec2.htm, accessed 8 September 2010

Mowry, Albert, 'Some Sexual Disorders in the Male: Impotency and Involuntary Seminal Emissions, *Illinois Medical Journal* (March 1913)

Muir, Ramsay, *Bygone Liverpool* (Liverpool: Henry Young and Sons, 1913)

Müller, F. M., 'On the Classification of Mankind by Language or by Blood', *Nature*, 44 (1891)

Müller, Max, 'Forgotten Bibles' (first pub. 1884), in *The Essential Max Müller on Language, Mythology, and Religion*, ed. Jon R. Stone (New York: Palgrave Macmillan, 2002)

——, *Lectures on the Science of Language Delivered at the Royal Institution of Great Britain in April, May, and June, 1861*, 4th edn (London: Longman, Green, Longman, Roberts, and Green, 1864)

Mundi Club, *A Pictorial History of the Royal Animal Terrorists. Time to Abolish the Monarchy and Expropriate the Windsors' Land Holdings* (London: mundi, 2001)

Munn, N. L., 'The Effect of Knowledge of the Situation upon Judgment of Emotion from Facial Expression', *Journal of Abnormal and Social Psychology*, 35 (1940)

Munson, Ronald, *Raising the Dead. Organ Transplants, Ethics, and Society* (Oxford: Oxford University Press, 2002)

Murray, Keith Anderson Hope, *Factors Affecting the Prices of Livestock. A Preliminary Study* (Oxford: National Institute of Agricultural Engineering, 1931)

Myers, Gene, *The Significance of Children and Animals. Social Development and Our Connections to Other Species*, 2nd (revised) edn (West Lafayette: Purdue University Press, 2007)

Mygind, Holger, *Deaf-Mutism* (London: F. J. Reban, 1894)

Myklebust, Helmer R., *The Psychology of Deafness. Sensory Deprivation, Learning, and Adjustment*, 2nd edn (1960; New York: Grune and Stratton, 1971)

Nahai, Foad, *The Art of Aesthetic Surgery. Principles and Techniques*, 3 vols (St Louis: Quality Medical ublishing, 2005)

'The Name of a Dog; or, Natural Rights', in Matthew Calarca and Peter Atterton (eds), *Animal Philosophy: Essential Readings in Continental Thought* (London: Continuum, 2004)

Napier, C. O. Groom, 'Resemblance Between Man and Animals', *Journal of the Anthropological Society of London*, 5 (1867)

National Society for the Prevention of Cruelty to Children, *Scottish Branch Report for the Year 1901. Moray, Nairn and Banffshire* (Edinburgh: Shelter, 1901)

'Neil from Shrewsbury', 'Speaking Out', *Arkangel for Animal Liberation*, 2 (spring 1990)

'Neil', 'A Retort', *Arkangel for Animal Liberation*, n.d. [1990 or 1991]

Niechajev, Igor and Per-Olle Haraldsson, 'Ethnic Profile of Patients Undergoing Aesthetic Phinoplasty in Stockholm', *Aesthetic Plastic Surgery*, 21 (1997)

Nietzsche, Friedrich, *Beyond Good and Evil. Prelude to a Philosophy of the Future*, trans. Helen Zimmern (Mineola, NY: Dover, 1997)

'NNDB – William Seabrook', at http://www.nndb.com/people/695/000113356/, accessed 8 September 2010

Noble, William and Iain Davidson, 'The Evolutionary Emergence of Modern Human Behaviour: Language and its Archaeology', *Man*, new series, 26.2 (June 1991)

Noblitt, James Randall and Pamela Sue Perskin, *Cult and Ritual Abuse. Its History, Anthropology, and Recent Discovery in Contemporary America* (Westport, CT: Praeger, 1994)

Nocella, Anthony J., http://student.maxwell.syr.edu/ajnocell/, accessed 8 September 2010

Nott, Josiah C., 'Two Lectures on the Natural History of the Caucasian and Negro Races' (first pub. 1844), in Drew Gilpin Faust (ed.), *The Ideology of Slavery. Proslavery Thought in the Antebellum South, 1830–1860* (Baton Rouge: Louisiana State University Press, 1981)

Nourmand, Tony and Graham Marsh, *Film Posters of the 60s. The Essential Movies of the Decade* (London: Aurum Press, 1997)

'Now, How Did I Come to Win That War?', *Our Empire. The Official Organ of the British Empire Service League*, vi.2 (May 1930)

Nuffield Council on Bioethics, *Animal-to-Human Transplants: The Ethics of Xenotransplantation* (London: Nuffield Council on Bioethics, 1996)

Oakley, Charles Selby, *Vivisection. Can It Advance Mankind?* (London: Dryden Press, J. Davy and Sons, 1895)

Oakley, H., *A Plea for Dumb Animals* (London: Whittaker and Co., 1865)

Office of the High Commissioner for Human Rights, http://www.ohchr.org/EN/UDHR/Documents/UDHR_Translations/eng.pdf, accessed 8 September 2010

Oldfield, Josiah, 'The Scientific View', in Henry Salt (ed.), *The New Charter. A Discussion of the Rights of Man and the Rights of Animals* (London: Charles Bell and Sons, 1896)

Oliver, Kelly, *Animal Lessons. How They Teach us to be Human* (New York: Columbia University Press, 2009)

'On Physiognomy', *Fun* (23 March 1881)

Opinions of Women on Women's Suffrage (London: Central Committee of the National Society for Women's Suffrage, 1879)

Oppenheimer, Mark, 'Who Lives? Who Dies?', Christian Century (19 December 2009), http://findarticles.com/p/articles/mi_m1058/is_14_119/ai _89580866/, accessed 19 December 2009

'The Origin of Species. A New Song', *Blackwood's Magazine*, 89 (1861)

Oswald, John, *The Cry of Nature; or, An Appeal to Mercy and to Justice on Behalf of the Persecuted Animals*, ed. Jason Hribal (1971; Lewiston: The Edwin Mellen Press, 2000)

Ouida, *The New Priesthood* (London: E. W. Allen, 1893)

'Our First Marriage', http://www.ourfirstmarriage.com/index.php/2009/07/23/ placenta-recipies/, 2009, accessed 8 September 2010

'Our Medical Corner', *Reynolds's Miscellany of Romance, General Literature, Science and Art*, 15.389 (22 December 1855)

'Our Simian Cousins', *Chambers's Journal of Popular Literature, Science and Arts*, 12.621 (23 November 1895)

'Outrages on Women', *Leader*, 3.128 (4 September 1852)

Oxenham, Henry Nutcombe, *Moral and Religious Estimate of Vivisection* (London: John Hodges, 1878)

Paley, Ruth, 'Imperial Politics and English Law: The Many Contexts of "Somerset"', *Law and History Review*, 24.3 (fall 2006)

Paley, William, *Natural Theology or, Evidence of the Existence and Attributes of the Deity Collected from the Appearance of Nature*, ed. Matthew D. Eddy and David Knight (1802; Oxford: Oxford University Press, 2006)

Panaman, Roger (Ben), 'How to Do Animal Rights – and Win the War on Animals', 2008, http://www.animalethics.org.uk/i-ch1-3-animalholocaust.html, accessed 23 January 2010

Papagaroufali, Eleni, 'Xenotransplantation and Transgenesis: Im-moral Stories about Human–Animal Relations in the West', in Philippe Descola and Gísli Pálsson (eds), *Nature and Society. Anthropological Perspectives* (London: Routledge, 1996)

Park, Marmaduke, *Aesop, in Rhyme; or, Old Friends in a New Dress* (Philadelphia: C. G. Henderson and Co., 1852)

Parks, Elizabeth S., 'Treatment of Signed Languages in Deaf History Textbooks', *Sign Language Studies*, 8.1 (fall 2007)

'Passing Events', *Hearth and Home. An Illustrated Weekly Journal for Gentlewomen* (28 September 1899)

Paterson, A. H., 'Toussaint L'Ouverture', *Young Folks Paper* (9 May 1885)

Patterson, Charles, *Eternal Treblinka. Our Treatment of Animals and the Holocaust*

(New York: Lantern, 2002)

Paulson, Ronald, *Representations of Revolution (1789–1820)* (New Haven: Yale University Press, 1983)

Pavletic, Michael M., *Atlas of Small Animal Reconstructive Surgery*, 2nd edn (Philadelphia: W. B. Saunders Co., 1999)

Payen, Nikòl, 'Lavalas. The Flood after the Flood', *Callaloo*, 25.3 (2002)

'The Pendleton Panther', Plastic Surgery for Animals', 29 October 2008, http://pendletonpanther.wordpress.com/2008/10/29/plastic-surgery-for-animals/, accessed 8 September 2010

Pennell, Elizabeth Robins, *Mary Wollstonecraft* (Boston: Roberts Bros, 1885)

Pepys, Samuel, *The Diary of Samuel Pepys* (1661; Coln St Aldwyns: Echo Library, 2006)

Percy, Samuel R., *What Effect Has the Meat or Milk from Diseased Animals Upon the Public Health?* (New York: John Medole, 1866)

Pernick, Martin S., *A Calculus of Suffering. Pain, Professionalism, and Anesthesia in Nineteenth Century America* (New York: Columbia University Press, 1985)

'Personal Examination of Prisoners Contrary to English Law', *Shield* (10 March 1877)

PETA, 'All Animals Have the Same Parts', https://secure.peta.org/site/Advocacy?cmd=display&page=UserAction&id=3205, accessed 15 October 2010

Phelps, A. M., 'Transplantation of Tissue from Lower Animals to Man, and a report of the Case of Bone Transplantation at Charity Hospital, Blackwell's Island, NY', *Medical Record*, 39 (21 February 1891)

Phillips, B., 'A Record of Monkey Talk', *Harper's Weekly*, 35 (1891)

'Physiognomy', *Anthropological Review*, 6.21 (April 1868)

Pinker, Steven, *The Language Instinct: How the Mind Creates Language* (New York: W. Morrow, 1994)

Playfair, Lyon, *Motion for the Repeal of the Contagious Diseases Acts. Speech of Dr Lyon Playfair, CB, MP, FRS, in the House of Commons, May 24th, 1870* (London: James Walton, 1870)

'Polling Report', http://www.pollingreport.com/terror5.htm, accessed 8 September 2010

Polwhele, Richard, 'The Unsex'd Females: A Poem', in *Poems; Chiefly The Local Attachment, The Unsex'd Females; The Old English Gentleman; The Pneumatic Revellers, and The Family Picture* (Truro: Messrs Rivingstons, 1810)

Pope, Alexander, *An Essay on Man* (1734; London: John and Paul Knapton, 1765)

Porter, Jennifer Parker, 'Analysis of the African American Female Nose', *Plastic and Reconstructive Surgery*, 111.2 (February 2003)

Porter, J. P., 'The Average African American Male Face: An Anthropometric Analysis', *Archives of Facial Plastic Surgery*, 6.2 (March–April 2004)

Porter, J. P. and K. L. Olson, 'Anthropometric Facial Analysis of the African American Woman', *Archives of Facial Plastic Surgery*, 3.3 (July–September 2001)

Posinsky, S. H., 'Cannibalism', *American Anthropologist*, 73.1 (February 1971)

Preece, Rod, 'Darwinism, Christianity, and the Great Vivisection Debate', *Journal of the History of Ideas* (2003)

President's Commission for the Study of Ethical Problems in Medicine and Biomedical and Behavioral Research, *Splicing Life: A Report on the Social and Ethical Issues of Genetic Engineering with Human Beings* (Washington DC: President's Commission for the Study of Ethical Problems in Medicine and Biomedical and Behavioral Research, 1982)

Preston Chronicle (1 September 1838)

Prichard, Hesketh, *Where Black Rules White. A Journey Across and About Hayti* (London: Archibald Constable and Co., 1900)

Primatt, Humphry, *A Dissertation on the Duty of Mercy and Sin of Cruelty to Brute Animals* (London: Rittett, 1776)

'The Progress of Science: From Complexes to Glands', *Scientific Monthly*, 15.2 (August 1922)

Pseudo-Dionysius, *The Complete Works*, trans. Colm Luibheid and Paul Rorem (London: SPCK, 1987)

Public Characters of 1798–1799. The Fourth Edition. Enlarged and Corrected to the First of June, 1803 (London: Richard Phillips, 1803)

Punch, Or the London Charivari (25 March 1914)

Purser, Frank C., *Current Theories on Aphasia* (Dublin: John Falconer, 1907)

'Quaero', 'Monkeying with Man', *Saturday Review* (9 June 1928)

Rachels, James, *Created from Animals: The Moral Implications of Darwinism* (Oxford: Oxford University Press, 1990)

Radick, Gregory, 'Primate Language and the Playback Experiment, in 1890 and 1980', *Journal of the History of Biology*, 38.3 (autumn 2005)

——, *The Simian Tongue. The Long Debate about Animal Language* (Chicago: University of Chicago Press, 2007)

Rae, William Shaw, 'The Black Demons of Hayti', *Big Budget* (7 October 1899)

Raff, Georg Christian, *A System of Natural History, Adapted for the Instruction of Youth, in the Form of a Dialogue*, vol. 2 (London: J. Johnson, 1796)

Ramus, Carl, *Outwitting Middle Age* (New York: Century Co., 1926)

Rawick, George P. (ed.), *The American Slave: A Composite Autobiography. Volume 7. Oklahoma and Mississippi Narratives* (Westport, CT: Greenwood, 1972)

Read, Piers Paul, *Alive: The Story of the Andes Survivors* (London: Arrow, 2002)

'A Reasonable Request. To the Poor Law Commissioners: The Humble Petition of the Inmates of the Andover Union Workhouse', *Punch* (30 August 1845)

'Record of Events', *Englishwoman's Review* (15 December 1885)

Redden, Laura, 'A Few Words about the Deaf and Dumb', *American Annals of the Deaf and Dumb*, 10.3 (1858)

Redfield, James W., *Comparative Physiognomy or Resemblances between Men and Animals* (New York: Redfield, 1852)

Reece, Henry, *The Public Health Act and the Contagious Diseases Acts* (London: W. Ridgway, 1875)

Regan, Tom, *The Case for Animal Rights* (London: Routledge and Kegan Paul, 1983)

——, 'The Other Victim', *Hastings Center Report*, 15.1 (February 1985)

'The "Rejuvenation" Treatment', *Anti-Vivisection Journal* (February 1925)

'Remarks on the Comparative Pleasures and Sufferings of Animals', *Universal Magazine of Knowledge and Pleasure*, 106 (May 1800)

Rhodes, G. M., *The Nine Circles or the Torture of the Innocent* (London: Society for the Protection of Animals from Vivisection, 1893)

Richards, Cynthia, 'The Body of Her Work, the Work of Her Body: Accounting for the Life and Death of Mary Wollstonecraft', *Eighteenth-Century Fiction*, 21.4 (summer 2009)

Richardson, Benjamin Ward, 'Public Slaughter-Houses. A Suggestion for Farmers', *New Review*, viii (January–June 1893)

Richardson, Ruth, *Death, Dissection and the Destitute* (London: Penguin, 1988)

Rickaby, Joseph, *Moral Philosophy: Ethics, Deontology and Natural Law*, 4th edn (London: Longmans, Green and Co., 1929)

———, *Moral Philosophy or Ethics and Natural Law* (London: Longmans, Green and Co., 1888)

Ricketts, Henry C., *Appeals for Mercy. Six Sermons Preached in the Diocese of Exeter in Behalf of Dumb Animals* (London: Skeffington and Son, 1898)

Ritchie, David G., *Natural Rights. A Criticism of Some Political and Ethical Conceptions* (London: Swan Sonnenschein and Co., 1895)

Rivard, Michael D., 'Toward a General Theory of Constitutional Personhood: A Theory of Constitutional Personhood for Transgenic Humanoid Species', *UCLA Law Review*, 39 (1991–92)

Robertson, Ritchie, *Kafka. Judaism, Politics and Literature* (Oxford: Clarendon Press, 1985)

Robinson, Edward Kay, *The Religion of Nature* (London: Hodder and Stoughton, 1906)

Rochet, M., 'Analytical Account of the Chief Characters Tending to Separate Man from Animals', *Anthropological Review*, 7.25 (April 1869)

Roe, John O., 'The Deformity Termed "Pug Nose" and Its Correction by a Simple Operation', *Medical Record* (4 June 1887)

Rollin, Bernard, *Animal Rights and Human Morality*, 2nd edn (New York: Prometheus, 1992)

———, *Science and Ethics* (Cambridge: Cambridge University Press, 2006)

Romanes, George John, 'Intellect in Brutes', *Nature*, 20 (1879)

———, *Mental Evolution in Animals, with a Posthumous Essay on Instinct by Charles Darwin* (London: Kegan Paul, Trench and Co., 1883)

Rondilla, Joanne L. and Paul Spickard, *Is Lighter Better? Skin-Tone Discrimination amongst Asian Americans* (Plymouth: Rowman-Littlefield, 2007)

Ross, Colin A. and Shaun Joshi, 'Paranormal Experiences in the General Population', *Journal of Nervous and Mental Disease*, 180.6 (1992)

Ross, Colin A., *Satanic Ritual Abuse: Principles of Treatment* (Toronto: University of Toronto Press, 1995)

Ross, James, *On Aphasia: Being a Contribution to the Dissolution of Speech from Cerebral Disease* (London: J & A Churchill, 1887)

Rothblatt, Martine, *Your Life or Mine. How Geoethics Can Resolve the Conflict between Public and Private Interests in Xenotransplantation* (Aldershot: Ashgate, 2004)

Royal College of Obstetricians and Gynaecologists, *Fetal Awareness. Working Party Report* (London: RCOG Press, 1997)

RSPCA, *Trustees' Report and Accounts. 2008* (London: RSPCA, 2008)

Rubinstein, William C., 'Franz Kafka: A Hunger Artist', *Monatscheft*, 44 (1952)

Russell, J. A., 'Is There Universal Recognition of Emotion from Facial Expressions? A Review of Cross-Cultural Studies', *Psychological Bulletin*, 115 (1994)

Ryder, Daniel, *Breaking the Circle of Satanic Ritual Abuse: Recognizing and Recovering from the Hidden Trauma* (Minneapolis: CompCare, 1992)

Ryder, Richard D., 'Sentientism', *Arkangel for Animal Liberation*, n.d. [1990 or 1991]

Ryder, Richard, 'Speciesism', in Robert M. Baird and Stuart E. Rosenbaum (eds), *Animal Experimentation: The Moral Issues* (Buffalo: Prometheus, 1991)

Rymer, Charles A. and Marion Reinhardt Rymer, 'Psychological Medicine as Practiced by the Quack', *American Journal of Psychiatry*, 92 (1935)

Salt, Henry S., *Consolations of a Faddist. Verses Reprinted from 'The Humanitarian'* (London: A. C. Fifield, 1906)

——, *The Humanities of Diet. Some Reasonings and Rhymings* (Manchester: Vegetarian Society, 1914)

——, *The Logic of Vegetarianism. Essays and Dialogues* (London: Ideal Publishing Union, 1899)

——, 'The Rights of Animals', *International Journal of Ethics*, 10.2 (January 1900)

——, *Seventy Years Among Savages* (London: George Allen and Unwin, 1921)

Salzmann, Rev. C. G., *Elements of Morality, for the Use of Children; with an Introductory Address to Parents*, vol. 2 (London: J. Johnson, 1790)

Sapontzis, S. F., *Morals, Reasons, and Animals* (Philadelphia: Temple University Press, 1987)

Sarwer, David B. and Leanne Magee, 'Physical Appearance and Society', in David B. Sarwer, Thomas Pruzinsky, Thomas F. Cash, Robert M. Goldwyn, John A. Persing and Linton A. Whitaker, *Psychological Aspects of Reconstructive and Cosmetic Plastic Surgery. Clinical, Empirical, and Ethical Perspectives* (Philadelphia: Lippincott Williams and Wilkins, 2006)

Savage-Rumbaugh, Sue, Stuart G. Shanker and Talbot J. Taylor, *Apes, Language, and the Human Mind* (New York: Oxford University Press, 1998)

Sax, Boria, *Animals in the Third Reich. Pets, Scapegoats, and the Holocaust* (New York: Continuum, 2000)

Scherer, K. and Paul Ekman (eds), *Approaches to Emotion* (Hillsdale, NJ: Lawrence Erlbaum Associates, 1984)

Schiebinger, Londa, 'The Gendered Ape: Early Representations of Primates in Europe', in Marina Benjamin (ed.), *A Question of Identity. Women, Science, and Literature* (New Brunswick: Rutgers University Press, 1993)

——, 'Why Mammals are Called Mammals: Gender Politics in Eighteenth-Century Natural History', *American Historical Review*, 98.2 (April 1993)

Schleifer, Harriet, 'Images of Death and Life: Food Animal Protection and the Vegetarian Option', in Peter Singer (ed.), *In Defence of Animals* (New York:

Harper and Row, 1985)

Schlosser, Eric, *Fast Food Nation. What the All-American Meal is doing to the World* (London: Penguin, 2002)

Schmitt, Carl, *Political Theology. Four Chapters on the Concept of Sovereignty*, trans. George Schwab (1922; Chicago: University of Chicago Press, 2005)

Schmitt, Martin, 'Meat's Meat: An Account of the Flesh-Eating Habits of Western Americans', *Western Folklore*, 11.3 (July 1952)

Schnurer, Maxwell, 'At the Gates of Hell: The ALF and the Legacy of Holocaust Resistance', in Steven Best and Anthony J. Nocella (eds), *Terrorists or Freedom Fighters? Reflections on the Liberation of Animals* (New York: Lantern Books, 2004)

Schorn, Daniel, 'Burning Rage', http://www.cbsnews.com/stories/2005/11/10/60minutes/main1036067_page2.shtml, accessed 26 January 2010

Scott, Fred Newton, 'The Genesis of Speech', *PMLA*, 22 (1907)

Scott, Joan Wallach, 'French Feminists and the Rights of "Man": Olympe de Gouges's Declarations', *History Workshop Journal*, 28 (1989)

Scott, W. R., *The Deaf and Dumb. Their Education and Social Position*, 2nd (revised) edn (London: Bell and Daldy, 1870)

Scoutetten, Robert Henri Joseph, *Eléments de Philosophie Phrénologique* (Metz: M. Alcan, 1861)

Seabrook, W. B., *The Magic Island* (London: George G. Harrap and Co., 1929)

Segerdahl, Pär, William Fields and Sue Savage-Rumbaugh, *Kanzi's Primal Language. The Cultural Initiation of Primates into Language* (Basingstoke: Palgrave Macmillan, 2005)

Seiss, Joseph A., *The Children of Silence; or, The Story of the Deaf* (Philadelphia: Porter and Coates, 1887)

Sellars, Kirsten, *The Rise and Rise of Human Rights* (Stroud: Sutton, 2002)

Senate Committee on Environment and Public Works, *Oversight on Ecoterrorism Specifically Examining the Earth Liberation Front (ELF) and the Animal Liberation Front (ALF)*, 109th Congress, 1st Session (2005)

Sengoopta, Chandak, *The Most Secret Quintessence of Life: Sex, Glands, and Hormones, 1850–1950* (Chicago: University of Chicago Press, 2006)

Serpell, James, *In the Company of Animals: A Study of Human–Animal Relationships* (Oxford: Basil Blackwell, 1986)

Seyfer, Tara, 'The Ethics of Chimeras and Hybrids', in http://www.lifeissues.net/writers/sey/sey_02ethicschimeras.html, accessed 5 December 2009

Sharp, Lesley A., 'Organ Transplantation as a Transformative Experience: Anthropological Insights into the Restructuring of the Self', *Medical Anthropology Quarterly*, 9.3 (September 1995)

Shaw, Charles, *When I was a Child* (1892–3; Firle: Caliban Books, 1977)

Shaw, George Bernard, *The Doctor's Dilemma, Getting Married, and the Shewing-up of Blanco Posnet* (London: Constable and Co., 1911)

Shaw, James, *The Physiognomy of Mental Disease and Degeneracy* (Bristol: John Wright and Co., 1903)

Shaw, Vero, *The Illustrated Book of the Dog* (London: Cassell and Co., 1890)

Shaw, W. C., 'Folklore Surrounding Facial Deformity and the Origins of Facial

Prejudice', *British Journal of Plastic Surgery*, 34.3 (July 1981)

Sheehan, Thomas, 'Heidegger and the Nazis', *New York Review of Books*, vol. xxxv, no. 10 (16 June 1988)

'Shell Shock in Cows', *Lancet*, 191.4297 (2 February 1918)

Shelley, Mary Wollstonecraft, *Frankenstein or The Modern Prometheus. The Original Two-Volume Novel of 1816–1817 from the Bodleian Library Manuscripts* (New York: Vintage Books, 2008)

Shelman, Eric A. and Stephen Lazoritz, *The Mary Ellen Wilson Child Abuse Case and the Beginnings of Children's Rights in 19th Century America* (Jefferson, NC: McFarland and Co., 2005)

Shepard, Odell, *Pedlar's Progress. The Life of Bronson Alcott* (London: Williams and Norgate, 1938)

Sher, Kathy L. Coffman Linda, Allen Hoffman, Sergio Rojter, Patricia Folk, Donald V. Cramer, John Vierling, Federico Villamel, Luis Podesta, Achilles Demetriou and Leonard Makowka, 'Survey Results of Transplant Patients' Attitudes on Xenografting', *Psychosomatics*, 39.4 (July–August 1998)

Sholtmeijer, Marian, *Animal Victims in Modern Fiction. From Sanctity to Sacrifice* (Toronto: University of Toronto Press, 1993)

Siegel, Laurel R., 'Re-Engineering the Laws of Organ Transplantation', *Emory Law Review*, 49.3 (summer 2000)

Siemionow, Maria, Selahattin Ozmen and Yavuz Demis, 'Prospects for Facial Allograft Transplantation in Humans', *Plastic and Reconstructive Surgery*, 113.5 (15 April 2004)

'Sigma', 'My Cousin the Gorilla. Considered in a Second Letter to Joseph Wagsby, Esq, of Little Pedlington', *Tinsley's Magazine*, 9 (September 1871)

Sinclair, Upton, *The Autobiography of Upton Sinclair* (New York: Harcourt, Brace and World, 1962)

Singer, Isaac Bashevis, *Enemies, A Love Story* (London: Jonathan Cape, 1972)

Singer, Peter, 'Animal Liberation' (n.d.), http://www.utsc.utoronto.ca/~psya01/RTCPpracYes.pdf, accessed 4 January 2010

——, *Animal Liberation. A New Ethics for our Treatment of Animals* (London: Cape, 1976)

——, *Animal Liberation. Towards an End to Man's Inhumanity to Animals* (1975; Wellingborough: Thorsons, 1983)

——, *Rethinking Life and Death. The Collapse of Our Traditional Ethics* (Oxford: Oxford University Press, 1995)

——, 'Severe Impairment and the Beginning of Life', *APA Newsletter on Philosophy and Medicine*, 99.2 (2000), http://www.stonybrook.edu/philosophy/faculty/ekittay/ articles/singer.pdf, accessed 19 December 2009

Skinner, E. Benjamin, *A Crime So Monstrous. Face-to-Face with Modern-Day Slavery* (New York: Free Press, 2008)

Slotki, Rev. Dr Israel W., *History of the Manchester Shechita Board, 1892–1952* (Manchester: Manchester Shechita Board, 1952)

Smil, Vaclav, 'Eating Meat: Evolution, Patterns and Consequences', *Population and Development*, 28.4 (December 2002)

Smith, Adam, *The Theory of Moral Sentiments*, ed. Knud Haakonssen (Cambridge:

Cambridge University Press, 2002)

Smith, Clive Stafford, 'Inside Guantanamo', *New Statesman* (21 November 2005)

Smith, David F. and H. Lesley Diack, *Food Poisoning, Policy, and Politics: Canned Beef and Typhoid in Britain in the 1960s* (Woodbridge: Boydell Press, 2005)

Smith, John, *Fruits and Farinacea. The Proper Food of Man; Being an Attempt to Prove from History, Anatomy, Physiology, and Chemistry, that the Original, Natural, and Best Diet of Man is Derived from the Animal Kingdom* (London: Ideal Publishing Union, 1897)

Smith, John Thomas, *Vagabondiana. Or, Anecdotes of Mendicant Wanderers Through the Streets of London; With Portraits of the Most Remarkable* (1817; London: Chatto and Windus, 1874)

Smith, Lewis, 'Pig Organs "Available" to NHS Patients in a Decade', *The Times* (7 November 2008)

Smyth, Albert Henry (ed.), *The Writings of Benjamin Franklin, Collected and Edited With a Life*, vol. v (New York: Macmillan Co., 1907)

Solis, Dianna, 'Plastic Surgery Wooing People Hoping to Move Up Career Ladder', *Wall Street Journal* (6 August 1985)

Spicer, Catherine, 'Not a Game of Cricket', *Arkangel for Animal Liberation*, 3 (1990)

Spiegel, Marjorie, *The Dreaded Comparison. Human and Animal Slavery* (London: Heretic Books, 1988)

Squires, P. C., '"Wolf Children" of India', *American Journal of Psychology*, 38(1927)

Stanford, Craig B., *The Hunting Apes: Meat Eating and the Origins of Human Behavior* (Princeton: Princeton University Press, 1999)

Starzl, Thomas E., Luis A. Valdiva, Noriko Marase, Anthony J. Demitris, Paulo Fontes, Abdul S. Rao, Rafael Manez, Ignazio R. Marino, Satoru Todo, Angus W. Thomson and John J. Fung, 'The Biological Basis of and Strategies for Clinical Xenotransplantation', *Immunological Reviews*, 141 (1994)

'Staying on Target and Going the Distance: An Interview with UK ALF Press Officer Robin Webb', *No Compromise*, 22 (fall 2003), www.nocompromise.org/issues/22robin-html, accessed 1 January 2010

Steeves, Peter, 'Lost Dog, or Levinas Faces the Animal', in Mary Sanders Pollock and Catherine Rainwater (eds), *Figuring Animals: Essays on Animal Images in Art, Literature, Philosophy, and Popular Culture* (New York: Palgrave Macmillan, 2005)

Stockdale, Percival, *A Remonstrance Against Inhumanity to Animals; and Particularity, Against the Savage Practice of Bull-Baiting* (Alnwick: M. & J. Graham, 1802)

Stokoe, William C., *Language in Hand: Why Sign Came Before Speech* (Washington DC: Gallaudet University Press, 2001)

——, *Sign Language Structure: The First Linguistic Analysis of American Sign Language* (1960; Silver Springs: Linstock Press, 1978)

Stone, Harvey B. and William J. Kennedy, 'Survival of Heterologous Mammalian Transplants. A Third Report', *Annals of Surgery*, 159.5 (May 1964)

Suckling, Horatio John, *Anti-Darwin: or, Some Reasons for not Accepting His Hypothesis* (Twickenham: privately, 1887)

Sully, James, *Studies of Childhood* (London: Longmans, Green and Co., 1895)

Sunday Times (5 July 1992)

'The Sunderland Election', *English Gentleman* (16 August 1845)

Sunstein, Cass R. and Martha C. Nussbaum (eds), *Animal Rights: Current Debates and New Directions* (New York: Oxford University Press, 2004)

Sztybel, David, 'Can the Treatment of Animals Be Compared to the Holocaust?', *Ethics and the Environment*, 11.1 (2006)

Taylor, Charles Bell, *The Contagious Diseases Act, Showing its Cruelty, Injustice, Demoralising Tendency, & Inexpediency in a Sanitary Point of View. Being the Substance of a Paper Read Before the Medical Society of London, January 17, 1870; with Report of the Debate*, part 1 (Nottingham: Frederick Banks, 1870)

Taylor, Thomas, *Vindication of the Rights of Brutes* (London: Edward Jeffrey, 1792)

Terrace, Herbert S., *Nim* (London: Eyre Methuen, 1980)

'Thinks Well of Gorillas: Professor Richard L. Garner Tells of his Life in a Cage', *New York Times* (26 March 1894)

Thomas, Keith, *Man and the Natural World: A History of the Modern Sensibility* (New York: Pantheon, 1983)

Thompson, Alton H., 'The Descent of Facial Expression', *Transactions of the Annual Meeting of the Kansas Academy of Science*, 13 (1891–92)

——, 'Facial Expression and its Psychology', *Transactions of the Annual Meetings of the Kansas Academy of Science*, 12 (1889–90)

Thorek, Max, *A Surgeon's World. An Autobiography* (Philadelphia: J. B. Lippincott, 1943)

Thornton, Robert, *Vaccinae Vindicia; or, Defence of Vaccination* (London: privately, 1806)

'Those Estimable People, the Vegetarians', *The Times* (13 January 1885)

Timberlake, William, 'The Attribution of Suffering', in Robert M. Baird and Stuart E. Rosenbaum (eds), *Animal Experimentation. The Moral Issues* (New York: Prometheus, 1991)

Tipper, Ernest H., *The Cradle of the World and Cancer: A Disease of Civilization* (London: Charles Murray, 1927)

Tomasello, Michael, Sue Savage-Rumbaugh and Ann Cale Kruger, 'Imitative Learning of Actions on Objects by Children, Chimpanzees, and Enculturated Chimpanzees', *Child Development*, 64.6 (December 1993)

Tomes, Nancy, 'The History of Shit', *Journal of the History of Medicine*, 56 (October 2001)

[Tonna], Charlotte Elizabeth, *The Happy Mute: or, the Dumb Child's Appeal*, 4th edn (London: L. B. Seeley and Sons, 1835)

——, *Kindness to Animals; or the Sin of Cruelty Exposed and Rebuked* (Philadelphia: American Sunday-School Union, 1845)

Tooley, Michael, 'Abortion and Infanticide', in Peter Singer (ed.), *Applied Ethics* (Oxford: Oxford University Press, 1986)

'The Tourist', *Pearson's Magazine*, xxviii (September 1909)

'T. P.', 'Rhymes for Youthful Readers, on Colonial Slavery', *The Tourist; or, Sketch Book of the Times* (31 December 1832)

Traill, Thomas Stewart, 'Observations on the Anatomy of the Orang Outang', *Memoirs of the Wernerian Natural History Society*, iii (1821)

Train, George Francis, *Train's Speeches in England, on Slavery and Emancipation,*

Delivered in London, on March 12th, and 19th, 1862. Also his Great Speech on the 'Pardoning of Traitors' (Philadelphia: T. B. Peterson and Brothers, 1862)

The Truth, (27 December 1894 and 12 November 1896)

Turner, James, Reckoning with the Beast. Animals, Pain, and Humanity in the Victorian Mind (Baltimore: Johns Hopkins University Press, 1980)

Twigg, Julia, 'The Vegetarian Movement in England, 1847–1981: A Study in the Structure of Ideology' (PhD thesis, 1981), http://www.ivu.org/history/thesis

'Twilight HQs. Placenta recipes', http://www.twilightheadquarters.com/placenta.html, accessed 8 September 2010

United Nations, 'Charter of the United Nations', http://www.un.org/en/documents/charter/, accessed 8 September 2010

Uniting and Strengthening America by Providing Appropriate Tools Required to Intercept and Obstruct Terrorism (USA PATRIOT Act) Act of 2001, 107th Congress, 1st Session (2001)

Van Cleve, John V. (ed.), Deaf History Unveiled: Interpretations for the New Scholarship (Washington DC: Gallaudet University Press, 1993)

Vanasseur, E. O., 'A Friend of Mine', Animals' Guardian (February 1916)

Vanderpool, H. Y., 'Critical Ethical Issues in Clinical Trials with Xenotransplants', Lancet, 351.9112 (2 May 1998)

'Vanessa', 'Vivisection is Demoralizing to Vivisectors and Spectators. Part III', Women's Penny Paper (13 December 1890)

Vayda, Andrew P., 'On the Nutritional Value of Cannibalism', American Anthropologist, 72.6 (December 1970)

'Vegetarianism', Woman's Herald (10 September 1892)

The Vivisector (London: Middlesex Printing Works, n.d.)

Voronoff, Serge, 'The Conquest of Old Age', in Dr. A. Forbath (ed.), Sidelights from the Surgery. Human Experiences in the Consulting Room (London: Pallas, 1939)

——, Love and Thought in Animals and Men (London: Methuen and Co., 1937)

——, Rejuvenation by Grafting, trans. Fred F. Imianitoff (London: Allen and Unwin, 1925)

——, The Study of Old Age and My Method of Rejuvenation (London: Gill, 1926)

Voronoff, Serge and George Alexandrescu, La Greffe Testiculaire du Singe à l'Homme (Paris: Gaston Dain and Ce, 1930)

——, Testicular Grafting From Ape to Man: Operative Technique, Physiological Manifestations, Histological Evolutions, Statistics (London: William and Norgate, 1933)

Vorzimmer, Peter J., 'The Darwin Reading Notebooks (1838–1860)', Journal of the History of Biology, 10.1 (spring 1977)

Waddington, Keir, The Bovine Scourge. Meat, Tuberculosis, and Public Health, 1850–1914 (Woodbridge: Boydell, 2006)

——, '"Unfit for Human Consumption": Tuberculosis and the Problem of

Infected Meat in Late Victorian Britain', *Bulletin for the History of Medicine*, 77 (2003)

Waldby, Catherine and Susan Squier, 'Ontogeny, Ontology, and Phylogeny: Embryonic Life and Stem Cell Technology', *Configurations*, 11 (2003)

Waldman, Murray and Marjorie Lamb, *Dying for a Hamburger. The Alarming Link Between the Meat Industry and Alzheimer's Disease* (London: Piatkus, 2004)

Walker, Edward, 'Current Studies of Animal Communication as Paradigms for the Biology of Language', in Edward Walker (ed.), *Explorations in the Biology of Language* (Hassocks: Harvester, 1978)

Wallis, Claudia, 'Baby Fae Stuns the World', *Time* (12 November 1984), http://www. time.com/time/magazine/article/0,9171,926947-3,00.html, accessed 8 September 2010

Walvin, James, *Black Presence. A Documentary History of the Negro in England, 1555–1860* (London: Orbach and Chambers, 1971)

Wantchekon, Leonard and Andrew Healy, 'The "Game" of Torture', *Journal of Conflict Resolution*, 43 (October 1999)

Warbasse, James Peter, *The Conquest of Disease Through Animal Experimentation* (New York: D. Appleton, 1919)

Wardle, Ralph M. (ed.), *Godwin and Mary: Letters of William Godwin and Mary Wollstonecraft* (Lawrence: University of Kansas Press, 1967)

Warren, Sir Charles, 'Dogs of London', *Contemporary Review*, li (January 1887)

Washburn, Emory, *Extinction of Villenage and Slavery in England; With Somerset's Case* (Boston: John Wilson and Son, 1864)

Watson, James D. (ed.), *Darwin: The Indelible Stamp. The Evolution of an Idea* (Philadelphia: Running Press, 2005)

Waugh, Benjamin, 'Letter to the Editor. Unwanted and Illtreated Children. A New Law and a New Departure for Them', *The Times* (8 January 1890)

——, 'Notes', *Child's Guardian*, 3.29 (May 1889)

——, 'Notes', *Child's Guardian*, 4.4 (April 1890)

——, 'Notes', *Child's Guardian*, 11.11 (October 1897)

'We Hardly Know How to Approach the Andover Inquiry', *John Bull* (13 September 1845)

Weedon, Chris, *Feminist Practice and Poststructuralist Theory* (Oxford: Basil Blackwell, 1987)

Weil, Simone, 'Human Personality', in *Simone Weil: An Anthology*, ed. Siân Miles (New York: Weidenfeld and Nicolson, 1986)

Wells, H. G., *The Island of Doctor Moreau* (1896; Harmondsworth: Penguin Books, 1971)

Wells, S. R., 'Cannibal of Central Australia', *Illustrated Annual of Phrenology and Physiognomy* (New York: privately, 1869)

Wesley, Robert B., 'Letter to the Editor. A Day's March', *The Times* (25 June 1870)

'What's For Dinner Tonight? Roast Placenta', http://www.birenandkris.com/serendipity/index.php?/archives/14-Whats-for-dinner-tonight-Roast-Placenta....html, accessed 8 September 2010

Wheeler, Roxann, *The Complexion of Race: Categories of Difference in Eighteenth-Century British Culture* (Philadelphia: University of Pennsylvania Press, 1999)

Wherry, Edgar T., 'Does a Low-Protein Diet Produce Racial Inferiority?', *Science*, new series, 37.963 (13 June 1913)

Whorton, James, 'Civilization and the Colon: Constipation as "the Disease of Diseases"', *Western Journal of Medicine*, 173.6 (December 2000)

——, *Inner Hygiene: Constipation and the Pursuit of Health in Modern Society* (Oxford: Oxford University Press, 2000)

Wierzbicka, Anna, *Semantics, Culture, and Cognition. Universal Human Concepts in Culture-Specific Configurations* (New York: Oxford University Press, 1992)

Winsten, Stephen, *Salt and His Circle* (London: Hutchinson and Co., 1951)

Winter, Roger, 'Journey into Genocide: A Rwanda Diary', *Washington Post* (5 June 1994), http://pqasb.pqarchiver.com/washingtonpost/access/8594938.html?FMT=ABS&FMTS=ABS&date=Jun+5%2C+1994&author=Winter%2C+Roger&desc=Journey+into+genocide%3A++A+Rwanda+diary

Wise, Steven, 'Animal Rights, One Step at a Time', in Cass R. Sunstein and Martha C. Nussbaum (eds), *Animal Rights: Current Debates and New Directions* (Oxford: Oxford University Press, 2004)

——, *Though the Heavens May Fall. The Landmark Trial that Led to the End of Human Slavery* (London: Pimlico, 2006)

——, *Towards Legal Rights for Animals* (London: Profile, 2000)

——, *Unlocking the Cage. Science and the Case for Animal Rights* (Oxford: Perseus Press, 2002)

Wise, Steven M., *An American Trilogy. Death, Slavery, and Dominion on the Banks of the Cape Fear River* (Philadelphia: Da Capo, 2009)

Wiswall, Sara A., 'Animal Euthanasia and Duties Owed to Animals', *McGeorge Law Review*, 30 (1998–99)

Wolff, Charlotte, 'The Form and Dermatoglyphs of the Hands and Feet of Certain Anthropoid Apes', *Proceedings of the Zoological Society*, series A, pt. 3 (1937)

Wolfson, David J. and Mariann Sullivan, 'Foxes in the Hen House: Animals, Agribusiness, and the Law. A Modern American Fable', in Cass R. Sunstein and Martha C. Nussbaum (eds), *Animal Rights: Current Debates and New Directions* (New York: Oxford University Press, 2004)

Wollstonecraft, Mary, *Letters Written During a Short Residence in Sweden, Norway and Denmark*, ed. Carol H. Poston (1796; Lincoln: University of Nebraska Press, 1976)

——, *A Vindication of the Rights of Woman: With Strictures on Political and Moral Subjects*, 3rd edn (1972; London: J. Johnson, 1796)

——, *A Vindication of the Rights of Woman*, ed. Deidre Shauna Lynch, 3rd edn (1792; New York: W. W. Norton and Co., 2009)

'The Woman About Town', *Sporting Times* (30 December 1871)

'Woman, The Slave of Man!', *Judy* (25 September 1872)

'Women Legislators. The Plea Made by an Englishman Against Them', *Aurora Daily Express* (30 November 1896), http://news.google.com/newspapers?nid=2329&dat=18961130&id=88EnAAAAIBAJ&sjid=5AQGAAAAIBAJ&pg=5965,879324, accessed 28 February 2010

Women's Franchise League, *Report of Proceedings at the Inaugural Meeting: London,*

July 25th, 1889 (London: Hansard Publishing Union, 1889)

Women's Social and Political Union, *Woman This, and Woman That* (London: WSPU, n.d.)

Wood, Marcus, *Blind Memory. Visual Representation of Slavery in England and America, 1780–1865* (Manchester: Manchester University Press, 2000)

Woods, Tania, 'Have a Heart: Xenotransplantation, Non-Human Death, and Human Distress', *Society and Animals*, 6.1 (1998)

Woolnoth, Thomas, *The Study of the Human Face* (London: William Tweedie, 1865)

'A Word for Children', *Home Journal* (20 June 1866)

'Working of the Workhouse System', *Satirist; or, The Censor of the Times* (14 September 1845)

Wright, R. George, 'Personhood 2.0: Enhanced and Unenhanced Persons and the Equal Protection of the Laws', *QLR*, 23 (2004–5)

Wynne-Tyson, Jon, *The Extended Circle: A Commonplace Book of Animals Rights* (New York: Paragon House, 1989)

Yellon, Evan, *Surdus in Search of his Hearing: An Exposure of Aural Quacks and a Guide to Genuine Treatments and Remedies, Electrical Aids, Lip-Reading and Employments for the Deaf* (London: Celtic Press, 1906),

Yerkes, Robert Mearns, *Almost Human* (New York: Century Co., 1925)

Young, Thomas, *An Essay on Humanity to Animals* (London: T. Cadell, 1798)

Young-Bruehl, Elisabeth, *Hannah Arendt. For Love of the World* (New Haven: Yale University Press, 1982)

Yousif, N. John, 'Introduction', *Clinics in Plastic Surgery. An International Quarterly*, 22.2 (April 1995)

Zangwill, Israel, *One and One are Two* (London: Women's Social and Political Union, 1907)

Index